THE ALBERT SHAW LECTURES ON
DIPLOMATIC HISTORY

Under the Auspices of the

WALTER HINES PAGE SCHOOL OF
INTERNATIONAL RELATIONS

By the liberality of Albert Shaw, Ph.D., of New York City, The Johns Hopkins University has been enabled to provide an annual course of lectures on Diplomatic History. The Lectures, while continuing to be included in the regular work of the Department of History, have since the establishment of the Page School of International Relations, in 1930, been placed under its auspices.

ALBERT SHAW LECTURES ON
DIPLOMATIC HISTORY

1899. JOHN H. LATANÉ. The Diplomatic Relations of the United States and Spanish America. 1900. (Out of print.)

1900. JAMES MORTON CALLAHAN. The Diplomatic History of the Southern Confederacy. 1901. (Out of print.)

1906. JESSE SIDDALL REEVES. American Diplomacy under Tyler and Polk. 1907. $1.75.

1907. ELBERT JAY BENTON. International Law and Diplomacy of the Spanish-American War. 1908. $1.75.

1909. EPHRAIM DOUGLAS ADAMS. British Interests and Activities in Texas, 1838-1846. 1910. (Out of print.)

1911. CHARLES OSCAR PAULLIN. Diplomatic Negotiations of American Naval Officers, 1778-1883. 1912. $2.25.

1912. ISAAC J. COX. The West Florida Controversy, 1798-1813. 1918. $3.00.

1913. WILLIAM R. MANNING. Early Diplomatic Relations Between the United States and Mexico. 1916. $2.50.

1914. FRANK A. UPDYKE. The Diplomacy of the War of 1812. 1915. $2.75.

1916. PAYSON JACKSON TREAT. The Early Diplomatic Relations Between the United States and Japan, 1853-1865. 1917. $2.75.

1921. PERCY ALVIN MARTIN. Latin America and the War. 1925. $3.50.

1923. HENRY MERRITT WRISTON. Executive Agents in American Foreign Relations. 1929. $5.00.

1926. SAMUEL FLAGG BEMIS. Pinckney's Treaty: A study of America's Advantage from Europe's Distress, 1783-1800. 1926. (Out of print.)

1927. BRUCE WILLIAMS. State Security and the League of Nations: A Survey of the Movement for State Security from the Treaty of Versailles to the Locarno Conference. 1927. $2.75.

1928. J. FRED RIPPY. Rivalry of the United States and Great Britain over Latin-America, 1808-1830. 1929. $2.75.

1931. CHARLES CALLAN TANSILL. The purchase of the Danish West Indies. 1932. $3.50.

1932. DEXTER PERKINS. The Monroe Doctrine, 1826-67. 1933. $3.50.

1933. CHARLES SEYMOUR. American Diplomacy During the World War. 1934. $3.00.

1935. FRANK H. SIMONDS. American Foreign Policy in the Post-War Years. 1935. $2.00.

1936. JULIUS W. PRATT. Expansionists of 1898. The Acquisition of Hawaii and the Spanish Islands. 1936. $3.00.

EXPANSIONISTS OF 1898

THE ACQUISITION OF HAWAII AND THE SPANISH ISLANDS

THE ALBERT SHAW LECTURES ON DIPLOMATIC HISTORY, 1936
THE WALTER HINES PAGE SCHOOL OF INTERNATIONAL RELATIONS

EXPANSIONISTS OF 1898

THE ACQUISITION OF HAWAII AND
THE SPANISH ISLANDS

BY

JULIUS W. PRATT

Emanuel Boasberg Professor of American History
University of Buffalo

GLOUCESTER, MASS.

PETER SMITH

1959

PREFACE

It is the purpose of this study to trace the rise and development in the United States of the movement for overseas expansion from hesitant beginnings under the Harrison Administration at the opening of the last decade of the nineteenth century to its surprising triumph in the ratification of the treaty with Spain in February, 1899. The first chapter analyzes the ideological background of the movement and surveys briefly the unsuccessful attempts of Harrison, Blaine, and Foster to secure for the United States a strategic foothold in the Caribbean. The next four chapters deal with the Hawaiian question—the immediate origins of the movement for annexation, the revolution of January, 1893, the Cleveland policy of refusal, and the repercussions to these events on the part of the American public and the American Congress. The heavy emphasis upon the Hawaiian question is, I believe, justified, in part by the lack, hitherto, of any adequate treatment of this theme, in part by the fact that the proposal to annex Hawaii focused public opinion for the first time upon the issues involved in the expansionist policy, produced a sharp cleavage between the advocates and opponents of that policy, and opened a debate which continued almost uninterruptedly for seven years. The sixth chapter traces the broadening program of the expansionist group from the temporary shelving of Hawaiian annexation to the beginning of the war with Spain. The seventh analyzes the attitude of American business toward the war with Spain and the opportunities for

expansion which it presented. The eighth presents a similar analysis of the attitude of religious bodies. The ninth describes the triumph of the expansionist policy in the annexation of Hawaii and the treaty of peace with Spain.

It is a pleasure to make the following acknowledgments of courtesies and assistance rendered: to Colonel Thomas M. Spaulding, of Washington, D. C., for valuable criticism of certain chapters of the manuscript; also to Colonel Spaulding and to Professor R. S. Kuykendall and Miss Maude Jones, of Honolulu, for invaluable assistance in securing photostatic copies of diplomatic documents from the Hawaiian Archives (copies now forming a part of the Stephen Spaulding Memorial Collection in the General Library, University of Michigan); to Dr. William W. Bishop and his staff for aid in using the materials in the Spaulding Collection; to Mrs. Natalia Summers and her assistants in the archives of the Department of State for generous and cheerful aid in using the manuscripts under their charge; to the Social Science Research Council for two grants-in-aid in furtherance of this study; to three of my former graduate students, Mrs. Bernice B. Shannon, Miss Elizabeth Ahern, and Mrs. Bernice H. Lee, for certain of the materials used in chapters VII and VIII; to the editors of the *Hispanic American Historical Review,* the *Mississippi Valley Historical Review,* and the *Pacific Historical Review,* for permission to republish in whole or in part material originally printed in those journals; and finally to my wife, who gave indispensable assistance in the preparation of the manuscript.

JULIUS W. PRATT.

Buffalo, August, 1936.

CONTENTS

CHAPTER   PAGE

PREFACE vii

I. THE NEW MANIFEST DESTINY.............. 1

II. HARRISON AND HAWAII.................. 34

III. REVOLUTION IN HAWAII................. 74

IV. ANNEXATION REJECTED 110

V. A WAR OF PROPAGANDA................. 146

VI. BROADENING HORIZONS 188

VII. THE BUSINESS POINT OF VIEW............. 230

VIII. "THE IMPERIALISM OF RIGHTEOUSNESS".... 279

IX. CONSUMMATION 317

BIBLIOGRAPHY 361

INDEX 377

I

THE NEW MANIFEST DESTINY

On March 24, 1895, there died obscurely in New York a one-time journalist and diplomat, John Louis O'Sullivan by name. Fifty years before, he had enriched the national vocabulary with the potent phrase, " manifest destiny," and had, as editor of the *Democratic Review* and as an acquaintance of Presidents Polk, Pierce, and Buchanan, urged energetically the policy of expansion which the phrase embodied.[1] Thereafter, both he and his idea had fallen upon evil times. O'Sullivan had been a Democrat and a Southern sympathizer, and the idea for which he stood had been too frequently connected with the cause of slavery-extension to escape a share of the discredit suffered by the latter. The close of the Civil War found O'Sullivan an exile in Europe. The efforts of Seward as Secretary of State and Grant as President to revive the expansionist policy of pre-war days met with little popular support.[2]

But while the passing years only deepened the obscurity surrounding the man, they brought a surprising resurrection of the idea which he had advocated and even of the

[1] Julius W. Pratt, " John L. O'Sullivan and Manifest Destiny," *New York History*, XIV, 213-234. Dr Albert K. Weinberg in his *Manifest Destiny: A Study of Nationalist Expansionism in American History*, has made an elaborate study of the ideas advanced at various periods in justification of the acquisition of new territory by the United States.

[2] T. C. Smith, " Expansion after the Civil War, 1865-1871," *Political Science Quarterly*, XVI, 412-436.

phrase which he had coined. Before O'Sullivan's death, " manifest destiny " was again in the air. There was new talk of expansion, which now found its chief support not as formerly among Democrats but in the other political camp—in what O'Sullivan had once described as the party of " wicked and crazy Republicanism." It was the Republican party which in 1892 pledged its belief in " the achievement of the manifest destiny of the republic in its broadest sense." [3] It was a Republican administration which gave most sympathetic support to the project of an American-controlled isthmian canal and which sought naval bases for the United States in Hawaii and Samoa and in various Caribbean islands. It was a Republican Senator who proclaimed, in an article which O'Sullivan may well have read just before his death, that the United States should extend its limits from the Rio Grande to the Arctic Ocean, should build a Nicaraguan canal, control Hawaii, maintain its influence in Samoa, and own Cuba; that, since " the great nations [were] rapidly absorbing for their future expansion and their present defence all the waste places of the earth," the United States, as one of the great nations, " must not fall out of the line of march." [4] In fact, the United States was about to embark, under Republican leadership, upon a new career of expansion, which was to be justified if not motivated by new interpretations of " manifest destiny."

The manifest destiny of the 1840's had been largely a matter of emotion. Much of it had been simply one ex-

[3] E. Stanwood, *A History of the Presidency from 1788 to 1897*, p. 496.

[4] H. C. Lodge, " Our Blundering Foreign Policy," *The Forum*, XIX, 8-17.

pression of a half-blind faith in the superior virility of the
American race and the superior beneficence of American
political institutions. In the intervening years, much had
been done to provide this emotional concept with a philosophic backing. The expansionists of the 1890's were able
to cite the lessons of science and of history in support of
their doctrine. Far-fetched and fallacious as their reasoning
may appear to us, it nevertheless carried conviction to some
of the best minds of the period.

Prominent among the conceptions which contributed to
the new expansionist philosophy was the Darwinian hy-
pothesis of evolution through natural selection. If the continuous struggle for existence among biological forms resulted in the elimination of the unfit and the emergence of
higher types, why might not the same law hold good in
human society? If the survival of the fittest was the law of
nature and the path of progress, surely the more gifted
races need offer neither apologies nor regrets when they
suppressed, supplanted, or destroyed their less talented
competitors. And who could doubt that the Anglo-Saxon
race, especially in its American branch, possessed those
superior talents which entitled it to survive? Certainly not
Charles Darwin, the founder of the creed. In his second
great work, *The Descent of Man,* the English scientist included a passage well calculated to flatter American self-
esteem.

There is apparently much truth [he wrote] in the belief
that the wonderful progress of the United States, as well
as the character of the people, are the results of natural
selection; the more energetic, restless, and courageous men
from all parts of Europe having emigrated during the last
ten or twelve generations to that great country, and having

there succeeded best. Looking to the distant future, I do not think that the Rev. Mr. Zincke takes an exaggerated view when he says: "All other series of events—as that which resulted in the culture of mind in Greece, and that which resulted in the empire of Rome—only appear to have purpose and value when viewed in connection with, or rather as subsidiary to, . . . the great stream of Anglo-Saxon emigration to the west." [5]

In thus hailing the American as " the heir of all the ages, in the foremost files of time," Darwin was merely recording what seemed to him a scientific fact. He was not preaching a message or advocating a policy. It was not difficult, however, to derive a practical lesson from such a premise, and this task was gladly undertaken by certain of Darwin's disciples in the United States. Among the foremost of these was the historian, John Fiske. A·convert to the theory of evolution since his undergraduate days at Harvard—where he had been threatened with expulsion for his unorthodox opinions—he became one of its chief popularizers in the United States.[6] In an essay entitled " Manifest Destiny," which he published in *Harper's Magazine* in 1885, it is easy to detect the working of the evolutionary theory. After stressing the superior character of Anglo-Saxon institutions and the overwhelming growth of Anglo-Saxon numbers and power, Fiske remarked:

It is enough to point to the general conclusion that the work which the English race began when it colonized North America is destined to go on until every land on the earth's

---

[5] Charles Darwin, *The Descent of Man, and Selection in Relation to Sex,* I, 179. The passage quoted and endorsed by Darwin is from Rev. F. B. Zincke, *Last Winter in the United States,* p. 29.

[6] See the sketch of Fiske by J. T. Adams in *Dictionary of American Biography,* VI, 420-423.

surface that is not already the seat of an old civilization shall become English in its language, in its religion, in its political habits and traditions, and to a predominant extent in the blood of its people. The day is at hand when four-fifths of the human race will trace its pedigree to English forefathers, as four-fifths of the white people of the United States trace their pedigree to-day. The race thus spread over both hemispheres, and from the rising to the setting sun, will not fail to keep that sovereignty of the sea and that commercial supremacy which it began to acquire when England first stretched its arm across the Atlantic to the shores of Virginia and Massachusetts.

Even the English language, he believed, would " ultimately become the language of mankind." [7]

Another widely read author whose ideas closely re-sembled Fiske's and whose indebtedness to Darwin was no less obvious was the Congregational clergyman, Josiah Strong. In 1885 he published a small volume entitled *Our Country: Its Possible Future and Its Present Crisis,* in which appeared a chapter on " The Anglo-Saxon and the World's Future." The Anglo-Saxon, he asserted, as the chief representative of two great ideas—civil liberty and " a pure *spiritual* Christianity "—was " divinely commis-sioned to be, in a peculiar sense, his brother's keeper. Add to this the fact of his rapidly increasing strength in modern times, and we have well-nigh a demonstration of his destiny." God, it appeared to Mr. Strong, was training this favored race for the final competition of races—the struggle for existence—which would arise from the continued pres-sure of population upon the means of subsistence.

[7] John Fiske, " Manifest Destiny," *Harper's New Monthly Magazine,* LXX, 578-590. This essay was also published in Fiske's *American Political Ideas Viewed from the Standpoint of Universal History,* pp. 101-152.

Then this race of unequaled energy, with all the majesty of numbers and the might of wealth behind it—the representative, let us hope, of the largest liberty, the purest Christianity, the highest civilization—having developed peculiarly aggressive traits calculated to impress its institutions upon mankind, will spread itself over the earth. If I read not amiss, this powerful race will move down upon Mexico, down upon Central and South America, out upon the islands of the sea, over upon Africa and beyond. And can any one doubt that the result of this competition of races will be the " survival of the fittest " ?

The extinction of weaker races before the all-conquering Anglo-Saxon might appear sad to some, but to Mr. Strong it seemed almost inevitable. Only adverse climatic conditions could hold the Anglo-Saxon in check, and the areas where he could not thrive were not extensive. " Is there room for reasonable doubt," he asked in conclusion, " that this race, unless devitalized by alcohol and tobacco, is destined to dispossess many weaker races, assimilate others, and mold the remainder, until, in a very true and important sense, it has Anglo-Saxonized mankind? " [8]

The reader may be tempted to attribute the rather sophomoric generalizations and prophecies of Fiske and Strong to their lack of broad and systematic scholarly training. Yet one of their contemporaries who possessed these advantages to a degree unusual among American scholars of his time arrived by a different road at quite similar conclusions. Professor John W. Burgess, after completing his undergraduate work at Amherst, had spent two years in the study of history and political science at Göttingen, Leipzig, and Berlin. Thence he returned to teach, first at Amherst

[8] Josiah Strong, *Our Country: Its Possible Future and Its Present Crisis*, chap. xiv, pp. 208-227.

and later at Columbia, where in 1880 he took a leading part in founding the School of Political Science.

It is significant that the two German scholars to whom Burgess acknowledged the heaviest debt were Gustav Droysen, historian of the rise of the Prussian state, and Rudolf von Gneist, profound student of the development of English constitutional law.[9] Whether the admiration for the political talents of the Teutonic race which Burgess must have derived from study under these men was strengthened by an acquaintance with Count Arthur Gobineau's work on the superiority of the Nordic stock can only be conjectured.[10] In any event, his most ambitious work, *Political Science and Comparative Constitutional Law,* published in 1890, contains a remarkable chapter on " National Political Character," in which Burgess virtually assigned world dominion to Germans and Anglo-Saxons.[11]

After analyzing the political character of Greek, Slav, Celt, Roman, and Teuton as exhibited in their political institutions, Burgess concluded that all but the last were deficient in the highest political talent. The successes of Greek, Celt, and Slav had been confined to the organization of local communities; the genius of the Roman was for world empire. Only Teutons had developed the true national state, which was, in Burgess's opinion, " the most modern and the most complete solution of the whole prob-

[9] John W. Burgess, *Reminiscences of an American Scholar,* pp. 126, 131.

[10] Gobineau's *Essai sur l'inégalité des races humaines* (4 vols., Paris, 1853-1855) was translated into English with the title *Moral and Intellectual Diversity of Races* (Philadelphia, 1856).

[11] John W. Burgess, *Political Science and Comparative Constitutional Law,* I, 30-39.

lem of political organization which the world has as yet produced." The fact that the national state was a Teutonic creation stamped the Teutonic nations "as the political nations *par excellence,* and authorize[d] them, in the economy of the world to assume the leadership in the establishment and administration of states." [12]

Having thus assigned the Teutons to their proper place in the hierarchy of races, Burgess proceeded, in the next chapter, to draw certain "conclusions of practical politics." [13] It followed easily from what had been said,

that the Teutonic nations are particularly endowed with the capacity for establishing national states, and are especially called to that work; and, therefore, that they are intrusted, in the general economy of history, with the mission of conducting the political civilization of the modern world.[14]

This meant, among other things,[15] that the Teutonic nations were "called to carry the political civilization of the modern

[12] *Ibid.,* p. 39.

[13] *Ibid.,* pp. 40-48.

[14] *Ibid.,* p. 44.

[15] Of some modern interest are Burgess's conclusions as to the proper attitude of the Teutonic rulers to alien elements within their own borders. In a state with heterogeneous population, he wrote, "the Teutonic element, when dominant, should never surrender the balance of political power, either in general or local organization, to the other elements. Under certain circumstances it should not even permit participation of the other elements in political power . . . the participation of other ethnical elements in the exercise of political power has resulted, and will result, in corruption and confusion most deleterious and dangerous to the rights of all, and to the civilization of society." *Ibid.,* pp. 44-45. Burgess was likely thinking of the South during the carpet-bag régime. The passage might, however, have been taken as a text by the rulers of the Third Reich.

world into those parts of the world inhabited by unpolitical and barbaric races; *i. e., they must have a colonial policy.*" [16] To North Americans, who were reluctant to undertake such responsibility and inclined to regard it as " unwarrantable interference in the affairs of other states," Burgess pointed out that

by far the larger part of the surface of the globe is inhabited by populations which have not succeeded in establishing civilized states; which have, in fact, no capacity to accomplish such a work; and which must, therefore, remain in a state of barbarism or semi-barbarism, unless the political nations undertake the work of state organization for them. This condition of things authorizes the political nations not only to answer the call of the unpolitical populations for aid and direction, but also to force organization upon them by any means necessary, in their honest judgment, to accomplish this result. There is no human right to the status of barbarism.[17]

To justify such interference in the interests of civilization, it was not necessary that the inferior race be wholly barbaric. In the case of populations " not wholly barbaric, which have made some progress in state organizations, but which manifest incapacity to solve the problem of political civilization with any degree of completeness," interference by the political nations would be justifiable.

No one can question that it is in the interest of the world's civilization that law and order and the true liberty consistent therewith shall reign everywhere upon the globe. A permanent inability on the part of any state or semi-state to secure this status is a threat to civilization everywhere. Both for the sake of the half-barbarous state and in the interest of the rest of the world, a state or states, endowed

[16] *Ibid.*, p. 45. Italics mine.
[17] *Ibid.*, pp. 45-46.

with the capacity for political organization, may righteously assume sovereignty over, and undertake to create state order for, such a politically incompetent population.

To undertake such interference was not only a right but an obligation. " Indifference on the part of Teutonic states to the political civilization of the rest of the world is, then, not only mistaken policy, but disregard of duty." [18]

Modern imperialism could ask for no more sweeping justification than Professor Burgess gave it. To a reviewer in the *Nation* this portion of Burgess's work seemed a surprising endorsement of " the political morality of Omar and Pizarro." " The war-cry of the modern State," remarked this writer, " is not ' The sword of the Lord and of Gideon,' it is true, but it conquers in the name of its ' world-duty,' which is practically the same thing." [19] It is little wonder that, as Burgess complained later, his discussion of the colonial question was widely condemned in Continental Europe and in America " as a justification of the existing system of British colonial empire and of its

---

[18] *Ibid.*, pp. 47-48. It is interesting to compare portions of the above passage with language subsequently used by one of Burgess's students at Columbia. In his annual message of December 6, 1904, President Theodore Roosevelt wrote, with reference to the Dominican Republic: " If a nation shows that it knows how to act with reasonable efficiency and decency in social and political matters, if it keeps order and pays its obligations, it need fear no interference from the United States. Chronic wrongdoing, or an impotence which results in a general loosening of the ties of civilized society, may in America, as elsewhere, ultimately require intervention by some civilized nation, . . . " *Congressional Record*, 58th Cong., 3d sess., p. 19. This was, of course, part of the famous Roosevelt Corollary to the Monroe Doctrine.

[19] *Nation*, LIII, 240 (September 24, 1891).

farther extension in Asia and Africa, if not elsewhere, as a permanent world condition. The British publicists," he remarked naively, " understood me better and defended this part of my book with distinct appreciation." [20] Why, one may ask, should they have done otherwise?

It may be remarked here, parenthetically, as a curious fact, that when in 1898 the United States embarked upon a war which led directly to the assumption of a portion of the " world-duty " which Burgess had held before its eyes, he himself heatedly opposed that course. The war with Spain was to him " the first great shock " that he had experienced since the founding of the School of Political Science, which he had looked upon as an agency for international peace. The atrocity stories which preceded the war he set down as the insidious work of British statesmen, who wished to embroil the United States in a war with Spain; and the extension of American authority over subject peoples he regarded as " disastrous to American political civilization " and as " a fatal move . . . bound to reach farther and finally compromise the liberties of all American citizens." [21] Burgess apparently saw no inconsistency between this attitude and his earlier advocacy of a colonial policy. To the student any attempt to reconcile the two seems hopeless.

From Burgess, who planted the seed of an expansionist policy only to abjure the ripened fruit, we may turn to a philosopher whose thought on this subject was consistent and who never shrank from the responsibilities which his ideas entailed for his country. In the same year in which

[20] Burgess, *Reminiscences*, p. 249.
[21] *Ibid.*, pp. 312-316.

Burgess's treatise on political science saw the light there also appeared *The Influence of Sea Power upon History*, by Alfred Thayer Mahan, at that time a captain in the United States Navy. The embodiment of a series of lectures on naval history which Mahan had been detailed to give at the Naval War College at Newport, Rhode Island, the volume put forth the thesis which Mahan was further to illustrate and defend through the remainder of his active life. This thesis was, in short, that sea power was the most potent factor in the making or breaking of nations, that without sea power no people, however gifted, had attained or could attain the fullest measure of well-being or of influence and importance in world affairs. This volume, which told the story of the rise of British sea power in the years from 1660 to 1783, was followed by others which carried the narrative to the close of the Napoleonic wars, with excursions into other periods and into the naval history of the United States.[22]

But Mahan was always the preacher as well as the historian. What he perhaps had most at heart, and what certainly most concerns us here, was his indoctrination of his own countrymen with the gospel of sea power. A patriotic American, he wished to see his nation profit by the lessons which he had discovered in history and which he drove home at every opportunity, in his books and in the numerous articles which he contributed to American periodicals.

The history of sea power, wrote Mahan in 1890, embraces " in its broad sweep all that tends to make a people

[22] For a partial bibliography of Mahan's writings see C. C. Taylor, *The Life of Admiral Mahan, Naval Philosopher*, pp. 336-338.

great upon the sea or by the sea." [23] While it is " largely
a military history," its fundamental significance is economic.
Sea power exists chiefly for the sake of commerce; it in-
cludes all that goes to make sea-borne commerce secure and
profitable—a merchant marine, that trade may not be in
alien hands; a navy capable of defending the merchant
marine and keeping the trade routes open in time of war;
colonies, which may both serve the interests of commerce
directly and also provide naval vessels with secure bases
and coaling stations the world over.

These things, in Mahan's mind, were the essential foundations of national prosperity and national greatness. How
desperate to him, in 1890, must have appeared the prospects
of his own country! There was, indeed, a growing foreign
trade, but it was carried in ships flying alien flags. There
was the beginning—a very feeble beginning—of a modern
navy. A dozen light cruisers were built or being built as
well as the two second-class battleships, " Maine " and
" Texas "; and in the year of the publication of *The Influence of Sea Power upon History,* Congress authorized the
construction of three first-class battleships. These small
beginnings did not impress Mahan. Without a great merchant marine, of which he saw little prospect, he doubted
whether an adequate navy would or could be built.

Even had the United States a great national shipping, it
may be doubted whether a sufficient navy would follow; the
distance which separates her from other great powers, in
one way a protection, is also a snare.[24]

[23] *The Influence of Sea Power upon History, 1660-1783,* p. 1.
[24] *Ibid.,* pp. 87-88.

As for colonies, which " afford . . . the surest means of supporting abroad the sea power of a country,"—

Such colonies the United States has not and is not likely to have. . . . Having therefore no foreign establishments, either colonial or military, the ships of war of the United States, in war, will be like land birds, unable to fly far from their own shores. To provide resting-places for them, where they can coal and repair, would be one of the first duties of a government proposing to itself the development of the power of the nation at sea.[25]

But Mahan was not without hope for the future. For a quarter of a century, it is true, America had turned her eyes inward, away from the sea—an attitude which, in the historian's mind had spelled disaster for France in the seventeenth and eighteenth centuries.[26] There were signs now, however, that the nation might be forced to " the turning of the eyes outward, instead of inward only, to seek the welfare of the country." The growing productivity of its farms and factories would compel a search for foreign markets and induce relations to the world " radically distinct from the simple idea of self-sufficingness." The competition for markets and colonies being carried on by the seaboard powers of Europe, especially the aggressiveness shown of late by Germany in the Pacific, in Africa, in South America, might bring those powers into collision with the United States; had, in fact, already done so in the recent Samoan complication. The prospective piercing of the Isthmus of Panama, which would be " nothing but a disaster to the United States, in the present state of her military and naval preparation "; the unsettled political conditions

[25] *Ibid.,* p. 83.
[26] *Ibid.,* p. 87.

prevalent in Haiti, Central America, and the Hawaiian Islands, places of great military or commercial importance, whose control might be productive of international quarrels —all these things might perhaps jar the United States from her wonted complacency, might lead her to "look outward" and to build up her sea power.[27]

In preparation for the day when such a change of attitude should come about, Mahan sketched the outlines of a program. In addition to constructing a modern navy and adequate coast defenses, the United States must be ready to take, when opportunity offered, such outlying positions as would confer mastery of the essential water routes. Of preeminent importance, when the isthmian canal should have been opened, would be the control of the Caribbean. Upon such control would depend freedom of interoceanic transit. What, then, were the necessary measures?

Control of a maritime region is insured primarily by a navy; secondarily, by positions, suitably chosen and spaced one from the other, upon which as bases the navy rests, and from which it can exert its strength. At present the positions of the Caribbean are occupied by foreign powers, nor may we, however disposed to acquisition, obtain them by means other than righteous; but a distinct advance will have been made when public opinion is convinced that we need them, and should not exert our utmost ingenuity to dodge them when flung at our head.[28]

Next to the isthmus and the Caribbean area, Mahan was concerned with the Pacific. That ocean was destined to be

[27] Mahan, "The United States Looking Outward," *Atlantic Monthly*, December, 1890, reprinted in *The Interest of America in Sea Power, Present and Future*, pp. 3-27.

[28] *Ibid.*, pp. 102-103 (from "The Isthmus and Sea Power," originally published in the *Atlantic Monthly*, September, 1893).

the scene not only of a thriving commerce but of a gigantic struggle of races, civilizations, and religions—of Orient against Occident. The day was approaching " when the vast mass of China—now inert—[might] yield to one of those impulses which have in past ages buried civilization under a wave of barbaric invasion. The great armies of Europe, whose existence is so frequently deplored, may be providentially intended as a barrier to that great movement, if it come." But China might " burst her barriers eastward as well as westward, toward the Pacific as well as toward the European Continent "; in that event, to be confronted not by the armies of Europe but, God willing, by the navy of the United States.

Whate'er betide, Sea Power will play in those days the leading part which it has in all history, and the United States by her geographical position must be one of the frontiers from which, as from a base of operations, the Sea Power of the civilized world will energize.[29]

In that approaching Armageddon, the United States would need not only the unobstructed use of the isthmian canal, but outposts in the Pacific as well, and the most logical outpost was in the Hawaiian Islands. As early as 1890 Mahan had remarked that for the defense of the west coast it was essential that no foreign power should acquire a lodgment in those islands.[30] Three years later he pre-

---

[29] *Ibid.*, pp. 31-32 (letter to New York *Times,* January 30, 1893) ; pp. 123-124 (from " Possibilities of an Anglo-American Reunion," *North American Review,* November, 1894). The " yellow peril " idea was more fully elaborated in " A Twentieth Century Outlook," *Harper's Magazine,* September, 1897. See *infra,* chap. vi, p. 222.

[30] *Ibid.*, p. 26.

dicted that the outcome of the contest between East and West in the Pacific might be determined by " a firm hold of the Sandwich Islands by a great, civilized, maritime power," and that the United States was " naturally indicated as the proper guardian for this most important position." [31]

While Mahan's arguments for expansion looked primarily to the national interest, he did not hesitate to identify that interest with the welfare of the world at large. With her frontage on the Pacific, the United States stood guard over the preservation of Western civilization. But it was her rôle not only to defend but to extend the blessings of that civilization. " How much poorer would the world have been," he exclaimed, " had Englishmen heeded the cautious hesitancy that now bids us reject every advance beyond our shore-lines! " [32] Indeed, such a policy of beneficent expansion seemed to him a part of divine destiny. When one reflects, he wrote, upon the chains of accidents by which Great Britain had taken and held both Gibraltar and Jamaica,—

one marvels whether incidents so widely separated in time and place, all tending towards one end—the maritime predominance of Great Britain—can be accidents, or are simply the exhibition of a Personal Will, acting through all time, with purpose deliberate and consecutive, to ends not yet discerned.[33]

Even more than Burgess's, Mahan's message seemed to sound the battle-cry: " The sword of the Lord and of Gideon! "

[31] *Ibid.*, p. 32.
[32] *Ibid.*, p. 50.
[33] *Ibid.*, pp. 307-308.

The basic ideas of all these men—Darwin, Fiske, Strong, Burgess, and Mahan—were in current circulation at the beginning of the 1890's, though Mahan's thesis was broadened as the decade advanced. In 1894 appeared another contribution to the new expansionist philosophy in Benjamin Kidd's *Social Evolution*. Kidd, an English sociologist, belonged, like Fiske, to the Darwinian school and, also like Fiske, attempted to apply the Darwinian formula to society. The part of his book that concerns us here is a chapter dealing with the relation of the white man to the tropics.[34] In the near future, Kidd predicted, the European races were certain to have utilized all available agricultural lands in the temperate zone. It would then be imperative that, in the interest of the food supply, the immense resources of the tropics should be developed. But since it was evident that the native peoples of the tropics had not the requisite " social efficiency " to insure such development, it would be necessary for the more efficient races (preeminently the Anglo-Saxons) to take control. The spirit of altruism and social responsibility which, since the Reformation, had developed to a high degree in England, was a guarantee that such Anglo-Saxon control would be exercised not for purposes of human exploitation but for the common good. The partition of Africa seemed to Kidd evidence that Europe realized the future importance of the tropics. In the western hemisphere—where Haiti and the Central American states were cited as horrible examples of " social inefficiency "—the same realization might be perceived,

[34] Benjamin Kidd, *Social Evolution,* pp. 303-329.

even in the United States, where the necessity for the future predominance of the influence of the English-speaking peoples over the American Continents is already recognised by a kind of national instinct that may be expected to find clearer expression as time goes on.[35]

All of these writers contributed to the "intellectual climate" of the United States in the decade in which it inaugurated a· program of overseas expansion. How far they influenced the popular thought of the period cannot, obviously, be determined with any high degree of exactitude. They were all, however, well known and widely read. John Fiske's lectures on "American Political Ideas"—of which that on "Manifest Destiny" was the conclusion— were given orally many times in the United States. In print, they enjoyed a circulation as wide as that of *Harper's Magazine;* and they were subsequently published in book form. Fiske was, according to one reliable student of his career, "one of the most important intellectual influences in America in the last quarter of the nineteenth century." [36] Josiah Strong's volume, *Our Country,* had a circulation of 170,000 copies in English, besides being translated into several foreign languages.[37]

[35] *Ibid.,* p. 324. The thesis set forth in this chapter Kidd elaborated at greater length in his *The Control of the Tropics* (1898). Another application of the evolutionary concept to society, which has significance for this study is found in Professor Simon N. Patten's *The Theory of Social Forces* (supplement to *Annals* of American Academy of Political and Social Science, VII, 1896). "The earth," he wrote (pp. 131-132), "has but one general environment and can bring to perfection but one type of man. Attempts to preserve lower types of men, or to bring them into organic relations with higher types, tend to make a society static and thus check its progress."

[36] Adams, *loc. cit.*

[37] *National Cyclopaedia of American Biography,* IX, 416-417.

Burgess's treatise was not written for popular consumption, but in the opinion of President Butler of Columbia University, it "made a most profound impression at the time of its publication, both in Europe and in the United States. It served as the basis of the lectures and interpretations which Professor Burgess gave at Columbia University for a generation to thousands of eager and interested students of law and political science."[38] Among these students was young Theodore Roosevelt, some of whose ideas bear more than a fancied resemblance to Burgess's teachings.[39] At least one newspaper cited Burgess's work in support of the annexation of Hawaii.[40]

Of Mahan's influence upon his contemporaries there is no dearth of evidence. His books were widely noticed.[41]

[38] Nicholas Murray Butler's "Foreword" to John W. Burgess, *The Foundations of Political Science*, p. v. This volume is a reprinting of certain of the chapters of *Political Science and Comparative Constitutional Law*, including those considered above. The republication was suggested by President Butler in 1917, in the hope that it might "be of commanding service for the guidance of public opinion when the issues of the great war . . . were presented for settlement upon its termination." *Ibid*. Professor Burgess relates that arrangements to that end were made with the publishers of the original work, but that the plan was suspended when a typesetter in the publishing establishment discovered that "everything done by the Germans in the present war found its justification in that book." *Reminiscences of an American Scholar*, pp. 256-257. The reprint was finally brought out in 1933 by the Columbia University Press. Professor Burgess died in January 1931.

[39] *Supra*, p. 10, note 18.

[40] New York *Commercial Advertiser*, February 11, 1893. For Burgess's influence on President Dole of Hawaii, see *infra*, chap. vi, note 8.

[41] E. g., *Literary World*, XXI, 218 (July 5, 1890); *Harper's New Monthly Magazine*, LXXXVII, 962 (November, 1893); *Political Science Quarterly*, IX, 171-173 (March, 1894).

Unlike the other writers, he addressed himself directly to the problems in hand, contributing to such periodicals as the *Atlantic Monthly,* the *Forum,* the *North American Review, Harper's Magazine,* and *McClure's Magazine* articles urging naval preparedness, the annexation of Hawaii, the control of the Caribbean, and related policies.[42] His arguments were repeatedly cited in Congress, by Henry Cabot Lodge and other expansionist Senators and Congressmen,[43] and printed in reports of Congressional committees.[44] Theodore Roosevelt reviewed his books with high appreciation,[45] praised his magazine articles,[46] and corresponded with him in regard to annexing Hawaii and the Virgin Islands.[47] Other expansionist publicists went to Mahan for their arguments.[49] To a British observer, on the eve of the Spanish-American War, it seemed that the spirit of America had been remade through Mahan's influence. Mahan's teaching, wrote " The Looker-on," in *Blackwood's,*

was as oil to the flame of " colonial expansion " everywhere leaping into life. Everywhere a new-sprung ambition to go

[42] See the thirteen essays, all published 1890 to 1899, collected in the two volumes, *The Interest of America in Sea Power, Present and Future,* and *Lessons of the War with Spain.*

[43] *E. g., Cong. Record,* 51st Cong., 2d sess., p. 1856; 53d Cong., 2d sess., pp. 1844-1849; 53d Cong., 3d sess., pp. 3082-3084, 3111, 3113. In not all of these speeches is Mahan mentioned by name, but in all the debt to his ideas is perfectly obvious.

[44] *Senate Report* No. 681, 55th Cong., 2d sess., p. 99.

[45] *Pol. Sci. Quart.,* IX, 171-173.

[46] H. C. Lodge (ed.), *Selections from the Correspondence of Theodore Roosevelt and Henry Cabot Lodge,* I, 274.

[47] H. F. Pringle, *Theodore Roosevelt, a Biography,* pp. 171, 293.

[48] *E. g.,* Lt. F. L. Winn, U. S. A., in *Overland Monthly,* XXIII, 496 (May, 1894); Truxton Beale, in *North American Review,* CLXVI, 760 (June, 1898).

forth and possess and enjoy read its sanction in the philosophy of history ennobled by the glory of conquest. . . . I doubt whether this effect of Mahan's teachings has gone deeper anywhere than in the United States.[49]

Controvert as it may current fashions in historical interpretation, the observation must be made that the rise of an expansionist philosophy in the United States owed little to economic influences. Of the writers mentioned, only Mahan had much to say of expansion as an aid to commerce, and Mahan's ideas were derived from the study of history, not from any contemporary economic pressure. In fact, as will be shown later,[50] business interests in the United States were generally opposed to expansion, or indifferent to it, until after May 1, 1898. The need of American business for colonial markets and fields for investment was discovered not by business men but by historians and other intellectuals, by journalists and politicians.

Among the public men who espoused expansion largely in the supposed interest of trade was James G. Blaine, Secretary of State during three and one-quarter years of Benjamin Harrison's administration. In Congress, twenty years before, Blaine had predicted with approval the " expansion of our flag and our sovereignty over insular or continental possessions, north or south." [51] But by the time of his first appointment as Secretary of State (under Gar-

[49] *Blackwood's Edinburgh Magazine*, CLXIII, 563-565 (April, 1898). For a recent appraisal of Mahan's influence, see L. M. Hacker, " The Incendiary Mahan: a Biography," *Scribner's Magazine*, XCV, 263-268, 311-320.

[50] *Infra*, chap. vii.

[51] Quoted by Joseph B. Lockey, *James Gillespie Blaine*, in S. F. Bemis (ed.), *The American Secretaries of State and Their Diplomacy*, VIII, 116.

field in 1881), his idea of expansion had, according to Professor Lockey, "suffered a radical change." He had already begun to formulate his Pan-American policy, of which one of the chief purposes was, in his own words, "to cultivate such friendly, commercial relations with all American countries as would lead to a large increase in the export trade of the United States, by supplying fabrics in which we are abundantly able to compete with the manufacturing nations of Europe." [52] Like President Hoover in later years, Blaine had come to realize that, in the words of Professor Lockey, "territorial aggrandizement at the expense of the neighbours, whose friendship was essential to the success of that policy, was no longer to be thought of." Hence, assurances that the United States would scrupulously respect the independence and territorial integrity of its southern neighbors. [53]

Yet the assumption of this attitude of friendliness and forbearance toward Latin America did not prevent Blaine from contemplating the eventual dominance of the United States in the Caribbean. He believed it essential to the welfare of the United States that there should be an isthmian canal under American control. His energetic efforts to secure, for that purpose, a modification of the Clayton-Bulwer Treaty are well known. [54] Cuba, because of its relation to the future canal and the Gulf trade, must never be permitted to pass out of the "American system." The actual

[52] Ibid., VII, 275.

[53] Ibid., VIII, 116-117.

[54] For a recent treatment of this subject see D. S. Muzzey, James G. Blaine, pp. 197-201. A standard account is in M. W. Williams, Anglo-American Isthmian Diplomacy, 1815-1915.

possession of Cuba might not be necessary, or even desirable, he wrote in 1881; [55] yet ten years later he believed
that the United States would one day need to annex both
Cuba and Puerto Rico,[56] if not, indeed, all the West India
islands.[57] That he was keenly interested in acquiring a
naval base in the Caribbean we shall presently see.

Blaine showed no less interest in the Pacific than in the
Caribbean. Like Mahan and others of his day, he saw in
that ocean the great theater of American trade in the years
to come. Two diverging lines, drawn from San Francisco
to the Aleutian Islands and to Honolulu, would mark " the
natural limit of the ocean belt within which our trade with
the oriental countries must flow." The southern side of
this triangle would be, moreover, " the direct line of communication between the United States and Australasia.
Within this line lies the commercial domain of our western
coast." [58] Hawaii, obviously, if held by a strong naval
power, would dominate this area. Blaine considered it, like
Cuba, a part of the American system, but because of both
the actual existence of international rivalries in Hawaii,
and its close cultural and commercial ties with the United
States, he regarded the annexation of Hawaii as more natural and more imperative than the acquisition of Cuba.
Should the maintenance of the independence of Hawaii
prove impracticable, he wrote in 1881, the United States
would " unhesitatingly meet the altered situation by seek-

[55] *Papers Relating to the Foreign Relations of the United States,
1881*, p. 638. The volumes in this series will hereafter be cited in
the abbreviated form, *U. S. For. Rel.* with the appropriate year.

[56] Muzzey, *op. cit.*, p. 394.

[57] C. C. Tansill, *The Purchase of the Danish West Indies*, p. 191.

[58] *U. S. For. Rel., 1881*, p. 636.

ing an avowedly American solution for the grave issues presented." [59] A decade later he wrote to President Harrison:

I think there are only three places that are of value enough to be taken; one is Hawaii and the others are Cuba and Porto Rico. Cuba and Porto Rico are not imminent and will not be for a generation. Hawaii may come up for decision at any unexpected hour, and I hope we shall be prepared to decide it in the affirmative.[60]

Such was the man who, in March, 1889, became Harrison's first Secretary of State. To what extent Blaine shaped the foreign policy of the Harrison administration is difficult if not impossible to determine.[61] Yet Harrison's foreign policies, so far as they concern us here, were in accord with ideas which Blaine had previously expressed. It seems safe to assume that in their desire to promote American interests and even American sovereignty in the Caribbean and the Pacific, Harrison, Blaine, and John W. Foster, who succeeded Blaine in June 1892, worked harmoniously.[62] Whoever was chiefly responsible, the Har-

[59] *Ibid.*, p. 639.

[60] Gail Hamilton (pseudonym for Mary Abigail Dodge), *Biography of James G. Blaine,* p. 692.

[61] *Cf.* Prof. A. T. Volwiler's review of Muzzey's *James G. Blaine,* in *American Historical Review,* XLI, 554-557.

[62] Two other men who are known to have been very close to Harrison and who may have influenced his foreign policy were Whitelaw Reid of the New York *Tribune,* an enthusiastic expansionist, and B. F. Tracy, Secretary of the Navy. Tracy was insistent upon a vigorous defense of American interests on the isthmus and in the Pacific. In his annual report for December, 1892, he complained that " the aggressive policy of foreign nations . . . has continued, and this country, whether it will or not, will soon be forced into a position where it cannot disregard measures which form a standing menace to its prosperity and security. On

rison administration adopted an expansionist policy which, though barren of results, foreshadowed in its purposes the " large policy " of 1898.

No attempt will be made here to present in detail all the features of this policy, most of which have been treated in other studies. It is important, however, to view them in relation to one another.

In the settlement of the Samoan question—the first problem that confronted the new administration in the field of foreign relations—Harrison and Blaine succeeded in preserving the nominal independence of the islands under the tripartite protection of the United States, Germany, and Great Britain, and in safeguarding American rights at Pago-Pago under the treaty of 1878. Though Blaine was acclaimed for having taken a stronger tone than his Democratic predecessor and thus having brought Germany to terms, it has been shown that he found the German Government disposed toward a reasonable compromise and that he did, in fact, little more than push ahead to a settlement along lines already sketched by Bayard.[63] That Harrison, at any rate, did not consider the Samoan question as one of first magnitude we may perhaps infer from the conservative tone of editorials on the subject in the New York

---

the Isthmus our commerce is engaged in a desperate fight to maintain its foothold. In the South Pacific repeated annexations and protectorates are extending the power and influence of the maritime states of the Old World. . . . " House Exec. Doc. No. 1, Pt. III, 52d Cong., 2d sess., p. 37.

[63] For several recent accounts of the Samoan affair see Muzzey, op. cit., pp. 394-402; G. H. Ryden, The Foreign Policy of the United States in Relation to Samoa; Alice Felt Tyler, The Foreign Policy of James G. Blaine, chap. ix.

Tribune, which, in the hands of Harrison's friend Whitelaw Reid, may almost be considered an administration organ. Samoa, according to the *Tribune*, lay " entirely outside the circle of American interests." It might well be a matter of concern to Australia and New Zealand, but not to us.

There has been a scramble for territorial acquisition in that quarter during the last decade, England, France, and Germany having either coveted or seized one island after another. America ought not to compete with those powers in rivalries that lie outside of its own sphere of activity [64]

Not in the Samoan incident are the evidences of a new policy to be found, but in the administration's attitude to the canal question, to the Caribbean, and to Hawaii.

[64] N. Y. *Tribune*, January 11, January 18, 1889. After the disastrous hurricane of March, 1889, however, the *Tribune* insisted upon retention of all American rights in the land-locked harbor of Pago-Pago. " Pago-Pago should neither be neglected nor surrendered, but intelligently and sagaciously utilized." *Ibid.*, March 31, 1889. While the Samoan incident is not particularly significant as an indication of the new administration's policy, it did call forth, in Congress and the press, some expressions which give an interesting foretaste of the expansionist talk which was to be heard in the next ten years. Senator Frye, of Maine, asserted that Pago-Pago was destined to be of the most vital importance to the commerce of the United States in the South Pacific. *Cong. Record*, 50th Cong., 2d sess., pp. 108, 1374. Senator Dolph, of Oregon, and Mr. G. H. Bates, invoked the Monroe Doctrine for the protection of Samoa against European covetousness. *Ibid.*, pp. 1325-1337. G. H. Bates, " Some Aspects of the Samoan Question," *Century Magazine*, XV, 945-949. Mr. U. S. Eddy, member of a New York exporting firm, declared that American policy in Samoa had " created a profound impression in Europe, where it was rightly regarded as the indication of a changed attitude." The United States, he thought, was " about to begin an aggressive movement in the campaign of commerce." U. S. Eddy, " Our Chance for Commercial Supremacy," *Forum*, XI, 419-428.

A treaty negotiated by Secretary Frelinghuysen with Nicaragua in December, 1884, had, in plain disregard of the restrictions of the Clayton-Bulwer Treaty, proposed to give to the United States exclusive rights in the construction and control of a Nicaraguan canal.[65] This treaty had not been acted upon by the Senate and had been withdrawn by Cleveland in December, 1885. The project of a Nicaraguan canal to rival the French canal under construction at Panama had then been taken up by American capitalists and promoters, who on February 20, 1889, secured from Congress a charter under the name of the Maritime Canal Company of Nicaragua.[66] But as the company met with difficulty in raising the money, the proposal arose to have the United States guarantee the bonds of the company and in return receive possession of all or a majority of the stock, thus securing indirectly, as the principal stockholder in the corporation, that control over the canal which, by the Clayton-Bulwer Treaty, it was estopped from securing directly.[67] To this scheme, certainly contrary to the spirit if not to the letter of the nation's treaty obligations, Harrison gave his cordial support, expressing the opinion, in December, 1891, that the completion of the canal was " a matter of the highest

[65] P. M. Brown, *Frederick T. Frelinghuysen,* in Bemis, *op. cit.,* VIII, 30-31.

[66] *U. S. Statutes at Large,* XXV, 673-675. J. B. Henderson, *American Diplomatic Questions,* pp. 75-101. There is a MS Master's thesis, The Maritime Canal Company of Nicaragua, by Margaret Stern Wilkinson, in the University of Buffalo Library.

[67] *Cong. Record,* 51st Cong., 2d sess., p. 1123. See *Senate Report,* No. 1944, 51st Cong., 2d sess., a report from the Senate Committee on Foreign Relations, January 10, 1891, recommending the government guarantee of the bonds.

concern to the United States." [68] A year later he again recommended that Congress give " prompt and adequate support " to the Maritime Canal Company, and added:

It is impossible to overstate the value from every standpoint of this great enterprise, and I hope that there may be time, even in this Congress, to give to it an impetus that will insure the early completion of the canal and *secure to the United States its proper relation to it when completed.*[69]

Whether the isthmus was to be pierced by an American canal at Nicaragua or a French canal at Panama, the control of the approaches to it was a matter of vital importance to the United States, and no sooner had Captain Mahan begun publishing his admonitions upon this subject, than the Harrison administration was fishing in the troubled waters of the Caribbean with that object in view. The first opportunity to present itself was in Haiti, where a new president, Hyppolite, had come into power encumbered with certain supposed obligations to the United States. Frederick Douglass was sent as minister to Haiti, evidently with verbal instructions to press upon Hyppolite the mutual advantages to be derived from a lease of Môle St. Nicholas to the United States for a naval station; and when Hyppolite proved obstinate, Harrison dispatched Rear Admiral Gherardi as a special envoy to assist Douglass. Gherardi was instructed to point out to Hyppolite that the presence of a part of the United States fleet in Haitian waters would " be equivalent to a guaranty of the autonomy and independence of the Haytian government without any treaty

[68] James D. Richardson (ed.), *A Compilation of the Messages and Papers of the Presidents,* IX, 189.
[69] *Ibid.,* p. 317. Italics mine.

relations which might appear as a subordination of one Republic to the other." [70] Gherardi went even further than this, promising the Haitian foreign minister the protection of the United States against any attempts at revolution that might be provoked by a grant of the coveted lease.[71] Unable to convince the Haitian government with these arguments, Gherardi suggested to Blaine that the United States might seize Môle St. Nicholas in order to " relieve the Haitian government of responsibility and embarrassment." [72]

The drastic policy suggested by Admiral Gherardi was not followed. Instead, the Washington government turned to the Dominican Republic, where Samana Bay presented a site for a naval base equally eligible with Môle St. Nicholas. In opening negotiations for a reciprocity treaty in May, 1891, the Dominican minister in Washington let it be known that he was empowered also to negotiate a lease for such part of Samana Bay as the United States might need for a naval station. As negotiations proceeded, President Heureaux intimated that he would need a cash payment of $200,000 immediately upon the execution of the treaty, in order to suppress possible armed opposition to such an infringement of Dominican sovereignty. This information was made known confidentially to the proper

[70] Tyler, op. cit., p. 94. The whole incident is treated in ibid., pp. 91-98. See also Frederick Douglass, " Haiti and the United States: Inside History of the Negotiations for the Môle St. Nicholas," North American Review, CLIII, 337-345; 450-459 (Sept., Oct., 1891).

[71] Tyler, op. cit., p. 96.

[72] Ibid., pp. 96-97, note 22, citing Gherardi to Blaine, February 9, 1891, MS Dispatches, Haiti, XXV.

committees of Congress, and that body incorporated in
the Sundry Civil Appropriation Bill of August 5, 1892,
an item of $250,000 " for providing coaling and naval
stations, . . . to be expended under direction of the President." [73] A convention was drawn up providing for a
lease to the United States for 99 years, renewable for a
like period, of the island of Carenero in Samana Bay, with
free use and occupancy of the waters and shores of the
bay and the right to erect any necessary defenses; the United
States to pay $250,000 within thirty days, $50,000 annually
for five years, and $25,000 annually thereafter.

Unhappily for the success of the plan, rumors of what
was afoot leaked out, and their reverberations in the Dominican Republic compelled Heureaux to break off negotiations. Subsequent efforts to secure action, in Secretary
Foster's words, met with " delays, subterfuges, and broken
promises." [74]

Môle St. Nicholas and Samana Bay did not exhaust the
list of possible naval bases in the Caribbean. In the summer of 1891, certain Danish officials sounded the United
States minister to Denmark, Mr. C. E. Carr, upon the possibility of reviving Seward's old project—the sale of the

[73] *U. S. Statutes at Large,* XXVII, 349.

[74] Memorandum by Secretary John W. Foster, February 23, 1893,
accompanied by copies of the proposed treaty. *Miscellaneous Letters,
1893,* Department of State. Before becoming Secretary of State in
June, 1892, Foster had been in charge of the reciprocity negotiations
authorized by the McKinley Tariff act of 1890. (W. R. Castle, Jr.,
John Watson Foster, in Bemis, *op. cit.,* VIII, 191). Apparently he
had handled the negotiations with the Dominican Republic from
start to finish. There is an excellent account of this episode in
Sumner Welles, *Naboth's Vineyard,* I, 468-495.

islands of St. Thomas and St. John to the United States.[75] Upon receipt of Carr's report, Blaine wrote Harrison that he was opposed to this purchase until the United States should be in possession of the larger islands, since the Danish islands lacked both commercial and strategic importance and would be difficult to defend. "They are destined to become ours," he wrote, "but among the last of the West Indies that would be taken." [76]

Blaine's refusal may have been due to the fact that at this time the prospects of obtaining Samana Bay seemed good. When Carr brought the matter anew to Foster's attention in the fall of 1892, he found Foster friendly to the idea but doubtful whether the transaction could be consummated before March 4, 1893, when the Harrison régime would terminate. Foster wrote Carr:

> The question of the acquisition of the Islands is one of far-reaching importance, the extent of which is appreciated by no one more than the President. As his administration is, however, drawing to its close, he considers it inadvisable to express any views or indicate any policy, the consummation of which he could not effect.[77]

Thus the Harrison administration was fated to pass into history without having materially strengthened the position of the United States in the Caribbean. Its purposes, however, now that the facts are revealed, are clear enough.

There is very good reason for believing [wrote a reporter for the Washington *Star*, February 1, 1893] that if he [Harrison] had been re-elected an aggressive foreign policy

---

[75] Tansill, *op. cit.*, p. 190.

[76] *Ibid.*, p. 191. Blaine to Harrison, August, 10, 1891. Gail Hamilton, *loc. cit.*

[77] Foster to Carr, December 20, 1892. Tansill, *op. cit.*, p. 195.

would have been the most marked feature of his administration and that the end of another four years would have found this country in possession of strong points of advantage, from a naval point of view, in the South Atlantic and in the Pacific, placing us in a position both to foster and protect American commerce and to check foreign aggression in this hemisphere.

This seems like an accurate characterization. It was called forth, however, by the arrival of the news that a revolution in Hawaii had overthrown the royal government and that the United States would be invited to annex the islands. Thus, thought the *Star* reporter, there was even yet a chance that what Harrison had failed to accomplish in the Caribbean he might be able to achieve in the Pacific before laying down the cares of office.

Upon Harrison's Hawaiian policy, the subject of much writing but little real understanding, we must now dwell at considerable length.

II

HARRISON AND HAWAII

The relations of the Hawaiian kingdom to the United States, intimate from the arrival in the islands of American missionaries and the first ships of the Pacific whaling fleet in 1820, were drawn immensely closer by the reciprocity treaty of 1875. That treaty, admitting free of duty to each country the principal products of the other, and pledging the Hawaiian Government not to alienate any port or territory in the kingdom to any other power, virtually made Hawaii an economic colony of the United States, and was thought of by many as a step preliminary to the political annexation which had already been a subject of negotiation between the two governments.[1]

The treaty of 1875 was to run for seven years, terminable thereafter by either party at one year's notice. By a new treaty, negotiated in 1884 and ratified in 1887, the life of the original treaty was extended seven years from the latter date, with the added provision that the United States should enjoy the exclusive right to utilize the harbor of Pearl River in the island of Oahu for a coaling and repairing station for its ships.[2] Thus the ties between the two countries were drawn closer still.

---

[1] Foster Rhea Dulles, *America in the Pacific*, chaps. ix, x, xi, gives a concise account of the relations of Hawaii and the United States.

[2] W. M. Malloy, *Treaties, Conventions*, etc., I, 915-917 (treaty of 1875), 919-920 (treaty of 1884). The first treaty was put in effect by protocol of September 9, 1876. *Ibid.*, pp. 918-919.

The reciprocity provisions proved a great stimulus to Hawaiian industry, especially the production of sugar, and to trade between Hawaii and the Pacific coast of the United States. Sugar production increased nearly five-fold from 1877 to 1887 and more than doubled again in the next ten years. Hawaii's foreign trade mounted from $5,230,000 in 1877 to $20,104,000 in 1890. In the latter year, three-fourths of Hawaii's imports came from the United States, which took, in turn, over 99 per cent of the exports of the islands.[3] A consistently favorable balance of trade facilitated the accumulation of capital in Hawaii. An estimate prepared in 1893 showed over $33,000,000 invested in the sugar industry alone.[4] Hawaii enjoyed a period of phenomenal prosperity, which was, however, largely dependent upon the continuance of the favored status enjoyed by Hawaiian sugar in the American market.

The principal beneficiaries of this boom in industry and trade were the sugar planters, most of them of American birth or descent. The better agricultural lands had passed largely into the hands of men of this class. Large plantations, owned by whites and worked to an increasing degree by Oriental laborers—Chinese and Japanese—came to typify Hawaiian economics. And since a modern system of property and economics did not comport well with the capriciousness, extravagance and corruption of the native monarchy, a party whose chief strength lay in the white property-owners forced King Kalakaua, in 1887, to accept a modernized constitution which made the government a parliamentary one and gave a preponderance of political

[3] *Statistical Abstract of the U. S.*, 1907, p. 555; 1925, p. 668.
[4] *U. S. For. Rel., 1894*, Appendix II, p. 921.

power to the property-owners.[5] Hawaii seemed destined
to enjoy both material prosperity and orderly, responsible
government. The loss or threatened loss of both these
blessings produced revolution in Hawaii and ultimately the
annexation of the islands by the United States.

The first threat to the economic prosperity of Hawaii
occurred in the consideration of tariff legislation in Washington in 1888-1889. The Mills bill—the Democratic tariff
bill passed by the House of Representatives—would have
reduced duties on raw sugar by approximately $18\frac{1}{2}$ to 20
per cent. The Senate substitute proposed a much greater
reduction, approximately 50 per cent, and in addition, at
the instance of the producers of Louisiana cane and California beet sugar, provided a bounty of one cent per pound
on American-grown sugar.[6] No legislation was enacted
at this time, but the trend was obvious. Equally obvious
was the menace to Hawaiian sugar growers, who were
threatened at the same time with the loss of their advantage
over other foreign producers and of their status of equality
with producers in the United States.

The Hawaiian government was quick to see the danger
and to lodge a protest in Washington. Complaining that
" it seems to be unjust and inequitable to depreciate the
value of a treaty while in force by any legislation of either
party," the Hawaiian minister of foreign affairs warned

[5] For the operation of the Hawaiian Government under the
Constitution of 1887, see Col. T. M. Spaulding's valuable study,
Cabinet Government in Hawaii, 1887-1893; also H. E. Chambers,
Constitutional History of Hawaii.

[6] *Senate Report* No. 2332, 50th Cong., 1st sess. *Cong. Record,*
50th Cong., 2d sess., pp. 927-931, 1013, 1180.

the United States that if the economic ties between the two countries were weakened and if Hawaiian products found a better market in Canada, for instance, than in the United States, the political leanings of the Hawaiians might be similarly diverted, and should the occasion ever arise for annexation or a protectorate by a stronger power, Hawaii might be led to seek refuge elsewhere than under the American flag.[7]

As a consequence of this protest, Minister Carter and Secretary Blaine undertook the negotiation of a new treaty, with the object of safeguarding and rendering permanent the advantages enjoyed by Hawaii in the markets of the United States, and on the other hand, of assuring similar permanence to American rights in Pearl Harbor. More than this was proposed, however—nothing less than the extension of a definite protectorate over Hawaii by the United States.

Following discussion of the subject between the two men, Carter sent to Blaine, on April 11, 1889, a project, as he wrote, " of a treaty of the nature as I understood it, of the proposition discussed between us personally to be proposed to our governments for consideration." [8] The purport of the proposed treaty was to establish complete reciprocity in trade between the United States and Hawaii, to grant, in each country, to imports from the other all bounties or im-

[7] Austin to Carter, March 8, 1889. Extract enclosed in Carter to Blaine, March 29, 1889. *Hawaii, Notes,* III. Jonathan Austin was at this time Hawaiian minister of foreign affairs. H. A. P. Carter was Hawaiian minister at Washington.

[8] Carter to Blaine, April 11, 1889. *Ibid.* The draft of the proposed treaty accompanies the note.

munities which should be granted to native products, and
to continue in force all provisions of this treaty and of
existing treaties not inconsistent therewith, either until
terminated by mutual consent, or (as an alternative) for
ten years from the date of its going into effect and thereafter
for three years after either party should give notice of its
termination. In addition, it was stipulated that the United
States should guarantee " positively and efficaciously, the
independence and autonomy of Hawaii in all its territory,"
and that in order to enable the United States to fulfill this
obligation, the King of Hawaii would enter ir to no treaties
or engagements with any foreign power " without the con-
currence and assent of the Government of the United
States." Furthermore, in the event of domestic disturbance
or difficulty with a foreign power, the armed force of the
United States might take whatever steps were necessary to
preserve peace, maintain Hawaiian sovereignty, and protect the just interests of foreign residents.[9]

There is no record of further conversations at this time
between Carter and Blaine, but in May, Carter returned

[9] Over a year later, when there had been a change in ministry
in Honolulu and Carter found it necessary to defend this treaty
negotiation to a new minister of foreign affairs, he implied that
Blaine had taken the initiative in the negotiation by asking that
a greater degree of permanence be given to American rights in
Pearl Harbor; that he (Carter) had replied that this could not be
without the assurance that Hawaiian sugar growers should share
equally with Americans in any bounty that might be granted, to
which Blaine had agreed; that the guarantee of independence was
introduced to disarm Hawaiian and foreign critics who suspected
the United States of aiming at the annexation of Hawaii. Carter
to J. A. Cummins, September 21, 1890. Copy in Spaulding Collection.

to Honolulu, where, during the summer of 1889, he discussed the proposed treaty with the cabinet. The result
was a modified draft providing for the guarantee of Hawaiian independence by the United States, full free trade
between the two countries in the native products of each,
and equal treatment in respect to bounties, etc., in each
country of domestic products with those imported free
from the other. The extension of American rights in Pearl
Harbor was made contingent upon the passage by Congress
of the legislation necessary to carry out the reciprocity
provisions. Finally, the life of the treaty was made of indefinite duration, and terminable only by mutual consent.[10]

The portion of the new draft providing for the guarantee
of Hawaiian independence differed in two respects from
Carter's original draft. Instead of stipulating for American
consent to all treaties made between Hawaii and other
countries, it provided merely that the government of the
United States should be informed of all such treaties; and
it omitted all mention of the right of the United States to
land its armed forces on Hawaiian soil. Two alternative
clauses embodying the right to land troops were, according
to a later statement by the ministers, discussed, and rejected
by them.[11]

[10] A copy of the proposed treaty is in *Letter Book* II, pp. 83-86,
Hawaiian Archives. Copy in Spaulding Collection.

[11] *Report of the Proceedings of the Committee on Foreign Relations to the Legislature of 1890, in regard to the Investigation of
Treaty Matters. Reply of Minister Austin to the Majority Report
of Committee on Foreign Relations, in the Legislative Assembly,
June 13, 1890.* In their account of the history of the " landing of
troops " clause, the members of the cabinet and Minister Carter
were not entirely frank. Austin, the foreign minister, withheld

With the new draft, and with instructions that permitted
him some leeway in negotiating with the United States,[12]
Carter departed for Washington at the close of September.
Even before his departure, however, an attempt was on foot
in Honolulu to defeat the negotiations. A copy of the
proposed treaty fell into the hands of the opposition, supposedly through the instrumentality of the King. As given
to the press, it included the two alternative " landing of
troops " clauses, which had been set aside by the cabinet,
as " proposed additions " to the treaty.[13] On September 26,
a mass meeting, attended chiefly by native Hawaiians,
petitioned the King to withhold his signature from any
treaty impairing the independence or autonomy of the Kingdom, at any rate until the wishes of the nation should have
been expressed through its elected representatives.[14] Statements by Austin and other members of the cabinet defending their program and denying that any proposal to permit
the landing of troops had ever been made either by the

---

from an investigating committee of the legislature all correspondence
with Carter in the spring of 1889, prior to Carter's return to
Honolulu, on the ground that this was private and not public
correspondence. He stated that the clause in question had been
merely suggested by Carter as something which the United States
might perhaps ask in the course of the negotiations, not as a
matter already discussed between him and Blaine. Carter himself,
in a letter to Austin's successor, stated that this clause had never
been mentioned between himself and Blaine, but had been suggested by occurrences in Honolulu in July, 1889—three months
after Carter had sent his draft to Blaine. Carter to J. A. Cummins,
September 21, 1890. Copy in Spaulding Collection.

[12] Austin to Carter, September 27, 1889. Spaulding Collection.

[13] *Daily Pacific Commercial Advertiser,* Honolulu (hereafter
cited as *Advertiser*), September 30, 1889.

[14] *Ibid.,* September 27, 1889.

United States or the Hawaiian government, failed to allay suspicion.[15] Though Austin assured Carter that opposition to the treaty was mainly personal and factious and was not shared by the King,[16] the latter, in December, refused to sign instructions authorizing Carter to conclude a treaty.[17] The question became an issue in the biennial election of the legislature on February 5, 1890, and so strong was the feeling against the treaty that the opposition—the so-called National Reform Party—captured every seat in the island of Oahu (where Honolulu is located) and enough elsewhere to make the control of the legislature a matter of doubt until its actual meeting on May 21.[18]

As a consequence of the King's opposition, of the partial defeat in the elections, and of the advice of a group of prominent citizens of Honolulu, the cabinet now dropped from the treaty all provision for a protectorate by the United States, leaving only the clauses on free trade and bounties. But at this point the attorney-general, C. W. Ashford, who had been in Canada during the winter and was alleged to be under Canadian influence, turned against his colleagues and refused to advise the King to authorize even a drastically modified treaty. As the King declined to give the authorization without the unanimous vote of the cabinet, Austin was finally compelled to inform Carter in Washington that no action upon the treaty would be

[15] *Ibid.*, October 5, 1889. *U. S. For. Rel., 1894,* App. II, p. 311.

[16] Austin to Carter, December 1, 1889. Spaulding Collection.

[17] *Report of the Proceedings of the Committee on Foreign Relations to the Legislature of 1890, . . .*

[18] H. W. Mist to Carter, February 13, 1890. Spaulding Collection. *U. S. For. Rel., 1894,* App. II, pp. 301-303.

taken until after the meeting of the legislature.[19] When
the legislature convened, the division in the cabinet, coupled
with distaste for the proposed treaty and for the way in
which it had been handled, resulted in the resignation of
the entire cabinet and its replacement by a new group of
ministers with J. A. Cummins as minister of foreign affairs.
Treaty negotiations lapsed for the time being. The idea of
an American protectorate, even with the bait of complete
free trade and a possible bounty for Hawaiian sugar, had
not found favor with the King or the rank and file of the
Hawaiian voters.[20]

Meanwhile, the McKinley tariff bill, putting raw sugar
on the free list and compensating American producers
with a bounty of two cents a pound, was under discussion
in Washington.[21] On May 1, 1890, Carter left at the State
Department a memorandum pointing out the injustice to
Hawaii involved in such action. The proposed legislation,
he said, " would be a violation of the equities of the exist-

[19] Austin to Carter, May 3, 1890. Spaulding Collection. *Advertiser*, April 2, 1890. *Minority Report, Committee on Foreign Relations*. Presented by Hon. H. P. Baldwin, June 14, 1890. *Cf.* L. A.
Thurston, *Memoirs of the Hawaiian Revolution*, pp. 209-214.

[20] *U. S. For. Rel., 1894*, App. II, pp. 321, 332. Carter, meanwhile, had received some encouragement from Blaine, but formal
discussion of the proposed treaty was postponed from time to time
and finally abandoned because of the situation in Honolulu. Carter
to Austin, November 28, December 26, 1889; February 20, March
26, 1890. Spaulding Collection. Whether a treaty promising
Hawaiian sugar growers equality in bounties, etc., with American
producers could actually have been made and ratified in Washington
is doubtful. J. Mott Smith, who succeeded Carter in Washington,
appeared to think the treaty proposals of 1889 had never had a
chance of fulfillment. Smith to Parker, November 5, 1892. *Ibid*.

[21] *House Report* No. 1466, 51st Cong., 1st sess., p. 14.

ing treaties . . . unless Hawaiian sugar were admitted to share in the bounties, as the obvious intent of the treaties was to put Hawaiian sugars upon the same footing as American sugars, and the proposed legislation would place Hawaii on the same footing as non-reciprocating nations." [22] This official protest was very mildly worded, but in interviews with the press Carter gave out the opinion that passage of the McKinley bill without giving the bounty to Hawaiian sugar would have the effect of abrogating the reciprocity treaty, and that thereby the United States would lose its exclusive rights to the use of Pearl Harbor.[23]

In spite of protests and threats, the McKinley tariff bill became law with the sugar schedule substantially as first proposed.[24] But for Hawaii further misfortunes befell. Apparently by a clerical error, there was omitted from the bill a section exempting imports from Hawaii from the operation of the new duties. This omission did not affect sugar, which was on the free list, but did have the effect of reimposing duties on certain other Hawaiian products, such as rice and tallow, which were entitled to free entry under the reciprocity treaty. Thus, while the free admission of sugar wiped out most of the substantial advantage enjoyed by Hawaii under the reciprocity treaty, an error in printing the bill threatened to destroy all remaining benefits and even the theoretical advantage accruing to the island-

[22] Unsigned Memorandum, May 1, 1890. *Hawaii, Notes*, III. Carter to Austin, May 1, 1890. Spaulding Collection.

[23] Carter to Austin, June 30, 1890, enclosing clippings from New York *Herald,* June 30, and Rochester *Chronicle,* June 25. Spaulding Collection.

[24] *Stat. L.,* XXVI, 583-584. Act approved October 1, 1890.

ers.[25] To make matters worse, a resolution was introduced in Congress for the appropriation of $500,000 for establishing a coaling and repair station at Pearl Harbor, suggesting that the United States, while destroying the value of the treaty to Hawaii, would claim all its own privileges under the same.[26]

Carter warned Blaine that if the error in the tariff law were not corrected, Hawaii would be compelled to abrogate the treaty, and that such action would result not only in the United States losing its exclusive privileges in Pearl Harbor, but very probably in Hawaii's being forced to turn to Great Britain for a reciprocity arrangement with Canada and perhaps Australia.[27] The legislative error was eventually corrected. The President noticed the matter in his annual message,[28] and the State Department forwarded Carter's protests to the proper committees of Senate and House. An act approved March 3, 1891, provided that nothing in the tariff act should be held to repeal or impair the provisions of the conventions of 1875 and 1887 respecting commercial reciprocity with the Hawaiian Islands.[29]

[25] Carter to Cummins, November 24, 1890. Spaulding Collection. Blaine's memorandum of conversation with Carter, January 6, 1891. *Hawaii, Notes,* III.

[26] Carter to Blaine, February 1, 1891. *Ibid.* Carter to Cummins, February 5, 1891. Spaulding Collection.

[27] Blaine's Memorandum, January 6, 1891, *Hawaii, Notes,* III.

[28] Richardson, *Messages and Papers of the Presidents,* IX, 110.

[29] Wharton to Carter, December 18, 1890. *Notes to Hawaii,* I, 157. *House Report* No. 3422, 51st Cong., 2d sess. *Stat. L.,* XXVI, 844. Mrs. Alice Felt Tyler, in her *Foreign Policy of James G. Blaine,* p. 206, assumes erroneously that the correspondence over this error in legislation and the passage in Harrison's message dealing with the same referred to the sugar schedule and its injury to Hawaii.

Thus Hawaiian products continued to enter the United States free of duty, as they were entitled to do under the treaties. But Hawaiian sugar must now compete with other foreign sugar, also admitted free, and with American-grown sugar enjoying a bounty of two cents a pound. The effect in the islands was serious. The United States minister alleged later that sugar prices in Honolulu fell from $100 to $60 a ton and that property in the islands depreciated by not less than $12,000,000.[30]

The Hawaiian sugar industry could, of course, have been saved from loss by the extension of the bounty to Hawaiian sugar, as proposed in the treaty negotiations of 1889. Whatever chance there may have been of that solution was destroyed by the opposition in Hawaii to the accompanying protectorate feature. After the McKinley Act became law, Carter explained to his government, the bounty could be extended to Hawaiian sugar only by action of both houses of Congress, whereas prior to the passage of the act, Senate action alone would have been required upon the treaty. All hope of the bounty ended with the passage of the McKinley Act.[31] Secretary Blaine, however, appeared anxious to do anything that circumstances permitted to " set things straight again " with Hawaii, and Carter believed there was a possibility of extending the reciprocity treaty to admit free all Hawaiian products instead of a limited list.[32] Such action was proposed in a resolution passed almost unanimously by the Hawaiian Legislative Assembly

[30] *U. S. For. Rel., 1894,* App. II, p. 382;
[31] Carter to Cummins, November 29, 1890. Spaulding Collection.
[32] Carter to Cummins, November 29, 1890, December 5, 1890. *Ibid.*

in November, 1890.[33] Carter at first counseled delay in arranging such a treaty, but in February, 1891, when action by Congress safeguarding the existing reciprocity treaty seemed assured, he advised that the attempt be made.[34] On March 10, Samuel Parker, the new Hawaiian minister of foreign affairs, wrote Carter that the cabinet would support any treaty favorable to Hawaiian commercial interests, and that the legislature would probably ratify such a treaty, provided it safeguarded the rights of the crown and the independence of the kingdom. Carter was therefore instructed to send to Honolulu a draft of such a treaty as he believed would be acceptable to both governments.[35]

Negotiation of a new treaty was accordingly begun in Washington, and on April 6, 1891, Carter sent to his government a draft which had been discussed and tentatively agreed to between himself, Blaine, and Moore, of the Department of State. It substituted complete for limited free trade between the two countries (thus admitting refined as well as raw sugar free of duty) and stipulated that existing treaties should be terminated only by mutual consent.[36] Carter had contemplated making a trip to Honolulu to discuss the treaty, as he had done two years previously, but because of ill health he decided to go to Europe for the summer, with the result that negotiations were at a standstill for some months.[37]

[33] U. S. For. Rel., 1894, App. II, p. 339.
[34] Carter to Cummins, December 21, 1890, February 15, 1891. Spaulding Collection.
[35] Parker to Carter, March 10, 1891. Ibid.
[36] Carter to Parker, April 6, 1891. Ibid.
[37] Carter to Parker, March 24, 1891. Parker to Carter, April 18, 1891. Ibid.

Carter returned to the United States in the late summer
or fall of 1891, but was too ill to take up his official duties
and died in New York on November 1. Meanwhile, the
Hawaiian Government, becoming impatient to conclude
the negotiations, had commissioned Mr. J. Mott Smith,
a Bostonian temporarily in the islands and serving as minister of finance, a special envoy to negotiate a treaty of
full free trade with the United States.[38] The proposed
treaty, drafted in Honolulu, differed little from that prepared by Carter in Washington. It, and other existing
treaties, were to be terminable only by mutual consent. All
native products (raw or manufactured) of each country
were to be admitted free of duty into the other, with the
exception of liquors, opium and preparations thereof, and
other prohibited articles. The article of the Convention of
1887, giving the United States exclusive right to the use
of Pearl Harbor, was to be subject to termination by the
Hawaiian Government if, after five years, the United States
should not have deepened the entrance sufficiently for the
passage of deep-sea ships and have entered upon the use
of the harbor.[39]

Within less than a month Blaine and Smith had reached
agreement on the form and wording of the treaty, and it

[38] Parker to Carter, August 25, September 26, 1891. *Ibid*.
Smith's commission as special envoy, dated October 15, 1891, and
another of same date as *chargé d'affaires pro tem.*, were presented
at the Department of State, November 6. *Hawaii, Notes*, III.

[39] *Ibid*. There are several slightly variant drafts of the proposed
treaty in the files. The final draft contains an additional article
pledging the President and the Queen " to urge upon their respective governments the speedy construction and operation of an ocean
cable between California and the Hawaiian Islands."

had been submitted to President Harrison for approval.[40]
Then followed weeks of perplexing inaction, ended with
the announcement that the President would not submit the
treaty to the Senate. His reasons, as they reached Smith
through the State Department, were his belief that the
Senate would not advise ratification, his feeling (together
with that of certain Republican Senators) that it was inconsistent for the party committed to protection to espouse, in
the proposed treaty, the principle of free trade, even with
one small country, and his objection to reopening the tariff
question by asking a modification of the McKinley Act.
Smith was further informed that pressure had been brought
to bear against the treaty by the fruit growers and sugar
refiners of California.[41]

Later conferences with Blaine, with Secretary Foster, who
succeeded Blaine in June, 1892, and with Senator Aldrich
convinced Smith that any further negotiation was futile
until after the presidential election in November. If the
Republicans were victorious, said Foster, they would renew
negotiations after the election.[42]

After the Democratic victory in November, Smith again
called upon Foster, who informed him that the President
would not again consider the free trade treaty and that the
chances would be better under the incoming Democratic
administration.[43] As Mott Smith penned this dispatch,
and apparently quite without his knowledge, events more
momentous than any free trade treaty were preparing in
Honolulu.

[40] Smith to Parker, December 2, 1891. Spaulding Collection.
[41] Smith to Parker, January 30, February 10, 1892. *Ibid.*
[42] Smith to Parker, April 22, May 6, July 15, 1892. *Ibid.*
[43] Smith to Robinson, December 30, 1892. *Ibid.*

Diplomatic correspondence between the United States and Hawaii, in these years, flowed through two channels, which seldom, if ever, touched. Official relations between the two governments—treaty negotiations and the like—were conducted almost exclusively in Washington between the Secretary of State and the Hawaiian minister. In the letters which passed between the Department of State and the Hawaiian Legation and between the latter and the Ministry of Foreign Affairs in Honolulu, the two nations appear as equally sovereign and independent, and likely to remain so. The possibility of annexation was mentioned, if at all, only to be refuted. Both Carter and Smith reported that Blaine had no desire to disturb in any way the relations between Hawaii and other nations, that his one desire was for a continuance of Hawaiian independence under a stable government. To that end, said Smith, in December, 1891, the United States would render assistance if necessary. But, he wrote to Parker, " you may rest assured that the United States will not interfere in our affairs except by desire of the Queen, in times of *pilikia* [domestic disorder], and then only to withdraw, when order shall have been restored." [44]

Very different was the correspondence between the Department of State and the American minister in Honolulu. Letters from the Department to the minister were of routine nature only, but the dispatches of Minister John L. Stevens, who took up his duties in Honolulu in September, 1889, were full of disturbing accounts of domestic turmoil and foreign intrigue in the islands, and as months passed, be-

[44] Carter to Austin, February 20, 1890; Carter to Cummins, September 21, 1890. Smith to the Queen, November 16, 1891; Smith to Parker, December 30, 1891. *Ibid.*

came more and more insistent that annexation to the United States was the only effective remedy for Hawaii's troubles.

Because of the prominent part that Stevens was to play in the dethronement of the Queen and the initial attempt at annexation to the United States, and because of the absence of any official instructions to Stevens in the State Department files, there has been considerable speculation as to whether Stevens received secret instructions from Blaine either before or after his departure for Hawaii. Blaine was on record as favoring eventual annexation of the islands.[45] Blaine and Stevens were old friends. Did Blaine, perchance, tell Stevens that his business would be to seek to bring about annexation during Blaine's term in the State Department? It seems certain that no such instructions were given, at least prior to the spring of 1892, for Stevens, in a personal letter to " Bro. Blaine," March 25, 1892, after analyzing the growing annexation sentiment in Hawaii, wrote:

> After carefully reading what I have herein expressed, I want you to write me in as few or many words as you please —are you for Annexation? [46]

Had there been any previous understanding on the subject between Blaine and Stevens, such an inquiry would hardly have been necessary. There is no record of any reply to this, or to more formal requests for instructions voiced by Stevens. Whether private communications were sent we do not know. The fairest assumption we can make seems to be that Blaine (and his successor, Foster,) were satisfied

---

[45] *Supra,* pp. 24-25.
[46] Stevens to Blaine, March 25, 1892. *Dispatches, Hawaii,* XXV.

with Stevens's fervor for annexation and, while not wishing
to commit themselves, were willing to allow the minister a
free rein.

Stevens had been in Hawaii barely six months when he
began urging upon Blaine the need for closer relations with
the United States—the utilization of Pearl Harbor, the
laying of a cable, the modification of the treaty, etc. The
United States, he said, must soon solve the question: Will
the Hawaiian Islands be American or Asiatic? [47] From
the time of Queen Liliuokalani's accession to the throne
(January, 1891) he complained of subversive and anti-
American influences about the Queen.[48] But it was not
until the spring of 1892 that Stevens began his real drive
for annexation. After the biennial Hawaiian elections in
February, he reported that the pro-American party had apparently secured enough seats in the legislature to insure
the ratification of the pending free trade treaty with the
United States. Annexation sentiment, he said, was growing, both among the responsible business men in the islands
and the less responsible whites and natives. " The present
political situation is feverish and I see no prospect of its
being permanently otherwise until these islands become a
part of the American Union or a possession of Great
Britain." He added that after the treaty should have been
ratified he should deem it his official duty " to give a more
elaborate statement of facts and reasons why a new departure ' by the United States as to Hawaii is rapidly becoming a necessity, that a ' protectorate ' is impracticable,

[47] *U. S. For. Rel., 1894,* App. II, pp. 315-317 (March 20, 1890).
[48] *Ibid.,* p. 343.

and that annexation must be the future remedy "—unless, indeed, the United States was willing to see the islands pass to Great Britain.[49]

A month later Stevens reported information that there was in the islands an organized revolutionary party (the Hawaiian Patriotic League), composed of native Hawaiians, whites and half-castes, which was determined either to force the Queen to choose a cabinet from among its members, or else to overthrow the monarchy and establish a republic, with the object of ultimate annexation to the United States.[50] He asked for special instructions to guide him and the officers of such naval force as might be present in the event of the success of such a movement. Should they, in line with ordinary practice, confine themselves to protection of life and property? Or, in view of the exceptional relations between Hawaii and the United States, should they assist in restoring the deposed government? [51] Subsequent letters played upon the same themes— the imminence of revolution, the growth of annexation sentiment. The annexationists were of two groups: the natives and irresponsible whites and half-castes, who favored revolution and the establishment of a republic as steps

[49] Ibid., pp. 353-354 (February 8, 1892). Stevens did not know as yet that President Harrison had rejected the new free trade treaty.

[50] Stevens's report is confirmed by the statement of Col. Volney V. Ashford. A leader in the revolution of 1887, Ashford was active in organizing, in the spring of 1892, secret leagues among both whites and natives, whose ultimate object, he claims, was the overthrow of the monarchy and either the creation of a republic or annexation to the United States. Ibid., pp. 637-638.

[51] Ibid., pp. 354-355 (March 8, 1892). As far as the records show, this inquiry went unanswered.

toward annexation; and the responsible business men and property owners, who hoped to reach the same end by peaceful, constitutional means. Could these two groups unite, said Stevens, "they would carry all before them, providing the latter could get any encouragement that the United States would take these islands as a territory." [52]

Would the United States give such encouragement? That was the question to which Stevens asked an answer in his private letter to Blaine, mentioned above. "What this involves in our national policy I have carefully considered," he said, in closing that letter. "But I think we should accept the issue like a great Nation, and not act the part of pigmies nor cowards. These Islands fully developed can be made gardens, sustaining 400,000 or 500,000 people, and the key of the North Pacific, which is fronted by the Pacific States with their vast American possibilities."

After the arrest, May 20, of a number of the radical leaders,[53] Stevens reported that the better element among the discontented, who wished to secure a change of government by peaceful means, were now looking to the legislature, "which was fairly and quietly elected, and is believed to have a safe majority of prudent men, several of

[52] *Ibid.*, pp. 356-357 (April 2, 1892).

[53] According to Ashford's statement, the Queen was at this time meditating a coup d'état for the overthrow of the Constitution of 1887 and attempted to induce R. W. Wilcox and other leaders of the League to support her plans. When they refused, she ordered their arrest. *Ibid.*, pp. 637-638. Those arrested were, however, discharged by a friendly judge. Wilcox participated actively in the ensuing session of the legislature. Ashford thought it safer to leave the islands. Statement of V. V. Ashford in San Jose *Mercury*, quoted in *Advertiser*, September 9, 1892.

them being of the chief men of the islands, of good American blood." [54] The legislature, then, was the agency through which peaceful annexation might be secured, given sufficient encouragement at Washington. A prominent member-elect of the legislature now came forward to second the efforts of Minister Stevens to convert the United States to the idea.

" Hon. Lorrin Thurston arrived here yesterday."

This bare statement closed Mott Smith's letter of May 6, 1892, to the Hawaiian minister of foreign affairs. Lorrin A. Thurston was a prominent member of the American group in the Hawaiian Islands, a lawyer by profession, a former minister of the interior in the ministry of 1887-1890, and a member-elect of the legislature chosen in February, 1892. His visit to the United States in May, 1892, was ostensibly in connection with the Hawaiian exhibit at the Chicago World's Fair.[55] In reality, however, he came to Washington as the representative of a secret Annexation Club, recently formed in Honolulu, and the purpose of his mission was to " get into contact with the authorities, and ascertain their disposition " as to the annexation of the islands.[56] Thurston's secret was poorly kept. Scarcely had

[54] *U. S. For. Rel., 1894*, App. II, pp. 357-359 (May 21, 1892).

[55] Washington *Evening Star*, May 3, 1892.

[56] Thurston, *op. cit.*, p. 229. On the same page Thurston states, of the Annexation Club: " Our object was not to promote annexation, but to be ready to act quickly and intelligently, should Liliuokalani precipitate the necessity by some move against the constitution, tending to revert to absolutism or anything of the nature." This statement, written long after the event, is contradicted by Thurston's memorandum to Secretary Blaine, discussed below. A year later, Thurston told Secretary Gresham that the Club had been

he reached Washington when the press became filled with rumors of the proposed annexation of Hawaii. The Washington correspondent of the London *Times* cabled to his paper that at the instance of the Secretary of State the chairman of the Foreign Affairs Committee of the House of Representatives had polled that committee as to their attitude, which was understood to be favorable. Similar reports appeared in the Boston *Transcript* and in the San Francisco papers. As carried in the latter, and copied in the *Advertiser* and *Bulletin* of Honolulu, they contained the additional information that Dr. Mott Smith, the Hawaiian minister, had said that " if the United States made Hawaii a fair proposition looking toward annexation it would be well received.": [57]

---

formed *after* he returned to Honolulu. *Infra,* note 60. The existence of the Annexation Club was known to American naval officers in Honolulu and, inferentially, to Minister Stevens. Rear Admiral George Brown, U. S. N., wrote to the Secretary of the Navy, September 6, 1892: " There now exists in Honolulu an organization comprising the most prominent Annexationists, which has for its object the formulation of some plan by which a change of Government can be effected quietly, and with the consent and co-operation of the Queen and the members of her Cabinet and Staff." It would not, he said, " countenance anything of a revolutionary character in the way of force," but expected that the Queen would consent to abdicate in return for a pecuniary settlement and that the majority of the Hawaiians would aid the movement. Letter enclosed in Secretary of Navy to Secretary of State, September 12, 1892. *Miscellaneous Letters,* September, 1892. Knowledge of the existence of such an organization was denied by a number of witnesses who later testified before a committee of the Senate. *Senate Report* No. 227, 53d Cong., 2d sess., pp. 174, 223-224, 243-244, 300, 356-357, 605. The statements of Thurston and Brown are sufficient to remove all doubt on the point.

[57] London *Times*, May 9, 1892; Boston *Transcript*, May 14, 1892; both enclosed in Smith to Parker, May 20, 1892. *Advertiser*, May

It is evident that Thurston had spent some very busy
days in Washington in behalf of annexation, and to some
extent had dragged Mott Smith along with him. Mr. James
H. Blount, of Georgia, chairman of the House Committee
on Foreign Affairs, testified later that Thurston and Smith
had come to the committee room and Thurston had asked
whether the Democratic party would consent to the annexation of the Hawaiian Islands, adding: " I am a member of
the Legislature and I mean to endeavor to bring about the
annexation of the islands." Blount stated that he made no
reply, other than advising Thurston to see the Secretary of
State. He thought Thurston " a pretty uppish sort of person " and gave the matter no further consideration.[58] Mott
Smith, however, in denying that there had been public
discussion of annexation in Congress, stated that Mr. Blount
had conversed privately on the subject " with fellow members during a morning Session of the House." [59] This,
apparently, was the foundation for the story of a discussion
in the Foreign Affairs Committee. But more than this had
occurred. Thurston had called on Blaine. "After advising
me to consult a number of leading men of both parties,"
Thurston stated later, " he said that if the people of the
Islands applied to the United States for annexation, he
did not see how the application could be rejected." [60]

18, *Bulletin,* May 17, enclosed in Parker to Smith, May 23, 1892.
Spaulding Collection.

[58] *Senate Report* No. 227, 53d Cong., 2d sess., p. 386. Thurston
(*op. cit.,* p. 479) makes a curious misstatement in regard to Blount's
testimony.

[59] Smith to Parker, July 13, 1892. Spaulding Collection.

[60] *Memoranda of Conversations with the Secretary of State, 1893-
1898.* Notes of conversation between Secretary Gresham and L. A.

He also saw Secretary Tracy, of the Navy, but, as he subsequently wrote Blaine, " did not call upon the President,
as both the President and Mr. Tracy thought it best that
the President should not commit himself in the matter,
saying that anything that was done in the matter could be
done through you." [61]

Thus if Thurston had secured no definite commitment
from any one in Washington, he had at least made himself
and his mission well known in the highest quarters. Not
content with this, before leaving San Francisco for Hawaii,
he sent to Blaine a detailed memorandum of the existing
political situation in the islands, the various groups who
favored and opposed annexation, and the procedure by
which he planned to dispose of the Queen and bring about
annexation to the United States.[62]

Thurston, June 14, 1893. It is not stated whether these are based
on stenographic notes or merely on the Secretary's memory. Thurston is made to say that he visited Washington in February, 1892.
Obviously May is meant.

[61] Thurston to Blaine, San Francisco, May 27, 1892. *Miscellaneous Letters,* May, 1892. The account of this episode contained
in Thurston's *Memoirs* (pp. 230-232) is substantially similar to
that here given. He states that he received word from the President
through Secretary Tracy that the Administration would be " exceedingly sympathetic."

[62] The memorandum accompanied the letter referred to in the
preceding note. Thurston wrote that business in Chicago and the
approaching meeting of the Hawaiian legislature had called him
away from Washington and prevented his seeing Blaine again. He
sailed from San Francisco May 28. San Francisco *Chronicle,* May 29.
Thurston's memorandum was discussed in my article, " The Hawaiian Revolution: A Reinterpretation," in the *Pacific Historical
Review,* I, 273-294.

Annexation, said Thurston, had developed in the past year or two " from a theoretical proposition to one of practical discussion and importance at the Islands." It was now favored by the following groups:

1. Those with money invested in the islands, and whose chief interest was financial. Prior to the McKinley tariff, the $33,000,000 invested in sugar was yielding a handsome profit. The effect of the McKinley bill had been a fall in the price of sugar from $100 to $60 a ton. Some plantations were now operating at a loss, and many would probably be forced out of business with loss of many millions of invested capital. These planters had formerly opposed annexation, which, they feared, by subjecting them to the immigration laws of the United States, would cut off the supply of cheap labor. They now believed that the advantage of the bounty, or of a reasonable tariff if that were done away with, would outweigh the disadvantage of interference with their labor arrangements.

2. Those foreigners, and some natives as well, who in addition to having a financial stake in the country, regarded it as their permanent home. The whites owned four-fifths of the property in the islands but cast only 4000 out of 15,000 votes. They were able to defend their property interests only because the property qualification in the election of nobles generally gave them control of the legislature. This situation had given rise to bitter feeling among the natives toward the whites and also toward the Queen, who they believed looked for support to foreigners rather than natives. Thus a color line was being drawn in politics. But in addition there were factional divisions between different foreign groups. " The result of this situation is a

dissatisfied native element, and an irresponsible foreign element which has everything to gain, and nothing to lose by a disturbance of the peace, who are constantly, more or less openly, threatening revolution and disturbance." Since the existing government lacked the power to defend itself against violent overthrow, there was a constant feeling of uncertainty and apprehension, which retarded new investments and the further development of the islands. The people of this second group saw no hope of stable government except through union with the United States or England. They greatly preferred the former, but if the United States would not have them, " a union with England would be preferable to a continuance under existing circumstances."

3. The leaders among the natives, known as the Liberal Party. These men were not in the confidence of the Queen, who would not appoint them to office. They could not control the legislature because the property qualifications prevented most of their native followers from voting for nobles. They favored annexation to the United States in the belief that under American rule universal suffrage would make them leaders of the majority and give them control of the patronage.

Opposed to annexation were the Queen and her personal following and an English faction rallying around the British commissioner. The majority of the common natives were undecided and could probably be swayed in either direction.

As to the form which union with the United States should take, Thurston recommended territorial status rather than statehood or other possible arrangements.

Thurston came then to the means by which the desired end was to be brought about. There were two difficulties to be overcome: (1) "the disposition to be made of the Queen, the Royal family," (2) "to overcome the opposition of the common natives." The Queen would be given an opportunity " to retire peaceably upon a liberal pension." If she refused, it would be necessary to use force and establish a provisional government pending the completion of union with the United States. It was believed that through the influence of the native leaders a majority of the common natives could be won for annexation. If not, it might be necessary to set up a provisional government by a coup d'état " against the common natives as well as against the Queen."

Finally Thurston described his " proposed line of action " upon returning to Honolulu.

Pending the Presidential election, it is proposed to hold the public developement of the subject in check; reorganize the Cabinet, and securing the appointment of a Cabinet at the Islands, committed to annexation; proceed with the education of the Island people in favor of annexation, and secure the adhesion of as many native leaders as possible; have the Legislature adjourn when it gets through business next August or September, instead of being prorogued as usual. This will allow the Legislature to assemble again upon their own volition without the necessity of being called together for extra session by the Queen; if the sentiment in Washington is found to be favorable to the proposition next December when Congress meets, assemble the Legislature and, according as circumstances at the time seem to dictate, either submit a general proposition to the people, allowing them to vote upon the one question of annexation or not, without going into detail, and thereupon appoint a commission with full powers to go to Washington and negotiate the terms of the annexation;

or in case this does not seem advisable, to take such action by the Legislature directly without submitting the question to the people.

This line of action is by way of suggestion, and may of course be subject to radical change if circumstances require it.

This memorandum accompanied Thurston's letter to Blaine from San Francisco, May 27, 1892. There is no record of any reply. Neither letter nor memorandum has the usual State Department stamp of date received. Blaine resigned the office of Secretary of State on June 4, and it is possible that he never saw it. Thurston, at any rate, had furnished the State Department with an explicit statement of his plans.[63] We must now follow him to Honolulu and

[63] The existence of Thurston's memorandum seems never to have been made public, even by Foster's Democratic successor, Gresham, who might easily have made political capital of it. At least one Democratic Senator, however, was almost certainly told of it. In a debate in the Senate in January, 1895, in which Senator Aldrich had attacked Cleveland for holding communication with representatives of the deposed Queen, who had come to Washington in her interest, Senator Gray, of Delaware, asked Aldrich if he did not know that prior to the Revolution of 1893, agents of the parties then conspiring against the Queen had conferred about their plans with the Secretary of State. When Aldrich and other Republican Senators denied that this was so, Gray replied:

" Before this debate is over I will show that the Senators are mistaken. . . . there was a communication to the Secretary of State, Mr. Foster, made by people there prior to any revolution in that island, or any overt act, which shows that the revolution was contemplated and contemplated with the countenance of the Administration then in power in this country." *Cong. Record,* 53d Cong., 3d sess., p. 1207. Gray did not carry out his threat, but it seems a safe guess that he had been told by Gresham of Thurston's communication. Gray was the leading defender of Cleveland's and Gresham's Hawaiian policy.

observe the course of political events there for the next six months.

It is pertinent at this point to give a brief résumé of political events in Hawaii, leading up to the legislative session of 1892-93. The Constitution of 1887 had been forced upon Kalakaua against his will. It had never been relished by him or by his sister Liliuokalani, who succeeded to the throne upon his death in January, 1891. In July, 1889, a party led by the half-caste, Italian-educated R. W. Wilcox, attempted to seize the government and the person of the King. Their real purpose, it seems, was to suppress the Constitution of 1887 and break the hold of the white capitalists on the government. It was rumored that they had the sympathy of the King himself, or his sister. The attempt was easily thwarted, and the King surrendered still more power to his ministers.[64]

The Reform Party, led by white business men among whom the descendants of American missionaries were prominent, had come into control through the revolution of 1887 and remained securely in power for three years. They were opposed by the National Reform Party, which drew its strength variously from native Hawaiians, friends of the king, anti-American and anti-missionary whites. As we have seen, this party won a partial victory in the legislative elections of February, 1890. In June, the Reform ministry resigned and was succeeded by one chosen from among the leaders of both parties. This ministry, which enjoyed the confidence of the business community, remained in office until after Kalakaua's death, when Liliuo-

[64] U. S. For. Rel., 1894, App. II, pp. 280-290, 295-298.

kalani claimed the right to dismiss the ministers and choose her own—a right in which she was sustained by an advisory opinion of the Supreme Court.[65] Thus Liliuokalanı, who was restive under the restraints imposed in 1887, was able to select her ministers from among her own personal adherents of the National Reform Party.

Meanwhile discontent had grown, as described in Thurston's memorandum, among both whites and native Hawaiians, especially ambitious and disgruntled half-castes; and in the elections of 1892 the latter group, with some white support, raised the standard of a new Liberal Party. The February elections gave no one party a clear majority in the legislature, but the Reform and Liberal parties together won enough seats to enable them, if they should combine, to oust the National Reform ministry. It appears that the leaders of both Reform and Liberal parties at this time favored annexation to the United States. They differed in that the Reform leaders hoped to reach their end by orderly legislative process, while the Liberals were ready for violence. The plan proposed by Thurston was to unite these dissimilar elements in the legislature, secure the appointment of a ministry favorable to annexation, and when the auspices at Washington should be favorable, proceed to put through an annexation program, with the consent of the Queen and the " common natives " if possible; otherwise by some sort of coup d'état. That he and his associates attempted to put this plan into effect is indicated by a study

[65] Normally the ministry would have held office until ousted by a vote of the legislature. The Queen held, and the Supreme Court agreed, that the death of the sovereign terminated the life of the ministry.

of the proceedings of the legislature during the summer and fall of 1892, which reveal a transitory alliance between the Reform Party and the Liberal leaders.[66]

The Liberal leaders with whom Thurston and his group now sought to work were the half-castes R. W. Wilcox and J. E. Bush. Wilcox had been sent to Italy in the days of King Kalakaua to receive a military education. He had returned after the Revolution of 1887, to find his ambitions thwarted and his advancement blocked, and had become a chronic agitator. He had been implicated in the uprising of 1889, when a native jury had failed to convict him, and had been arrested in May, 1892, on a charge of treasonable conspiracy. Bush was the editor of a paper in the native tongue, *Ka Leo*. Both appear to have had a considerable following and influence among the natives. Both were members of the legislature.

During the summer the flirtations of these men with the Reform Party were perfectly evident. Several articles in the *Advertiser*, the newspaper which spoke the sentiments of the white business community, suggested that only a union of Reform and Liberal groups could secure a ministry that would unite the country and effect closer relations with the United States and lamented that an unjustified distrust of Bush and Wilcox had prevented such a union.[67] Wilcox,

[66] The proceedings of the Hawaiian legislature were reported in detail in the *Daily Pacific Commercial Advertiser* of Honolulu. The files of this paper in the University of Michigan Library do not include January-June, 1892. The writer was, therefore, unable to follow the first month of the legislative session.

[67] *Advertiser,* July 9, August 3, 1892. Two articles signed by D. L. Huntsman.

on his part, made undisguised gestures toward an alliance
with the Reform party. On July 9 he offered resolutions
in the legislature for a commission to visit Washington
and seek closer relations with the United States, and two
days later explained and defended this proposal before a
mass meeting of natives. On the 13th he offered a resolution of want of confidence in the ministry.[68] Significantly,
his course was commended by Thurston,[69] while from other
quarters came charges that he was seeking a post in a new
ministry and that he was aiming at annexation to the United
States.[70] Bush likewise received the praise of Thurston
and of the *Advertiser* for his stand on legislative matters
and for the policy of his paper.[71]

What dickerings and intrigue went on behind the scenes
there is no way of knowing.[72] But on August 30, Bush,
Wilcox, and other natives in the legislature joined with
the Reform members in voting out the ministry by the large
majority of 31-10.[73] The first step in Thurston's program

[68] *Ibid.,* July 11, 13, 14, 1892.

[69] *Ibid.,* July 15, 1892.

[70] *Ibid.,* July 13, 15, 1892. Nothing came of these moves at
this time.

[71] *Ibid.,* August 4, September 1, 1892. Thurston remarked that
he had had three libel suits against Bush at different times; " but if
the member were Gladstone himself he could not take a sounder
position than he had in the present case." Bush had opposed an
appropriation of $50,000 for the Queen's Guards.

[72] C. B. Wilson, marshal of the kingdom, who was ousted after
the revolution of January, 1893, stated that the Reform leaders used
" shameless bribery and corruption " to win the Liberals. *U. S. For.
Rel., 1894,* App. II, pp. 1025-1026. The statement is from a hostile
source and is not to be taken too seriously. Each side was in the
habit of attributing bribery to the other.

[73] *Advertiser,* August 31, 1892.

was accomplished. The next was to secure the appointment of a new ministry whose attitude could be relied upon when the opportunity for annexation should come.

To bring this about, the victorious majority adopted a resolution to the effect that the Queen ought to call upon a leader of the opposition to form the new cabinet.[74] This principle the Queen at first refused to accept. Two cabinets were formed headed by persons amenable to her. One of these was allowed to exist slightly over a month; the other was voted out at once.[75] At length she yielded, and on November 8 named a cabinet headed by G. N. Wilcox and composed of substantial members of the Reform Party enjoying the confidence of the business community.[76]

That the appointment of the Wilcox ministry was regarded by the annexationists as a victory there can be little doubt. The word had been freely used during the political squabbles of the fall, and while no public man had openly espoused the idea, it was a recognized issue in the contest for control of the ministry.[77] Mr. Wilcox stated officially

[74] *Ibid.,* September 6, 1892.

[75] *Ibid.,* September 13, October 18, November 2, 1892.

[76] *Ibid.,* November 9, 1892. The other members of the cabinet were Mark P. Robinson, P. C. Jones, and Cecil Brown. Minister Stevens reported with satisfaction that their property aggregated nearly a million dollars. *U. S. For. Rel., 1894,* App. II, p. 376.

[77] The Queen had appointed to one of her short-lived ministries two members of the legislature—nobles from Honolulu. In the election to fill the vacancies thus created Bush and Wilcox joined with Thurston and other Reformers to support two candidates who were friendly to the United States. Thurston said the issue was not annexation, but " bread and butter." *Advertiser,* September 27, 1892. Speakers for the opposing candidates denounced Bush and Wilcox for joining the annexationists, charged that there were already twenty-four annexationists in the legislature, and warned

that the ministry, while seeking closer commercial relations
with the United States, would maintain the autonomy and
independence of Hawaii.[78] But it is evident that Mr.
Stevens, the United States minister, felt that the time for
annexation was approaching.

It will be recalled that in February, 1892, Stevens had
promised that after the ratification of the proposed treaty
he would make a full report on the situation in Hawaii and
give the reasons why the islands must either be annexed
to the United States or become a British possession. The
treaty had failed to meet with the approval of President
Harrison, and the complete victory of the pro-American
party in the Hawaiian legislature had been delayed, as we
have seen, until November. Stevens's reports in October,
while the contest continued between the Queen and her
opponents, had been full of charges that the British commissioner at Honolulu and another Englishman, who represented Canadian Pacific interests, were intriguing against
the American party in the hope of bringing British and
Canadian influence into the ascendant.[79] The appointment
of the Wilcox ministry, November 8, he described as " especially a proof of American ascendancy over ultra English
and other anti-American elements and sentiments." And

---

against electing two more. *Ibid.*, September 30. The anti-American
candidates were elected. *Ibid.*, October 5.

[78] *Ibid.*, November 15, 1892.

[79] See his reports No. 71 (October 19) and No. 72 (October 31),
U. S. For. Rel., 1894, App. II, pp. 362-363, 374-375. His report
No. 70 (October 8) described the intriguing of the British commissioner and his wife in such outspoken language that it alone of
all Stevens's important dispatches was withheld from Congress in
the subsequent investigation. It is printed in Mrs. Tyler's *Foreign
Policy of James G. Blaine*, pp. 370-372.

he added significantly: " This new cabinet is justly considered the most positively American there has been since
the Reform ministry went out two and a half years ago." [80]

Evidently thinking that the time had come to place his
full views before the State Department, Stevens followed
this brief report with a long dispatch, dated November 20,
giving a detailed description of the islands, their area,
products, commercial and naval importance, the extravagance and corruption of the existing government, the straits
to which the sugar industry was reduced by the McKinley
tariff, the danger that white civilization would be sub-
merged by the growing number of Orientals—all leading
up to an argument for annexation by the United States.
" Destiny and the vast future interests of the United States
in the Pacific clearly indicate who, at no distant day, must
be responsible for the government of these islands. . . .
Hawaii has reached the parting of the ways. She must now
take the road that leads to Asia, or the other, which outlets
her in America, gives her an American civilization and
binds her to the care of American destiny." Only " wise,
bold action by the United States," said Stevens, could
rescue the islands from the perils that hung over them.
There must be either annexation or a protectorate, and of
the two, annexation was much to be preferred.[81]

In a private letter to Secretary Foster a few days later,
Stevens expressed the hope that Foster would not only give
his long report a careful reading, but would also lay it
before the President, the Secretary of the Navy, and certain

[80] *U. S. For. Rel., 1894*, App. II, p. 376.
[81] *Ibid.*, pp. 377-384. Dispatch No. 74.

prominent Senators. " I am not sure," he said, " that our statesmen are yet ready to grapple boldly with this Hawaiian question. I am, however, very confident that the sooner it is firmly taken hold of, the better it will be for the United States as well as for Hawaii." [82]

So far as the records show, the State Department made no reply to Mr. Stevens's communications, other than routine acknowledgments and one warning to separate his confidential reports from his " narrative of public affairs in their open historical aspect." [83] It seems evident, however, that the administration sympathized with Stevens's ideas and wishes, and took steps to prepare public opinion for a change in the Hawaiian situation.

President Harrison, in his annual message, December 6, 1892, declared: " Our relations with Hawaii have been such as to attract an increased interest, and must continue to do so." He urged the laying of a cable to Honolulu, to meet the need for quick communication for both commercial and naval purposes, and the establishment of a naval base at Pearl Harbor. He spoke of the past friendliness of the two countries, and remarked that it was " gratifying to believe that the advantage and necessity of a continuance of very close relations is appreciated." [84]

[82] Stevens to Foster, November 28, 1892. *Dispatches, Hawaii.* XXV. This letter was stamped as received December 23, 1892.

[83] Foster to Stevens, November 8, 1892. *U. S. For. Rel., 1894,* App. II, p. 376. " Many of your dispatches," Foster wrote, " combine these two modes of treatment to such a degree as to make their publication, in the event of a call from Congress or other occasion therefor inexpedient and, indeed, impracticable, without extended omissions."

[84] Richardson, *op. cit.,* IX, 316.

Secretary Foster, meanwhile, had denied newspaper rumors that he had discussed annexation with the Hawaiian minister, but said nothing of what might have passed between him and Minister Stevens.[85]

American newspapers now began to carry articles on the approaching crisis in Hawaii, the interest of the United States in the islands, and the menace of British intrigue in Honolulu. Some, at least, of these articles were quite evidently inspired in Washington. The New York *Tribune,* on November 20, said editorially that events occurring in the islands might soon compel the United States to decide upon its future relations to them. " Indeed," it said, " the occasion might present itself at any moment when readjustments would be unavoidable." [86] Within a few days, other papers were reporting on the growth of annexation sentiment in Hawaii, and printing rumors that there had been correspondence on the subject between the State Department and the Hawaiian minister.[87] But it was toward the end of December, after the State Department had received not only Stevens's long dispatch on Hawaii but also his subsequent letter asking that it be shown to the President,

[85] Clipping from unnamed paper, November 21, 1892, enclosed in Smith to Robinson, November 26, 1892. Spaulding Collection.

[86] There is no proof that this editorial was suggested by the State Department. *The Nation* attributed it to a " tip " from that quarter. *The Nation,* LVII, 381 (November 23, 1893). Stevens's long dispatch No. 74 was not yet available, but earlier dispatches describing British intrigues in Honolulu must have been in the Department for some time. It was significant that the *Kennebec Journal,* the paper which Stevens had edited before going to Honolulu, published similar hints at this time. *Ibid.*

[87] Clipping from unnamed paper, November 21, 1892, enclosed in Smith to Robinson, November 26, 1892. Spaulding Collection.

the Secretary of the Navy, and leading Senators, that some obviously "inspired" articles appeared in the Washington *Post*. The first of these, on December 29, warned of efforts being made in Honolulu to undermine American influence, divert trade from the United States to Canada, and prevent the utilization of Pearl Harbor by the United States. Two days later, the *Post* published a summary of a confidential report on the value of Pearl Harbor, made in 1873 by General J. M. Schofield and Lt. Col. B. S. Alexander,[88] which it seems could hardly have been obtained except from official sources. Editorially, the *Post* remarked:

Some very important dispatches have been received by the Department of State from the Hawaiian Islands, but the Department officials are not prepared to divulge their contents. They relate to the machinations of agents of foreign governments to prevent the advancement of American interests in the Hawaiian Islands. . . . Diplomatic and naval officers report that affairs in Hawaii are fast approaching a serious political crisis. . . .[89]

[88] This report was first published in full in 1925 in the *American Historical Review*, XXX, 561-565.

[89] Washington *Post*, December 29, 31, 1892. Upon one point the *Post* was in error. In the article published December 31, it stated that the item of $250,000 " for providing coaling and naval stations," incorporated in the Sundry Civil Appropriation bill of the preceding summer was designed for the development of Pearl Harbor. This item was, in reality, intended for the negotiation over Samana Bay. See *ante,* chap. i, p. 31. Mott Smith, falling into the same error, had lodged a protest against this appropriation as improper in view of the possible termination of the Hawaiian reciprocity treaty in 1894. Smith to the Acting Secretary of State, June 9, 1892. *Hawaii, Notes,* III. That there was, nevertheless, some thought in Washington of using this $250,000 in connection with Hawaii is suggested by a curious detail related by Thurston. Archibald Hopkins, who was employed in Washington as an agent of the Annexa-

We may infer that "the Department officials" were "prepared to divulge" so much of the contents of Stevens's dispatches as they wished the public to know. The *Post* articles had echoes in newspapers in widely separated parts of the United States.[90] It can hardly be doubted that the information was given out with the purpose of preparing public opinion for approaching annexation.[91]

In December Rear Admiral Skerrett was ordered to San Francisco to take command of the Pacific squadron and eventually to proceed to Honolulu. Calling upon Secretary Tracy before his departure, he asked whether the government was still opposed to annexation and was informed that "the wishes of the Government have changed. They will be very glad to annex Hawaii." [92] When the news of the

tion Club, wrote Thurston, November 15, 1892, that the United States Government was willing to pay "to Queen Liliuokalani, and those connected with her, the sum of two hundred and fifty thousand dollars, for the assignment to the United States of the Sovereignty of Hawaii." Thurston, *op. cit.,* p. 234.

[90] *Cf.* San Francisco *Call,* January 1, 1893; Portland *Oregonian,* January 3, 5, 1893.

[91] Mott Smith reported to Robinson, December 31, 1892: "The sudden and strong interest manifested by newspaperdom in this subject seems to have arisen from dispatches received by the State and Naval Departments from their officials in Honolulu by the last mail." Spaulding Collection.

[92] *U. S. For. Rel., 1894,* App. II, p. 476. In Chicago en route to the West Coast, Admiral Skerrett stated that his ship would probably soon be ordered to Honolulu; that there was discontent among the natives, "a strong movement to place the islands under the government of the United States," and a probability that there would be friction with Great Britain over such an attempt. Portland *Oregonian,* January 3, 1893. Skerrett arrived in Honolulu February 10.

revolution of January 17, 1893, and of the application for annexation reached Washington, the Washington *Star* asserted (January 31) that one of its reporters " was informed to-day that the administration has not been suddenly confronted by a new situation in this Hawaiian matter, but that everything that has happened has been expected for months by the President and his cabinet has been fully prepared for it." Undoubtedly the administration had been prepared, since the preceding spring, for a revolution of some sort in Hawaii, followed by an offer of annexation. The precise time, however, when these things would come about, and the exact manner of their coming, could not well have been foreseen.

III

REVOLUTION IN HAWAII

Events in Honolulu developed more rapidly than Stevens or Thurston had foreseen, and took an unexpected course. The appointment of the Wilcox ministry, November 8, was a victory for Thurston's annexation policy. It was so considered by Stevens, who, as we have seen, proceeded to prepare the way for annexation in his correspondence with the Department of State. G. N. Wilcox and his cabinet colleagues, however, took no hasty steps. The attitude of the United States now appeared to them uncertain. While they knew very well what they could expect from the Harrison administration, the November elections, ensuring Democratic control of the government on March 4, created a new element of doubt. They also felt a lack of confidence in their ability to control the situation in Hawaii.[1] On January 5, 1893, however, a committee of the legislature headed by R. W. Wilcox brought in a report recommending that a commission be sent to Washington to ascertain American sentiment in regard to full free trade, the utilization of Pearl Harbor, and other matters, and to report to an adjourned session of the legislature. A motion to place Thurston, R. W. Wilcox, and three others on the commission was finally lost in favor of a substitute making the commission appointive by the Queen with the approval

[1] Both elements of doubt appear clearly in letters between Thurston and his Washington correspondent, Archibald Hopkins. Thurston, *Memoirs of the Hawaiian Revolution*, pp. 235-243.

of the Cabinet, and directing that it report to a special or adjourned session of the legislature if the information brought back seemed to the Cabinet sufficient to justify such a course.[2]

A comparison of this procedure with the line of action sketched by Thurston in his memorandum of the preceding May will show an almost complete correspondence, and we may surmise that the Wilcox ministry, had it remained in power, would first have canvassed the prospects in Washington and, if they proved good, would then have inaugurated an annexation program, perhaps attempting to persuade the Queen to abdicate and retire on a pension. There was, however, a fatal defect in the ministry's position. The Reform Party had failed to cement the alliance with the Liberals, upon which depended its control of the legislature. No Liberal was given a seat in the cabinet. Furthermore, the marshalship of the kingdom was left in the hands of C. B. Wilson, popularly known as " King Bolabola," a Tahitian half-caste against whose administration and alleged influence over the Queen, both Reformers and Liberals had leveled their bitterest attacks. Even the *Advertiser,* friendly as it was to the ministers, warned them that if they failed to remove Wilson they would lay themselves open to a charge of bad faith and would have no right to claim Liberal support.[3] Weeks passed, and it became evident that Wilson was to retain his office. Bush and

---

[2] *Advertiser,* January 6, 7, 1893. In opposing the naming of Thurston and Wilcox as members of the commission, a native member complained that they were " still on the fence as to the question of annexation."

[3] *Ibid.,* November 10, 1892.

R. W. Wilcox turned against their former allies. Both supported, against the ministry, a bill for a constitutional convention, Wilcox making a personal attack upon Thurston.[4] On January 4, Bush introduced and Wilcox supported a resolution of want of confidence in the ministry, which was, however, defeated by a vote of 19 ayes and 22 noes.[5]

So far, Bush and Wilcox had been unable to carry with them enough of their native colleagues to defeat the ministry, and after the vote of January 4, with adjournment but a few days off, the latter's position seemed secure—so secure that Minister Stevens and the "Boston," the only United States naval vessel at Honolulu, departed for a cruise among the islands.[6] On January 9, however, the *Advertiser* complained that a dishonorable backstairs intrigue was going on against the cabinet. Two days later the opposition carried by a vote of 23 to 20 a bill to license a lottery company,[7] and on the following day (January 12)

[4] *Ibid.*, December 29, 1892.

[5] *Ibid.*, January 5, 1893.

[6] In the debate in Congress which followed the Hawaiian Revolution, at least one critic of Minister Stevens voiced the suspicion that Stevens and the "Boston" had left Honolulu for the very purpose of giving the Queen an opportunity to try a coup which might result in her overthrow. *Cong. Record*, 53d Cong., 2d sess., pp. 2284-2288. The present writer expressed a similar suspicion in a recent article. Pratt, *Pacific Historical Review*, I, 273-294. Further study of the sources has yielded nothing to corroborate this theory. Lucien Young, at the time an officer on the "Boston," warned Stevens before the ship sailed that there was an intrigue on foot against the Wilcox ministry. Stevens gave no credence to the report. He impressed Young as believing sincerely that the ministry was safe. Lucien Young, *The Boston at Hawaii*, pp. 145-146.

[7] *Advertiser*, January 12, 1893. Among the charges brought against Liliuokalani after her dethronement was her signature of

mustered the twenty-five votes necessary to oust the ministry.[8]

Thus the Reform Ministry, upon which presumably the annexationists were counting to carry out their program after the adjournment or prorogation of the legislature, fell from power, and the legislative session had but two days to run. At first there was little excitement, and the *Advertiser* confidently predicted that the Queen would choose ministers who deserved the confidence of the community.[9] When the names of the new cabinet were announced, however, this expectation was not borne out. The

---

this lottery bill and also of a bill licensing the sale of opium in the islands, which had passed the legislature December 31. The opium bill, however, had been passed by a large majority, including two of the ministers and a number of the respectable white members of the legislature. *Ibid.,* January 3, 1893. R. W. Wilcox and Bush, in supporting the lottery bill, charged the Reform leaders with hypocrisy for their support of the opium bill. For an analysis of these and other moral charges against the Queen, see *infra,* pp. 160-170.

[8] *Advertiser,* January 13, 1893. By a Supreme Court opinion, a want of confidence resolution to be successful must receive a majority of the entire 48 votes in the legislature. The resolution of January 4 had received only 19 votes. A comparison of the vote on that date with the vote of January 12, shows that six native members changed their votes from No to Aye, while one who had been excused from voting January 4 voted Aye January 12. One of the original 19 was absent January 12. How the native members were induced to change their votes is not known. Charges of bribery were freely made on both sides. The *Advertiser* claimed that the vote exonerated the Reform party of corruption; they " allowed the Cabinet to be dismissed by a single vote, when they could have purchased half a dozen at prices ranging from $50 down to a calabash of poi." *Ibid.,* January 13, 1893. The remark is typical of the opinion which the whites held of many of the native politicians.

[9] *Ibid.*

new ministry, said the *Advertiser*, " does not possess, because it does not deserve, the respect of any section of the
community." W. H. Cornwell, minister of finance, did not
" know enough about accounts to keep those of a poi-shop."
A. P. Peterson, attorney-general and the only man of capacity, " has forfeited by his political course every claim to
confidence." About J. F. Colburn, secretary of the interior,
" perhaps the less said the better. It is sometimes charity
to be silent." Against " genial Sam " Parker, minister of
foreign affairs, there was nothing to be said personally, but
despite the " Hawaiian tradition that brains are not needed
in the Foreign Office," the *Advertiser* thought in the existing crisis something more was needed there than a good-
natured smile.[10] The appointment of such a cabinet, said
the *Advertiser*, " must hasten the downfall of the Hawaiian
Monarchy." It compared the Queen's playing of politics
with that of Kalakaua in 1886-1887, and gave plain warning that she would bring on revolution, just as her brother
had done.

Whether revolution would have come about if the Queen
had rested content with this victory it is difficult to say, but
the Queen played directly into the hands of her enemies
by herself taking a revolutionary step.

Revision of the Constitution of 1887 in the interest of
the native Hawaiians and the sovereign had been a subject of discussion ever since the time of its adoption. It
had been the motive of the abortive uprising of 1889. Resolutions for the calling of a constitutional convention had
been defeated in the legislature in the fall of 1890.[11] It

10 *Ibid.*, January 14, 1893.
11 McCurley to Secretary of Navy, August 22, 1890, in Secretary
of Navy to Secretary of State, September 5, 1890; Brown to

had been rumored that Liliuokalani was implicated in the affair of 1889. Undoubtedly, as Queen, she had been restive under the restrictions imposed by the constitution. In the spring of 1892 she had tried to enlist the support of the Liberal leaders for constitutional change. An unsuccessful move for a convention had been made in the legislature at the end of December, 1892,[12] and it seems certain that before the voting out of the Wilcox ministry there had been an understanding between the Queen and some of the native leaders that she would take advantage of her victory to bring about a revision of the constitution.[13]

Now, on the day set for the proroguing of the legislature (Saturday, January 14, 1893), Liliuokalani attempted the wholly unconstitutional act of proclaiming a new constitution by royal edict.[14] But her ministers—weak men who

Secretary of Navy, October 24, 1890, in Secretary of Navy to Secretary of State, November 6, 1890. Spaulding Collection.

[12] *Advertiser*, December 29, 1892.

[13] *Ibid.*, January 13, 1893. In the debate on the resolution to oust the Wilcox ministry, one of the native members, Kamauoha, remarked that the ministers were excellent men. " But," he asked, " would they carry out the wishes of the Queen? Would they do what the Queen and the Hawaiian people wanted in regard to the Lottery, the Constitutional Convention, etc.? " In a subsequent statement to Commissioner Blount, Liliuokalani said that the men who became her ministers in January and through whom she tried to put the new constitution in effect had had the document for a month. *U. S. For. Rel., 1894,* App. II, pp. 864-865. Colburn implied that he heard of the constitution for the first time on January 14. *Ibid.*, p. 498.

[14] The only mode of amending the constitution provided for by the constitution of 1887 was proposal of amendments by a majority vote of one session of the legislature and adoption by a two-thirds vote in the following session. Art. 82, Constitution of 1887. *Ibid.*, p. 816.

either had not understood what was expected of them or, if they had understood, now lost their nerve—hesitated at participating in the plan. One of them, J. F. Colburn, brought a report of the impending event to Thurston and other leaders of the business community and asked their advice. This was at about eleven in the morning. Thurston and his confrères advised the frightened minister that he and his colleagues should stand firm against the Queen's demands—should refuse, that is, either to countersign the proposed new constitution or to resign their posts—and assured him of the support of the white community. Meanwhile the "Boston," with Minister Stevens on board, had most opportunely returned from her cruise.[15] Her commander, Captain Wiltse, was promptly informed of the situation and gave assurance of his willingness to protect the life and property of American citizens. The Queen, having prorogued the legislature at noon, demanded that her ministers countersign the new constitution. Three of them escaped from the palace in fear of their lives, and sought another conference with the business men. With their courage thereby effectually reinforced, they returned to the palace.

Meanwhile, preparations had been made for an impressive ceremony. The Queen's Guard was drawn up, armed and in military array, before the palace; a large crowd of

[15] The "Boston" went to Hilo, Hawaii, for target practise. She then returned to Lahaina on the island of Maui. Here, on the night of Friday, January 13, Stevens and Wiltse received news of the fall of the Wilcox ministry. Anticipating trouble, they got under way at once and reached Honolulu at 10:30 a. m., January 14. Lucien Young's testimony before the Senate Committee on Foreign Relations. *Senate Report* No. 227, 53d Cong., 2d sess., p. 326.

natives had assembled in anticipation of the happy event;
and by prearrangement the native society, *Hui Kalaiaina,*
marched to the palace with a draft of the new constitution
and a petition that it be promulgated. This document, if
we may accept as genuine the draft of it later secured by
Commissioner Blount, would have greatly enhanced the
power of the Queen, while proportionately lessening that
of the white owners of island property.[16] It would have
undone the work of 1887. Nothing could better illustrate
the political naïveté of Liliuokalani and her advisers than
their expectation that such a revolution could be peaceably
effected—or indeed effected at all.

Rapidly the drama moved on to its anti-climax. The tim-
orous ministers, returning from their conference with the
" enemy," gave their final refusal. Without their support
the Queen feared to persist. First to the members of the
Hui Kalaiaina, gathered in the Throne Room, and then to

[16] The principal innovations in the proposed constitution were
that nobles were to be appointed by the Queen instead of being
elected by the property-owners; that the suffrage was to be limited
to subjects of the kingdom; and that justices of the Supreme Court
were to be appointed for six-year terms instead of life. *U. S. For.
Rel., 1894,* App. II, pp. 1047-1055. The authenticity of this draft
is not entirely above suspicion. It was secured from the Queen by
Commissioner Blount. The Queen had stated earlier that all copies
of the draft had been destroyed. *Ibid.,* p. 1059. *Cf. Senate Report*
No. 227, 53d Cong., 2d sess., pp. 393-394; S. B. Dole, *Memoirs of
the Hawaiian Revolution,* pp. 71-73. Dole (p. 71) states that a
draft taken from the Queen's residence in 1895 and corresponding
almost exactly with that obtained by Blount was "made up of
printed matter from the constitution of 1864, pasted in, with
marginal amendments, supplemented by written matter. . . . "
The draft printed in Blount's report closely resembled the constitution of 1864. *Cf. U. S. For. Rel., 18^4,* App. II, pp. 804-816.

the assemblage in the palace grounds, she announced that because of the desertion of her ministers she was compelled to postpone for a time the promulgation of the new constitution which she and her native subjects had at heart. A native orator, from the steps of the palace, denounced both the Queen and her ministers for their betrayal of the popular cause, but the flow of oratory was soon cut off and about 3:30 the crowd dispersed quietly.[17]

In the meantime, the office of W. O. Smith had become a rendezvous of the Queen's opponents. Crowds of white men gathered there to take counsel and to formulate plans to defeat her designs. From the beginning, however, they had more than that in mind. While there is no evidence that Thurston and his supporters had formulated any plans for revolution at this time, the Queen's false step furnished an occasion for the measures of revolution which they had rather vaguely contemplated for possible use in the future. One of the participants in the conferences at Smith's office stated later that several of those present, including himself, had voiced the sentiment that the Queen's action was " a very good thing and a splendid opportunity to get rid of the whole old rotten Government concern and now to get annexation to the United States."[18] Shortly after the close of the proceedings at the palace, the gathering

[17] There is little disagreement as to the events of Saturday, January 14. The foregoing account is based on the *Advertiser* of January 16, 1893, and on the statements of W. O. Smith, J. F. Colburn, and Liliuokalani herself, in *U. S. For. Rel., 1894,* App. II, pp. 955-963, 496-501, 856-869.

[18] Affidavit of C. Bolte. *Senate Report* No. 227, 53d Cong., 2d sess., pp. 452-453.

at Smith's office was organized, with H. E. Cooper as chairman and Smith as secretary. Upon Thurston's motion, Cooper appointed thirteen men, all of them members of the Annexation Club, as a committee of safety, with power to form a plan of action, call meetings, and report to the larger body. The office was then cleared of all except the committee. Thurston moved that " steps be taken at once to form and declare a provisional government," and a subcommittee consisting of Thurston, W. C. Wilder, and H. F. Glade was appointed to ascertain the attitude of Minister Stevens and report to the full committee at nine o'clock Sunday morning.[19] The meeting then adjourned. In the evening, however, Thurston, Smith, and Castle from the committee, together with other interested persons, including Sanford B. Dole, associate justice of the Supreme Court and future head of the Provisional Government, who was not yet committed to the cause of revolution, met at Thurston's home, where they worked to a late hour drafting the essential revolutionary documents—a declaration of abrogation of the monarchy, a constitution for a provisional government, and a form to be used in requesting the United States minister to land troops, should that be deemed advisable.[20]

Early Sunday morning Thurston paid a visit to Colburn and Peterson, the two members of the Queen's cabinet who were least in sympathy with her and who had been present at the meeting Saturday afternoon when the committee

[19] W. O. Smith's account in *U. S. For. Rel., 1894*, App. II, pp. 961-962. Thurston, *op. cit.*, pp. 249-250.
[20] *U. S. For. Rel., 1894*, App. II, p. 963.

of safety was appointed. Thurston informed them that
the committee was determined to depose the Queen and
establish a provisional government. He invited them, in
their official capacity, to lead the movement and to appeal
to Minister Stevens to land troops upon the ground that
the Queen's revolutionary aims were likely to be supported
by force, with resulting danger to life and property.[21]
This attempt to legitimatize the proposed revolution by giving it a foothold in the existing cabinet was frustrated
by Colburn's and Peterson's refusal to cooperate with the
committee.

Meetings of the committee were held Sunday morning,
Sunday evening, and Monday morning at the homes or
offices of different members. At the first of these, the committee determined to call a mass meeting for 2:00 p.m.
on Monday to secure as wide a backing as possible for
their plans. At this time, too, Thurston made known his
ideas for the structure of the proposed provisional government, but when it was suggested that he become the head
of it, he objected that he was likely to be called away on
business and further, that "he was considered such a
radical mover that he believed it was wise to have some one
who was more conservative." His name was thereupon
dropped as a candidate, and it was not until Monday night
that Judge Dole was asked to accept the post.[22] At the
meeting on Monday morning, preparations for the mass

[21] Affidavit of Colburn and Peterson. *Ibid.*, p. 631. Their account is corroborated, except in some details, in the statement
published by Thurston in the New York *World* and other papers,
November 22, 1893.

[22] *U. S. For. Rel., 1894,* App. II, pp. 963-964.

meeting were perfected, and a request for the landing of troops from the " Boston " was adopted and signed by the members of the committee, with the idea that a copy should be placed in the hands of Mr. Stevens, but not to be acted upon till a further request should be made.[23]

On Monday morning, too, the committee rejected overtures from the alarmed supporters of the Queen. The committee's plans had been no secret from any one. Colburn and Peterson, as has been seen, had attended the meeting on Saturday afternoon, and had been invited by Thurston to participate in the overthrow of the Queen. The committee's posters calling the mass meeting for Monday afternoon had been displayed about the city. The meeting on Monday morning was held at Thurston's office, within two hundred feet of the police station where presided C. B. Wilson, marshal of the kingdom. Warned by her supporters of the danger, and to all appearances powerless to combat it by force, Liliuokalani consented to a retreat in the hope of saving her throne. In her speech on Saturday she had plainly intimated that she was merely postponing for a short time the granting of the new constitution.[24] On Monday morning, with her consent, her ministers issued a signed statement declaring that her measures of Saturday had been taken " under stress of her native subjects," and that in future any changes desired in the constitution would be sought " only by methods provided in the constitution

[23] *Ibid.*, p. 966.

[24] Speaking in the native tongue of her intention to grant the constitution at a future time, the Queen had used an expression which might mean a few days, a few months, or a few years. It was equivalent to " one of these days." *Ibid.*, pp. 1004-1005.

itself." [25] This assurance the ministers now requested the committee to accept as an adequate guarantee for future security. Marshal Wilson went even further. Coming to Thurston's office during the committee meeting, he demanded of Thurston that the mass meeting be called off, offering in return to guarantee that the Queen would not again undertake to change the constitution, and promising to lock her up if necessary to prevent it.[26] It was too late for compromise. The promises of the Queen and her vacillating and weak-willed ministers carried little conviction. Liliuokalani had played directly into the hands of the men who had for months been seeking the means and the excuse for forcing her abdication. Confident in their ability to carry through their program, they could hardly be expected to permit her to retrieve the card.

On Monday afternoon occurred two mass meetings. One, called by the Queen's supporters and composed largely of natives, met at Palace Square, was addressed temperately by several Hawaiian or half-caste orators, and adopted resolutions accepting and endorsing the promise of good behavior issued by the Queen and ministers in the forenoon.[27] Very different was the meeting at the armory held under the auspices of the committee of safety, where 1,260 people gave unanimous endorsement to resolutions condemning the Queen's action, ratifying the steps already taken by the

[25] *Ibid.*, p. 582.

[26] *Ibid.*, p. 966. Thurston's statement, New York *World*, November 22, 1893. Wilson stated later that he had previously attempted to dissuade the Queen from her purpose of granting a new constitution. *U. S. For. Rel., 1894*, App. II, p. 1027.

[27] *Advertiser*, January 17, 1893.

committee, and empowering it "to further consider the situation and further devise such ways and means as may be necessary to secure the permanent maintenance of law and order and the protection of life, liberty and property in Hawaii." The vote meant, said the *Advertiser,* that "the foreign community is weary of aboriginal dynasty." [28] A copy of the request for troops, adopted at the morning committee meeting, had probably already been sent to Minister Stevens. Other copies had been prepared with a view to getting additional signatures at the mass meeting, but this plan had been abandoned.[29] During the mass meeting, however, Thurston sent a note to Stevens, who was at the time on board the "Boston," advising that if the troops were to be landed they come ashore at once.[30] Shortly after the mass meeting, however, the committee of safety resolved that the landing of the troops ought to be postponed. The situation, as described by W. O. Smith was as follows:

. . . it was then nearly 4; our plans had not been per-fected, papers had not been completed, and after a hasty discussion, the time being very short, it was decided that it was impossible for us to take the necessary steps, and we should request that the troops be not landed until next morning, the hour in the morning being immaterial, . . . but we must have further time to prevent bloodshed, and Mr. Thurston and I were appointed to proceed at once to the American minister and inform him of our decision.[31]

[28] *Ibid.; U. S. For. Rel., 1894,* App. II, pp. 716-717.

[29] *Ibid.,* p. 966.

[30] *Senate Report* No. 227, 53d Cong., 2d sess., p. 489. This incident was recalled by Lieut. De Witt Coffman of the "Boston."

[31] *U. S. For. Rel., 1894,* App. II, p. 966. Thurston (*op. cit.,* p. 268) states that "a landing might precipitate action by the Queen's government, before the committee had evolved a plan."

Perhaps no incident of the revolution is more difficult to interpret than this. The ostensible reason for asking for troops, as stated in the committee's request, had been to protect life and property against the menace created by the supposed designs of the Queen. " We are unable," said the document, " to protect ourselves without aid, and therefore pray for the protection of the United States forces." [32] Yet now the committee of safety asked that this " protection " be deferred until the following morning! The most plausible explanation seems to be the following: The committee of safety was about to create a provisional government. They counted upon the presence of the United States troops to give at least moral support to that government. But if the troops should be landed before the new government was proclaimed, might not the Queen, with considerable logic, demand of Stevens that the troops support her against those seeking to overturn her government?

[32] *U. S. For. Rel., 1894*, App. II, p. 1056. The entire communication from the Committee of Safety to Stevens was as follows:
" Sir: We, the undersigned citizens and residents of Honolulu, respectfully represent that, in view of recent public events in this Kingdom, culminating in the revolutionary acts of Queen Liliuokalani on Saturday last, the public safety is menaced and lives and property are in peril, and we appeal to you and the United States forces at your command for assistance.
" The Queen, with the aid of armed force, and accompanied by threats of violence and bloodshed from those with whom she was acting, attempted to proclaim a new constitution; and, while prevented for the time from accomplishing her object, declared publicly that she would only defer her action.
" This conduct and action was upon an occasion and under circumstances which have created general alarm and terror.
" We are unable to protect ourselves without aid, and therefore pray for the protection of the United States forces."

Obviously it would be convenient to have the new government existing *de facto* when the troops landed. Another possibility is that the committee hoped to have the troops create a diversion by landing at the very moment when they proclaimed the provisional government.

At all events, Stevens refused to comply with this request for delay. He said, according to Smith, " that as a precautionary measure, and to protect American life and property, he had ordered the troops to be landed at 5 o'clock, and that they would come." [33] At the hour named, Captain Wiltse sent ashore a landing party of 154 bluejackets and marines, with ten officers and two light cannon.[34] Detachments were stationed at the legation and consulate. The remainder, after some marching about the city, were finally quartered in a vacant building known as Arion Hall, directly across the street from the Government Building and little more than a stone's throw from the royal palace. Here they remained throughout the night and the crucial events of the following day.

The landing of troops without request or even permission from the legitimate government was protested by Samuel Parker, the Queen's foreign minister, and by the governor of the island. To the former Stevens replied cryptically if not ominously:

. . . In whatever the United States diplomatic and naval representatives have done or may do at this critical hour of

[33] *Ibid.*, p. 966. Stevens maintained that he would have landed the troops Monday afternoon even had there been no request for them since he feared an outbreak of incendiary fires during the night. New York *World*, November 30, 1893.

[34] *Senate Report* No. 227, 53d Cong., 2d sess., p. 338.

Hawaiian affairs, we will be guided by the kindliest views and feelings for all the parties concerned and by the warmest sentiments for the Hawaiian people and the persons of all nationalities.[35]

We may now view briefly the events of the next twenty-four hours, and then examine more critically the part played by the United States minister and troops in these events. The committee of safety at a meeting on Monday night invited Judge Sanford B. Dole to become the head of the new government. Dole, who had not yet decided upon his attitude to the movement, asked some hours to consider and gave his consent on Tuesday morning. At the same meeting one J. H. Soper was tendered the command of the as yet non-existent military forces, and a " finance committee " was appointed " to collect the lists of arms and ammunition and buy or otherwise procure the same." [36] Meeting again at 10:00 a. m. on Tuesday, January 17, the committee determined finally upon the form and personnel of the provisional government and adjourned to meet once more at one-thirty, when they were joined by such members of the new government as were not also members of the committee. After signing the necessary papers, the committee of safety and the two councils constituting the new government made their way from Smith's office to the Government Building, which they had discreetly ascertained to be undefended. From the steps of the building a member of the committee read a proclamation announcing the abroga-

[35] *U. S. For. Rel., 1894,* App. II, pp. 1057-1059. The protests were made January 16; Stevens's replies were dated January 17.

[36] *Ibid.,* p. 967. Thurston, W. R. Castle, and W. C. Wilder were all ill and absent from this meeting.

tion of the monarchy and the institution of a provisional government—an executive council of four, headed by Dole, and an advisory council of fourteen—to exist until terms of union with the United States should have been agreed upon. All officers of the existing government, except the Queen, her cabinet, and the marshal, were requested to continue in the performance of their duties, and all laws not inconsistent with the change in government were to remain in force until further notice.[37]. The new government at once asked recognition from the United States minister and other members of the diplomatic corps and invited the members of the Queen's cabinet to a conference.[38]

When the Provisional Government thus asked recognition as a *de facto* government, it was supported by an improvised military force of 150 or 200 men.[39] At the same time, according to affidavits of the commanders of the Queen's troops and police force, there were at the palace, barracks, and police station 496 armed men, of whom 182 were regularly trained troops or police and 314 volunteers,

[37] *Ibid.*, pp. 210-211.

[38] *Ibid.*, pp. 967-968.

[39] J. H. Soper told Blount that the troops came in in squads during the reading of the proclamation; first about 15, probably 60 or 75 by the time the proclamation was finished, and soon thereafter a total of 150 to 200. *Ibid.*, p. 971. In a subsequent affidavit he stated that the supporters of the provisional government had a larger number of effective rifles than the Queen's forces. *Senate Report* No. 227, 53d Cong., 2d sess., pp. 450-451. Thurston told Gresham the provisional government's troops numbered about 274 men, "mostly armed" with Springfield rifles. *Memoranda of Conversations with the Secretary of State, 1893-1898.* August 4, 1893.

with 500 Springfield and Winchester rifles, over 50,000 rounds of ammunition, twelve Austrian breech-loading cannon, and two Gatling guns.[40] Despite this apparent superiority of force upon the Queen's side, the United States minister accorded prompt recognition to the Provisional Government and upon inquiry informed the Queen's ministers that he had done so.[41]

In the meantime, negotiations had been opened between the members of the Provisional Government at the Government Building and the Queen's ministers at the police station. The ministers, according to the affidavit of two of them, were urged to yield on the ground that the United States forces would support the Provisional Government and that resistance would result only in useless bloodshed.[42] They were not difficult to convince, but the Queen, with more at stake and greater courage to defend it, was less tractable. About five-thirty, the ministers, accompanied by others of her friends and advisers and by Mr. S. M. Damon of the Provisional Government, visited her at the palace, where they advised her to surrender. It is evident that the considerations which determined the Queen's decision were

[40] Affidavits of Samuel Nowlein and C. B. Wilson. *U. S. For. Rel., 1894,* App. II, pp. 640, 643. Lucien Young, of the " Boston," was sure there were not more than 140 troops and police under arms. *Senate Report* No. 227, 53d Cong., 2d sess., p. 338. Even if we accept the larger figures (which are probably correct), this force was perhaps less formidable than it appeared. Hawaiian military morale, in a contest with whites, had never been high.

[41] *U. S. For. Rel., 1894,* App. II, p. 228. An entry by Stevens on the legation records indicates that between 4:00 and 5:00 p. m. he notified the Queen's ministers of his action. *Ibid.,* p. 589.

[42] Affidavit of Peterson and Colburn. *Ibid.,* p. 524.

the knowledge that Stevens had recognized the new government, the presence of United States troops, and the belief, whether justified or not, that the troops would support the new government in the event of conflict. Upon the advice of her friends, and of Mr. Damon, that " she could surrender or abdicate under protest," [43] she signed a declaration that she yielded

to the superior force of the United States of America, whose minister plenipotentiary . . . has caused United States troops to be landed at Honolulu, and declared that he would support the said Provisional Government.

Now, to avoid any collision of armed forces [the statement continued] and perhaps the loss of life, I do, under this protest, and impelled by said force, yield my authority until such time as the Government of the United States shall, upon the facts being presented to it, undo the action of its representative and reinstate me in the authority which I claim as the constitutional sovereign of the Hawaiian Islands.[44]

Orders were now sent to Marshal Wilson to surrender the police station, and by seven o'clock the Provisional Government was in undisputed control of the city. Thus an

[43] *Ibid.*, p. 509. Damon's statement to Blount.

[44] *Ibid.*, p. 1279. This statement was signed by Liliuokalani and her four ministers and addressed to Sanford B. Dole *et al.* It was endorsed as received January 17, 1893, by Sanford B. Dole. The theory subsequently adopted by the Cleveland administration that the presence of Damon at this conference and the acknowledgment of the protest by Dole created an agreement of both parties to submit their controversy to the determination of the President of the United States seems to have little logical foundation. See Dole to Willis, December 23, 1893, *ibid.*, pp. 1276-1282. Liliuokalani's letter of protest to President Harrison makes no claim to any such agreement. *Ibid.*, p. 1278.

almost bloodless revolution was accomplished.[45] Following the example of Minister Stevens, representatives of
other foreign governments promptly recognized the new
régime.[46]

We may now attempt an appraisal of the influence exerted upon the events of these four days, January 14-17,
1893, by the minister and armed forces of the United States.
Such an appraisal is rendered difficult by the extremely
partisan character of the controversy to which the episode
gave rise. In Hawaii, bitter enmity arose between the supporters of the Provisional Government and the friends of
the Queen. In the United States, the conduct of Stevens
became an issue of party politics, denounced by the Democratic administration and its adherents and warmly defended by Republicans. Under such circumstances, impartial witnesses were very rare and most of the testimony
taken by Commissioner Blount in Honolulu and by the
Senate Committee on Foreign Relations in Washington
was given by men who were trying to prove a case, men
who wished to show that there was or was not improper

[45] Apparently only one shot was fired and one person wounded.
A native policeman was shot by a Provisional Government supporter while attempting to interfere with the transportation of a
wagon load of arms from a store to the armory for the use of the
Provisional Government. This incident occurred a few minutes
before the committee of safety and Provisional Government occupied the Government Building and read their proclamation. The
work of this policeman and of several others who assisted him was
the only instance of forcible resistance to the revolution. *Ibid.*, pp.
786-787. The man who fired the shot was Captain John Good. His
decisive action was, in Judge Dole's opinion, an important factor
in the easy victory of the revolutionists. Dole, *op. cit.*, p. 80.

[46] *U. S. For. Rel., 1894*, App. II, pp. 228-232.

collusion between the American minister and the committee of safety or the Provisional Government. Through such testimony the historian must pick his way with considerable care.

It was charged by Stevens's critics that long before the events of January 14 he was working with residents of Honolulu to perfect an annexation scheme,[47] that from the time of his return to Honolulu in the "Boston" on the morning of that day he gave definite encouragement to those seeking to overthrow the Queen, that he promised recognition and support to the proposed provisional government as soon as it should be in possession of the Government Building or, as some maintained, of *any* building in the city,[48] and should read a proclamation therefrom, and that he promised protection to members of the com-

[47] Liliuokalani stated that she had been warned of such activity on his part in November, 1892. *Ibid.,* p. 862. Stevens's hostile attitude toward the Queen is further illustrated by his Fourth of July oration of the preceding summer, in which he had referred to Hawaii as "a monarch-cursed country." *Nation,* LVII, 381 (November 23, 1893). As a public utterance of a diplomatic officer, it is to be hoped this is unique.

[48] F. W. Wundenberg, who attended the meeting of the committee on Monday night, told Blount it was his understanding that Stevens had told the committee he would immediately recognize and support them if they would take possession of the Government Building and read their proclamation, "or failing to get the Government building, any building in Honolulu. They deny that, but I understood *any building in Honolulu.*" *U. S. For. Rel., 1894,* App. II, p. 561. After publication of Blount's report, Wundenberg was prosecuted for making "malicious, untrué and misleading" statements. He was found guilty by the Hawaiian Supreme Court, which recommended his removal from his position as court clerk. New York *World,* December 17, 1893.

mittee of safety pending such recognition. Stevens, on the other hand, asserted that during all his residence in Honolulu, prior to the days of the revolution, he had kept his views on annexation to himself, that, as he said, " nobody except the United States Government knew what my real view was "; [49] that he had made no promises of protection to members of the committee of safety, and no promises of recognition beyond saying that he would recognize whatever government was in power *de facto;* that to all proper inquiries he had stated that United States troops, if landed, would not take sides but would confine themselves to the protection of American life and property and the preservation of order; and he claimed that everything he had done had been warranted by the instructions of Secretary Bayard to his predecessor, Merrill, of July 12, 1887, which directed that the aid of both the minister in Hawaii and the naval officers present should " be promptly afforded to promote the reign of law and respect for orderly government in Hawaii." [50]

Of the respective merits of these claims it is not altogether easy to judge. That Stevens promised to recognize a government which would read a proclamation from any building in Honolulu there is the evidence of but one witness, and he made no claim to have heard Stevens himself make such a statement.[51] That Stevens said he would recog-

[49] *Senate Report* No. 227, 53d Cong., 2d sess., p. 550.

[50] *Ibid.,* p. 532. See two statements issued by Stevens November 12 and 29, 1893, and widely published in the newspapers; *e. g.*: Buffalo *Courier,* November 13, 1893; New York *World,* November 30, 1893.

[51] *Supra,* note 48.

nize a *de facto* government is unquestioned. Whether he said
that he would consider the mere occupation of the Government Building as evidence that such a government existed it
is impossible to determine from the available evidence.[52]
That in practise he accepted such occupation as sufficient
does not prove that he had promised to do so. Nor is it
possible to be sure how far Stevens went in promising
protection to members of the committee of safety. W. O.
Smith, a member of the committee, recorded that on Sunday,
January 15, he and Thurston visited Stevens to discuss
the situation.

> Among other things we talked over with him what had
> better be done in case of our being arrested or extreme or
> violent measures being taken by the Monarchy in regard
> to us. . . . Mr. Stevens gave assurances of his earnest
> purpose to afford all the protection that was in his power
> to protect life and property; . . . He repeated that the
> troops when landed would not take sides with either party,
> but would protect American life and property.[53]

If this is a faithful report of the interview, it hardly
warrants the statement that Stevens promised protection to
Smith and Thurston against such measures as the Queen's
government might take in self-defense.[54]

[52] According to W. O. Smith, Thurston reported to the meeting
on Saturday night, January 14, that Stevens had said that " whatever government was established, and was actually in possession
of the Government building, the executive departments and archives,
and in *possession of the city,* that was a *de facto* government proclaiming itself as a government, would necessarily have to be recognized." *U. S. For. Rel., 1894,* App. II, p. 963. Smith's natural
desire to protect Stevens must be considered in weighing his statement.

[53] *Ibid.,* p. 964.

[54] It is related by C. B. Wilson that Ministers Parker and Peterson
visited Stevens Sunday evening and were told that " he was ready

But it can hardly be denied that for the minister of a friendly power, accredited to the Queen's government, Stevens's relations with members of the committee were of an entirely improper character. Stevens's enthusiasm for annexation is well known to us. Despite his statement to the contrary, it was well known in Honolulu.[55] His antagonism to the monarchy had been plainly revealed in public speeches in the past and had been again demonstrated Saturday morning immediately after his return to Honolulu.[56] It is evident that from Saturday to Tuesday the members of the committee of safety regarded him as their confidential and most valued friend. Thurston and Wilder visited him Saturday night, Thurston and Smith on Sunday and again on Monday afternoon. Dole, the president-elect, dropped in to see him on Tuesday afternoon, a few minutes before the Provisional Government was proclaimed, and was told: " I think you have a great opportunity." [57] Even if Stevens gave these men no indiscreet promises, even though

to support a provisional government with United States troops from the *Boston." Ibid.*, p. 1031. It is obviously impossible to determine just what Stevens said in conversation.

[55] Thurston, in a letter of December 14, 1892, wrote of " the American Minister, with the fullest knowledge of the facts, and himself an enthusiastic advocate of annexation." Thurston, *op. cit.*, p. 235.

[56] *U. S. For. Rel., 1894*, App. II, p. 498. According to Colburn, in a conference of the ministers with the diplomatic corps just after the proroguing of the legislature on Saturday, Stevens, when informed that the Queen had signed the lottery bill, pounded his cane on the floor, said this was " a direct attack upon the United States," and left the conference in anger.

[57] Dole, *op. cit.*, p. 78.

he refused their request to postpone the landing of troops
from Monday afternoon till Tuesday morning, there is nothing, I believe, in the code of international amenities to justify
a minister in holding such confidential relations with men
seeking to overthrow the government to which he is
accredited.

It seems fair to say then, that Stevens's attitude from
Saturday to Tuesday was such as to give improper encouragement to the revolutionists. But was this encouragement a decisive factor in the success of the revolution?
It may be observed first that the revolution followed rather
closely the pattern of one of the alternatives sketched in
advance by Thurston in his memorandum of May 27, 1892.
In that memorandum he had proposed, if it proved impossible to persuade the Queen to abdicate, to create a
provisional government by a coup d'état. At that time,
apparently, he felt confident that the groups for whom he
spoke would be capable of deposing the Queen without
aid from the United States. So, after the revolution had
occurred, Thurston and his friends maintained that they
would and could have carried it through without any sort
of assistance from Minister Stevens. In his statement
given to the papers in the United States, Thurston asserted
that while the landing of the troops Monday afternoon
had a quieting effect upon the city, their presence was not
essential to the success of the revolution. He pointed out
that when the troops were landed, the movement for revolution had been in progress two days, with no attempt at
concealment, that the Queen, her cabinet, and supporters
were demoralized, suspicious of one another, and devoid of
leadership, while " the committee and their supporters were

united, had ample force to execute their purpose, knew precisely what they wanted, and proceeded with intelligent deliberation, thoroughness and confidence to do it." He recalled the ease with which the whites had worked their will upon Kalakaua in 1887 and had suppressed the Wilcox rising in 1889 and argued from these facts that a show of force was all that was necessary to overawe the Queen's supporters in 1893.[58]

So much of this statement as pertains to the demoralization, division, and paralysis of the Queen's supporters must be admitted. They had ample time to act against the committee of safety before the troops were landed. Yet their impression of Stevens's hostile attitude may have been one of the elements that imposed this paralysis. Thurston's claims for the strength, firm purpose, and self-confidence of the committee are less convincing. The situation was not that contemplated in his May memorandum. He had lost the support of native leaders like Bush and R. W. Wilcox. The crisis had come unexpectedly, and there had been no adequate time for perfecting plans or resurrecting the military organization that had proved so effective in 1887 and 1889. At the first meeting of the committee of safety on Saturday afternoon there was a painful realization that the Queen's military forces were well organized and well armed, while the committee had no military organization, few arms, and little knowledge of what arms were available. Hence the appointment of Thurston, Wilder, and Glade to visit Stevens and ascertain what protection might be af-

[58] Thurston's statement of November 21, 1893, in New York *World*, November 22, 1893.

forded by the " Boston." [59]   At the meeting on Sunday morning Messrs. Wundenberg and Soper, who had been asked to make an inventory of available arms, reported that the prospect was very discouraging, that only some sixty stand of arms could be found not in the possession of the government.[60]   It is easy to understand why Smith and Thurston went immediately thereafter to Stevens to express solicitude for the committee's safety.   There is no reliable evidence that the situation had greatly improved in this respect by Tuesday.   As late as Monday night a " finance " committee was named to procure arms, and at one-thirty on Tuesday rifles were being transported from a store to the armory for the use of the revolutionists.   We must, therefore, take with a grain of salt the statements of Soper and Thurston of the adequacy of the Provisional Government's military force.

Under these circumstances, the Provisional Government, when it took possession of the undefended Government Building and watched its armed supporters drift in by twos and threes, must have derived considerable comfort from the presence, just across the street, of the friendly marines and bluejackets from the " Boston."   The troops, as previously stated, had been landed Monday afternoon and later had been quartered in Arion Hall for the night.   Stevens was no doubt within his rights in exercising his own judgment as to the propriety of landing troops for the protection of American life and property, even against the protest of the Government.   His request to Captain

[59] From Smith's narrative. *U. S. For. Rel., 1894,* App. II, p. 962.
[60] *Ibid.,* p. 964.

Wiltse for the troops, and Wiltse's orders to Lieutenant Commander Swinburne, who commanded the landing party, betrayed no political motive, no hint of favoritism to either faction in the existing controversy.[61] Swinburne was directed to protect " our legation, consulate, and the lives and property of American citizens, and to assist in preserving order." But why were the troops stationed at Arion Hall, far from the legation, the consulate, and the bulk of American property? Stevens maintained stoutly that the site was selected without thought of political effect; in fact, that it was the only building available where he could find shelter for the troops, who had landed without tents.[62] If we accept this statement as true—and its truth was questioned [63]—we may still ask why it was necessary that they should remain there throughout Tuesday, unless they were indeed intended to overawe the Queen. Several officers were questioned by Blount or the Senate committee as to the significance of the Arion Hall location. Lieutenant Commander Swinburne and Lieutenant Coffman, both of whom were present, agreed that the troops stationed there would probably have been exposed to any firing that oc-

[61] *Ibid.*, pp. 553, 474.

[62] Buffalo *Courier*, November 13, 1893. Stevens stated that he had first tried to secure the Opera House and had turned to Arion Hall when that proved unavailable. The statement is interesting in view of the fact that in a conflict between the Palace and the Government Building the Opera House would have been even more exposed than Arion Hall. See sketch, p. 103.

[63] Lt. Coffman, U. S. N., one of the officers of the landing party, stated that there was a large, unoccupied hotel building about half-way between the legation and consulate which in his judgment would have been a more suitable place for the troops than Arion Hall. *Senate Report* No. 227, 53d Cong., 2d sess., pp. 639-640.

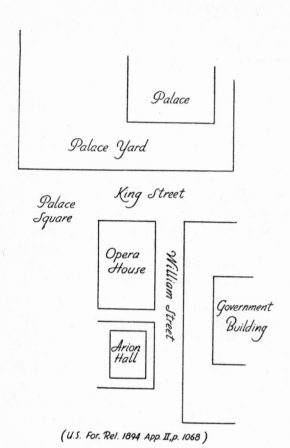

Palace

Palace Yard

Palace
Square

King Street

Opera
House

William Street

Arion
Hall

Government
Building

(U.S. For. Rel. 1894 App. II, p. 1068)

curred between Royalist troops and those of the Provisional Government.[64]   Rear Admiral Skerrett, who arrived in Honolulu soon after the revolution, thought the location poorly chosen if the purpose of the troops was to protect American life and property, but wisely " if they were landed with a view to support the Provisional Government troops, then occupying the Government building." [65]   Whatever the purpose of the troops—and it seems certain that they had no orders to support the Provisional Government [66]— there can be little doubt that their presence at Arion Hall created the impression that they were ready to support that government and so helped to intimidate the Queen. It seems, indeed, very doubtful whether the leaders of the revolutionary movement would have carried it through had they not been able to count upon the presence of the United States troops and the impression their presence would make upon the Queen's supporters. C. Bolte, one of the com-

[64] *Ibid.*, pp. 486, 645. Lucien Young, on the other hand, thought fighting could have occurred in Palace Square and about the Government Building without affecting the troops. *Ibid.*, p. 346. Yet the same officer reported that Captain Wiltse had said to him: " I will not allow any fighting in the city." *U. S. For. Rel., 1894,* App. II, p. 1139.

[65] *Ibid.*, p. 538.

[66] Swinburne told a resident of Honolulu that he was expected to assist in preserving order. " If the Queen calls on me to preserve order I am going to do it." Later, before the Senate committee, he said: " I did not know that I was there to fight her battles any more than anybody else's." When asked by Senator Gray whether, if Dole and the others had been attacked while on their way to the Government Building, he would have protected them, he replied that that question was very difficult to answer. *Senate Report* No. 227, 53d Cong., 2d sess., pp. 470, 475, 483.

mittee, when asked by Blount what they would have done
if Stevens had not landed troops, said he could not answer,
as they had not made any plans.[67] Another member of the
committee, Henry Waterhouse, was asked if the committee
expected Stevens to do more than protect American citizens
who went to the consulate or legation. He replied:

> That in case there was any bloodshed that they [the
> troops] would, if called upon, protect the party in power,
> and I expected we were going to be in power forthwith.
> How did you expect to get into power without a little
> bloodshed?
> We knew the feeling of those who were in power then—
> that they were cowards; that by going up with a bold front,
> *and they supposing that the American troops would assist
> us,* that would help us out.[68]

Lieutenant Coffman, who may be regarded as an un-
prejudiced witness, said it was common opinion in Honolulu that the Provisional Government would not have been
established except for the presence of the American troops.

> My opinion is that everybody believed that the entire
> American force and the American minister were in accord
> and sympathy with the movement, and I do not think the
> movement would have been undertaken had they not
> thought so beforehand. . . . If you say to them, " Would
> you have taken possession of that building had you not
> known that the sympathy of the United States troops and
> minister was with you," some of them will say, " Well,
> perhaps not: but they were there." [69]

In view of Stevens's improper intimacy with the leaders
of the revolution and of the aid which the movement derived from his attitude and from the presence of the

[67] *U. S. For. Rel., 1894,* App. II, p. 723.
[68] *Ibid.,* p. 521. Italics mine.
[69] *Senate Report* No. 227, 53d Cong., 2d sess., pp. 642-643.

" Boston's " marines and sailors, the question of whether Stevens recognized the Provisional Government prematurely may seem rather academic. It was, nevertheless, a much disputed question at the time, and a glance at it now may not be out of place.

Recognition was proper (leaving aside the question of antecedent improprieties) if the government when recognized actually exercised a *de facto* authority capable of maintaining order and compelling obedience. This situation could exist only if any formidable opposing force had surrendered or had been defeated, dispersed, or otherwise nullified. In reporting to Washington his recognition of the Provisional Government, Stevens wrote that he and Captain Wiltse had " recognized only accomplished facts and [had] not allowed the use of the United States forces for any but the most conservative reasons." [70] The five Hawaiian commissioners who at once went to Washington to seek annexation made the following official declaration to Secretary Foster:

No public recognition was accorded the Provisional Government by the American minister until they were in possession of the Government buildings, the archives, and the treasury, supported by several hundred armed men, and after the abdication by the Queen and the surrender to the Provisional Government of her forces.[71]

The latter part of this statement is redeemed from the realm of plain falsehood only by the word " public " at the beginning. It is probably true that there was no public recognition of the Provisional Government, in the sense of

[70] *U. S. For. Rel., 1894,* App. II, p. 209.
[71] *Ibid.,* p. 237.

a proclamation or announcement in the newspapers, until after the Queen had surrendered her authority and ordered the marshal to do likewise, but as we have seen, the recognition had been made known to the Queen and her ministers and was a major if not the determining factor in her decision. That recognition actually preceded the surrender of the Queen and her military force is placed beyond dispute by a letter from Dole to Stevens, which acknowledges Stevens's letter according recognition, expresses " deep appreciation of the same," and continues:

We have conferred with the ministers of the late government and have made demand upon the marshal to surrender the station house. We are not actually yet in possession of the station house, but as night is approaching and our forces may be insufficient to maintain order, we request the immediate support of the United States forces, and would request that the commander of the United States forces take command of our military forces so that they may act together for the protection of the city.[72]

A government which found it necessary to make such an admission and such a request could hardly claim to be exercising *de facto* authority.

Confronted with this evidence of a somewhat hasty act of recognition, Stevens fell back upon two claims in justification of his action. In his statements to the press he asserted that at the time of recognition the Provisional

[72] *Ibid.,* p. 565. Stevens replied as follows: " Think Capt. Wiltse will endeavor to maintain order and protect life and property, but do not think he would take command of the men of the Provisional Government. Will have him come to the legation soon as possible and take his opinion and inform you as soon as possible." *Ibid.,* p. 607. The request was endorsed by Stevens: " The above request not complied with."

Government " was complete master of the situation, had
full control of the city and of the Government archives,
the police station being surrounded and at the mercy of the
provisional Government. . . . The provisional Government knew its power to possess the station at once, but
wished not to take a single life of its occupants." [73] Let
him who will attempt to reconcile this statement with the
description of the situation in Dole's letter. Stevens's other
argument, advanced at the same time, was that the Queen's
government was practically dead after January 14—killed
by her own attempt at revolution—and that the only government capable of maintaining law and order was such an
one as the Provisional Government of January 17.[74] In a
measure this claim may seem plausible, for as we have
seen, the Queen's government appeared completely para-
lyzed in its capacity to cope with revolution. But again the
guess may be hazarded that this paralysis was the product
of the strong suspicion that Stevens and the " Boston "
would support the revolutionists.[75] That suspicion may

[73] New York *World*, November 30, 1893. No other witness,
so far as I know, goes so far as to claim that the station house
was actually surrounded and at the mercy of the Provisional Government forces.

[74] *Ibid., Cf.* also Stevens's statement to the Senate Committee:
" The Queen's government ended on Saturday afternoon. There
was no government of the Queen's for more than forty-eight hours;
from 4 o'clock Saturday afternoon, the 14th of January, the
Queen's government was absolutely dead. . . . " *Senate Report*
No. 227, 53d Cong., 2d sess., pp. 539-540.

[75] Marshal Wilson stated that on Sunday he had proposed that
the ringleaders of the movement be arrested and all arms and
ammunition in the town seized. " Messrs. Peterson and Neumann
both objected, on the grounds that it would precipitate a conflict,

have weakened the morale of one party as much as it strengthened that of the other. In all other respects, the life of the city went on normally and undisturbed. There were no disorders. On Monday, both before and after the mass meeting, and before the troops were landed, J. O. Carter saw women and children going about the streets as usual. " It was," he said, " the most peaceful, law-abiding community you would see anywhere." [76] The Queen's government was not dead, as Stevens asserted. It was capable of coping with ordinary situations. It was not a strong or wise or coherent government, and it knew not which way to turn when confronted by a band of revolutionists who were seen to be enjoying confidential relations with the United States minister.

---

as Minister Stevens had already declared himself, and we must at all hazards avoid a conflict with the United States troops." *U. S. For. Rel., 1894,* App. II, p. 1031. Wilson also proposed to defend the Government Building against the revolutionists, but was dissuaded by Peterson. Dole, *op. cit.,* pp. 81-82. *Cf.* Thurston, *op. cit.,* p. 254.

[76] *U. S. For. Rel., 1894,* App. II, pp. 738-739.

IV

ANNEXATION REJECTED

The avowed purpose of the men who had led the revolution and organized the Provisional Government was annexation to the United States. The declaration proclaiming the Provisional Government had stated that it should exist until terms of union with the United States should have been agreed upon. The committee of safety, at its Monday night meeting, had determined that the " Claudine," a steamer owned by the Inter-Island Steamship Company, should proceed at once to San Francisco with dispatches for Washington.[1] The new government lost no time in initiating measures for annexation. A commission of five was promptly named to visit Washington, and on January 18 the Executive Council completed and signed instructions empowering the commissioners to negotiate a treaty of union with the United States. The commission, consisting of Messrs. L. A. Thurston, W. C. Wilder, W. R. Castle, J. Marsden, and C. L. Carter, sailed for San Francisco at 9:00 a.m., January 19, on the " Claudine."[2] A request from the deposed Queen that she be permitted to send a representative by the same steamer was refused, and she

[1] *U. S. For. Rel., 1894*, App. II, p. 967. The president of the steamship company was W. C. Wilder, a member of the committee of safety and one of the commissioners sent to Washington. *Ibid.*, p. 397.

[2] *Ibid.*, p. 237. For details of instruction see *infra*, p. 118.

was compelled for the time being to confine her representations to a written protest to President Harrison.[3]

The " Claudine " arrived at San Francisco in the early
morning of January 28, bearing not only the commissioners
but the first news of the revolution to reach the outside
world. The commissioners spent a very busy day in the
coast city, lining up business and newspaper men for their
cause. Among others they found there Claus Spreckels,
leading Hawaiian sugar grower, and his two sons, Adolph
and John. " They were much interested," wrote Thurston,
" and immediately sided with us and proposed a meeting
of all interested in Honolulu be held in the evening at
the Palace Hotel. . . . Mr. Spreckels," added Thurston,
" has gone into the matter with both feet and is going on
from here next Tuesday to Washington to back us in every
way that he can." [4] Having spent, as they thought, a profitable day in San Francisco, the commissioners departed for
Washington, where they arrived February 3, and at once
entered into negotiations with Secretary Foster.

Stevens, meanwhile, had done and was doing everything
in his power to smooth the way for the Washington negotiations and ensure the consummation of his pet project.
The Hawaiian commissioners he described to Foster in terms
of high praise. They were all men of the " highest re-

[3] *U. S. For. Rel., 1894,* App. II, p. 867.

[4] Thurston to Dole, January 29, 1893. Spaulding Collection.
The San Francisco *Examiner,* January 29, 1893, printed a statement
from Spreckels that with such information as he possessed he
favored annexation and a territorial form of government. For
Spreckels's later opposition to annexation and support of the Queen,
see *infra,* pp. 156-157.

spectability." Thurston was "one of the most, if not *the* most, talented and influential man on the islands." Castle was a lawyer of eminence, born in Hawaii of western New York parentage. Carter was "an accomplished and most reliable gentleman, American to the core, and has a Michigan wife." As a group, the commissioners represented "a large preponderating proportion of the property holders and commercial interests in the islands. They are backed," he added, "by the influences which will enable them to fully carry out their agreements with the United States Government." [5] Not content with vouching for the "respectability" and substantial property interests of the commissioners, Stevens thought it prudent to call attention to the low character and reputation of the men who were going or might go to Washington to represent the deposed Queen. Paul Neumann, who was to go as her attorney, Stevens characterized as a lawyer who had had an unsavory reputation in San Francisco and a pernicious influence in Hawaii; who had been a boon companion in revelry and corruption of Kalakaua, from whom he was reputed to have won money at cards. He was also supposed to have been the chief agent in putting the lottery bill through the recent legislature.[6] Others who might go to Washington, or who were engaged in the use of bribery or false representations to secure native signatures to a remonstrance against annexation, were likewise, Stevens warned, members of the old "palace gang." They wished to discredit the Provisional Government because it had cancelled the lottery charter

[5] *U. S. For. Rel., 1894,* App. II, pp. 397-398. Stevens here speaks of *six* commissioners. Only five were sent.

[6] *Ibid.,* p. 398.

which they had hoped to sell for $500,000.[7] Most of the opponents of annexation, wrote Stevens, were of " the lower class of natives, led by unscrupulous foreigners, of little property, . . . who wish to maintain the Hawaiian monarchy and its corruption for their own unworthy purposes." In favor of annexation, on the other hand, were most of the native Christian ministers, an influential native newspaper, and a number of the native political leaders. Specifically Stevens mentioned R. W. Wilcox, who, he said, "has more fighting ability than any other native Hawaiian, and will be proud to become an American citizen and at a future time to serve in the army or civil service of the United States." [8]

A long report containing such details as the above and various suggestions as to terms of annexation Stevens concluded with the following paragraph:

The Hawaiian pear is now fully ripe, and this is the golden hour for the United States to pluck it. If annexation does not take place promptly, all is held in doubt and suspense for six or ten months, there certainly will be here a revulsion to despair, and these people, by their necessities, might be forced towards becoming a British colony, for the English here of the monarchial type would then avail themselves of their opportunity and stir up all possible opposition to annexation. . . .[9]

On the same day that Stevens wrote this advice to the Department of State he announced that he had placed the

---

[7] *Ibid.,* pp. 402-403.

[8] Here, perhaps unwittingly, Stevens appears to have touched the key to Wilcox's character. A man of thwarted ambition, he seemed ever ready to give his allegiance to any party that would reward him with place and power.

[9] *Ibid.,* pp. 400-402. Stevens to Foster, February 1, 1893.

Hawaiian Islands temporarily under the protection of the
United States. A note to Stevens from the Executive Council, dated January 31, expressed the belief that the Government was "unable to satisfactory [*sic*] protect life and
property, and to prevent civil disorders in Honolulu and
throughout the Hawaiian Islands," and requested, therefore, that Stevens raise the United States flag "for the protection of the Hawaiian Islands for the time being." It
conferred upon the United States Government, through the
minister, the right to occupy the public buildings and the
soil of Hawaii, so far as should be necessary for the exercise
of such protection, "but not interfering with the administration of public affairs by this Government." [10] Accordingly, at 9:00 a.m. on February 1, Stevens caused the
United States flag to be raised over the Government Building and announced the protectorate in a proclamation to the
Hawaiian people.[11]

In a letter to Foster of the same date, Stevens explained
the reasons for his action. The Provisional Government,
he said, needed time to organize a new police and to dis-
cipline a small, permanent military force. So far, the Government had been "sustained by the uprising and union of
the business men and best citizens. Bankers, merchants,
clerks, professional men, respectable mechanics have stood
manfully by the new Government and kept guard at night.
This kind of defence must give place to a small, reliable
military force." But such a force would require time to

[10] *Ibid.*, p. 405. This communication throws a backward light
upon the *de facto* status of the Provisional Government two weeks
before.
[11] *Ibid.*, p. 792.

organize and train, and in the meantime there was peril
from the 40,000 Chinese and Japanese in the islands, who
might be stirred to disorder by "evil-disposed persons,"
and from certain vicious elements in Honolulu, both white
and native. But there was another reason for the protectorate, in line with Stevens's habitual distrust of British
intentions. There was a probability, he wrote, that a British
naval vessel would arrive on the scene, and a danger in that
event that the British commissioner "might try to press
unduly" the Provisional Government.

With the islands under our protection we think the
English minister will not attempt to insist that his Govern-
ment has the right to interfere while our flag is over the
Government building.[12]

Stevens's persistent arguments for annexation were su-
perfluous. The Harrison administration had, in all probability, determined long beforehand what its policy would be
in such a contingency as had now arisen,[13] and its action
was prompt and unequivocal. In a telegram of January 28,
Secretary Foster had not only approved of Stevens's recognition of the Provisional Government, but had added:

It is trusted that the change, besides conducing to the tran-
quility and welfare of the Hawaiian Islands, will tend to
draw closer the intimate ties of amity and common interests which so conspicuously and necessarily link them to
the United States.[14]

Four days later (February 1) the Secretary sought to fore-
stall any foreign opposition to annexation by reminding

[12] Ibid., pp. 403-404. A telegram of the same date gave a brief
statement of the facts. Ibid., p. 399.
[13] Supra, pp. 69-73.
[14] U. S. For. Rel., 1894, App. II, p. 399.

foreign governments of the long-established predominance of American interests in Hawaii and of repeated declarations of "the paramount interest of the United States in these Islands." The identic cablegrams to American ministers in London, Paris, Berlin, and St. Petersburg continued:

They constitute an essential and important element in our commercial system, and their proximity and situation make them a potential factor, which we could never see transferred to any other control without the gravest concern. The President directs me to recall this historical attitude to your attention, and to say that recent events have fortified our position and made our paramount concern more evident.[15]

On the following day, February 2, the Secretary of State received members of the diplomatic corps. The ministers of Japan, France, Russia, and Germany brought up the subject of Hawaii, and each in turn expressed the opinion that his government would interpose no objection to the annexation of the islands by the United States. The Russian minister, however, warned Foster to expect opposition from Great Britain. The British minister made no reference to the subject,[16] but dispatches from Minister Lincoln in London indicated that no trouble was to be expected from that quarter.[17]

Foster was ready enough to forward the cause of annexation. He was not willing in the meantime, however, to assume a full-fledged protectorate over the islands, with

[15] Text in *Instructions, France,* XXII, 461.

[16] The memorandum of these conversations is filed in *Hawaii, Notes,* IV, under date of February 2, 1893.

[17] *Infra,* pp. 125-126.

all that the term implied. To Stevens's message of February 1, announcing the raising of the United States flag in Honolulu, Foster replied that the action was commended, so far as it accorded to the *de facto* Government " the material coöperation of the United States for the maintenance of good order and protection of life and property from apprehended disorders "; but, he added:

so far as it may appear to overstep that limit by setting the authority of the United States above that of the Hawaiian Government in the capacity of protector, or to impair the independent sovereignty of that Government by substituting the flag and power of the United States, it is disavowed.[18]

On the day that this message was sent (February 14), Foster signed with the Hawaiian commissioners a treaty for the annexation of the islands to the United States. Negotiations had been opened promptly after the arrival of the commissioners in Washington. Formal conferences with Foster were held on February 4th, 7th (two meetings), and 9th. Meanwhile Thurston had three private interviews with the secretary, lasting, as he wrote, from an hour and a half to three hours each. Foster's attitude was friendly and encouraging from the start.

He states [wrote Thurston, February 9] that since we have been here, the President, Attorney General and several other members of the Cabinet besides himself, together with members of the House and Senate Committee on Foreign Relations have done little else but devote themselves to this question. He informed us on Tuesday that he was instructed by the President to say that the President and Cabinet had made up their minds to annex the Islands; that they were willing to do so on as nearly the lines that

[18] *U. S. For. Rel., 1894,* App. II, pp. 406-407.

we asked as was possible, . . . They have made up their minds to act immediately through the Senate by means of a Treaty, which will secure the annexation, although the financial part of it will require further action by Congress.[19]

There were, however, several points upon which the commissioners were forced to abandon a part of their hopes in order to quiet probable opposition in the Senate. Their instructions from the Provisional Government directed them, if possible, to incorporate in the treaty promises that the United States would lay and maintain a cable to the islands and would open the entrance to Pearl Harbor and establish a naval and coaling station there; a provision that sugar and other Hawaiian products should be entitled to all bounties, benefits, and exemptions enjoyed by similar products in the United States; and a further provision exempting the islands from the operation of the laws against importation of Chinese laborers.[20] All of these provisions Foster found to be objectionable. The laying of a cable must be left to private initiative. The United States must be left free, if it annexed the islands, to develop whatever ports or harbors it saw fit. But it was the provisions regarding the sugar bounty and Chinese immigration that presented the greatest difficulty. Foster was at first willing

[19] Thurston to Dole, February 9, 1893. Spaulding Collection.

[20] The Executive Council to the Commissioners, January 18, 1893. Spaulding Collection. Subsequent instructions of January 31 directed the commissioners not to insist upon either the cable or the full sugar bounty if such insistence threatened to embarrass the negotiations. *Ibid.* It is doubtful whether these latter instructions were received prior to the signing of the treaty. Stevens advocated a bounty of six mills per pound for Hawaiian sugar instead of the full bounty of two cents. *U. S. For. Rel., 1894,* App. II, p. 400.

to consent to a small bounty of one-half a cent a pound
on sugar, but when Thurston revealed that the Hawaiian
planters had been coerced by the Sugar Trust into signing
contracts whereby the Trust would receive one-half of any
bounty that might be paid, Foster concluded that it was
politically inexpedient to send to the Senate a treaty con-
ferring any bounty whatsoever. A bounty clause and a
clause permitting importation of Oriental laborers under
contract " would have the same effect upon the opposition
that a red flag would have upon a bull." [21] To persuade
the commissioners to forego the bounty, Foster pointed to
the probability that the bounty provision would be repealed
within a year, and a duty substituted, and he added, as
reported by W. R. Castle:

> The great difficulty is the first, that of securing admission
> to the Union. After you become American citizens no Con-
> gress will treat you differently from any other American
> citizen. It will be the object and aim of Congress to make
> the Hawaiian portion of the Union as prosperous as any
> other part.[22]

Foster thereupon presented a draft of a treaty which
made all the concessions which he thought it safe or politic
to grant. With some difficulty he had succeeded in over-

[21] Minutes of Meeting of Hawaiian Commission at Wormley's
Hotel, Washington, February 10, 1893. Spaulding Collection. The
Protocols of the conferences, in MS in the Dept. of State, are well
summarized in Castle, *John Watson Foster*, pp. 213-217. The sugar
contract referred to had been made with the Western Sugar Refining
Company, owned jointly by the Spreckels family and the eastern
combination known as the Sugar Trust. E. Jones, *The Trust Problem in the United States*, pp. 93-94.

[22] Castle to Dole, February 25, 1893. Spaulding Collection.

coming certain inconvenient scruples of President Harrison, who wished an expression by the voters of the Hawaiian state in regard to annexation, and who as late as the morning of February 10 " asked if something could not be inserted giving it the semblance of having been the universal wish of the people." [23] Thurston called a meeting of the commissioners and certain of their friends in Washington at Wormley's Hotel on February 10. He presented Foster's draft, together with Foster's opinion that a treaty in this form would be unanimously approved by the Senate Committee on Foreign Relations and acted upon at the current session, whereas the chances of getting quick action on any other form were very slight. All present agreed that Foster's draft should be accepted, since the alternative seemed to be to return to Honolulu empty-handed.[24]

The treaty thus agreed upon and signed by Foster and the five commissioners on February 14 provided for the annexation of the Hawaiian Islands as " an integral part of the territory of the United States," the cession to the United States of all government buildings and government and crown lands, the continuance of the existing government and laws, " subject to the paramount authority of the United States," until Congress should otherwise provide, the extension to the islands within one year of the laws of the United States respecting duties on imports, internal revenue, and commerce and navigation, the prohibition of further immigration of Chinese laborers to the islands or from the islands to the mainland, the assumption by the United States of the Hawaiian debt, not to exceed $3,250,000, the

[23] Minutes of a Meeting . . . *Loc. cit.*
[24] *Ibid.*

payment of an annuity of $20,000 to Liliuokalani for life and of a lump sum of $150,000 to Princess Kaiulani, the ex-heir presumptive.[25] On the following day (February 15) President Harrison sent the treaty to the Senate with a report by Foster and a message urging prompt and favorable action.[26] Both message and report disclaimed all responsibility for the revolution on the part of the United States. Harrison's statement that "the overthrow of the monarchy was not in any way promoted by this Government" expressed a belief which the President, with the information in hand, could no doubt honestly hold. Foster's report contained a statement of facts ingeniously worded so as to give an erroneous impression. His assertion that the revolution "was entirely unexpected so far as this Government was concerned" was true of *the* revolution which had occurred. Advices from Hawaii had, he said, for some time "indicated political uncertainty, party intrigues, and legislative opposition," but these had not suggested "an overthrow of the monarchy through popular resistance to the unconstitutional acts of the late sovereign." *This* revolution had been unexpected. That *a* revolution had been unexpected the Secretary did not say.

The treaty was promptly approved by the Senate Committee on Foreign Relations and favorably reported to the Senate.[27] Its fate then hung upon the attitude of the

[25] *U. S. For. Rel., 1894,* App. II, pp. 202-205.
[26] *Ibid.,* pp. 197-202.
[27] *Journal of the Executive Proceedings of the Senate,* 52d Cong., p. 398. It is significant that the Senate, in considering the treaty, requested the President to send all correspondence with the U. S. minister to Hawaii *since the preceding May*—the month of Thurston's visit to Washington. *Ibid.,* p. 399.

Democratic Senators, since without some Democratic votes a two-thirds majority was not obtainable. Foster had made an effort to assure Democratic support, consulting with Senators Morgan, of Alabama, and Gorman, of Maryland, who reported that there would be no serious opposition.[28] Foster also approached Mr. James H. Blount, of Georgia, chairman of the House Foreign Affairs Committee, showing him Stevens's report of the preceding November on the Hawaiian situation. Blount showed the report to others but did not express an opinion.[29] Democrats, however, looked to the incoming administration for guidance. On February 22 Cleveland held a conference at Lakewood, N. J., with Walter Q. Gresham and John G. Carlisle, who were to be respectively his Secretaries of State and Treasury. They considered, says Mrs. Gresham, " the case of the Hawaiian Queen." [30] Their conclusions are not recorded, but it was presumably after this conference that Carlisle came to Washington and was reported to have made known the wish of the President-elect that the treaty be left for the new administration to deal with.[31] On February 25, Mott Smith and W. R. Castle were writing Dole that action on the treaty would probably be delayed until after March 4. Smith reported a conversation with Senator Platt, of Connecticut, who thought that if there were a full attendance in the Senate it would be easy to obtain a two-thirds vote, but that with an average daily

[28] John W. Foster, *Diplomatic Memoirs,* II, 168.

[29] *Senate Report* No. 227, 53d Cong., 2d sess., pp. 404-405.

[30] Matilda Gresham, *Life of Walter Quintin Gresham,* II, 684-685.

[31] Foster, *loc. cit.*

attendance of only fifty Senators, the margin was so close
that it would be unsafe to force a vote. With this turn
in affairs, the commissioners thought it expedient to cultivate the incoming administration, and Thurston and Carter
both set out in an effort to find Gresham, one going to
Chicago and the other to New York.[32]

The session of Congress ended March 4 with the Hawaiian treaty still awaiting action in the Senate. Cleveland
and Gresham, his Secretary of State, had learned enough,
apparently, to make them suspicious of the part played by
Stevens in the revolution and the creation of the Provisional
Government.[33] Cleveland was distrustful of the " vigorous

[32] Castle to Dole, Smith to Dole, February 25, 1893. Spaulding
Collection. Smith considered it unfortunate for the treaty that
Foster had resigned (February 23) and gone to Paris for the
Bering Sea arbitration. Paul Neumann, the former Queen's attorney, arrived in Washington on February 17 and was reported
to be seeing individual senators and priming them with arguments
against the treaty. New York Herald, February 19, 1893. It is
doubtful, however, whether he exerted any real influence against
ratification. In an interview at the State Department February 21
he told Foster that restoration of the Queen would be practicable
only under American protection, that the great majority of Hawaiians
were opposed not to annexation but to the rule of the faction represented by the Provisional Government, and that his power of attorney was broad enough to permit him to accept annexation with
a reasonable compensation for the Queen and heir presumptive.
Hawaii, Notes, IV. Stenographic notes of interview. Upon landing
in San Francisco, Neumann had been reported as saying that the
Queen was willing that the islands should be annexed if it were
done in the right way. New York Herald, February 10, 1893.

[33] Liliuokalani had addressed a letter to Cleveland January 31,
promising that a full statement of her case would be laid before him
by Paul Neumann and begging his friendly assistance in granting
redress for a wrong. U. S. For. Rel., 1894, App. II, pp. 867-868.

foreign policy" inaugurated by James G. Blaine. Gresham, in addition to a chivalrous desire to succor a Queen in distress, may have been animated partly by hostility to Harrison and a desire to put him in the wrong.[34] On March 9, Cleveland requested that the Senate return the treaty to him " for the purpose of reexamination." [35] Two days later he appointed James H. Blount, until March 4 Congressman from Georgia and chairman of the House Committee on Foreign Affairs, a special commissioner to visit the Hawaiian Islands and investigate conditions there, the causes of the revolution, the sentiment of the people toward the existing government, and " all that can fully enlighten the President touching the subjects of your mission." Blount was given " paramount " authority in all matters touching the protection of American citizens. He was to use the naval force at Honolulu for that purpose if necessary but was not to interfere in domestic affairs. He was informed that the United States would adhere to its established policy in the maintenance of its treaty and other rights in the islands and would " not acquiesce in domestic interference by other powers." [36] Blount talked with both Gresham and Cleveland, formed the opinion that Cleveland at least had an

[34] Allan Nevins, *Grover Cleveland, A Study in Courage,* pp. 549, 550, 553. Foster, *loc. cit.* Gresham, *op. cit.,* II, 738-739. Mrs. Gresham writes: " If my husband was actuated only by resentment towards President Harrison, the Republican leaders, and the Republican party, he had the satisfaction of knowing that he embarrassed them greatly. . . . "

[35] Richardson, *Messages and Papers of the Presidents,* IX, 393.

[36] *U. S. For. Rel., 1894,* App. II, pp. 1185-1187. These instructions were signed by Gresham.

open mind in the matter, and forthwith set out upon his difficult mission.[37]

On March 16, Secretary Gresham held conversations on the Hawaiian question with the diplomatic representatives of three leading Pacific powers, Japan, Russia, and Great Britain. In none of these did he find much to deter him had he wished to proceed along the road marked out by Foster. Mr. Tateno, of Japan, expressed an interest in the islands because of the presence there of more than 20,000 Japanese. His government, he said, would be very reluctant to see the islands fall under the control of any European power, but " would be pleased to see the sovereignty of the United States extended over them." Prince Cantacuzene read a communication from the Russian Government, expressing its pleasure at seeing the United States extend its authority in the direction of the islands. The prince then dropped a word of warning about Great Britain, who, he was convinced, was really scheming to get the islands for herself—" that she might, cat-like, purr at our feet, and rub against our legs, but we should remember that she had claws." The United States should remember that Russia was its firm and trustworthy friend in any effort at westward extension in the Pacific.

The " purring " of Great Britain was evident in the remarks of Sir Julian Pauncefote on the same day, but there is no indication that that nation had any hidden intention of using its claws. The British Government and press had, according to the reports of Minister Lincoln, taken the Hawaiian episode calmly from the beginning. In the House

[37] Nevins, *op. cit.,* p. 553.

of Commons on February 2, Sir Edward Grey, Under-
Secretary for Foreign Affairs, had stated that the Government had no intention of sending war vessels to Hawaii
or of making a protest of any kind at Washington, that
it considered the lives and property of British subjects safe
under American protection. The principal London newspapers were inclined to recognize the " predominance of
interests of the United States." [38] Now, on March 16, Sir
Julian said to Gresham

that his Government was only interested in seeing stable
authority maintained on the Islands; that it had no desire
or intention to interfere in the domestic affairs of the
Islands and that it knew of the close relations existing between the government of the Islands and this country, and
of the exceptional interests that the Government of the
United States had in the Islands. . . .

Sir Julian referred to the need that Great Britain and
the United States should maintain friendly relations in
Hawaii and elsewhere, and when Gresham intimated that
such relations would be made easier by the removal of Mr.
Wodehouse, the British commissioner in Honolulu, promised that " he would be very promptly relieved should the
Secretary of State say that in his judgment he deemed it
necessary for the maintenance of harmony and good
feeling."

Sir Julian also referred reminiscently to the suggestion he
had once made to Secretary Blaine that the United States
and Great Britain join with other powers to guarantee the
independence of the Hawaiian Islands and recalled that

[38] Lincoln to Foster, February 3, 10, 1893. *Dispatches, Great
Britain,* CLXXIII.

Mr. Blaine " in a very emphatic way said the United States would do nothing of the kind." [39]

It is fairly obvious from this conversation that while Great Britain preferred to see Hawaii remain independent, she had no purpose of contesting the establishment there of American sovereignty if that course should be adopted.

The Cleveland administration, then, might determine upon its Hawaiian policy without fear of interference from foreign powers. What that policy should be would depend largely upon the answers to two questions. Had Minister Stevens taken an improper part in the overthrow of the Monarchy? Was annexation desired by any large group of the native people, or only by the ruling clique of whites? It was to seek the answers to these questions that Blount had been sent to Honolulu.

The second question might, of course, have been answered by submitting the proposal for annexation to a plebiscite. It will be recalled that such a measure had been suggested by Harrison but abandoned under the persuasion of Foster and the commissioners. Paul Neumann, who was in Washington as representative of the former Queen, now reported to Thurston information that the new administration would agree to annexation if it could be ratified by a popular vote in the islands and said he could guarantee that the former Queen would use her influence for a favorable vote if she were permitted to keep possession of the crown lands during her life. Thurston replied that the

[39] Records of the conferences with Tateno, Cantacuzene, and Pauncefote are in *Memoranda of Conversations with the Secretary of State, 1893-1898.*

commissioners would never agree to a treaty with a plebiscite provision, and he warned Neumann that if annexation were defeated the President might agree to a protectorate, under which the former Queen would get nothing
instead of the annuity provided in the treaty. In reporting
the incident to Dole, Thurston added:

> We had to go over the entire plebiscite question with the
> former administration, and convinced them of the impos-
> sibility of carrying it out. I feel sure that as soon as the
> office-seeking rush is over, and we can fairly and squarely
> get at Mr. Gresham we can convince him of the impos-
> sibility of the plebiscite, and the inadvisibility of the pro-
> tectorate. At the same time if we cannot secure annexation,
> a protectorate will be the next best thing.[40]

Afraid to stake the cause of annexation upon the doubtful, if not certainly adverse, result of a popular vote, the
commissioners trusted that Mr. Blount, with his Southern
background, would sympathize with their position.

> As a southerner [wrote Thurston] he is thoroughly
> familiar with the difficulties attendant upon government
> with an ignorant majority in the electorate and will thor-
> oughly appreciate the situation upon this point.[41]

[40] Thurston to Dole, March 10, 1893. Spaulding Collection.
That Cleveland was considering a protectorate as a possibility was
stated to Thurston by Rear Admiral Brown after a conference with
Gresham. Thurston to Dole, March 10, 1893. *Ibid.* Congressman
W. M. Springer stated that he had had several talks with the
Hawaiian commissioners in Washington about submitting the an-
nexation question to a popular vote. " In every instance," he said,
" I was informed that the people of the islands were not capable
of self-government, and if the question were submitted to them
that they would be hostile to this movement." *North American
Review,* CLVII, 748 (December, 1893).

[41] Thurston to Dole, March 16, 1893. Spaulding Collection.
C. L. Carter, one of the commissioners, had an interview with

At the same time, it was important to convince Mr. Blount
that the movement had a backing among the more responsible natives. Thurston, therefore, took it upon himself to write letters to such prominent half-castes as Colburn,
the former cabinet minister, and Antone Rosa, arguing that
postponement of annexation would mean prolonged division and ill feeling along racial lines, whereas annexation
under the United States flag would mean equal rights for
all, as well as a great commercial development where advantages would be confined to no one class in the community.[42] Thurston informed the Provisional Government
of the course he was pursuing and added:

> It seems to me that it is very important to try and pull
> the teeth of some of those boys, so that you can get a num-
> ber of the more prominent Hawaiians to go before Blount
> and express their desire for annexation. If it is promptly
> rubbed into them that the only alternative is annexation or
> the provisional government, I think it would go a long
> way, especially in view of the fact that they know what
> the benefits of annexation would be as well as you and I do.

He suggested other prominent natives and half-castes who
might be induced to go before Mr. Blount and plead for
annexation—even if it should be necessary to pay their

Hoke Smith, of Georgia, Cleveland's Secretary of the Interior.
Smith was evidently opposed to annexation until Carter made some
inquiries about the availability of Negro labor for the sugar plantations. "When I left," wrote Carter, "he seemed to think that if
Annexation would help them get rid of a portion of their colored
population that it might not be altogether bad." Carter to Dole,
March, 21, 1893. *Ibid.*

[42] *U. S. For. Rel., 1894,* App. II, pp. 478-479. Colburn and Rosa
obligingly turned over these letters to Commissioner Blount.

expenses—in order to offset the former Queen's charge that annexation was a white man's movement.

But it was not through Mr. Blount's reason alone that he was to be won over to a proper attitude. He might be approached also through his stomach and his wife's supposed enjoyment of the amenities of polished society. " He is a genial, pleasant man," Thurston wrote to Dole, " one who would appreciate attention, . . . He is a thorough gentleman and it is of course unnecessary for me to suggest that he be given every opportunity to meet the best people in Honolulu." [43] Thurston's colleague, W. R. Castle, advised Dole to remember that

People in Washington are very much accustomed to social communion. . . . Let Mr. Blount be well entertained. If his wife is with him have the ladies see that she has a good time. It is the after dinner talk over the cigar, when one feels comfortable and well filled that effective work is done.[44]

Alas for all such pleasant plans! Mr. Blount was careful to guard himself against the perils of post-prandial persuasion, and such few demonstrations as there were of native interest in annexation failed to carry conviction.

Blount arrived in Honolulu March 29. Even before leaving the ship he found it necessary to decline courtesies extended by both parties in the city. With Stevens, when the latter came on board to greet the commissioner, was a committee of the newly formed Annexation Club. These men had come to offer him " an elegant house, well furnished," together with servants, carriage, and horses. For

[43] Thurston to Dole, March 16, 1893. Spaulding Collection.
[44] Castle to Dole, March 16, 1893. *Ibid.*

this he might pay, as Blount recalled the invitation, " just what I chose, from nothing up." Blount declined the offer and stated that he would go to a hotel. He also declined the courtesy, offered by the former Queen through her chamberlain, of her carriage to convey him to his hotel.[45] Having thus, at the beginning, avoided entanglement with either party, Blount installed himself at the Hawaiian Hotel and proceeded to carry out his duties as he understood them.

One of his first official acts was to terminate the limited protectorate instituted by Stevens on February 1. By virtue of the " paramount " authority with which his instructions endowed him, Blount directed Admiral Skerrett, who had succeeded Captain Wiltse in command of the naval forces at Honolulu, to lower the American flag over the Government Building and reembark the sailors and marines who had been ashore since January 16. These orders were executed at 11:00 a.m., April 1.[46] Stevens, who though still United States minister must needs yield authority to the " commissioner paramount," could only watch with chagrin this repudiation of his policy. He had tendered his resignation on March 7, and on April 4 made known his intention to leave Honolulu the latter part of May. On May 9, Blount was appointed to succeed him.[47]

Blount conducted himself, while in Honolulu, with exemplary discretion. He heard all opinions and expressed

[45] *U. S. For. Rel., 1894,* App. II, p. 568. Stevens denied that Blount had been offered these accommodations at any price he might name. He was told, said Stevens, that he might pay the same that he would otherwise pay for hotel accommodations. *Senate Report* No. 227, 53d Cong., 2d sess., p. 560.

[46] *U. S. For. Rel., 1894,* App. II, pp. 1060-1061.

[47] *Ibid.,* pp. 413, 419, 421.

none, thereby tempting punsters to dub him the " minister reticent." As a Georgian and a former Confederate soldier, he even bore with fortitude the playing of " Marching through Georgia " in the course of the July Fourth celebration over which he presided.[48] He refused all tenders of hospitality and made few public appearances. Mr. Stevens charged later that the Hawaiian Hotel, where Blount lived and conducted his interviews, was a hotbed of royalist sentiment, and intimated that in this environment others than royalists were not free to visit him.[49] Yet Stevens himself admitted that the Hawaiian Hotel was the natural place for a visitor in Honolulu to reside.[50] Rev. Sereno E. Bishop of Honolulu, an enthusiastic annexationist, commented upon Blount's accessibility to " leading men of all parties, and from different parts of the Islands," and added:

Mr. Blount has highly commended himself to us all by his wise and candid temper, by his discriminating penetration, and by his manifestly impartial search for truth. With great reticence he has, throughout the whole, scarcely betrayed in any degree his own leanings. It is, however, now quite generally surmised that he favors annexation.[51]

[48] *Senate Report* No. 227, 53d Cong., 2d sess., p. 414. President Dole records that this air was played at the pier as Blount was departing for the United States. He may have confused this with the July Fourth episode. Dole, *Memoirs of the Hawaiian Revolution,* p. 97.

[49] New York *World,* November 30, 1893.

[50] *Senate Report* No. 227, 53d Cong., 2d sess., p. 560.

[51] *Independent,* XLV, 666 (May 18, 1893). President Dole stated later: " During his stay in Honolulu, his relations with the Provisional Government were uniformly pleasant, and his attitude toward me was always one of courtesy." Dole, *op. cit.,* pp. 96-97.

The student who peruses the voluminous testimony taken by Mr. Blount will feel that he gave each party to the controversy its day in court. But in reading Blount's report to Gresham he will probably doubt whether the commissioner's attitude was throughout that of an impartial judge. Blount stated later to a Senate committee that he had had no fixed opinions about the revolution before going to Hawaii, but at the same time he confessed to having formed an unfavorable opinion of Thurston when the latter had called on him to talk annexation in the spring of 1892, and one can read between the lines that he had been annoyed by Foster's importunities in behalf of the annexation treaty.[52] As a Southerner and ex-Confederate, one would expect, as Thurston had expected, to find in him a predisposition in favor of the white race and a skepticism as to the political capacity and the right to equal status of the dark-skinned Polynesian. Yet as one reads his report and compares it with the evidence upon which it is based, one feels that wherever a doubt existed, Blount resolved it against Stevens and the revolutionists and in favor of the former Queen and her native subjects. Blount's attitude is an example of the peculiar reversal of party positions on the race question that marked the whole affair.

Blount's long report was dated at Honolulu, July 17, 1893.[53] After narrating in some detail the story of the rise to power of the American group in the Hawaiian Islands, he proceeded to answer the two chief questions which had been committed to him—the part played by Stevens

[52] *Senate Report* No. 227, 53d Cong., 2d sess., pp. 386, 404-405.
[53] *U. S. For. Rel., 1894,* App. II, pp. 567-605.

and the armed forces from the "Boston" in the revolution, and the attitude of the people of the islands toward annexation. It is in his answer to the first of these that the document resembles more nearly the philippic of a prosecuting attorney than the reasoned conclusion of a judge. It is evident that he took satisfaction in pointing out the vulnerability of some of the assertions of Stevens and the Hawaiian commissioners; and while he could hardly have done otherwise than fix upon Stevens a large responsibility for the success of the revolution, portions of his verdict exhibit a dogmatism for which the historian can hardly find warrant in the evidence.

The leaders of the revolutionary movement [he wrote] would not have undertaken it but for Mr. Stevens's promise to protect them against any danger from the Government. But for this their mass meeting would not have been held. But for this no request to land the troops would have been made. Had the troops not been landed no measures for the organization of a new Government would have been taken. The American minister and the revolutionary leaders had determined on annexation to the United States, and had agreed on the part each was to act to the very end.[54]

In regard to the native attitude toward annexation, Blount concluded that the great preponderance of opinion was adverse, and while it is evident that he found it easier to believe opponents than advocates of annexation, there seems little reason to take issue with his conclusions on this point. Thurston's attempt to produce a show of native sentiment for annexation had failed signally. Colburn and Rosa, half-castes to whom he had written persuasive letters, made hostile statements, and placed the letters in Blount's

[54] *Ibid.*, p. 594.

hands.[55] J. A. Cummins another prominent part-Hawaiian for whose support Thurston had hoped, appeared as honorary president of the Hawaiian Patriotic League, the chief anti-annexationist organization.[56] So far as the records show, the only one of those mentioned by Thurston as possible native advocates who said a word for annexation was J. W. Kalua, and he stated that the few Hawaiians for whom he spoke would favor annexation only if assured of the ballot.[57] Even the Annexation Club, which claimed to have 5,500 members, counted among them only 1,022 Hawaiians, the remainder being predominantly American and Portuguese.[58] The Hawaiian Patriotic League, on the other hand, claimed to have over 7,500 native Hawaiian voters (out of a total electorate of 13,000) aligned against annexation and for the perpetuation of the monarchy.[59]

It was alleged that such natives as signed annexation petitions were coerced into doing so through fear of losing their jobs as government employees or as workers on sugar plantations.[60] In fact, the annexationists made no claim to have any very large section of native opinion on their side. Their plea was rather that the native Hawaiians were incapable of knowing what was good for them and that their wishes in the matter should therefore not be given weight.[61]

[55] *Ibid.*, pp. 496-501, 939-945.
[56] *Ibid.*, pp. 911-914.
[57] *Ibid.*, pp. 846-847.
[58] *Ibid.*, p. 1137.
[59] *Ibid.*, p. 911.
[60] *Ibid.*, pp. 532-533, 943.
[61] *Cf. supra*, p. 128, note 40.

This plea for white supremacy made less impression than might have been expected upon the Georgian. He saw no reason, in Hawaii, for disfranchising a colored race or disregarding its votes. He believed that if the annexation issue could be put to the test of a secret ballot, with the suffrage qualifications as under the Constitution of 1887, it would be defeated by at least two to one, and that if persons owing allegiance to foreign countries were excluded, the adverse majority would be more than five to one.

The undoubted sentiment of the people [he wrote] is for the Queen, against the Provisional Government, and against annexation. A majority of the whites, especially Americans, are for annexation.[62]

The conflict of parties in Hawaii, Blount wrote a few days later, would remain in abeyance until the attitude of the United States was determined. Should the proposal for annexation be rejected, it was not likely that there would be any sudden commotion in the islands. But—

The present Government can only rest on the use of military force, possessed of most of the arms in the islands, with a small white population to draw from to strengthen it. Ultimately it will fall without fail. It may preserve its existence for a year or two, but not longer.

Having thus discharged his duty, as he wrote, " the best I could, considering I was surrounded by persons interested in misleading me, and in my inability to compel answers from witnesses," Blount announced that his personal affairs necessitated his return to the United States, and took his

[62] *U. S. For. Rel., 1894*, App. II, pp. 598-599. Blount explained that nearly all the Portuguese and a majority of the whites of European or American origin who had signed annexation petitions were subjects or citizens of the countries of their origin.

departure from Honolulu on August 8.[63] His attitude and
his conclusions he successfully concealed until the end. At
the time of his departure it was widely believed in Honolulu
that he was friendly to the Provisional Government and
would advocate at least a strong protectorate by the United
States.[64]

Blount's report was not given to the public until the
latter part of November.[65] In the meantime, Cleveland and
Gresham, with the advice of other members of the cabinet,
were deliberately formulating a policy. Thurston, who had
succeeded Mott Smith as Hawaiian minister at Washington,
had made no progress in his effort to convert Gresham to
the cause of annexation. The Secretary of State was not
amenable either to Thurston's argument against a plebiscite
or to his warning that if the United States declined to take
the islands they must look elsewhere for protection.[66]

[63] Ibid., p. 630. Blount to Gresham, July 31, 1893. Buffalo
Courier, August 24, 1893. Blount was not alone in predicting an
early collapse of the Provisional Government. Charles Nordhoff,
special correspondent of the New York Herald, made even gloomier
forecasts. New York Herald, June 29, 1893. Rear Admiral Skerrett
reported that the Provisional Government maintained its authority
only by " the iron heel of Military Law." Skerrett to Secretary of
Navy, June 28, 1893. Navy Department MSS.

[64] Buffalo Courier, August 13, 24, 1893.

[65] Ibid., November 21, 1893.

[66] Memoranda of Conversations with the Secretary of State, 1893-
1898. Gresham recorded conversations with Thurston on June 14
and June 16, 1893. Whether the memoranda are based on stenographic notes or on Gresham's memory is not apparent. In connection with the intimation that Hawaii, if rejected by the United
States, might seek another alliance, it is interesting to note that in
the preceding February W. R. Castle had urged upon Dole the
expediency of ascertaining unofficially how the British Government

Just when Gresham reached the conclusion that the Queen should be reinstated it is impossible to say. In the spring he had told both Mott Smith and C. L. Carter that he had no such intention.[67] Probably the purpose matured in his mind after the receipt of Blount's full report. In a report to the President, dated October 18, 1893, Gresham summarized Blount's findings and endorsed his view of the culpable part played by Minister Stevens in the revolution. He advised against resubmitting to the Senate the treaty of annexation, and asked:

> Should not the great wrong done to a feeble but independent State by an abuse of the authority of the United States be undone by restoring the legitimate government? Anything short of that will not, I respectfully submit, satisfy the demands of justice.
> Can the United States consistently insist that other nations shall respect the independence of Hawaii while not respecting it themselves? Our Government was the first to recognize the independence of the Islands and it should be the last to acquire sovereignty over them by force and fraud.[68]

Apparently the President and Gresham's colleagues in the Cabinet accepted his conclusions as ethically sound.

---

would receive overtures from Hawaii. Many Americans, he said, felt that no European power was interested in the islands, and hence that the United States could make any terms that it chose. " If we could know beforehand that any terms offered by Hawaii would be entertained by England, it would very materially strengthen our position in this country." Castle to Dole, February 25, 1893. Spaulding Collection.

[67] Smith to Dole, April 6, 1893; Carter to Dole, April 17, 1893. Spaulding Collection.

[68] *U. S. For. Rel., 1894*, App. II, pp. 459-463.

But serious difficulties, both ethical and practical, were involved in carrying out the course which he suggested. Richard Olney, the Attorney-General, had already pointed out in a letter to Gresham that the use of force for the restoration of the Queen would amount to war and could not properly be resorted to without the consent of Congress. He also argued that, since the Provisional Government had been placed in power through the aid of the minister and armed forces of the United States, and since the preceding administration had approved the action of its representatives, the United States had incurred obligations to the revolutionists who had enjoyed its support, and was responsible for their safety. To allow them to suffer punishment for behavior in which the American minister had encouraged them would, wrote Olney, " be grossly unjust and unfair, and would deservedly bring the Government of the United States into great discredit both at home and abroad." He urged, therefore, first, that an earnest effort be made to restore the Queen to her throne by diplomatic means; second, that if such peaceful restoration should prove impracticable, no force be used without the authorization of Congress; and third, that the United States require from the Queen full power to negotiate for restoration upon such terms as it might approve and find practicable.

Among such terms and conditions [he added] must be, I think, full pardon and amnesty for all connected with the Stevens Government [sic] who might otherwise be liable to be visited with the pains and penalties attending the crime of treason.[69]

[69] Henry James, *Richard Olney and His Public Service.* The letter to Gresham (October 9, 1893) is printed in full on pp. 212-216. Other letters dealing with the Hawaiian questions are on pp.

Even Olney, however, while he envisioned the possibility that the Dole government might refuse to step down and believed that in that event the proper course for the United States would be to make some pecuniary compensation to the Queen for the injury done her through Minister Stevens,[70] did not expect that events would take this course. With all fear of royal vengeance removed, the Provisional Government would, he predicted, "readily follow the course recommended by the United States." It is probable that he, Gresham, and Cleveland were all misled by Blount's estimate of the inherent weakness and short life expectancy of the Provisional Government. Not one of the four, it is clear, realized the force and determination of the men who now ruled Hawaii.

The Cleveland policy was formed upon lines sketched by Gresham and amended by Olney. In September Albert S. Willis had been named to succeed Blount as minister to Hawaii, accredited to the Provisional Government.[71] His mission was explained in instructions from Gresham dated October 18, 1893. He was to express to the Queen the President's regret at the "flagrant wrong" inflicted upon her as a result of the "reprehensible conduct of the American minister and the unauthorized presence on land of a military force of the United States," but was to make it plain to her that the President expected her, when reinstated, to grant full amnesty to all who had participated in the revolution or had been connected with the Provisional

217-220, and Olney's part in the whole affair is discussed in chap. ix, pp. 81-95.

[70] *Ibid.*, p. 218.

[71] *U. S. For. Rel., 1894,* App. II, p. 1189.

Government, and to assume all obligations created by that government. Having obtained the Queen's assent to these conditions, Willis was to inform the Provisional Government " of the President's determination of the question which their action and that of the Queen devolved upon him, and that they are expected to promptly relinquish to her her constitutional authority." Should the Queen refuse to agree to the stipulated conditions, or should the Provisional Government " refuse to abide by the President's decision," Willis was simply to " report the facts and await further directions." [72]

Willis's task proved far less simple than his superiors had anticipated. After arriving in Honolulu, November 4, and presenting his letter of credence to the Dole government, he sought an interview with Liliuokalani. Their first meeting occurred November 13, at the American legation. Willis informed the Queen of the President's decision and then asked her directly whether, if restored to the throne, she would grant full amnesty to all who had been concerned in the revolution or the conduct of the Provisional Government.

She hesitated a moment and then slowly and calmly answered: " There are certain laws of my Government by which I shall abide. My decision would be, as the law directs, that such persons should be beheaded and their property confiscated to the Government." [73]

[72] *Ibid.*, pp. 463-464.

[73] Liliuokalani subsequently denied that she had prescribed beheading her enemies. " That is a form of punishment which has never been used in the Hawaiian Islands, either before or since the coming of foreigners." That, however, is a technical detail. She admitted having insisted upon the death penalty. *Hawaii's Story by Hawaii's Queen*, pp. 247-248.

From this position the Queen refused, for the time being, to recede, further than to say that she might leave the matter to her ministers. She would make no promise of amnesty as a condition precedent to restoration. " These people," she told Willis, " were the cause of the revolution and constitution of 1887. There will never be any peace while they are here." Her attitude and Willis's conversations with native leaders—Bush, Wilcox, and Joseph Nawahi—convinced him that she would not be satisfied with a restoration of the situation of a year before.

> I feel satisfied [he wrote] that there will be a concerted movement in the event of restoration for the overthrow of that constitution [of 1887] which would mean the overthrow of constitutional and limited government and the absolute dominion of the Queen.[74]

To Willis's brief telegraphic summary of this interview, Gresham replied that he must insist upon amnesty and recognition of the obligations of the Provisional Government as essential conditions to restoration.[75] Subsequently he wrote that if the Queen refused to accept these conditions, the President would " cease interposition in her behalf." [76] As the passing weeks brought no news of any concessions on the Queen's part, the President resolved to submit the whole matter to Congress. In a message of December 18, 1893, Cleveland restated the history of the revolution as already told by Blount and Gresham, referred to the landing of troops on January 16 as " an act of war,"

[74] *U. S. For. Rel., 1894,* App. II, pp. 1241-1243. Willis to Gresham, November 16, 1893.

[75] *Ibid.,* p. 464. November 24, 1893.

[76] *Ibid.,* p. 465. December 3, 1893.

expressed the conviction that the Provisional Government owed its existence "to an armed invasion of the United States," and rehearsed the recent attempts to restore the Queen upon conditions that would secure the safety of the revolutionists. Since the Queen had refused these conditions and since, evidently, Cleveland and Gresham were at the end of their resources, Cleveland commended the subject "to the extended powers and wide discretion of the Congress," with the assurance of his willingness to cooperate "in any legislative plan which may be devised for the solution of the problem before us which is consistent with American honor, integrity, and morality." [77] Thus the President, in effect, washed his hands of the affair, confessing that he and the Secretary of State were unable to see the end of the path upon which they had, with good intentions but somewhat illadvisedly, set out.

Meanwhile, in Honolulu, the Queen's better counsellors had prevailed upon her to accept the conditions required by the President. At first, while waiving the demand for the death penalty for revolutionists, she proposed instead perpetual banishment, together with certain modifications of the constitution in the interest of the native Hawaiians. When informed that these concessions were insufficient, she at length apprised Willis of her full acceptance of the President's conditions.[78] Liliuokalani's decision was in

[77] *Ibid.*, pp. 445-458.

[78] The conferences leading to the above result were reported in Willis's letters to Gresham of December 18, 19, and 20, 1893. *Ibid.*, pp. 1262-1270. Joseph O. Carter, brother of the former minister at Washington and a sincere and judicious friend of the Queen, was instrumental in effecting her capitulation.

Willis's hands December 18, the day on which President
Cleveland laid the problem on the Congressional doorstep.
Uninformed of contemporary developments in Washington, Willis on December 20 called at the Government
Building and presented to the Executive Council a memorandum summarizing his instructions and announcing that,
since the Queen had now agreed to grant complete amnesty
and assume all obligations of the Provisional Government,
the President would expect that government " to promptly
relinquish to her her constitutional authority." He closed
by submitting in the name and by the authority of the
United States the question: "Are you willing to abide by
the decision of the President? " [79]

Three days later Dole presented a firm and dignified
reply. He denied that the Provisional Government had ever
agreed to submit the question of its continued existence to
the President's arbitration, and that, even if it had so agreed,
it had had any real opportunity to state its side of the
case. He denied that the revolution owed its success to
Stevens and the armed forces from the " Boston " and
argued (logically, it would seem) that even had this been
true, the issue would have been solely one between the
United States and the former Queen.

This Government, a recognized sovereign power . . .
can not be destroyed by it [the United States] for the sake
of discharging its obligations to the ex-Queen. . . .
Though the Provisional Government is far from being " a
great power " and could not long resist the forces of the
United States in a hostile attack, we deem our position to be
impregnable under all legal precedents, under the principles

[79] *Ibid.*, pp. 1270-1275.

of diplomatic intercourse, and in the forum of conscience.
. . . I am instructed to inform you, Mr. Minister, that the
Provisional Government of the Hawaiian Islands respectfully and unhesitatingly declines to entertain the proposition of the President of the United States that it should
surrender its authority to the ex-Queen.[80]

There was no disposition in Washington to accept the
challenge thus flung down by the Provisional Government.
Gresham wrote Willis that while the President did not
claim the position of an arbitrator, he had felt obligated
" to endeavor to restore the lawful authority " subverted
" by an abuse of the authority of the United States," but
that he had now " submitted the subject to the more extended powers and wider discretion of Congress," and must
await their pleasure. He added the innocuous assurance
that the President would keep Congress fully advised of the
situation and would lay before them from time to time
reports received from the minister in Honolulu.[81] With this
anticlimax, ended Cleveland's and Gresham's adventure in
international knight-errantry.

[80] *Ibid.*, pp. 1276-1282.
[81] *Ibid.*, pp. 1283-1284. January 12, 1894.

V

A WAR OF PROPAGANDA

The Congress to which President Cleveland referred the Hawaiian question for a final decision could not plead ignorance of the facts and issues involved. The documents bearing upon the question, with a few exceptions, were laid before it by the President.[1] All aspects of the affair, moreover, had been debated with increasing heat in American newspapers and magazines throughout the months that had elapsed since the preceding January. In Congress itself, the subject had received some attention during the closing weeks of the Harrison administration. The special session called by Cleveland (August 7 to November 3, 1893) had given little time to anything other than the repeal of the Sherman Silver Purchase Act. With the meeting of the regular session in December, 1893, Hawaiian affairs at once took a prominent place. Before examining the proceedings of that session, we may profitably investigate the effect which the revolution and the proposal of annexation had produced upon American public opinion.

Promptly upon receipt of the news of revolution in Hawaii, Senator William E. Chandler had introduced in the Senate a resolution requesting the President to enter into negotiations for the annexation of the islands.[2] While

---

[1] Thurston's letter and memorandum of May 27, 1892, were not made known; nor was Stevens's dispatch No. 70, reflecting severely upon the British minister (*supra*, p. 67, note 79.)

[2] *Cong. Record*, 52d Cong., 2d sess., p. 929.

President Harrison, as we have seen, needed no goading, the Chandler resolution gave occasion for some interesting expressions of opinion in the Senate. Senator Dolph, of Oregon, for example, declared the time had come when the United States " must abandon the doctrine that our national boundaries and jurisdiction should be confined to the shores of the continent," and must boldly grasp such opportunities as the present one before they were seized by rival powers.[3]

From a portion of the press, a loud chorus of welcome greeted the Hawaiian commissioners and their proffer of union. The commercial and strategic value of the islands to the United States was accepted as almost axiomatic.

Hawaii is the central point of the North Pacific [declared the San Francisco *Evening Bulletin* (January 30, 1893)]. It is in, or near to, the direct track of commerce from all Atlantic ports, whether American or European, via Nicaragua, and from all Pacific ports, whether of North or South America, to China and Japan. . . . It is the key to the whole system. . . . In the possession of the United States it will give us the command of the Pacific.

As a " key to the Pacific " the islands were seen also by the Washington *Post,* the *Commercial Advertiser* of New York, and Albert Shaw, editor of the *Review of Reviews.* The *Journal of Finance,* New York, thought the question " of interest to every business man, for the political change would certainly make a greater opening for American manufactures." The New York *Independent,* a semi-religious weekly which had close ties with the missionary group in the islands, painted their attractiveness in glowing colors:

The ripe apple falls into our hands, and we should be very foolish if we should throw it away. . . . The soil is

[3] *Ibid.,* pp. 977-980, 997-1002 (January 31, 1893).

fertile, the climate wonderfully equable and salubrious; it has excellent harbors, and the most wonderful volcano in existence. The possession of Hawaii gives perfect control of the ocean route across the Pacific, and Honolulu is the only natural station between America and Japan.

And the New York *Tribune,* long favorable to annexation, declared: " The popular verdict is clear, unequivocal, and practically unanimous. Hawaii is welcome." [4]

Such enthusiasm was, however, far from unanimous; many papers assumed a cautious or hostile attitude from the beginning. The New York *Times,* for example, was frankly skeptical.

We should annex Hawaii, if at all, as we should buy a ham. Let us first determine whether we want it or have any use for it; then whether it is worth the price, and thirdly whether the pretended owners are the real owners and can deliver the goods. We have serious doubts on all these points.

The same paper was highly critical of the haste with which the treaty was concluded, and later approved Cleveland's course in recalling it for further study. The Portland *Oregonian,* too, thought there should be a careful investigation, perhaps by a commission to be sent to the islands, to determine whether annexation was really the desire of the

[4] Washington *Post,* January 30, 1893; *Commercial Advertiser,* January 30, 1893; *Review of Reviews,* VII, 131-136 (March, 1893); *Journal of Finance,* February 7, 1893; *Independent,* XLV, 150 (February 2, 1893); New York *Tribune,* February 5, 1893. Other papers favoring annexation were the New York *Sun, Morning Advertiser, Mail and Express, Observer,* and *Christian at Work,* the Brooklyn *Standard Union,* Philadelphia *Inquirer* and *North American,* Rochester *Democrat and Chronicle,* Richmond *State,* Detroit *Journal* and *Tribune. Literary Digest,* VI, 389-390, 412-413, 500 (February 4, 11, March 4, 1893).

people. The islands, it believed, were sure to be annexed some time, and it mattered little whether they came to us now or a generation hence.[5]

But could the United States safely postpone action for a generation, or even for a much shorter time? A chorus of loud " Noes " arose from the nation's Anglophobes. The Washington *Post* reminded its readers of its previous exposure of British attempts to undermine American influence in the islands [6] and declared that the problem facing the United States was " made all the more grave because the threatening hand of Great Britain is a factor to be considered in its solution." [7] An anonymous writer in the New York *Tribune* analyzed the British system of naval bases—at Halifax, Bermuda, Kingston, and elsewhere—which threatened the coasts and communications of the United States, warned of the danger that England might add Hawaii to this system, thereby controlling the routes from the west coast and the isthmus to the Orient, and declared that a government mindful of these facts could not do otherwise than accept the proffered union.[8] The San Francisco *Call* told Cleveland that he could win " commendation from London journals " by refusing annexation,

[5] New York *Times*, January 31, February 17, March 10, 1893. Portland *Oregonian*, February 3, 1893. Cautious or hostile sentiment was expressed also by the New York *World, Evening Post,* and *Herald;* the Brooklyn *Citizen,* Washington *Star,* Boston *Advertiser* and *Herald,* Troy *Times,* Richmond *Times,* Cincinnati *Journal and Messenger,* and San Francisco *News Letter. Literary Digest, loc. cit.*

[6] *Supra,* pp. 70-71.

[7] Washington *Post,* January 29, 1893.

[8] New York *Tribune,* February 6, 1893.

and that should he follow that course, " the English Government would doubtless consent to establish a protectorate over the islands rather than see anarchy prevail." [9] It was expected that a British protest would expedite favorable action on the treaty,[10] and some journals attributed the Senate's failure to approve it to the absence of such a protest. England's " provoking indifference " and " calm unconcern," said the *Nation,* had " robbed the enterprise of all its glamour." [11] One Washington correspondent remarked that the unexpected British complaisance

arouses the suspicion in the minds of many public men that Great Britain is playing some deep and occult game of diplomacy which cannot at the present juncture be raveled, and hence the Senate feels compelled to act with extraordinary caution, feeling the way carefully in order to avoid falling into any trap.[12]

Most inconsiderately the British declined to promote annexation by opposing it.

But the most significant feature of this early discussion was the fact that many of those who favored the annexation of Hawaii hailed it as merely the first step in a comprehensive program of expansion. On the day after the arrival of the news of the revolution, the San Francisco *Call* printed a cartoon captioned " Uncle Sam catches the Ripe Fruit," picturing Uncle Sam seated under an apple tree, the apple Hawaii falling into his hat, while Canada, Mexico, Haiti, Samoa, and Cuba still hung upon the boughs, presumably not ripe but ripening. The thought thus graphically

9 San Francisco *Call,* March 10, 1893.

10 San Francisco *Examiner,* February 1, 1893.

11 *Nation,* LVI, 154 (March 2, 1893).

12 New York *Journal of Commerce,* February 21, 1893.

presented was spread abroad in many an editorial. Our
decision in regard to Hawaii, said the New York *Tribune,*
would have a significance as a precedent which would be

apparent to all the islands south of us and to every European
cabinet that thinks itself concerned in the political relations
of the States and dependencies near our borders. . . . It
must be recognized, at least, that we are close upon the time
when the traditional hostility of the United States toward
an extension of authority, if not also of territory, among
the islands near our coasts must to some extent give way to
the necessities of our increasing commerce.[13]

The Philadelphia *Press* rejoiced that the presentation of
the Hawaiian question would " familiarize the public mind
with the acquisition of other territory " which would soon
be necessitated by " the commercial development and the
political obligations of the country." The opening of the
Nicaraguan canal would make it imperative for the United
States to command both eastern and western approaches.
The Gulf of Mexico should become " practically an American lake," and to that end we should find it expedient to
possess ourselves of Santo Domingo and St. Thomas, both
once rejected, and of Cuba, " the greatest prize of that
quarter." Events were clearly ripening also for the annexation of Canada, which was indispensable for the safety of
our northern border. " Thus," the editor concluded, " our
manifest destiny is bound to work itself out." With similar
enthusiasm, the *Commercial Advertiser,* which, like the
Philadelphia *Press,* believed the acquisition of Cuba to be
manifest destiny, announced exultingly: " Our nation
stands on the threshold of a new policy as surely as it did

[13] New York *Tribune,* January 29, 1893.

in 1803, when Jefferson annexed Louisiana and the United States realized that it must govern it." [14]

The Philadelphia *Press* was not alone in recalling wistfully the spacious policies of Seward and Grant. Albert Shaw, in the *Review of Reviews,* predicted that Grant's Santo Domingo policy would yet be revived and that the United States would go on to acquire Canada, construct a Nicaraguan canal, and build a big navy.[15]

Senator Dolph, of Oregon, in a speech cataloguing the past mistakes of American foreign policy—the failure to take all of Oregon, the rejection of opportunities to annex Santo Domingo and Samoa, the shelving by Cleveland of Arthur's treaty for an American-controlled Nicaraguan canal—declared that in all Grant's brilliant career the Santo Domingo treaty " was the act which reflected more credit upon his foresight, sagacity, ability, and patriotism than any other." Grant's ideas must now find acceptance, past mistakes must be rectified. " We must abandon the doctrine that our national boundaries and jurisdiction should be confined to the shores of the continent." [16]

It was not to be expected that Captain Mahan, who three years previously had found few signs that his country was awake to its need of distant colonies or naval bases, would keep silent when a concrete issue had presented itself. He,

[14] Philadelphia *Press*, copied in *ibid.*, February 6, 1893. New York *Commercial Advertiser*, March 13, May 3, 1893.

[15] *Review of Reviews, loc. cit.*

[16] *Supra*, note 3. The Portland *Oregonian*, which had at first been rather indifferent about the Hawaiian offer, was soon following the Oregon Senator in advocating immediate annexation and in holding up Grant's policy as a model to be followed. March 8, 1893.

too, looked upon the Hawaiian question as important both in itself and in the precedent it would create. Entering the lists at once, he published in the March *Forum* an article on " Hawaii and our Future Sea Power." The Hawaiian Islands, he argued, had importance " as a position power-fully influencing the commercial and military control of the Pacific, and especially of the Northern Pacific, in which the United States, geographically, has the strongest right to assert herself." They had also, for the United States, a negative importance,—

the immense disadvantage to us of any maritime enemy having a coaling-station well within twenty-five hundred miles, as this is, of every point of our coast-line from Puget Sound to Mexico. . . . Shut out from the Sandwich Islands as a coal base, an enemy is thrown back for supplies of fuel to distances of thirty-five hundred or four thousand miles— . . . an impediment to sustained maritime operations well-nigh prohibitive.

But Mahan hoped that his countrymen would not view the Hawaiian opportunity too narrowly.

This is no mere question of a particular act, for which, possibly, just occasion may not have offered yet; but of a principle, a policy, fruitful of many future acts, to enter upon which, in the fulness of our national progress, the time has now arrived. The principle being accepted, to be conditioned only by a just and candid regard for the rights and reasonable susceptibilities of other nations, . . . the annexation, even, of Hawaii would be no mere sporadic effort, irrational because disconnected from an adequate motive, but a first-fruit and a token that the nation in its evolution has aroused itself to the necessity of carrying its life—that has been the happiness of those under its in-fluence—beyond the borders which heretofore have sufficed for its activities. . . . Comparative religion teaches that creeds which reject missionary enterprise are foredoomed to decay. May it not be so with nations? [17]

Mahan's whole line of reasoning was promptly challenged by Carl Schurz. To annex Hawaii or other islands, he maintained, would weaken, not strengthen, our military position. As long as we confined ourselves to the continent we were practically unassailable, and a foreign power would think twice before making war upon us. But by acquiring vulnerable island possessions we should invite attack. By entering the tropics, moreover, we should incur even graver dangers. Experience showed that democracy could not flourish there. " No candid American would ever think of making a State of this Union out of such a group of islands with such a population as it [Hawaii] has and is likely to have." It would of necessity be governed as a mere dependency—an arrangement wholly contrary to American ideals and traditions. If the American people yielded to the lure of tropical expansion, warned Schurz in Cassandra-tones,

their " manifest destiny " points with equal certainty to a total abandonment of their conservative traditions of policy, to a rapid deterioration in the character of the people and their political institutions, and to a future of turbulence, demoralization, and final decay.[18]

[17] Originally published in the *Forum,* March, 1893, this essay was reprinted in Mahan's *The Interest of America in Sea Power, Present and Future,* pp. 32-55.

[18] C. Schurz, " Manifest Destiny," *Harpers New Monthly Magazine,* LXXXVII, 737-746. Like Schurz, George W. Merrill, former United States minister to Hawaii, argued that social and political conditions in the islands presented difficulties which the United States would do better to avoid. His article in the *Californian Magazine* for March, 1893, is summarized in the *Literary Digest,* VI, 511 (March 11, 1893).

But was there even a constitutional warrant for the acquisition of such outlying possessions? Judge T. M. Cooley, formerly a member of the Michigan Supreme Court and of the Interstate Commerce Commission, argued that there was not; for while the Constitution itself imposed no limit upon the treaty-making power, that power, he reasoned, was in reality limited by the conditions under which the Constitution was made and the purposes of its makers; and the founding fathers, he was sure, had in mind neither states nor territories of non-homogeneous people, nor the erection of a colonial system. Nor did a mere provisional government, existing for an emergency only, have a right, without popular consent, to cede territory and sovereignty to a foreign power.[19] The proposal to take the islands without the consent of the natives seemed to another critic an exemplification of "the ethics of international piracy."[20]

Such reasoned arguments upon issues of policy and law probably attracted less popular notice than the bitter attacks upon the character and the motives of those concerned upon either side in the Hawaiian question, and the American public, instead of being enlightened as to the wisdom or folly of expansion, was too often regaled with denunciations, upon one side, of the "sugar conspiracy" of the planters, and upon the other, of the bad morals of Queen

[19] T. M. Cooley, "Grave Obstacles to Hawaiian Annexation," *Forum*, XV, 389-406. A somewhat similar argument against the constitutionality of annexing non-contiguous territory had previously been presented by George Ticknor Curtis in the *North American Review*, CLVI, 282-286 (March, 1893). Curtis's assumption that Alaska was contiguous seems hardly warranted.

[20] Gen. M. M. Trumbull, in *Open Court*, VII, 3556 (February 9, 1893).

Liliuokalani and her native subjects. Since much of this vituperative material has been accepted as sober fact by historians of the period, it merits some examination here.

That the revolution and the movement for annexation were simply the outgrowth of a conspiracy of the sugar interests to get the bounty of two cents a pound paid to domestic sugar growers was suggested at the very beginning of the controversy. The New York *Herald,* on February 7, 1893, and for some days thereafter interlarded between its editorials the pointed query, emphasized by italics: *" Is Spreckels & Co. the little nigger in the fence of the sugar islands? "* The *Nation* called attention to the contract between the Hawaiian planters and the Western Sugar Refining Co.—the Spreckels concern in San Francisco, a branch of the Sugar Trust—whereby the corporation would receive one-half of any bounty that might be paid to the planters, and expressed the opinion that the revolution was " of sugar by sugar and for sugar." [21] The New York *Times,* while less dogmatic, also pointed a finger of suspicion at the sugar men and advised that there be a thorough investigation of the relation of the sugar interests to the revolution.[22]

Plausible enough—this simple economic interpretation of the revolution. Yet a very cursory examination of the evidence shows it to have been, while perhaps not entirely false, at any rate an extreme oversimplification of the facts. In the first place, Claus Spreckels, who at one and the same time was the leading producer of Hawaiian sugar and a dominant figure in the Western Sugar Refining Company,

[21] *Nation,* LVI, 151 (March 2, 1893).
[22] New York *Times,* March 11, 1893.

which monopolized the refining industry on the West Coast, was found to be strongly opposed to annexation.[23] This was not his initial attitude. In May, 1892, Thurston had found him favorable to the idea of annexation, and the Hawaiian commissioners had found him disposed to work with them when they reached San Francisco in January, 1893.[24] But further reflection worked a complete change in his view of the question, and by May, 1893, he was talking openly against annexation and pointing out the injury it would do to the sugar interests. The island plantations, he argued, were dependent upon Oriental labor imported under contract. A continuation of this system would be impossible under the laws of the United States, and its abandonment, he believed, would ruin the sugar industry and reduce the islands to a cow pasture.[25] Either a restoration of the monarchy or an independent state ruled by an oligarchy was in his mind greatly to be preferred to annexation.[26]

Thus the myth that " Spreckels & Co." had made the revolution for the sake of the sugar bounty seems effectually disposed of. But Spreckels, while by his own statement he produced fully one-third of all the sugar grown in the

[23] Cf. Jones, The Trust Problem in the United States, pp. 93-94.
[24] Thurston to Blaine, May 27, 1892, Miscellaneous Letters, May, 1892, and supra, p. 111.
[25] New York Herald, May 13, 1893. Report of interview with Claus Spreckels by Charles Nordhoff, special correspondent of the Herald. Cf. his statement to Blount, U. S. For. Rel., 1894, App. II, pp. 973-980. His son, J. D. Spreckels, talked in a similar strain to Palmer of the Boston Transcript in January; 1894. Julius A. Palmer, Jr., Memories of Hawaii and Hawaiian Correspondence, p. 14.
[26] Independent, XLV, 814, 905 (June 15, July 6, 1893).

islands,[27] could not, perhaps, speak for the numerous other planters. Certainly not all of them were opposed to annexation, and it is not to be supposed that they viewed the chances of the bounty with indifference. Thurston, in the analysis which he prepared for Blaine in May, 1892, stated that the planters' fear of United States immigration laws was " offset by the fact that annexation . . . would give the planters the immediate benefit of the bounty now paid for sugar "; but he added that they did not believe the bounty system would last long, and his emphasis was on the need for stable government in the islands rather than on the hope of the bounty.[28] An inquiry undertaken in Hawaii in November, 1892, by a representative of the San Francisco *Examiner* elicited the fact that most planters still viewed annexation with distrust because of its probable effect on the labor supply.[29] The men active in the dethronement of the Queen represented the professional and business classes of the city of Honolulu rather than the planting interests.[30] Two men whose views were generally as wide apart as the poles—Claus Spreckels and Rev. Sereno E. Bishop of Honolulu—agreed that the planters did not instigate the revolution but were led to acquiesce in it after it was set on foot—Spreckels said by delusive promises of the bounty and exemption from unfavorable labor laws; Bishop said by the growing conviction " that the only valid prospect of permanently stable government lay in annexation." [31]

[27] *U. S. For. Rel., 1894*, App. II, p. 975.
[28] *Supra*, pp. 57-59.
[29] *Independent*, XLV, 814 (June 15, 1893).
[30] Nordhoff, in New York *Herald*, May 4, 1893.
[31] *Ibid.*, May 13, 1893; *Independent*, XLV, 814 (June 15, 1893).

This view is corroborated by the testimony of one William Blaisdell, manager of a million dollar sugar plantation on Kauai, who told Blount that up to the time when the Queen was overthrown very few of the sugar men were in favor of annexation, " in view of the contract-labor system which is our mainstay "; but, he added, " we came to the conclusion that we would rather take our chances on the labor question than to take the chances of an independent government." [32]

Naturally, sugar planters and others in the islands hoped that if they were annexed they would get the bounty, and the commissioners sent to Washington were instructed to secure the full bounty if possible and otherwise to compromise on a fraction of it. But when they found that they could get no guarantee of any bounty at all, they unhesitatingly signed an annexation treaty containing no mention of it. Thurston wrote from Washington in March that " the most cursory examination of the situation here shows the utter impossibility of our ever getting a cent of bounty out of the U. S. Treasury on our sugars," but this discovery did not in the least weaken his desire to consummate annexation.[33] Thurston claimed to have convinced Godkin,

[32] *U. S. For. Rel., 1894,* App. II, p. 705. Charles A. and Mary R. Beard, in their *Rise of American Civilization,* II, 359-360, assert that " it was mainly sugar that precipitated the crisis," and cite in evidence " a sugar planter of Lanai " who, when asked by Blount as to the cause of the revolution, replied: " Simply two cents a pound on sugar." A check-up of this evidence shows that the man who made this statement was not a sugar planter at all, but a wool grower and former sheriff of Lanai who had been dismissed from office by the Provisional Government for his royalist leanings. *U. S. For. Rel., 1894,* App. II, pp. 820-821.

[33] Thurston to Dole, March 10, 1893. Spaulding Collection.

of the New York *Nation* and *Evening Post*, of the falsity
of the sugar conspiracy theory and to have secured from
him a promise that he would no longer use this argument
against annexation.[34]

It seems safe to conclude that the very doubtful prospect
of the sugar bounty was not the mainspring of the annexation movement in the islands, that the material benefits
expected from annexation were the more general ones that
would flow from the displacing of the erratic royal government with the more stable rule of the United States.

The annexationists, on their side, were not content with
resting their case upon the Queen's attempt at revolution
and her temperamental unfitness to reign over a modern
state such as Hawaii had become, or upon the advantages
which would accrue from annexation, both to Hawaii and
to the United States. They felt it necessary to present their
cause to the American public as one in which Christianity
and good morals on one side were opposed to heathenism
and immorality upon the other. Thus the *Independent*, in
its first issue after receipt of news of the revolution, informed its readers that the revolution was " the result of a
long succession of events in which the Queen has been
largely under the influence of the *kahunas* or sorcerers of
the Hawaiians " and of her attempt to " strengthen the
hands of the native faction, over which the *kahunas* held

---

[34] Thurston to Dole, April 7, 1893. *Ibid.* Examination of the
Nation's comments on Hawaii through the remainder of 1893 reveals no further mention of any alleged conspiracy of the sugar
planters. Thurston stated that his explanation of this angle of the
question had also been accepted as satisfactory by other hostile
editors—those of the New York *World* and the Chicago *Herald*
and *Post*.

almost undisputed sway." It was reported, said the same paper a month later, that the Queen was not, as had been claimed, a member of the Christian church, but was " a very superstitious woman, frequently consulting the sooth-sayers or Kahunas."[35] A correspondent of the New York *Herald* portrayed the Queen's character in even more lurid hues.

> The true cause of Queen Liliuokalani's dethronement [he wrote] was the partial relapse to heathenism, into which she and her brother, the late King, had caused this little kingdom to sink. . . . The Queen's superstitious nature caused her to make sacrifices to Pele, the dreadful goddess of the volcanoes, and she has had constant recourse to the kahunas. . . . The Queen simply went from bad to worse, and the white people rebelled at further degradation. Hence her deposition.[36]

There was some confusion in the minds of the annexa-tionists in regard to the character of the native faction whom the Queen had wished to restore to power. Had not the kanakas all been Christianized by the devoted efforts of the early missionaries? The *Independent* gave a glowing account of missionary work in the islands and, in an edi-torial urging annexation, asserted that

> a larger proportion of the native Hawaiians can read and write than of native Georgians or Virginians or Pennsyl-vanians. . . . They are civilized, respectable people.[37]

Had the editor forgotten that just a month previously his periodical had stated that over the native faction " the *kahunas* held almost undisputed sway "? If so, he was in

---

[35] *Independent*, XLV, 149, 288 (February 2, March 2, 1893).
[36] New York *Herald*, February 16, 1893.
[37] *Independent*, XLV, 291 (March 2, 1893).

due time called back to earth by his Honolulu correspondent, Rev. Sereno E. Bishop, who wrote of " the lewd and
drunken majority of the native race." [38]

Such talk was depressing to Americans who had believed
in the efficacy of missionary work, and an American clergyman pointed out the damage likely to be inflicted upon the
cause of missions by these confessions that " after fifty years
of active missionary effort " the majority of the Hawaiians
were still steeped in vice and superstition.[39] To this com-
plaint the every ready Mr. Bishop replied that the Christian
character of the Hawaiians had once indeed been established, but alas!

Where are the 12,000 converts whom Mr. Coan baptized,
and the 400 converts whom I saw my father baptize in two
hours with a sponge? Not one in a hundred of them all
survives, and they have left few to take their places. . . .

That good Protestant Christianity had been beaten down
by " the terrible pressure of adverse influences from Roman-
ism and Mormonism," the unfortunate social consequences
of the introduction of Orientals, " and even worse the
deadly heathenizing of the Royal Court." [40]

But the moral obliquities with which Liliuokalani was
charged were not limited to consulting *kahunas,* sacrificing
to the dreadful goddess Pele, and favoring over-much the
recreant sons and daughters of the early Christian converts.
She was accused of even greater crimes against both public
and private morals. Much capital was made, by Stevens,

[38] *Ibid.,* XLVI, 5 (January 4, 1894).
[39] *Ibid.,* p. 164 (February 8, 1894).
[40] *Ibid.,* p. 391 (March 29, 1894).

Bishop, and others, of her signing of the opium and lottery
bills passed by the recent legislature, and of her alleged
alliance with the corrupt " rings " favoring these measures.[41]
But the former Queen's enemies added the accusation,
which was repeated with apparently increasing gusto as the
months passed, that her private life was grossly immoral.
In this form of abuse Mr. John L. Stevens easily excelled.
For months before the revolution he had regaled thé State
Department with Honolulu gossip to the effect that C. B.
Wilson, marshal of the kingdom, was attached to the Queen
by more than an official tie. Scandal of this type evidently
appealed strongly to the mind of the Puritan diplomat, for
he rarely mentioned Wilson without referring to him as
the Queen's paramour.[42]

The same charge was recklessly repeated elsewhere.[43]
The Reverend Mr. Bishop thought it proper to go even
further than an exposition of the Queen's personal morals
and to enlighten his American audience in regard to her
disreputable parentage. Her official parents, he asserted,

[41] Stevens to Foster, February 1, 1893. *U. S. For. Rel., 1894*, App.
II, pp. 400-403. Bishop wrote of the " debauched ex-Queen, who
attempted to . . . establish the Louisiana Lottery in Honolulu,"
and added that on her side were " those who wish to make Honolulu
a center for the manufacture and distribution of opium. . . . "
Independent, XLVI, 5 (January 4, 1894).

[42] *U. S. For. Rel., 1894*, App. II, pp. 356, 358, 362; Buffalo
Courier, November 13, 1893; New York *World*, November 30,
1893. Stevens di.: r.ot hesitate to hurl similar charges at others
who had incurred his ill will. See his statement in New York
World, just cited. Stevens had been a Universalist clergyman before entering the newspaper world. *Dict. Am. Biog.*, XVII, 618.

[43] *Cf.* New York *Herald*, February 16, 1893; *Independent*, XLVI,
11 (January 4, 1894), etc.

were not of truly royal descent but "only second rate chiefs"; but still worse, her mother, Keohokalole,

rather exceeding the usual latitude of Hawaiian morals, bore two older children, Kalakaua and Liliuokalani, to a mulatto paramour named John Blossom, a well-known shoe-maker here fifty years ago. This has always been matter of general notoriety.[44]

Not only by example but by direct encouragement, the Queen was charged with lowering moral standards in the islands. Her fault here was nothing less than having continued to countenance the immoral dances favored by her deceased brother. Thus Mr. Bishop, who seemingly vied with Minister Stevens in a taste for being shocked and shocking others with salacious gossip, quoted a statement made to him "by an intelligent and earnest Christian man in humble life," who said:

I was living at the further part of this island when the Queen was making her royal progress after her accession in 1891. There was a large gathering of the people to greet her. An old deacon offered prayer. Then a company of *hula* dancers came forward and performed. The Queen distributed six dollars to them. The performance was very vile, and I had no esteem for the Queen after that.[45]

This *ex parte* picture of the "corrupt and vicious monarch,"[46] since it has been in large part accepted by later writers,[47] deserves a critical examination. Fortunately, ma-

[44] *Independent*, XLV, 905 (July 6, 1893).

[45] *Ibid.*, XLVI, 102 (January 25, 1894).

[46] *Ibid.*, XLV, 288 (March 2, 1893).

[47] *Cf.* L. M. Sears, *History of American Foreign Relations*, p. 415; A. L. P. Dennis, *Adventures in American Diplomacy, 1846-1906*, p. 101; M. Schuyler, *Walter Q. Gresham*, in Bemis (ed.), *American Secretaries of State*, VIII, 250.

terial is not lacking. Attempts to sift the charges against
the former Queen were made not only by Commissioner
Blount but by several American newspaper men who were
sent to Hawaii, notably Messrs. Charles Nordhoff of the
New York *Herald* and Julius A. Palmer, Jr., of the Boston
Transcript. Blount, as we have seen, was perhaps predis-
posed to believe testimony favorable to the Queen and
adverse to the revolutionists. Nordhoff seems to have har-
bored a similar prejudice. Palmer, however, went to the
islands with an open mind and a disposition favorable, if
anything, to the revolutionary party.[48] The agreement of
the three in repudiating all the moral and religious charges
against the Queen is impressive.

The idea that the Queen was in any way culpable' for
signing the bill to license the sale of opium may be dismissed at once. The bill had been passed before the fall
of the Wilcox ministry and had been supported by two
members of that ministry, Messrs. Wilcox and Robinson,
and by several of the white members of the Reform Party.[49]
The bill was intended in part as a revenue measure, in part
as an improvement upon a system of prohibition copiously
tempered by smuggling. It was, wrote Palmer, after investi-

[48] *Cf.* his dispatch written en route to Honolulu in *Memories
of Hawaii and Hawaiian Correspondence,* pp. 18, 22. Thurston's
description of Palmer as " a lick-spittle person, worshipping at the
feet of his royal patron," seems grossly unfair. Thurston, *Memoirs
of the Hawaiian Revolution,* p. 180.

[49] *Advertiser,* January 3, 1893. Of the other members of the
ministry, Jones had voted against the bill, while Brown was absent.
The votes are those on a motion for indefinite postponement of the
bill, a vote against postponement being equivalent to a vote for
the bill. The vote on the actual passage was not recorded.

gation, " an attempt to regulate a traffic which cannot be suppressed, on account of the large Chinese population." [50] Good men differed honestly upon its merits. To charge the Queen with wrongdoing for appending her signature was not only unjust but dishonest.

For the lottery bill no similar justification can be found. It was backed almost solely by the less reputable native and half-caste elements in the legislature, and vigorously opposed by the four members of the Wilcox ministry, all but one of the white members, and the little group of natives who habitually voted with the Reform Party.[51] Yet it is not difficult to see why it appealed to the Queen. The parties seeking the franchise—said to be connected with the defunct Louisiana Lottery Company, recently driven from the United States—offered the Hawaiian government a bonus of $500,000 to be expended in public works. The bait was a tempting one, especially at a time when business was depressed and unemployment rife. It was peculiarly tempting to the Queen, who saw in the proposed public works program benefits for her native subjects, who, she complained, profited not at all from the prosperity of the sugar plantations.[52] But it was not only the Queen and

[50] Palmer, *op. cit.*, p. 113. *Cf. U. S. For. Rel., 1894*, App. II, pp. 495-496.

[51] *Advertiser*, January 11, 12, 1893.

[52] *Hawaii's Story by Hawaii's Queen*, pp. 239-240; Charles Nordhoff in New York *Herald*, May 4, 1893. The Queen's statement to Blount that she had at first declined to sign either the opium or the lottery bill because she desired to please her " lady friends," but had yielded to the argument of her ministers (the Cornwell cabinet) that since the legislature had passed both bills by large majorities she had no choice in the matter, need not, perhaps, be taken too seriously. *U. S. For. Rel., 1894*, App. II, p. 862.

the native element who were attracted by the proposal. In April, 1893, when Liliuokalani had for three months been vilified as the signer of this measure, Mr. Nordhoff unearthed the fact that petitions for the lottery had been circulated in Honolulu and signed by numbers of respectable white merchants and others, many of whom joined in the outcry against the Queen after she had signed the bill.[53] Regrettable as the passage of the bill may have been, it was with somewhat ill grace that the white community taxed the Queen with bad morals for signing it.

But what of the charges that the Queen's personal morals were low, that she was under the influence of native medicine men, that she sacrificed to " the dreadful goddess Pele," that she was, in short, a monster of vice and superstition?

Among the most persistent purveyors of such stories was, as we have seen, the Rev. Sereno E. Bishop, of Honolulu, whose correspondence in the *Independent* in 1893 and 1894 was a continual tirade against the deposed Queen. Mr. Bishop must have been embarrassed when he was reminded that he had written for the *Review of Reviews* in 1891, at the time of Liliuokalani's accession to the throne,

---

[53] New York *Herald,* May 4, June 1, 1893. Nordhoff's revelations were confirmed by Palmer several months later (Palmer, *loc. cit.*), and the substance of them was admitted by spokesman for the revolutionists. " The truth was," wrote Sereno E. Bishop, " that five months before, and prior to the introduction of the bill, a few hundred signatures were obtained from men, many of whom became active opponents of the measure, as soon as it was publicly discussed." *Independent,* XLV, 813 (June 15, 1893). A similar statement was made by Prof. W. D. Alexander to the Senate Foreign Relations Committee. *Senate Report* No. 227, 53d Cong., 2d sess., pp. 323-324.

a long article in which he had borne abundant testimony
to her excellent character and her zeal in Christian good
works. She had " long held a prominent place in Honolulu
society," wrote Mr. Bishop in 1891; she had associated
" from youth with the more cultivated ladies of the capital,
among whom . . . she received her early education. She
has a perfect use of English, a good literary, and an especially good musical culture. The Queen's manner is peculiarly winning, her bearing noble and becoming." She
was an adherent of the missionary, or Congregational
Church, a member of the Woman's Board of Missions and
" an interested participant in their meetings." She had
long been " a very active and munificent patroness of the
large Kawaiahae Seminary for training native girls, and
greatly looked up to by teachers and pupils." She gave
evidence, thought Mr. Bishop, " of having deeply at heart
the moral welfare of her people," and had used her influence against drunkenness, the hula dances, and the
kahunas.[54]

Had the Queen's character changed so remarkably between 1891 and 1893, or had Mr. Bishop, in the latter
year, been betrayed into distorting the truth for political
ends? Most of the testimony from what seem relatively
unbiased sources points to the conclusion that at the time
of the revolution the Queen still possessed the good quali-
ties described by Mr. Bishop two years previously. Of the
witnesses examined by Commissioner Blount, only one,
so far as I have discovered, credited the charges against her

[54] S. E. Bishop, " The Hawaiian Queen and Her Kingdom,"
Review of Reviews, IV, 147-163.

personal morals, and his evidence was purely circumstantial and hearsay.[55] Others, who had known her well, certified to their belief in her excellent character.[56] Nordhoff of the *Herald* and Palmer of the *Transcript* showed unmistakably that the "best people" of Honolulu had thronged to her receptions and delighted to welcome her in their own homes, and both gave impressive details of her religious and charitable activities. Even the latter, Palmer implied, had been used against her since the revolution: "her charity for fatherless children was never misconstrued until it was necessary to find something of ill report to say about her."[57] As for her "heathen practices," she may perhaps have sacrificed a black pig and sundry other offerings to Pele at the crater of Kilauea, as Henry Adams was informed in 1890;[58] she herself explained that such ancient practices were still kept up by the native people, but only as "a harmles sport, not by any means an act of worship"; she compared them to the custom of hurling rice and old shoes after a bridal pair.[59] With her religious life such things had nothing to do. "My own church is the old stone church of the missionaries," she told Palmer; "there is where I was educated, there I have always worshipped, and my faith is just the same as it ever was."[60]

[55] *U. S. For. Rel., 1894,* App. II, pp. 673-674.

[56] *Ibid.,* pp. 729, 735-736, 996.

[57] New York *Herald,* June 2, 1893; Palmer, *op. cit.,* pp. 109, 111, 113, 129. *Cf.* Blount's statement to Gresham, May 24, 1893. *U. S. For. Rel., 1894,* App. II, p. 534.

[58] W. C. Ford (ed.), *Letters of Henry Adams,* p. 410.

[59] *Hawaii's Story by Hawaii's Queen,* pp. 71-72.

[60] Palmer, *op cit.,* p. 130. Later the former Queen abandoned the "old stone church of the missionaries" and united with the

Mr. Palmer reached the firm conclusion that there was
no moral blemish on the Queen's character.

> To this day [he wrote] it can be asserted of her by
> women who have associated with her in all the intimacy
> possible to two individuals of like sex—women who have
> had the entry, unannounced, of her apartments—that not
> an impure word, not the suspicion of a concealed action has
> ever met their notice.[61]

The moral charges against Liliuokalani appear to have
been for the most part if not altogether the product of
irresponsible gossip, magnified and spread abroad for political ends. It is not unlikely that they helped to defeat
the purposes of those who made them. Grover Cleveland's
heart can hardly have warmed to the cause of men who
hurled personal abuse at a public official, and Gresham's

Anglican Church in Honolulu; but for this she is hardly to be
charged with recreancy, since the reason for it was that of all the
clergymen in the city only the Anglican rector had visited her
during her imprisonment in 1895, or had shown her any kindness
in the days of her misfortune. *Hawaii's Story by Hawaii's Queen*,
p. 269.

[61] Palmer, *op. cit.*, pp. 54-55. Senator Hoar, in his *Autobiography*, attempted to make amends for an injustice which he had
once done the former Queen. He was the author of the Massachusetts Republican platform of 1894, which contained the clause:
" No barbarous Queen beheading men in Hawaii." This expression,
he said, was in accord with the common impression at the time.
" . . . I learned afterward, from undoubted authority, that the
Queen is an excellent Christian woman; that she has done her best
to reconcile her subjects of her own race to the new order of things;
. . . and that she expended her scanty income in educating and
caring for the children of the persons who were about her court and
who had lost their own resources by the revolution. I have taken
occasion, more than once, to express, in the Senate, my respect for
her, and my regret for this mistake." G. F. Hoar, *Autobiography
of Seventy Years*, II, 264-265.

chivalrous attitude toward the deposed Queen may well have arisen from the belief that she was the victim of slander as well as conspiracy. The advocates of annexation would have done well had they rested their case on the proved fact of the Queen's light regard for the constitution she had sworn to uphold, culminating, as it did, in an attempted act of revolution on her part.[62]

The announcement of Gresham's plan to restore Liliuokalani to her throne reopened the debate which had been quiescent during the summer and early fall.[63] As was to have been expected, no one was more vehement in denouncing the proposal than John L. Stevens. "A public crime," he lamented, " is about to be committed in the name and under the authority of the American Government, a public crime of less proportions but its moral type similar to the stifling of National life and the reform aspirations of Poland and Hungary a few years ago by the Imperial despots." It was a crime against " an insulted, threatened and struggling American colony, planted as righteously and firmly on the North Pacific isles as our Pilgrim Fathers established themselves on Plymouth Rock." [64] The President's policy, said the editor of the *Independent,* " is properly called a policy of infamy." [65] Even worse, perhaps, it

[62] It is proper to say, in this connection, that Thurston and, so far as I have seen, the other commissioners to the United States, did not, in their published statements at any rate, indulge in this form of personal abuse. The chief offenders were Stevens, Sereno E. Bishop, and the editors of the *Independent.*

[63] The *Literary Digest* published practically nothing on the subject from May to November, 1893.

[64] Buffalo *Courier,* November 13, 1893; New York *World,* November 30, 1893.

[65] *Independent,* XLV, 1756 (December 28, 1893).

was a British policy. To Stevens it was plain that Blount had been deceived " by the shrewd, sharp, long-experienced British diplomatic agent " in Honolulu, while the Reverend Mr. Bishop saw evidence " of a well-arranged conspiracy between the President of the United States and the British Government, to trample down this American Colony, and maintain this debased and treacherous woman on the throne by the aid of American bayonets." What but foreknowl-edge of the President's plans could explain " the perfect passivity which England has maintained on the Hawaiian business since Mr. Cleveland came into office "? [66]

Republican newspapers, practically without exception, condemned the administration's proposal, and in language no more moderate than that employed by Stevens and the *Independent*. "A source of universal ridicule," " doubly stupid and outrageous," "the crowning infamy of the forcible restoration," " an act of national self-stultification," " political suicide "—were a few of the choice phrases culled from the Republican press in November.[67] While there was a tendency among Democratic papers to come to the defense of the Democratic President,[68] an impres-sive number even of these warned him that they could not support a restoration of the Hawaiian monarchy.[69] Possibly

[66] New York *World*, November 30, 1893; *Independent*, XLVI, 5 (January 4, 1894).

[67] *Literary Digest*, VIII, 58-60 (November 18, 1893).

[68] *Ibid.*, pp. 76-78 (November 25, 1893).

[69] The New York *Tribune* (November 23, 1893) listed the fol-lowing Democratic papers as hostile to the President's policy: New York *Sun* and *World*, Brooklyn *Eagle*, Philadelphia *Record* and *Ledger*, Chicago *Record*, Washington *Post* and *Star*, Atlanta *Constitution*, Springfield *Republican*, San Francisco *Examiner*, Provi-dence *Journal*, Hartford *Times*, Rochester *Post Express*.

the attitude of the New York *World* was typical of this group of papers. " The President's considerations of ' right and justice,' " it thought, " . . . might apply in Utopia. They are not applicable to the affairs of nations in this hardheaded, workaday world." [70]

A few significant journalistic voices were raised not merely in defense but in warm praise of the policy of the President and his Secretary of State. " Nothing," said the New York *Times*, " could more strengthen the Administration in the confidence of fair-minded and right-thinking men than the act of justice to Hawaii which is announced in the letter of Secretary Gresham." The *Nation*, likewise, highly approved Gresham's stand, and two of New York's most influential business journals, the *Journal of Commerce* and the *Commercial and Financial Chronicle*, were equally warm in their words of praise. Said the latter:

It appears to us that the stand which it is proposed to take in the matter is fully justified by the facts of the case, and is in consonance with personal honor and national dignity. Moreover, we have no hesitation in saying that to our minds the principle which this policy embodies is the only one that can or should be accepted for guidance in the conduct of our national affairs.[71]

Little was said, in these discussions, about annexation. Obviously, under Cleveland, there could be no hope of that. The issue for the present was whether Hawaii should be ruled by a restored Queen or by the elements represented

[70] *Literary Digest*, VIII, 146 (December 23, 1893).
[71] New York *Times*, November 11, 1893; *Nation*, LVII, 359 (November 16, 1893); *Journal of Commerce and Commercial Bulletin*, November 28, 1893; *Commercial and Financial Chronicle*, LVII, 826-828 (November 18, 1893).

by the Provisional Government. But the advocates of annexation refused to accept their defeat as permanent. The
administration might postpone a settlement of the Hawaiian question, said the San Francisco *Call,* but could not
change the final result. " The American people," it added,
" will not permit the islands to pass into the possession of a
foreign power and independence is out of the question.'
" There will be no annexation at present," said the Portland
Oregonian; nor would there be any restoration of the
Queen. The Hawaiian people would be left free to establish an independent republic, which would eventually come
under the protection of the United States, " when a wiser
and better American shall succeed Mr. Cleveland as
president." [72]

The President's reference to Hawaii in his regular message to Congress on December 4 was brief.[73] He reported
that, as a result of Commissioner Blount's investigation, he
had concluded that the only honorable course for the
government to pursue was to undo the wrong inflicted
through the action of the former minister " and to restore
as far as practicable the status existing at the time of our
forcible intervention." Appropriate instructions had been
given to the present minister, but as yet no definite accom-

[72] San Francisco *Call,* November 12, 1893; Portland *Oregonian,*
December 19, 1893. *Cf.* letter of Senator W. E. Chandler in New
York *Tribune,* November 15, 1893, outlining future Republican
policy—" eventual adhesion to the American Union of the whole
North American Continent, the Sandwich Islands, and a reasonable
and sufficient number of the West Indies."

[73] Richardson, *Messages and Papers,* IX, 441-442.

plishments had been reported. The President promised full information and a more extended treatment of the entire subject in a special message, which, as we have seen, he sent in on December 18, when he laid the whole question upon the doorstep of Congress.[74]

The Republican Senators, however, did not await the special message before opening their attack upon the President. Assuming the leadership of the party cohorts, Senator Hoar, of Massachusetts, introduced on December 5 a resolution requesting the President to send copies of instructions given to any representative of the United States, or any naval officer, in regard to Hawaiian affairs since March 4, 1893.[75] With this agreed to, Hoar brought forward another resolution questioning the legality both of Cleveland's appointment of Blount without the advice and consent of the Senate, and of Blount's conduct in Hawaii. This resolution, after debate, was referred to the Committee on Foreign Relations.[76] Upon receipt of the President's special message on Hawaii, Senator Morgan, chairman of the Committee on Foreign Relations, proposed that the message be referred to his committee, with instructions to inquire and report " whether any, and if so, what irregularities have occurred in the diplomatic or other intercourse between the United States and Hawaii in relation to the recent political revolution in Hawaii." The proposal was promptly adopted, and the committee was empowered " to

[74] *Supra,* pp. 142-143.

[75] *Cong. Rec.,* 53d Cong., 2d sess., p. 19. The resolution was agreed to December 6. *Ibid.,* p. 73.

[76] *Ibid.,* pp. 127, 206.

send for persons and papers and to administer oaths to witnesses." [77]

The Committee on Foreign Relations was thus launched upon the investigation which was to produce much valuable evidence bearing upon the revolution. Its report,[78] however, was not presented until late in February, and in the meantime several resolutions were brought in, seeking to define the attitude of the Senate to the Hawaiian imbroglio, and numerous Senators found occasion to debate the issues involved. In fact, the Hawaiian debate occupied the Senate intermittently from early in December to the end of May, when a resolution acceptable to nearly all factions was at length agreed upon.

For the most part, the debate followed partisan lines, and the bulk of it consisted of denunciation and defense of the chief personages involved—Stevens, Cleveland, Gresham, and Blount—rather than of discussion of the broader issue of expansion policy. Republican Senators complained that Cleveland had overstepped the limits of his constitutional powers—that he had illegally, without the consent of the Senate, appointed Blount and conferred upon him powers superior to those of regularly appointed diplomatic and naval officers, and that, in his attempt to displace the Provisional Government and restore the Queen, he had virtually assumed the power to make war without

[77] *Ibid.*, p. 434 (December 20, 1893).

[78] *Senate Report* No. 227, 53d Cong., 2d sess. The testimony taken and affidavits received by the committee, printed with the report, have been drawn on heavily for the chapter on the revolution.

consent of Congress.[79] They poured bitter ridicule upon
the concern shown by Cleveland and Gresham for a de-
cayed monarchy. The Queen's government, said Senator
Davis, of Minnesota, was like a puppet show played out,
and Cleveland and Gresham were Don Quixote and Sancho
Panza, coming in at the curtain and demanding that the
play go on.[80] Still more bitter things were said of Blount.
Cullom, of Illinois, likened his lowering of the United
States flag in Honolulu to the acts of rebels and traitors
during the Civil War, and described his relation to the
Provisional Government as that of a spy, meriting the fate
usually accorded to such characters.[81] Naturally enough,
too, Republican Senators felt called upon to defend the acts
of Minister Stevens as patriotic and proper and his truth-
fulness as unimpeachable.[82]

Democratic Senators, meanwhile, came to the defense
of their President and his commissioner paramount and
vented their wrath upon the head of Stevens. The brunt
of the battle upon this side was borne by Mills, of Texas,
Gray, of Delaware, Turpie, of Indiana, Vest, of Missouri,
Vilas, of Wisconsin, Daniel, of Virginia, George, of Mississippi, and Gordon, of Georgia—the last-named speaking
for Blount as Frye spoke for Stevens.[83] To a large extent

[79] E. g., Cong. Rec., 53d Cong., 2d sess., pp. 61-73, 128-132.
Senator Hill, of New York, joined the Republicans in denouncing
Cleveland's course.

[80] Ibid., p. 698.

[81] Ibid., pp. 1231-1237.

[82] Senator Frye, of Maine, felt special responsibility for defending
Stevens. Ibid., pp. 72, 189-199. Cf. also Davis, of Minnesota,
ibid., pp. 621-628, 694-702.

[83] Ibid., p. 204.

these speeches merely analyzed the evidence taken by Commissioner Blount and argued therefrom that Stevens had improperly abetted revolution and that Cleveland was right in trying to undo the wrong.[84] Senator Vest cited numerous precedents for the appointment of a special commissioner without confirmation by the Senate.[85] An unintended touch of humor was injected into the debate when Senator Call, of Florida, to whom all Pacific islands were evidently very much alike, announced that the President was obligated to defend the Hawaiian monarchy because it was guaranteed by the tripartite treaty of Berlin of 1889. Obviously it was the Samoan treaty which the Senator had in mind.[86]

But partisan discussion of the legal and ethical aspects of the Hawaiian drama did not entirely engross the attention of Senators, several of whom undertook to pass upon annexation as a national policy. Senator Cullom read into the record, with his endorsement, a letter from " a distinguished gentleman of the Pacific coast," who believed that " as a strategic point commercially, to say nothing of war, the value of the Hawaiian islands is beyond computation. . . . For our country this is a moment that may decide our destiny." [87] Platt, of Connecticut, believed that a nation of seventy million people could not be confined within the narrow limits of the past, and that any territory necessary

[84] Cf. ibid., pp. 702-707, 2080-2093, 2120-2130, 2280-2291, 3128-3139, etc.

[85] Ibid., pp. 196-198. The legal aspects of Blount's appointment are discussed in H. M. Wriston, Executive Agents in American Foreign Relations, pp. 292-303.

[86] Cong. Rec., 53d Cong., 2d sess., p. 73.

[87] Ibid., p. 1234.

for defense or commercial development should be taken, when that could be done "without injustice to other nations and other people." [88] Senator Teller, of Colorado— he who in April, 1898, was to offer the celebrated resolution against annexing Cuba—chided the Democratic party for having abandoned its expansionist policy of earlier years. He recalled its official declaration for the annexing of Cuba in 1856, and continued:

It was the height of wisdom, and it indicated then that the Democratic party was looking at the general welfare of the people of the United States and its general interests. . . . I am in favor of the annexation of the [Hawaiian] islands. I am in favor of the annexation of Cuba. I am in favor of the annexation of the great country lying north of us. I expect in a few years to see the American flag floating from the extreme north to the line of our sister republics on the south. I expect to see it floating over the isles of the sea—not only these, but in the Great Gulf and in the West Indian seas. [89]

Of the Democratic Senators at least one, Vest, of Missouri, spoke out against annexation of Hawaii at any time. [90] Others, like Turpie, of Indiana, and Mills, of Texas, were content to oppose annexation under existing circumstances, which, they felt, would be profiting from Stevens's misdeeds in violation of the rights of the Queen and the wishes of her people. Mills did not doubt the inherent superiority of the Saxon race or their destiny to rule the world, but he thought they should show a becoming decency and consideration for others in their progress. The present episode

[88] *Ibid.*, p. 1310.
[89] *Ibid.*, p. 1578.
[90] *Ibid.*, p. 1308.

reminded him of old Roman days, when queens came to Rome laden with golden chains.

Is that day coming [he asked] when along Pennsylvania Avenue we shall see a Hawaiian queen, not loaded with golden chains, but weighed down with sugar sacks on her back, coming to the Congress of the United States pleading in behalf of her poor, miserable, ignorant people for the right that we claim to have come direct from God to us, inalienable in its nature—the right to institute a government for themselves? [91]

All or nearly all of this debate took place before the Committee on Foreign Relations submitted its report. The House of Representatives, in the meantime, had produced less talk but more action. On February 7, 1894, the House adopted, by a vote of 177 to 78, a set of resolutions introduced on January 23 by McCreary, of Kentucky. The resolutions condemned the action of Stevens, approved the principle of non-interference in the domestic affairs of an independent nation, opposed annexation of Hawaii as " uncalled for and inexpedient," and declared

that the people of that country should have had absolute freedom and independence in pursuing their own line of policy, and that foreign intervention in the political affairs of the islands will not be regarded with indifference by the Government of the United States.[92]

Thus the House repudiated both Stevens's part in overthrowing the monarchy and Cleveland's attempt to restore it, and reaffirmed the nation's historic policy toward foreign interference in the islands. Of the speeches made in the

[91] *Ibid.*, pp. 62-67. *Cf.* Turpie's speech, *ibid.*, pp. 702-707.
[92] Text of resolutions, *ibid.*, p. 2001; vote on adoption, *ibid.*, pp. 2007-2008.

course of the debate on these resolutions, the most elaborate was that of W. F. Draper, of Massachusetts. One may infer that Draper was a student of Mahan's writings on sea power; at any rate, his exposition of the need of the United States for island outposts would have been thoroughly approved by the naval historian. He told the story of the recent rapid advance of Great Britain, France, and Germany in the island groups of the Pacific.

It has not been [he said] a blind grab for territory which has been going on in the South Pacific for six years past, but a working out of strategical schemes with definite ends in view; and the United States is the only great power interested in the Pacific trade which has not had the wisdom to acquire territory in localities where the great trade of the future will need guarding and supplying.

Hawaii and Samoa, advantageously situated from the point of view of our needs, had been " ripe to our hands for years." Thus far our " moral force " had prevented European powers from seizing them, but moral force would not long suffice should any one of those powers find them strategically necessary. By taking Hawaii now, we should provide for the safety of our Pacific trade and the protection of our Pacific coast. The trade of the Pacific, he continued,

is just opening on an era of activity which will be vastly augmented on the completion of an isthmian canal, and this trade belongs to the United States, if we are wise enough to secure it.

But trade must have assurances of protection.

If the United States aim at commercial supremacy in the Pacific, its trade must have such assurances, and a first necessity is the acquisition of bases for the protectors. Not only Hawaii is needed, but Samoa (distant 2,260 miles) ;

a station at the mouth of the canal (say, 4,200 miles from Honolulu and 3,000 from San Francisco) ; and another at the Straits of Magellan (distant 4,000 miles from the isthmus, and 5,000 from Samoa). With these bases, a properly organized fleet, of sufficient size to keep the communications open between them, will hold the Pacific as an American ocean, dominated by American commercial enterprise for all time.[93]

Draper expounded the doctrine of sea power in its relation to the Hawaiian Islands more fully than any other speaker in either house. He was seconded by Van Voorhis, of New York, and, on the Democratic side, by D. E. Sickles of the same state, who recalled that when he was a young man the annexation of Cuba was good Democratic doctrine and declared that no Congressional resolutions could " change the decree of Destiny that the Hawaiian Islands sooner or later shall become a part of these United States." [94]

But neither the philosophy nor the rhetoric of such speeches could sway the action of the House, and with Rayner, of Maryland, declaring his opposition " to the whole policy of annexation, either of these islands or of any other islands or places," and with Turner, of Georgia, announcing his belief " that an entrance upon that system of imperialism is inconsistent with the spirit of our institutions," [95] the House adopted the McCreary resolutions, thereby recording its unqualified opposition to either annexation of or protectorate over the Hawaiian Islands.

[93] *Ibid.*, pp. 1844-1849 (February 3, 1894). This speech was published in the *Social Economist* for June, 1894, whence it was condensed and republished in the *Literary Digest*, IX, 187 (June 16, 1894).

[94] *Cong. Rec.*, 53d Cong., 2d sess., pp. 1907-1908 (Van Voorhis), p. 1960 (Sickles).

[95] *Ibid.*, pp. 1831, 1959.

The Senate Committee on Foreign Relations presented its report on February 26, 1894.[96] The report was written by the chairman, Senator Morgan, of Alabama, an expansionist Democrat—or, as the New York *Times* termed him, an " antique Southern Whig," [97] and he alone accepted it *in toto*. It was a remarkable report—" evidently," said one paper, " an attempt to whitewash everybody "— everybody except the unfortunate Queen.[98] It accepted Stevens's theory that the Queen's government fell by the Queen's own act on Saturday, January 14, 1893. It therefore approved of Stevens's action in landing troops and recognizing the Provisional Government (though not in the subsequent declaration of a protectorate). It approved the action of Harrison and Foster in negotiating a treaty of annexation; it also approved Cleveland's action in withdrawing it from the Senate. It approved Cleveland's appointment of Blount, with paramount authority. It found that Blount had " executed his instructions with impartial care " and had " presented a sincere and instructive report "—though his conclusions were wrong. As to the policy toward the monarchy, the report announced sententiously:

When a crown falls, in any kingdom of the Western Hemisphere, it is pulverized, and when a scepter departs, it departs forever; and American opinion can not sustain any American ruler in the attempt to restore them, no matter

[96] *Senate Report* No. 227, 53d Cong., 2d sess. The chairman's report and the brief statements of other members of the committee occupy pp. 1-36. The remainder of the large volume comprises evidence taken by the committee.

[97] *Literary Digest,* VIII, 455 (March 8, 1894).

[98] *Ibid.*

how virtuous and sincere the reasons may be that seem to justify him.[99]

Yet a few pages farther on it held that so long as Cleveland intended to restore Liliuokalani without resort to force, he was fully justified in attempting it, as well as in abandoning the effort when both the Queen and the Provisional Government proved hard to manage. Willis's attempts to carry out his instructions were also, of course, correct. Everyone had done well except the Queen.

American relations with Hawaii, said Morgan's report, were not to be judged by the same principle as relations with other states. The United States had always exercised there a right of interference not paralleled elsewhere.

The cause of this departure from our general course of diplomatic conduct is the recognized fact that Hawaii has been all the time under a virtual suzerainty of the United States, which is, by an apt and familiar definition, a paramount authority, not in any actual sense an actual sovereignty, but a *de facto* supremacy over the country.[100]

The Republican members of the committee—Senators Sherman, Frye, Dolph, and Davis—expressed themselves as in accord with " the essential findings " of the chairman's report, but dissented strongly from those passages approving the actions of Cleveland and Blount, in which they found much that was unconstitutional and illegal.[101] The Democratic members, other than Morgan—Butler, Turpie, Daniel, and Gray—dissented from Morgan's endorsement of Stevens [102]; while Butler (with Turpie concurring)

[99] *Senate Report* No. 227, 53d Cong., 2d sess., p. 17.
[100] *Ibid.,* p. 21.
[101] *Ibid.,* pp. 33-34.
[102] *Ibid.,* pp. 35-36.

filed yet another statement to the effect that he believed
in the annexation of the islands but was unwilling to take
advantage of internal dissension there to secure it.[103]
" This," said the New York *Times*, " leaves the ancient
Whig in a position all his own." [104]

The report was accompanied by neither resolutions nor
proposals for a course of action. Some time previously,
however, Senator Turpie had brought in, with the endorsement of the committee, a resolution declaring that further
consideration at the time of any project of annexation was
unwise and inexpedient, that the Provisional Government
should be left free to pursue its own line of policy, and
that any foreign intervention would be regarded as unfriendly to the United States.[105] Debate on this resolution
occurred intermittently both before and after the presentation of the committee's report. An attempt, on March 20,
to set a date for voting on it was blocked,[106] and it was not
further considered.

Late in May Senator Kyle, of South Dakota, introduced
a new resolution, the essential feature of which was an expression of the sense of the Senate that the United States
should not use force for the restoration of the Queen or the
destruction of the existing Hawaiian government.[107] He
explained that some of the Hawaiian royalists were still expecting interference in the Queen's behalf and that in
the interest of peace and tranquillity in the islands it was

[103] *Ibid.*, p. 36.
[104] *Literary Digest, loc. cit.*
[105] *Cong. Rec.*, 53d Cong., 2d sess., p. 1220.
[106] *Ibid.*, p. 3128.
[107] *Ibid.*, p. 5127.

important that the Senate put an end to all doubt upon this point.[108] Various objections were raised to the language of this resolution,[109] and on May 31, Turpie brought in a substitute which had the unanimous approval of the Committee on Foreign Relations. It read as follows:

> *Resolved,* That of right it belongs wholly to the people of the Hawaiian Islands to establish and maintain their own form of government and domestic polity; that the United States ought in nowise to interfere therewith, and that any intervention in the political affairs of these islands by any other government will be regarded as an act unfriendly to the United States.

Unanimous consent for an immediate vote was asked and obtained, and the resolution was adopted by a vote of 55

[108] *Ibid.,* pp. 5193-5194. Rear Admiral Walker had reported in April that many natives had refrained from registering for the approaching election of a constitutional convention because of fear of the consequences to them in the event of the restoration of the Queen. "If the native Hawaiians could be fully assured that the Monarchy would not be restored by outside interference it is believed that they would readily participate in all steps for organizing a new form of government." Walker to Secretary of Navy, April 28, 1894. Navy Dept. MSS.

[109] *E. g.,* Gray wished a definite commitment against annexation; Palmer objected to a clause which seemingly endorsed recognition of the Provisional Government. *Cong. Rec.,* 53d Cong., 2d sess. pp. 5246, 5434. Palmer's objection to the language of Kyle's resolution and the change of wording in that brought in by Turpie and adopted were in accord with Cleveland's ideas. Cleveland wrote Senator Vilas, May 29, 1894: "The thing I care the most about is the declaration that the *people* of the islands instead of the *Provisional Government* should determine the policy, etc. . . . Can you not nail the endorsement of the Provisional Government, by putting in its place the more American and Democratic reference to *the People* as the source of power and control?" A. Nevins (ed.), *Letters of Grover Cleveland, 1850-1908,* p. 353.

to 0 with thirty Senators not voting. Only one dissenting voice was raised. Mills, of Texas, rose to say that if he had not been paired with another Senator he would have voted against the resolution, because, said he, he thought it the duty of the United States " to tear down that oligarchy which it has established by force, and permit the people of the Hawaiian Islands to institute their own government." [110]

At last the Senate had spoken. There would be, so far as it was concerned, neither restoration of the Queen, nor interference with the Provisional Government, nor—for the time being at least—annexation of the islands.

[110] The resolution and all proceedings in connection with it are in *Cong. Rec.,* 53d Cong., 2d sess., pp. 5499-5500 (May 31, 1894).

VI

BROADENING HORIZONS

On the day preceding the Senate's declaration of policy regarding Hawaii, a constitutional convention had met in Honolulu for the purpose of placing the Hawaiian state upon a more permanent and regular basis than that provided by the Provisional Government. The speedy collapse of the existing régime, so confidently prophesied by Blount, had not come to pass, but with all hope for immediate annexation at an end, there was no justification for further continuance of a self-appointed oligarchy. Even supporters of the Provisional Government began to grumble at their exclusion from all voice in its affairs and at the monopolization of political power by what they dubbed the missionary group.[1]

The creation of some sort of *de jure* republican government was plainly in order. The difficulty lay in devising republican forms which would operate successfully in a community where a majority of the former electorate presumably desired a restoration of the monarchy. To entrust the ballot to those who had exercised it before the Revolution might result in a speedy undoing of all that the Revolution had accomplished. To the men in power such an outcome was unthinkable. They solved their problem with considerable skill.

[1] Palmer, *Hawaiian Memories,* pp. 46, 75, 97.

On March 15, 1894, the Provisional Government passed an act " to provide for a constitutional convention." This body was to be composed of the nineteen members of the Provisional Government itself (the President and the members of the Executive and Advisory Councils) and eighteen delegates chosen by the voters. Thus the ruling oligarchy would constitute a majority of the convention. Male residents of the islands, of Hawaiian, American, or European birth or descent might vote for delegates, upon taking an oath to " support and bear true allegiance to the Provisional Government " and to " oppose any attempt to reestablish monarchical government in any form in the Hawaiian Islands." [2] As interpreted by the attorney-general, this oath pledged the voter not to vote for a delegate favorable to restoration of the monarchy, and likewise bound delegates to work in the convention against any provision which might result in such restoration.[3] Thus participation in the election of the delegates who would constitute but a minority of the convention was restricted to those willing to forego all thought of restoring the monarchy. It is not surprising that a royalist mass meeting in Honolulu, estimated to number two or three thousand, denounced the plan as calculated to prevent a full and fair representation of the people at the convention and the oath in particular as amounting to a disenfranchisement of the Hawaiian people and of all who remained loyal to the ancient form of government.[4] A copy of the resolutions adopted at this meeting was sent to Minister Willis, with the request that he

[2] *U. S. For. Rel., 1894*, App. II, pp. 1311-1312.
[3] *Ibid.*, pp. 1313-1314.
[4] *Ibid.*, p. 1316.

forward it to Washington. This and subsequent protests lodged with the minister indicate that the Queen and her followers were still hoping for some action by the United States to prevent the permanent shelving of the monarchy. Such hope did not entirely die until June 21, when Willis made known to the Provisional Government and also to Samuel Parker, as a friend of the Queen, the non-interference resolution passed by the United States Senate three weeks previously, and expressed to Parker the belief that this was the final decision of the Senate.[5]

Meanwhile, delegates to the convention had been chosen on May 2, in an election which Willis described as quiet and orderly,[6] and on May 30 the convention began its labors. By the beginning of July the assembled statesmen had achieved a result which seemed to meet admirably all the needs of the situation. What these needs were was stated with perfect frankness, while the convention was deliberating, by a writer in the *Hawaiian Gazette*:

It must be distinctly understood that, besides ruling themselves, the whites must create a form of government through which they can rule natives, Chinese, Japanese, and Portuguese, in order to prevent being " snowed under." That is, we need two distinct forms of government made up into one form; one for ourselves and one for aliens, who outnumber us.

This end was to be attained by creating " an uncommonly

[5] *Ibid.*, pp. 1318, 1341-1342.

[6] *Ibid.*, pp. 1317-1318. Among the eighteen delegates chosen were five native Hawaiians, of whom three—Iosepa, Kalua, and Kauhane—were members of the little group in the legislature of 1892-1893 who had stuck by the Reform Party through thick and thin. *Ibid.*, p. 1371.

strong central government with very large powers in the hands of a few." [7]

The new constitution provided for a legislature of two houses, Senate and House of Representatives, each of fifteen members, and an executive consisting of a President and four cabinet members appointed by him. A Council of State of fifteen members, five each named by the President, Senate, and House, should exercise certain emergency legislative powers between sessions of the legislature. Dole was confirmed in the presidency to serve until December 31, 1900; thereafter, the President was to be chosen by the legislature. The first regular session of the legislature should be held in February, 1896; until then, or until an earlier meeting of a special session, the existing Advisory Council should continue with full powers.

The real key to the nature of the new government, however, is found in the qualifications for suffrage and office-holding. Both voters and office-holders must subscribe to an oath not only to support the constitution, laws, and government of the Republic of Hawaii, but also neither directly nor indirectly to " encourage or assist in the restoration or establishment of a monarchical form of government." Voters must be able to speak, read, and write understandingly either Hawaiian or English. In addition, those voting for Senators, as well as candidates for either Senate or House, must meet property or income qualifications of varying amounts. [8] Few native Hawaiians, under these provisions,

[7] W. N. Armstrong in *Hawaiian Gazette,* June 15, 1894, quoted in *The Nation,* LIX, 57 (July 26, 1894).

[8] A voter in a Senatorial election must own real property worth $1500 or personal property of $3000 or have had a money income

would be able to sit in either house or even to vote for
Senators. To a greater degree than the constitution of 1887,
the new instrument placed political power in the hands of
the white, propertied classes.

Nor were the voters of the islands, however limited in
number, given an opportunity to pass upon the new constitution. It was simply promulgated by proclamation of
President Dole on July 4, 1894.[9] In words that clearly reveal the attitude of the ruling group, the Reverend Mr.
Bishop explained why there could be no popular referen-
dum. If the constitution were submitted to the people,
he wrote,

> the voting must be confined to the 4,700 who were regis-
> tered and participated in the election of delegates. This
> would not be submission to the whole people. Again upon
> most of the debatable points in the Constitution, it is im-
> possible for the mass of the voters to be well-informed,
> or to decide intelligently. It is necessary for the people to
> trust their delegates and leave the decision to them. . . .

for the preceding year of $600 or more. A Representative must
own property worth not less than $1000 or have a money income
of $600. A Senator must own property worth $3000 or more or
have a money income of $1200. The text of the constitution is
found in *U. S. For. Rel., 1894,* App. II, pp. 1350-1371. The Constitution of 1887 had required that a noble, or one voting in an
election of nobles, own taxable property worth $3000 or more, or
have an annual income not less than $600. *Ibid.,* p. 252. The new
constitution was based upon a draft prepared jointly by Messrs. Dole
and Thurston. Dole, *Memoirs of the Hawaiian Revolution,* p. 164.
In preparing it, Dole asked the advice of Professor John W.
Burgess, who gave suggestions for placing " the government in
the hands of the Teutons." H. M. Madden (ed.), " Letters of
Sanford B. Dole and John W. Burgess," *Pacific Historical Review,*
V, 71-75.

[9] *U. S. For. Rel., 1894,* App. II, p. 1371.

It is of great importance that there should be no uncertainty attending the final adoption of this Constitution
and no delay in putting it into operation. Any such delay
and uncertainty as would be caused by the useless form
of a popular vote upon it would be highly prejudicial to
the public confidence. It would be sacrificing important
and most essential practical results to a farcical carrying
out of Democratic theory.[10]

The aristocratic republic thus inaugurated on July 4,
1894, was to experience four years of success, prosperity,
and comparative tranquillity. "The year 1896," wrote a
member of the American group two and one-half years
later, "has been the most peaceful and prosperous one that
these islands have known for a great while."[11] The
Wilson-Gorman tariff of 1894, which abolished the sugar
bounty and restored the duty on foreign sugar, while leaving the Hawaiian reciprocity treaty intact, probably meant
quite as much to the islands as "strong" government. It
is, however, no part of this study to follow the internal
history of the Hawaiian Republic. We must note only certain features of its relations with the United States.

Minister Willis granted prompt recognition to the new
government, subject to the approval of the President of the
United States,[12] and President Cleveland in due time sent
a formal message of congratulation to his "Great and Good
Friend," President Dole.[13] A clause in the new constitu-

[10] Sereno E. Bishop in *Independent*, XLVI, 950 (July 26, 1894).

[11] W. D. Alexander to F. P. Hastings, December 9, 1896. Spaulding Collection.

[12] *U. S. For. Rel., 1894*, App. II, p. 1374.

[13] Nevins, *Letters of Grover Cleveland, 1850-1908*, p. 363
(August 17, 1894).

tion expressly empowering the President, with the approval of Cabinet and Senate, to make a treaty of political and commercial union with the United States [14] was not of interest to the Cleveland administration, though it would be so to a future one. In fact, though holding formal and apparently friendly intercourse with the Dole Government, Secretary Gresham permitted himself to confer informally with representatives of the former Queen and to give them, perhaps unwittingly, what they apparently considered encouragement in their still lingering schemes to restore her to the throne.

Shortly after the proclamation of the new constitution, a commission of three men—Messrs. Cummins, Widemann, and Parker—representing Liliuokalani visited Washington. In a note to Gresham they asked an audience with the President in order to ask him " whether there is any hope of his doing anything for the restoration of the constitutional [i. e., Royal] government of the Hawaiian Islands." [15] Cleveland consented to see them as individuals, but on the day set for the interview was confined to his bed. He therefore signed and sent to them a statement which he had planned to read them, to the effect that the attitude of Congress and the recent recognition of the new Government led to " an absolute denial of the least present or future aid or encouragement on my part to an effort to restore any government heretofore existing in the Hawaiian Islands." [16]

[14] Article 32.

[15] *Cong. Rec.*, 53d Cong., 3d sess., p. 718. *Cf. Hawaii's Story by Hawaii's Queen*, pp. 258-259.

[16] *Cong. Rec., loc. cit.*

This statement was explicit enough. Probably the commissioners had expected no different answer. Meanwhile, however, they had secured from Gresham satisfactory assurances that the United States would not interfere if the Queen's friends themselves undertook to restore her to power. In an interview with Gresham, August 2, Widemann had said: " The Hawaiian people would like to know precisely the attitude of the United States toward them. They do not wish to encounter the opposition of your Government." To this Gresham replied: " You will encounter no opposition from this Government. We claim no right to meddle in the domestic affairs of your country."

Three days later, Samuel Parker called at the Department of State. After stating to Gresham that the existing Government was unstable and could not long endure, he complained that the presence of United States warships at Honolulu had been a " constant moral support to the Provisional Government," creating in the minds of the people the impression that the ships were " there to support the existing government in case it should need help."

The attitude of this government ought to be understood at Honolulu [replied Gresham]. Our warships were sent there not to uphold the provisional government or its successor, but to afford protection to such of our own citizens as did not participate in the local strifes.

I am glad to hear you say that [said Parker]. All our people desire to know is that the government of the United States is not on the side of the existing government and against them. I see that Admiral Walker has been ordered back with your war ships from Honolulu. That will please our people very much.[17]

[17] Gresham's memorandum of these conversations is found in *Memoranda of Conversations with the Secretary of State, 1893-1898.*

It is quite clear from the words of both Widemann and Parker that they were meditating an attempt to overthrow the Dole Government and restore the Queen by force, provided they could count upon the neutrality of the United States. That was now assured; and there was the further encouraging fact, alluded to by Parker, that the U. S. S. "Philadelphia," which had for some months been stationed at Honolulu, had been recalled and not replaced. Throughout the latter part of 1894 and into January, 1895, there was, for the first time in many years, no United States war vessel stationed at Honolulu.[18] It seems probable that this policy was deliberately adopted with a view to determining whether the Dole Government could stand upon its own feet. The order to Admiral Walker to bring the "Philadelphia" to San Francisco without awaiting the arrival of another ship was dated July 20, 1894.[19] The "Philadelphia" sailed August 12. While at sea, Walker penned an alarmist report to the Secretary of the Navy, expressing the fear that, in the absence of an American warship while a British ship remained at Honolulu, British intrigue might bring about a royalist restoration.[20] This suggestion was scouted by Minister Willis, who reported that he had no reason to suspect the British of any hostile intent—in fact, their commissioner, Mr. Wodehouse, whose

[18] Cf. Secretary Long's letter to Senator Morgan in *Senate Report* No. 681, 55th Cong., 2d sess., p. 117. See also the report of the Bureau of Navigation in the Annual Report of the Secretary of the Navy, November 27, 1895. *House Document* No. 3, 54th Cong., 1st sess.

[19] *Senate Exec. Doc.* No. 16, 53d Cong., 3d sess., p. 4.

[20] *Ibid.,* pp. 19-22.

attitude had given concern to Minister Stevens and even to Gresham, was at this very time recalled—and that the Hawaiian foreign minister had said to him, apropos of the departure of the "Philadelphia," that his Government "welcomed the opportunity to prove to the world that they were able to take care of themselves." [21]

Heartened, presumably, by Gresham's statements to the commissioners and by the unwonted absence of an American man-of-war, the Queen's friends and other discontented elements planned an uprising for January 7, 1895. They imported and secreted arms, arranged for the landing of a further supply along the Honolulu waterfront, and proposed to take possession of the city and storm the Government Building. They pieced together a constitution and drew up a list of cabinet and other officers who were to assume control upon the success of the revolution. They had, certainly, the consent of the Queen to their plans.[22] But the fatal incompetence that had marked all previous attempts of this kind on the part of natives and half-castes again asserted itself. Rumors of the intended revolt leaked out some days in advance. On the night of January 6, a party of police in search of concealed arms stumbled upon an armed band of revolutionists at Waikiki Beach. After an exchange of shots the rebels fled to the mountains, where within a few days they were captured or dispersed. Three lives were lost. On the 7th the country was placed under

[21] *U. S. For. Rel., 1894,* App. II, pp. 1376-1378.

[22] It is impossible to reconcile Liliuokalani's denials of complicity before the military court (*U. S. For. Rel., 1895,* p. 825) with her subsequent statements in her book, *Hawaii's Story by Hawaii's Queen,* pp. 262-265.

martial law, and the Honolulu jail was filled with persons suspected of complicity in the uprising.[23]

For some weeks after the outbreak there was intense feeling in Honolulu. Supporters of the Government demanded the extreme penalty for the revolutionists, and there was talk of mob violence and the shooting of the prisoners without trial. A word of warning from Minister Willis and the arrival, January 29, of the "Philadelphia," which had been dispatched from San Francisco at the first news of the disorder, were sufficient to remove any possibility of such an outcome.[24] A military court was created for the trial of the conspirators. Among those haled before it was Liliuokalani, who upon signing a formal abdication,[25] was let off with the comparatively light sentence of five years' imprisonment and a fine of $5000.[26] Three ringleaders in the movement, originally sentenced to death by the military court, had their sentences commuted to fines and long prison terms. Similar sentences were imposed upon a number of other conspirators, among them that chronic trouble-

[23] The above account is based chiefly on the reports of Minister Willis in *U. S. For. Rel., 1894*, App. II, pp. 1391-1397, and *U. S. For. Rel., 1895*, pp. 818-820, 823. There is a good summary by W. R. Farrington in W. D. Alexander, *History of the Later Years of the Hawaiian Monarchy and the Revolution of 1893*, pp. 222-224. See also Dole, *op. cit.*, pp. 169-174.

[24] *U. S. For. Rel., 1895*, pp. 818-820, 852. The fact that several of the prisoners were or claimed to be American citizens was the excuse of Willis's intervention. *Cf.* Julius A. Palmer, Jr., *Again in Hawaii*, p. 11. Palmer came to Honolulu this time as correspondent of the New York *Evening Post*.

[25] *U. S. For. Rel., 1895*, pp. 820-823. *Cf. Hawaii's Story by Hawaii's Queen*, pp. 267-277.

[26] *U. S. For. Rel., 1895*, p. 835.

maker, R. W. Wilcox.[27] Another group of suspects, including the brothers C. W. and V. V. Ashford, who
for years had been energetic and picturesque figures in
Hawaiian politics, accepted the option of deportation in pref-
erence to standing trial.[28] One may hazard a guess that
the erstwhile Reform Party utilized the occasion of the
rebellion to make as clean a sweep as possible of their
traditional opponents.[29]

Julius Palmer, visiting Honolulu in March, reported the
city under military rule, full of fear and suspicion, infested
with spies and informers, and resounding with the noise of
young men at target practice with repeating rifles.[30] Better
feeling came speedily. On July 4, 1895, forty-five political
prisoners, serving five-year terms, were released on suspended sentences, while at the same time the sentences of
graver offenders were commuted. In September, forty-four
pardons were granted, and on January 1, 1896, all remaining political prisoners were released on parole.[31] Liliuokalani, who had been released on parole in September,
1895, subject to restrictions that were gradually relaxed,
received full pardon with restoration of full civil rights in

[27] *Ibid.*, pp. 818-820, 835.

[28] Palmer, *op. cit.*, pp. 37-38; Alexander, *op. cit.*, pp. 226-228.

[29] It is an interesting fact that C. B. Wilson, the former marshal,
whose régime had been bitterly assailed by Reform and Liberal
elements in 1892, was now in the good graces of the Dole Government—so much so that he was made custodian of the former Queen
during her imprisonment. *Hawaii's Story by Hawaii's Queen*,
pp. 289 ff.

[30] Palmer, *op. cit.*, p. vi.

[31] *U. S. For. Rel., 1895*, pp. 861-862, 864-865, 867.

October, 1896.[32] Such liberality betokened a growing self-confidence on the part of the Government of the Republic.[33]

Largely as a result of events in Hawaii, the short session of the Fifty-Third Congress (December, 1894-March, 1895) witnessed a spirited renewal of the debate between the expansionists and the defenders of the administration's "little America" policy. The discussion was opened by Senator Lodge, December 22, with the introduction of a resolution instructing the Secretary of the Navy to inform the Senate why all ships of war had been withdrawn from the Hawaiian Islands, and whether the interests of the United States and its citizens did not require that a war vessel be stationed at Honolulu.[34] In speaking to this resolution, Lodge referred to the correspondence of Admiral Walker, and predicted a royalist rising encouraged by British influence.[35] Fuel was added to the flames when on January 9, 1895, President Cleveland sent to Congress a special message urging that consent be given to the lease by the Hawaiian Government to Great Britain of uninhabited Necker Island to serve as a station for a cable to connect Canada and Australia.[36] The project of a cable to

[32] U. S. For. Rel., 1896, p. 388; Hawaii's Story by Hawaii's Queen, p. 303.

[33] The legislature provided for by the new constitution was called to meet in special session June 13, 1895, thereupon succeeding the Advisory Council which had held over from the Provisional Government. U. S. For. Rel., 1895, pp. 858, 861.

[34] Cong. Rec., 53d Cong., 3d sess., p. 555.

[35] Ibid., p. 622.

[36] Senate Exec. Doc. No. 31, 53d Cong., 3d sess. The consent of the United States was necessary because of Section 4 of the reciprocity treaty of 1887.

connect Hawaii directly with the United States had been discussed between the two governments as far back at least as 1889 and had been viewed as having decided political implications.[37] That the proposal for a British cable now came to Congress with Cleveland's endorsement seemed to Senators like Lodge to confirm their suspicions both of British designs upon Hawaii and of Cleveland's indifference to them. The same men found further reason for their fears in Cleveland's desire to withdraw from the tripartite Samoan arrangement. In his first annual message (December 4, 1893) he had referred to the Samoan situation as illustrating " the impolicy of entangling alliances with other powers." [38] In May, 1894, he had sent to Congress a long report from Gresham on Samoa, in which the Secretary intimated that the only fruits of the Berlin treaty had been expenses, responsibilities, and entanglements.[39] Now, in his message of December 3, 1894, he had proposed a complete withdrawal by the United States from its engagements there " on some reasonable terms not prejudicial to any of our existing rights." [40] This proposal,

[37] *E. g.,* the Hawaiian foreign minister had written, in support of a proposal for a cable to be sponsored by the two governments: " This country now is thoroughly American but if we should get our news from abroad through British channels sifted by British minds and made to suit British views I fear that the sentiment of our people would gradually tend to the views thus brought to us and that the American feeling would lose its predominance." Austin to Carter, January 15, 1889; extract enclosed in Carter to Blaine, March 29, 1889. *Hawaii, Notes,* III.

[38] Richardson, *Messages and Papers of the Presidents,* IX, 439.

[39] *U. S. For. Rel., 1894,* App. I, pp. 504-513.

[40] Richardson, *op. cit.,* IX, 531-532. For a convenient summary of the operation of the Treaty of Berlin and Cleveland's attitude

coupled with Cleveland's Hawaiian policy, seemed to Senator Lodge ample proof that the administration was bent upon abandoning American interests in the Pacific to Great Britain.[41]

While these matters were agitating the Senate, came the news of the royalist rebellion in Hawaii, which bore out, in part at least, Lodge's earlier predictions. Unfriendly Senators were to a slight degree mollified by the prompt dispatch of the " Philadelphia " to Honolulu, but the opportunity for an intensified attack upon the administration was not lost, and resolutions reflecting various shades of opinion were introduced. Of the hostile resolutions, all condemned, by implication if not directly, the withdrawal of United States warships from Honolulu; one expressed " profound indignation " (later changed to " regret ") at the attempt to restore the Queen; two (introduced by Lodge and by Allen of Nebraska) advocated annexation; and one (Lodge's) favored prompt measures for the construction of an American cable to Honolulu and opposed any steps which would permit another government " to secure a foothold or lease upon any part of the Hawaiian Islands." [42] None of these came to a vote. Instead, the Senate adopted as a substitute for Allen's resolution one proposed by Vest,

thereto, see G. H. Ryden, *The Foreign Policy of the United States in Relation to Samoa,* chap. xiv.

[41] *Cong. Rec.,* 53d Cong., 3d sess., p. 622. This speech was made on January 4, 1895, before the cable proposal had been sent in.

[42] The resolutions referred to were introduced by Frye (January 19, 1895, *Cong. Rec.,* 53d Cong. 3d sess., p. 1133); by Kyle (January 19, *ibid.*); by Lodge (January 21, *ibid.,* p. 1167); by Allen (January 24, *ibid.,* p. 1277).

of Missouri, which merely reaffirmed the policy of non-
interference for which the Senate had spoken in the preceding May and approved the position taken by the Cleveland administration as embodying that policy.[43] The vote
on the substitution stood 24 to 22, with 39 not voting.
It meant little more than an expression of opinion by
twenty-four Senators. Possibly a better index to the attitude of the Senate was the adoption, February 9, of an
amendment to the Diplomatic and Consular Appropriation
Bill providing $500,000 toward the cost of construction
of a cable between Hawaii and the United States.[44] The
House of Representatives, however, refused to concur in the
amendment, and the Senate, facing a hint from Senator
Blackburn that the President would veto a bill with this
provision, with a resulting need for an extra session, thought
best to yield.[45]

The debate on these various proposals called forth new
avowals of their faith on the part of both expansionist and

[43] *Ibid.*, pp. 1411-1412 (January 26, 1895). The vote was on
substituting Vest's resolution for Allen's. Vest's was in the form
of a concurrent resolution. There is no record of further action
upon it in either Senate or House.

[44] *Ibid.*, p. 1986.

[45] *Ibid.*, pp. 3126, 3127. The hint of a veto was well founded.
February 13, 1895, Cleveland wrote Thomas F. Bayard that he did
not see how he could make himself responsible for " such a departure from our traditions " as was involved in the proposed
appropriation for a cable, adding: " I do not believe we should in
present circumstances boom the annexation craze by entering upon
Government cable building." This is followed by a reference to
the possibility of an extra session of Congress. *Letters of Grover
Cleveland*, pp. 377-378. For a summary of the Hawaiian cable
question see L. B. Tribolet, *International Aspects of Electrical
Communications in the Pacific*, pp. 161-180.

anti-expansionist Senators. Caffery, of Louisiana, declared his "unalterable opposition" to incorporating into the American Union "that heterogeneous mixture of all the nations of the earth"—Hawaii.[46] Gray opposed annexation in general and that of Hawaii in particular.

> I believe [he said] that our policy is a continental one, and that we are not called upon by anything in our past history or by anything in the necessities of our situation to step off this continent in a career of colonial aggrandizement. That belongs to a past age; it belongs to other forms of government.[47]

On the other side, Teller, of Colorado, reaffirmed his belief in the propriety of flying the American flag over Cuba—"over that great island and over other islands."[48] Platt, of Connecticut, visioned the continued westward progress of the Caucasian race, "carrying civilization and blessing in its march," and declared his faith that "neither narrow statesmanship nor political prejudice can prevent or long hinder it in its continued progress westward, still westward."[49]

But it was Senator Lodge—accused by Gray of having embarked upon a "scheme of annexation and colonial empire"[50]—who preached with greatest fervor the twin gospels of expansion and sea power. Lodge, as has been indicated, was active throughout the session, but his supreme oratorical flight came on March 2, in a desperate effort to save the appropriation for the Hawaiian cable. He

[46] *Cong. Rec.*, 53d Cong., 3d sess., p. 1139.
[47] *Ibid.*, p. 628.
[48] *Ibid.*, pp. 628, 629.
[49] *Ibid.*, p. 1829.
[50] *Ibid.*, p. 1172.

considered this item, he said, "the most important thing
involved in any appropriation bill before Congress," since
upon the Hawaiian Islands depended "a great part of the
future commercial progress of the United States." Lodge
thereupon launched upon an exposition of Mahan's doctrine of sea power.

The sea power has been one of the controlling forces in
history. Without sea power no nation has been really great.
Sea power consists, in the first place, of a proper navy and
a proper fleet; but in order to sustain a Navy we must
have suitable posts for naval stations, strong places where
a navy can be protected and refurnished.

At this point the speaker exhibited to the Senate a map
of the world, upon which he had marked in red the location of the naval stations of Great Britain—a line of them
on the Atlantic coast of North America and in the neighbor-
ing islands, others in European, Asiatic, and African waters
—and indicated the relative naval strength of Great Britain
and the United States in the Atlantic and Pacific. Pointing
to the British stations at Vancouver and in the Falkland
and Fiji Islands, he continued:

In that great triangle marked by these three points Great
Britain does not hold a naval station. There in the center
of that triangle, in the heart of the Pacific, where I am
now pointing, lie the Sandwich Islands. They are the key
of the Pacific. . . .

He did not believe that England desired war with us; but
we were her natural commercial rivals; she had always
thwarted and opposed us; she desired to keep control of
the great commercial highways and to put us in a position
where we could fight, if at all, only at a disadvantage. We
had now the opportunity to strengthen our position against

her in the Pacific. Lodge disclaimed any desire to see his country "enter on an unlimited career of acquisition of colonial possessions. . . . But, Mr. President, . . . we hold the citadel of our greatness here on this continent within the borders of the United States, but we should not neglect the necessary outworks."

After another encomium upon the historic rôle of sea power, the Senator concluded:

Mr. President, I desire an extra session as little as any man in this body, but I would never vote to strike out that cable as the first step toward the development of American commerce, toward the taking of what belongs as of right to the American people in their onward march. I would never vote to strike it out if it meant ten extra sessions. It is part of a great policy. It is not a mere appropriation of $500,000.[51]

Anxious, apparently, to appeal to a wider audience than that reached by the *Congressional Record*, Lodge formulated his ideas in an article entitled "Our Blundering Foreign Policy," published in the *Forum* for March, 1895.[52] Characterizing the foreign policy of the preceding two years as "everywhere a policy of retreat and surrender," Lodge denounced Cleveland's attitude to Hawaii at every point, accused him of wishing to give Samoa to Great Britain, and charged him with dabbling ineffectually in the affairs of the Near and Far East, while abandoning true American interests nearer home and permitting the British to violate the Monroe Doctrine in Venezuela. Under Cleveland's leadership, said Lodge, the Democratic Party had abandoned the expansionist policies of Jefferson and Jackson for a

[51] *Ibid.*, pp. 3082-3084.
[52] *Forum*, XIX, 8-17.

policy of retreat coupled with the deplorable heresy of free trade. It had, in fact, become thoroughly "Cobdenized."

Lodge then proceeded to state, in no mincing words, what the foreign policy of the United States ought to be. There should be no further extension on the mainland to the south,

for neither the population nor the lands of Central and South America would be desirable additions to the United States. But from the Rio Grande to the Arctic Ocean there should be but one flag and one country. Neither race nor climate forbids this extension, and every consideration of national growth and national welfare demands it. In the interests of our commerce and of our fullest development we should build the Nicaragua canal, and for the protection of that canal and for the sake of our commercial supremacy in the Pacific we should control the Hawaiian Islands and maintain our influence in Samoa. England has studded the West Indies with strong places which are a standing menace to our Atlantic Seaboard. We should have among those islands at least one strong naval station, and when the Nicaragua canal is built, the island of Cuba . . . will become to us a necessity.

Adding to his list of desiderata "a navy strong enough to give protection to Americans in every quarter of the globe," Lodge concluded:

The tendency of modern times is toward consolidation. . . . Small states are of the past and have no future. . . . The great nations are rapidly absorbing for their future expansion and their present defence all the waste places of the earth. It is a movement which makes for civilization and the advancement of the race. As one of the great nations of the world, the United States must not fall out of the line of march.

There can be no doubt that the Massachusetts Senator was, in his own mind at least, defining the political issues of the next campaign. On no issue, not even the tariff, was Republican criticism of Cleveland more bitter than upon his foreign policy. In the *Forum* article Lodge sought rather skilfully to combine the two. Republicans, if Lodge had his way, would stand for a sturdy protection of American interests, at home by the tariff, abroad by a judicious naval and territorial expansion, in contrast with the alleged Democratic policy of free trade and territorial restriction.

Obviously, here was a real issue. It is true that before the year 1895 ran its course, Cleveland was to satisfy even the jingoes in his firm stand for the Monroe Doctrine in the Venezuela affair. It is true that he favored the upbuilding of the Navy, when the state of the treasury permitted,[53] and that he looked not wholly without sympathy upon the Nicaragua canal project.[54] But to all plans for the over-

[53] *Cf.* his annual messages of 1893, 1894, and 1896. Richardson, *op. cit.*, IX, 451, 540, 733.

[54] Throughout the years under discussion, Senator Morgan, of Alabama, was continually pressing a measure by which the United States would guarantee a bond issue of the moribund Maritime Canal Company of Nicaragua, receiving in return a majority of the stock of that company. *Cf. Cong. Rec.*, 53d Cong., 3d sess., pp. 158-160; *ibid.*, 54th Cong., 2d sess., p. 795; *ibid.*, 55th Cong., 1st sess., p. 40; *ibid.*, 55th Cong., 2d sess., p. 4063. Lodge (January 4, 1895) praised the "distinguished ability" and "most far-sighted patriotism" with which Morgan was championing the measure. *Ibid.*, 53d Cong., 3d sess., p. 622. Cleveland, in his message of December 4, 1893, stated that the United States was "especially interested in the successful achievement" of the task undertaken by the company and that this task ought to be "accomplished under distinctively American auspices." Richardson, *op. cit.*, IX, 438. This, apparently, was as far as he ever went in advocacy of this canal project. His unfavorable attitude to the canal treaty negotiated with Nicaragua under Arthur's administration is well known. *Supra*, p. 28.

seas expansion of American sovereignty he was unalterably opposed. The schemes for acquiring naval bases or insular possessions in the Caribbean, with which President Harrison and his Secretaries of State had dallied,[55] were, during Cleveland's four years, entirely discarded. Such interest as he or either of his Secretaries of State, Gresham and Olney, displayed in the Danish West Indies or the Dominican Republic was aimed solely at preventing those islands from passing under the control, respectively, of Germany and France—in other words at the enforcement of the Monroe Doctrine. Of the acquisition by the United States of the islands, or even of a naval base within their boundaries, there was, apparently, never a thought.[56] Cleveland's attitude on the subject was well summarized in a statement given to the press some months after the close of his term of office.

I regarded, and still regard [he said] the proposed annexation of these [the Hawaiian] islands as not only opposed to our national policy, but as a perversion of our national mission. The mission of our nation is to build up and make a greater country out of what we have, instead of annexing islands.[57]

Cleveland displayed the same conservatism in dealing with the Cuban question, which arose to bedevil his last two years in office as Hawaii had bedeviled the two years preceding. The Cuban insurrection began in February,

[55] *Supra,* pp. 29-32.

[56] Tansill, *Purchase of the Danish West Indies,* pp. 197-207; Welles, *Naboth's Vineyard,* II, 505-506.

[57] *Letters of Grover Cleveland,* pp. 491-492. This statement, dated January 24, 1898, was given out in reply to an assertion of Senator Morgan that Cleveland was not opposed to Hawaiian annexation *per se.*

1895, and within a few months the yellow press was in-
flaming the country with exaggerated and one-sided reports
of Spanish atrocities.[58] Popular sympathy with a people
struggling for their liberty found prompt reflection in Congress, and the long session of 1895-1896 was marked by the
introduction of a variety of resolutions expressing sympathy
for the insurgents and advocating recognition of their status
as belligerents. A concurrent resolution adopted by the
Senate in February, 1896, and accepted by the House in
April, declared that in the opinion of Congress a state of
public war existed in Cuba; that the United States ought
to accord belligerent rights impartially to both parties in
the conflict; and that " the friendly offices of the United
States should be offered by the President to the Spanish
Government for the recognition of the independence of
Cuba." [59]

Neither in these resolutions nor in the debate upon them
can one discover evidence of any clear plan to annex Cuba
to the United States. Several advocates of the resolutions
expressly disavowed any desire for annexation.[60] Senators
and Congressmen, nevertheless, were not unmindful of advantages which the United States might derive from liberat-
ing the Cubans, and there was some plain talk of actual
annexation, or some relationship closely akin thereto. Mr.
Sulzer, of New York, described Cuba as " a natural part of

[58] The part played by the yellow press in bringing on the war
is set forth in M. M. Wilkerson, *Public Opinion and the Spanish-
American War; a Study in War Propaganda,* and J. E. Wisan,
The Cuban Crisis as Reflected in the New York Press (1895-1898).

[59] *Cong. Rec.,* 54th Cong., 1st sess., pp. 2256, 2257, 3627-3628.

[60] *E. g.,* Senator Morgan, *ibid.,* p. 1975; Senator Sherman, *ibid.,*
p. 2246; Representative McCreary, *ibid.,* p. 2344.

our Geographical domain . . . a possession rich beyond the dreams of avarice and essential to our control of the Gulf of Mexico, our continental supremacy, and our national destiny." [61] Lodge, who a year before had written of Cuba as being a " necessity " to the United States, still retained the opinion that the island was of vast commercial and strategic importance to this country, but he no longer considered absolute possession essential, provided it were " in friendly hands."

Cuba in our hands or in friendly hands, in the hands of its own people, attached to us by ties of interest and gratitude, is a bulwark to the commerce, to the safety, and to the peace of the United States.[62]

Against all pressure for intervention or for the recognition of the belligerent status of the insurgents Cleveland stood firm. To the concurrent resolution of April, 1896, he paid no attention, viewing it as merely an expression of opinion on the part of the legislative branch. Yet Cleveland was genuinely perplexed as to the best solution of the unfortunate Cuban situation. The suggestion, made by Consul-General Fitzhugh Lee at Havana, that the United States purchase the island from Spain, he thought would not " suit at all, though it is perhaps worth thinking of." It would be absurd to buy the island and turn it over " to the people

[61] *Ibid.*, p. 2350. *Cf.* also speeches by Smith and Thomas, of Michigan, *ibid.*, pp. 2352, 2353, 2358, and by Senator Vest, of Missouri, *ibid.*, p. 2210. Vest declared that he had opposed the annexation of Hawaii because of his belief that it could be held only by greatly increasing the navy. He cited no less an authority than Thomas Jefferson for the possibility of holding Cuba without a navy, and therefore declared himself in favor of taking it.

[62] *Ibid.*, p. 1972.

now inhabiting it "; yet to incorporate it into the system of the United States " would be entering upon dangerous ground." [63] He did everything within his power to avoid the necessity of intervention or of war with Spain; yet in his last annual message he intimated plainly that the United States could not see the struggle drag on indefinitely, and added: " The United States is not a nation to which peace is a necessity." [64] But by the time Cleveland made this cautious admission that war might be the only solution of the Cuban question, he had seen the triumph at the polls of the party which had incorporated in its platform not only a demand for Cuban independence but an endorsement of the program of territorial expansion which for three and one-half years Cleveland had earnestly opposed.

By the end of the year 1896, the United States was unquestionably, in the words Mahan had used in 1890, " looking outward." The Fifty-Fourth Congress, besides showing a tendency to assert American rights in the western hemisphere against all comers, had been ready to lecture the Great Powers of Europe upon their duty elsewhere. It had given enthusiastic support to the President's determination to defend the Monroe Doctrine at all hazards [65]; it had resolved that Cuba ought to be independent,[66] and that

[63] To Richard Olney, July 16, 1896. *Letters of Grover Cleveland*, p. 448.

[64] Richardson, *op. cit.*, IX, 719. As late as April 6, 1898, Cleveland still believed that war with Spain would be avoided. *Letters of Grover Cleveland*, pp. 498-499.

[65] It took the House and Senate but two days to pass an appropriation of $100,000 to enable the President to determine the " true divisional line " between Venezuela and British Guiana. *Cong. Rec.*, 54th Cong., 1st sess., pp. 234, 235, 265.

[66] *Supra*, p. 210.

the parties to the treaty of Berlin—Great Britain, Germany, Austria-Hungary, France, Italy, and Russia—ought to live up to their obligations by protecting Armenian Christians against Turkish atrocities; and in the last connection it had pledged full support to the President in any action for the protection of American citizens in Turkey.[67] Big navy men dwelt with satisfaction upon this " revival of nationalism " and demanded naval increases which would enable the nation to back up its demands with force. Said one of them:

Why, Mr. Chairman, a failure at the present time to strengthen our Navy in a superlative degree would be tantamount to making an apology to the world for our actions during the past two months.[68]

Acting in this spirit, the House voted to authorize four new battleships instead of the two asked for by the Secretary of the Navy, and eventually compromised with the Senate on three.[69]

This spirit of aggressive self-assertion found enthusiastic expression in the Republican platform of 1896. " Our foreign policy," declared that document, " should be at

[67] *Cong. Rec.*, 54th Cong., 1st sess., pp. 854, 965, 1016.

[68] P. B. Low, of New York, in House of Representatives. *Ibid.*, p. 3197. *Cf.* speeches of Hawley, of Connecticut, and Hanly, of Indiana, *ibid.*, pp. 2487, 3240-3242.

[69] *Ibid.*, pp. 3194, 6326. The ships authorized at this time (1896) were the " Illinois," " Alabama," and " Wisconsin." The first modern battleships (other than the second-class " Maine " and " Texas," provided for in 1886) authorized by Congress were the " Indiana," " Massachusetts," and " Oregon " (1890). These three, with the " Iowa " (1892), were completed before the war with Spain. The " Kearsarge " and " Kentucky " were authorized in 1895. J. D. Long, *The New American Navy*, I, 53-54.

all times firm, vigorous, and dignified, . . . We reassert the Monroe Doctrine in its full extent, and we reaffirm the right of the United States to give the doctrine effect by responding to the appeal of any American State for friendly intervention in case of European encroachment." The United States should use its influence to restore peace in Cuba and to give independence to the Cuban people. It should do all in its power to stop the Armenian massacres and to protect American citizens and their property everywhere. And, in order to maintain peace and security at home and " its rightful influence among the nations of the earth," it must have " a naval power commensurate with its position and responsibility."

Such a program clearly called for an isthmian canal and for naval bases at strategic points in relation to it, and the platform was by no means silent upon these points. " The Hawaiian islands should be controlled by the United States, . . . ; the Nicaragua Canal should be built, owned and operated by the United States; and by the purchase of the Danish islands we should secure a proper and much-needed naval station in the West Indies." Then, with a glance northward, the platform added:

We hopefully look forward to the eventual withdrawal of the European powers from this hemisphere, and to the ultimate union of all English-speaking parts of the continent by the free consent of its inhabitants.[70]

In competition with this ambitious program of aggressive foreign policy and territorial expansion, the Democrats could offer only an endorsement of the Monroe Doctrine

[70] Stanwood, *History of the Presidency from 1788 to 1897*, pp. 535-536.

and a tender of " sympathy to the people of Cuba in their heroic struggle for liberty and independence." [71]

Yet this contrast of foreign policies probably attracted little attention in the ensuing campaign. After all, it was the year of Bryan and the Free Silver menace; and after Free Silver it was the historic debate over the tariff which held second place in popular interest.[72] Even McKinley, the Republican candidate, appears to have given little thought to the foreign policy to which the party imperialists had committed him. A reading of the dry " front-porch " addresses which he delivered during the campaign,[73] reveals scarcely a word upon that theme. Soon after his inauguration he assured Carl Schurz that there was to be no scheming for the annexation of Hawaii, and added: "Ah, you may be sure that there will be no jingo nonsense under my administration." [74] John Sherman, who became his Secretary of State, shared this attitude. To the Hawaiian minister he said, in March, 1897, that " he was opposed to all acquisitions of territory not on the main land. Cuba, Hawaii [,] San Domingo or any other. . . ." [75]

Friends of Hawaiian annexation undertook at once the task of converting McKinley to a belief in that cause.[76]

[71] *Ibid.*, p. 546.

[72] *Cf.* H. Croly, *Marcus Alonzo Hanna*, pp. 212-217.

[73] *E. g.*, Buffalo *Courier*, July to November, 1896, *passim.*

[74] C. M. Fuess, *Carl Schurz, Reformer (1829-1906)*, p. 349.

[75] F. M. Hatch to H. E. Cooper, March 27, 1897. Spaulding Collection.

[76] Carl Schurz was informed that McKinley was won to the annexation of Hawaii by the arguments of " a gang of sugar speculators in pursuit of profit." Fuess, *op. cit.*, p. 350. If so, they must have been Hawaii sugar men, for the Hawaiian minister considered the

As early as March 15, Senator Frye and John W. Foster, the former Secretary of State, who had negotiated the annexation treaty of 1893, had seen the President and received encouragement.[77] Ten days later, McKinley granted an interview to F. M. Hatch, the Hawaiian minister, and W. O. Smith, of Honolulu, who had been sent to Washington to promote the cause of annexation, listened to their arguments for immediate action, and expressed a great interest in the subject.[78] Hatch and Smith were evidently well satisfied with the result of the interview. The next day Smith was writing:

The difference between the attitude of the present administration and the last one is like that of the difference between daylight and darkness. The present is the friendly one, waiting for the best opportunity and most favorable means of presenting the matter. The other was irrevocably opposed to it.[79]

Nevertheless, Hatch and Smith had ample cause for worry. Even before Congress convened in special session to revise the tariff, it was evident that sugar interests in the United States would put up a vigorous fight not only against annexation but against even the continuance of the reciprocity

---

sugar interests in the United States the most formidable opponents of annexation. *Infra,* note 107.

[77] Hatch to Cooper, March 15, 1897. Spaulding Collection.

[78] Memorandum of an Interview of F. M. Hatch and W. O. Smith with President McKinley, March 25, 1897. *Ibid.* Hatch and Smith reverted to the time-worn argument that British influence was at work in Hawaii to prevent annexation. Smith had arrived in Washington March 2, with commission and instructions empowering himself and Hatch to conclude a treaty of annexation. Lorrin A. Thurston and General A. S. Hartwell, another annexationist, were also there—all very busy, as Smith reported. Smith to Cooper, March 15, 26, 1897. *Ibid.*

[79] Smith to Cooper, March 26, 1897. *Ibid.*

treaty.[80] Both McKinley and Mark Hanna, though favorable to annexation, insisted that tariff revision must be put ahead of all else in the special session, and, as it turned out, only the President's personal intervention saved the reciprocity treaty from destruction at the hands of Congress in the course of the new tariff legislation.[81] Meanwhile, the Hawaiian Republic was facing a serious situation in its relations with Japan. The Island Empire had lodged a vigorous protest over the Hawaiian Government's measures to restrict Japanese immigration—restriction to which, as Hatch wrote from Washington, the only alternative was to " abandon the country to Japan " [82]—and a crisis in this quarter seemed rapidly approaching. More than ever before, annexation seemed a matter of life or death to Occidental civilization in Hawaii. " It is the white race against the yellow, . . ." said the Honolulu *Star*. " Nothing but annexation can save the islands." [83]

In reality, we may well believe that Japan was unintentionally providing the incentive to annexation which Great Britain had refrained from contributing in 1893.[84] The potential utility of the Japanese attitude was clear to Mr. Hatch in Washington, who advised that all newspaper correspondents in Honolulu be kept informed of the Japanese negotiations.[85] Certainly one young member of McKinley's

[80] Hatch to [Cooper (?)], February 6, 1897. *Ibid.*

[81] Hatch to Cooper, March 15, April 2, July 1, 1897. *Ibid.*

[82] Hatch to Cooper, April 13, 1897. *Ibid.* See T. A. Bailey, " Japan's Protest against the Annexation of Hawaii," *Journal of Modern History*, III, 46-61.

[83] Quoted in *Literary Digest*, XIV, 771 (April 24, 1897).

[84] *Supra*, pp. 149-150.

[85] Hatch to Cooper, April 13, May 11, 1897. Spaulding Collection.

administration reacted in the desired manner. Theodore
Roosevelt, Assistant Secretary of the Navy, was almost in
a state of panic.

> If I had my way [he wrote Captain Mahan] we would
> annex those islands tomorrow. . . . I have been getting
> matters in shape on the Pacific Coast just as fast as I have
> been allowed. My own belief is that we should act instantly
> before the two new Japanese warships leave England. I
> would . . . *hoist our flag over the island leaving all de-*
> *tails for after action.* . . . I believe we should build the
> Nicaragua Canal at once, and . . . should build a dozen
> new battleships, half of them on the Pacific Coast. . . . I
> am fully alive to the danger from Japan.[86]

Possibly some of Roosevelt's alarm was shared by his
official superiors. At any rate, with work on the tariff bill
nearing completion McKinley gave his consent to the negotiation of a treaty of annexation with Hawaii.[87] Secretary
Sherman was not at first informed of the decision. The
negotiation was placed in the hands of Assistant Secretary W. R. Day, who in turn entrusted the drafting of the

[86] Pringle, *Theodore Roosevelt, a Biography,* p. 171. May 3,
1897. The italics are Pringle's.

[87] W. O. Smith had reported in March that Foster, Senator Frye,
and President McKinley, in their conference on Hawaiian annexation, had all agreed that annexation by joint resolution was preferable
to the negotiation of a treaty. Smith to Cooper, March 15, 1897.
Spaulding Collection. Why this plan was given up is unknown.
Foster, in referring to the subsequent shift, in 1898 (see *infra,*
p. 225), from treaty to joint resolution, states that he was
reluctant to see the latter method used " because of its evasion of
the constitutional provision and the creation of a bad precedent,"
but that he felt that the action was justified by the exigencies of
war. Foster, *Diplomatic Memoirs,* II, 174. The transcripts in the
Spaulding Collection contain nothing from Hatch on the actual
negotiation of the treaty.

treaty to Foster.[88] The treaty thus drawn was signed June 16, 1897, by Secretary Sherman and F. M. Hatch, Lorrin A. Thurston, and Wm. A. Kinney for the Hawaiian Government, and was sent to the Senate on the same day with a report signed by Sherman and a special message from the President.[89] The treaty resembled closely that of 1893, the principal difference being its omission of provision for compensation to the former Queen and the heir presumptive.[90]

On July 14, Senator Davis, from the Committee on Foreign Relations, reported the treaty to the Senate with a resolution consenting to ratification,[91] but no further action upon it was taken before the adjournment of Congress —a result which McKinley had perhaps expected [92]—but

[88] L. B. Shippee and R. B. Way, *William Rufus Day,* in Bemis (ed.), *American Secretaries of State,* IX, 34.

[89] *Senate Report* No. 681, 55th Cong., 2d sess., contains the text of the treaty, Sherman's report, and the Presidential message.

[90] Liliuokalani, at the time resident in Washington, was quick to file with Secretary Sherman a protest against the treaty. *Hawaii's Story by Hawaii's Queen,* pp. 354-356. The comment of another objector is worth recording. " Did you ever see such a preposterous thing as the Hawaiian business?" wrote Cleveland to Richard Olney. " . . . there ought to be soberness and decency enough in the Senate to save us from launching upon the dangerous policy which is foreshadowed by the pending treaty; but I am prepared for almost anything." *Letters of Grover Cleveland,* p. 478.

[91] *Journal of the Executive Proceedings of the Senate,* 55th Cong., p. 230.

[92] Carl Schurz recorded a conversation with McKinley July 1, 1897, in which Schurz reminded the President of his earlier expression adverse to annexation. McKinley replied that there was no chance of ratification during the summer and that he had sent the treaty to the Senate in order to test public opinion. This reply seems less than ingenuous. Fuess, *op. cit.,* p. 350.

the issue was again placed before the public, and, what was perhaps more important, notice was given to Japan of the intentions of the United States. Upon being informed of the signing of the treaty, the Japanese minister at Washington at once protested to Secretary Sherman, complaining that annexation would disturb the international balance in the Pacific and would endanger certain rights of Japanese subjects in Hawaii. The Department of State undertook to mollify the Japanese Government with assurances that all vested rights would be respected by the United States,[93] but in the meantime preparations were made to employ force if it should prove necessary. The commanding officer of the naval force at Honolulu was given secret instructions to do everything in his power to cultivate friendly relations with the Japanese and to promote an amicable settlement of the difficulty; but at the first sign of a resort to force on the part of Japan, he was to take possession of the islands, hoist the United States flag, and proclaim a provisional protectorate.[94] Meanwhile, the commanding officer of the battleship " Oregon," on the Pacific coast, was instructed to keep his ship coaled and ready to proceed at short notice to Honolulu,[95] and the naval attaché at Yokohama was told to " forewarn Department by telegraph of increase if any of Japanese fleet at Hawaii or other sig-

[93] The correspondence with Japan is summarized in John Bassett Moore, *Digest of International Law*, I, 504-509. See also Bailey, *loc. cit.*

[94] Long to Commander in Chief, U. S. Naval Force, Pacific Station, July 12, 1897. *Confidential Correspondence*, II, 314 (MS in Navy Dept.). Similar instructions went to the U. S. Minister in Honolulu. Bailey, *op. cit.*, p. 50.

[95] *Confidential Correspondence*, II, 317.

nificant movements of Japanese forces." [96] These preparations were made known to Hatch, who, after a conference
with the Assistant Secretary of State reported that the United
States would give full protection to Hawaii while the treaty
was pending.[97] Fortunately, no drastic action was required.
The Japanese Government accepted the friendly assurances
of the United States and in December withdrew its protest.

Hawaiian annexation was not the only expansionist
scheme that revived under the blessing of the Republican
platform and the complacency of William McKinley.
W. O. Smith had been informed in March that " the Nicaraguan Canal matter [was] to be taken up at the point
where it was left when Mr. Cleveland withdrew it from
Congress during his first term." [98] Senator Lodge, on
March 18, 1897, introduced a resolution calling upon the
Senate Foreign Relations Committee to inquire into the
chances of purchasing from Denmark the islands of St.
Thomas, St. John, and St. Croix.[99] President Heureaux, of
the Dominican Republic, recalling the friendly attitude of
the last Republican administration, was presently to renew
his attempt to dispose of Samana Bay to the United States
at a profit to himself.[100] Looking in a different direction
and to a much greater distance, Assistant Secretary Roosevelt was initiating those preparations which, in the event
of war with Spain over the Cuban question, would launch

[96] *Ciphers Sent,* I, 461, July 14, 1897 (MS in Navy Dept.).

[97] Hatch to Cooper, July 10, 17, 1897. Spaulding Collection.

[98] Smith to Cooper, March 15, 1897. *Ibid.*

[99] Tansill, *op. cit.,* p. 209. Lodge had introduced a similar resolution January 3, 1896, and had tried in vain to interest Olney in
the subject. *Ibid.,* pp. 207-208.

[100] Welles, *op. cit.,* II, 528-529.

an attack upon the Philippine Islands and lay an Asiatic empire at the feet of the United States.[101]

The time was not yet ripe for these things; the country was not ready. And, as if in a deliberate attempt to prepare it in spirit for coming events, a group of able writers let loose upon the American public a flood of expansionist propaganda. In *Harper's Magazine* for September and October, 1897, Captain Mahan published two articles entitled, respectively, "A Twentieth-Century Outlook" and "Strategic Features of the Caribbean Sea and the Gulf of Mexico." [102] In the first, he predicted, for the twentieth century, a colossal struggle of European and American against Asiatic civilization and religion. While European armies held the land frontier, American sea power would be the natural defender on the Pacific side, but to function effectively American sea power must hold securely the isthmian canal, the approaches to it through the Caribbean, and its western outpost, the Hawaiian Islands. With its philosophic tone, its strong undercurrent of religious mysticism, and its militaristic lesson, this seemed to Theodore Roosevelt "a really noble article." [103] The second article

[101] September 20, 1897, Roosevelt wrote to his superior, Secretary Long, of the advisability of a naval campaign against the Philippines. J. B. Bishop, *Theodore Roosevelt and His Time*, I, 83. At the same time he was pulling wires to have Dewey appointed to the command of the Asiatic squadron. *Cf.* Pringle, *op. cit.*, p. 178. Whether Roosevelt was at this time contemplating the actual conquest of the Philippines or merely the most effective means of waging war against Spain, is not entirely clear.

[102] Both are reprinted in *The Interest of America in Sea Power, Present and Future*, pp. 217-268 and 271-314.

[103] Lodge (ed.), *Selections from the Correspondence of Theodore Roosevelt and Henry Cabot Lodge*, I, 274. Excerpts from this article

was an analysis of the relative strategic value of the various naval strongholds, actual or potential, upon the eastern approaches to the isthmus, and reached conclusions highly favorable to Cuba and somewhat less so to Samana Bay and St. Thomas. There was no preaching in this article, but since the author had previously demonstrated that control of the Caribbean was essential to the preservation of Western civilization, his scientific analysis of how that area could be controlled led to practical conclusions which only a dull American could miss.

A civilian who fully shared Mahan's enthusiasm for expansion was Albert Shaw, editor of the *Review of Reviews*. From May, 1897, to February, 1898, the editorial pages of that magazine played frequently upon the importance of annexing Hawaii, constructing a canal, and acquiring or controlling key islands in the Caribbean—all as means toward the eventual domination of the Pacific, which was to be " the theater of great events in the coming century." [104] On the Pacific Coast, the *Overland Monthly,* edited by Horatio Bridge, was equally imbued with expansionist sentiment. Declaring frankly for a breaking away from the ancient tradition embodied in Washington's Farewell Address, the *Overland* announced itself an advocate " of the new doctrine of America's interest in external affairs, whether in the Caribbean sea, the Pacific islands, or the Orient." The subjugation of a continent had kept the American people occupied for a century.

---

occupied one and one-half pages in the *Literary Digest*, XV, 571-572 (September 11, 1897).

[104] *Review of Reviews,* XVII, 143-144 (February, 1898). *Cf. ibid.,* XV, 528 (May, 1897) ; XVI, 135 (August, 1897) ; XVII, 13 (January, 1898).

But now that the continent is subdued, we are looking for fresh worlds to conquer; and whether our conservative stay-at-homes like it or not, the colonizing instinct which has led our race in successive waves of migration is the instinct which is now pushing us out and on to Alaska, to the isles of the sea,—and beyond.[105]

To what extent such literature expressed or influenced public sentiment, it is obviously impossible to determine. It is significant, however, that a Trans-Mississippi Congress, meeting at Salt Lake City in July, 1897, and presided over by William Jennings Bryan, although chiefly concerned with the interests of agriculture, mining, and the development of the natural resources of the West, passed resolutions favoring the construction of the Nicaragua Canal as an American enterprise, the annexation of Hawaii, and the independence of Cuba.[106]

A new spirit of self-assertiveness was animating the American people as the year of 1898 dawned. The elements that would produce a new America were present,

[105] *Overland Monthly,* XXXI, 177-178 (February, 1898). For other magazine articles expressing a similar spirit see John R. Procter, "Hawaii and the Changing Front of the World," *Forum,* XXIV, 34-45, Commodore G. W. Melville (Chief Engineer, U. S. N.), "Our Future in the Pacific—What We Have There to Hold and Win," *North American Review,* CLXVI, 281-296.

[106] *Literary Digest,* XV, 428 (August 7, 1897). Delegates at the Congress represented eighteen states and three territories, and, in addition, the prospective territory of Hawaii. The Hawaiian delegates were Lorrin A. Thurston and William A. Kinney, who had just served as annexation commissioners in Washington. They were given ample time in which to present the cause of annexation. Thurston, *Memoirs of the Hawaiian Revolution,* pp. 579-580. The *Review of Reviews* (XVI, 135) welcomed the adoption of the resolutions mentioned as demonstrating that expansionist ideas were not confined to the Republican Party.

but as in the case of certain chemical reactions, heat was
necessary to precipitate the new combination—in this instance, the heat of war. This was clearly seen by some as
the events of February and March pointed more and more
toward war with Spain. It was seen specifically by the
Hawaiian minister in relation to the annexation treaty. The
united force of the anti-imperialists on principle and the
representatives of American sugar interests proved too
strong in the Senate to be overcome.[107] After nearly three
months of fruitless effort to make sure of the necessary
sixty votes, the friends of the treaty, early in March, confessed defeat,[108] and turned to the alternative plan. On
March 16, the Senate Foreign Relations Committee reported
to the Senate a joint resolution of annexation.[109] Several
weeks earlier, Hatch had expressed the opinion that intervention by the United States in Cuba "would carry our
treaty through on the jump." [110] Now, referring to the
probable action by joint resolution and the prospect that
the report on the sinking of the "Maine" would delay
matters, he wrote:

---

[107] Hatch attributed opposition to the treaty chiefly to Claus
Spreckels, who had now become deeply involved in the California
beet sugar industry (New York *Journal of Commerce,* May 26,
1897), to other spokesmen for that industry, and to the Sugar
Trust. Hatch to Cooper, July 21, December 22, 1897; Memorandum
by Hatch on Spreckels's sugar interests, December 27, 1897. Spaulding Collection. The American Federation of Labor also adopted
resolutions against annexation—wholly, Thurston believed, because
of the contract labor situation in Hawaii. L. A. Thurston to S. B.
Dole, December 23, 1897. *Ibid.*

[108] Hatch to Cooper, March 3, 6, 1898. *Ibid.*

[109] *Senate Report* No. 681, 55th Cong., 2d sess.

[110] Hatch to Cooper, February 10, 1898. Spaulding Collection.

We can well afford to wait until that matter is disposed of. If I mistake not, developments in that connection are sure to help us.[111]

" Developments in that connection " would forward other expansionist plans as well. On January 31, Senator Lodge had written to Henry White, with an apparent prescience that must have startled Lodge himself two weeks later: " There may be an explosion any day in Cuba which would settle a great many things." [112] The explosion he had in mind was presumably political—not the kind that destroyed the " Maine." But some things might be settled even while the explosion was preparing, and the Massachusetts Senator was more than ready to do his part. It was he and Roosevelt who, on February 25, in the absence of Secretary Long, sent off orders to Dewey, in Hongkong, directing him, in the event of war, to begin " offensive operations in the Philippine Islands." [113] Contemporaneously, Lodge's other scheme, for the purchase of the Danish West Indies, seemed on the point of consummation. The consent of the Danish Government was secured, a price of $5,000,000 was agreed upon, and on March 25, 1898, McKinley's Cabinet gave its approval to the proposed transaction. On March 31, Lodge introduced in the Senate a bill giving authority for the purchase and providing the necessary funds. With the bill he submitted a report, drawn by himself, declaring that the islands " occupy a commanding strategic position, and are of incalculable value to the United States," [114] and in

---

[111] Hatch to Cooper, March 6, 1898. *Ibid.*

[112] Nevins, *Henry White, Thirty Years of Diplomacy*, p. 130.

[113] W. Millis, *The Martial Spirit*, pp. 111-112; Bishop, *op. cit.*, I, 86; Lodge, *op. cit.*, I, 349.

[114] Lodge's Report is printed in the appendix to *Senate Exec. Report* No. 1, 57th Cong., 1st sess.

the ensuing debate he assured the Senate that he had talked with the President, who deemed the Danish islands of inestimable value in the event of hostilities with Spain. Apparently the purchase would have been consummated at this time but for the unwillingness of the Danish Government to commit what, after war began, it considered would constitute a " diplomatic discourtesy to Spain." [115]

No such scruples deterred President Heureaux of the Dominican Republic, who at this time suggested to the United States consul at Santo Domingo that if the United States cared to take forcible possession of Samana Bay for a base of operations against Spain, he would interpose no serious objection. This proposal the State Department thought worth referring to the Secretary of the Navy, who replied that his department did not " care to acquire a coaling station in Samana Bay by a process of seizure." [116] We may guess that Roosevelt, had he been in charge, would have answered differently.

McKinley's war message went to Congress on April 11th. On the 19th Congress issued its ultimatum to Spain, and on the 25th declared the existence of a state of war. On the first of May Dewey destroyed the Spanish fleet in Manila Bay. In the interim between the declaration of hostilities and Dewey's opening shot at Manila, an orator in Boston and an editor in San Francisco undertook to interpret the meaning of the war to the United States. On April 27, Albert J. Beveridge delivered an oration upon President

[115] For this whole episode, see Tansill, *op. cit.*, pp. 212-215.

[116] Secretary of Navy to Secretary of State, May 12, 1898. Dept. of State, *Miscellaneous Letters*, 1898, May, II. Welles, *op. cit.*, II, 528-531.

Grant at the Middlesex Club in Boston. Declaring that Grant "never forgot that we are a conquering race, and that we must obey our blood and occupy new markets and new lands," the speaker led up to the existing crisis.

American factories are making more than the American people can use; American soil is producing more than they can consume. Fate has written our policy for us; the trade of the world must and shall be ours. And we will get it as our mother [England] has told us how. We will establish trading-posts throughout the world as distributing points for American products. We will cover the ocean with our merchant marine. We will build a navy to the measure of our greatness. Great colonies governing themselves, flying our flag and trading with us, will grow about our posts of trade. Our institutions will follow our flag on the wings of commerce. And American law, American order, American civilization, and the American flag will plant themselves on shores hitherto bloody and benighted, but by those agencies of God henceforth to be made beautiful and bright.

Rejoicing that the stars and stripes were about to float " over an Isthmian canal, . . . over Hawaii, . . . over Cuba and the southern seas," the orator went on to point out that " the true field of our earliest operations " was Spain's weakly defended island empire in the Philippines: " The Philippines are logically our first target." [117]

[117] Claude G. Bowers, *Beveridge and the Progressive Era,* pp. 67-70. Mr. Bowers remarks: " At that moment, unknown to a single man in the room, and to few in the Nation, Admiral Dewey was moving on the waters upon the Philippines. . . . " If Beveridge's audience were ignorant of Dewey's plans, it was because they did not read the papers. The New York *Sun,* for example, had predicted the attack on Manila Bay on March 6, 1898, and again on April 3, and on April 27, the day of Beveridge's speech, had printed a dispatch from Hongkong, dated April 26, to the effect that Dewey would sail from Mirs Bay for Manila on the 27th.

In similar strain, the *Overland Monthly,* of San Francisco, in an editorial written before Dewey's victory, predicted the annexation of Cuba, the Philippines, and Hawaii:

So that almost without knowing it we shall have started forth on our colonizing ventures fully equipped with widely scattered possessions, a navy strong enough to protect them, and a newly roused martial spirit in our hearts made strong and enduring by victory. And if what is bred in the bone breaks out in the flesh, our British ancestry will see to it that we keep what we get, and get more when we can.[118]

The spirit embodied in Beveridge's speech and the *Overland* editorial was apparent to observers across the Atlantic. In the April issue of *Blackwood's Edinburgh Magazine,* " The Looker-on," had commented upon

the rising spirit in American affairs, which, with its fleets building, and its enthusiasms kindling, and its hidden spark in the heart of the most orthodox citizen, is preparing as much of a change as we saw in Japan the other day, and perhaps as sudden.[119]

Now, with the opening of the war with Spain, the same writer remarked:

Unless all signs deceive, the American Republic breaks from the old moorings, and sails out to be a " world-power." [120]

[118] *Overland Monthly,* XXXI, 472 (May, 1898).
[119] *Blackwood's Edinburgh Magazine,* CLXIII, 563-565.
[120] *Ibid.,* p. 703 (May, 1898).

VII

THE BUSINESS POINT OF VIEW

The joint resolutions of Congress embodying the ultimatum to Spain had, in the amendment offered by Senator Teller, disclaimed any intention of exercising " sovereignty, jurisdiction or control " over Cuba and had declared it to be the purpose of the United States, after pacifying the island, to leave its government and control to the Cuban people.[1] To some, at least, of the expansionist group, this act of renunciation seemed unfortunate[2]; yet they considered it no very serious obstacle to their plans. Whitelaw Reid, of the New York *Tribune,* in an interview published in the Paris *Matin,* announced that the United States had assumed responsibility for the maintenance of good government in Cuba, and that if the insurgents should prove incapable of conducting such a government, American responsibility would continue.[3] But the Teller Amendment referred to Cuba alone; it said nothing of Spain's other possessions, and it is apparent that no serious expansionist felt bound to apply the spirit of the amendment elsewhere than in Cuba.

[1] *Stat. L.,* XXX, 738-739. That Senator Teller, whose enthusiasm for expansion has been noted above (pp. 179, 204) should have been the one to propose this amendment is curious. A plausible account of its origin is given in Horatio Rubens, *Liberty, the Story of Cuba,* pp. 339-341.

[2] *Cf.* Whitelaw Reid to McKinley, April 19, 1898. R. Cortissoz, *The Life of Whitelaw Reid,* II, 222-223.

[3] *Ibid.,* p. 224.

Beveridge's speech, delivered a few days after the declaration of war, was quoted in the last chapter. Heartily in accord with him were such other young enthusiasts as Theodore Roosevelt and Henry Cabot Lodge—men thoroughly imbued with the concept of the "new manifest destiny." Three days after the battle of Manila Bay, Lodge wrote to Henry White: "We hold the other side of the Pacific, and the value to this country is almost beyond recognition." On no account, he said, must we "let the islands go . . . they must be ours under the treaty of peace." [4] Shortly thereafter, in response to an appeal from Roosevelt not to "make peace until we get Porto Rico, while Cuba is made independent and the Philippines at any rate taken from the Spaniards," Lodge assured his Rough Rider correspondent that a substantial military force would be sent to the Philippines, that Puerto Rico would surely not be forgotten, and that

Unless I am utterly and profoundly mistaken the Administration is now fully committed to the large policy that we both desire.[5]

A few days later he made it clear that Hawaii, too, was embraced in the "large policy." [6] Whitelaw Reid, also, undertook to inform the European public that the United States had no thought of relinquishing either the Philippines or Puerto Rico.[7]

[4] Nevins, *Henry White*, p. 136.

[5] Lodge, *Selections from the Correspondence of Theodore Roosevelt and Henry Cabot Lodge*, I, 299, 300.

[6] *Ibid.*, p. 302. *Cf.* Roosevelt to Lodge (*ibid.*, p. 309): "You must get Manila and Hawaii; you must prevent any talk of peace until we get Porto Rico and the Philippines as well as secure the independence of Cuba. . . ."

[7] Cortissoz, *op. cit.*, II, 224.

In other words, the young imperialists who had espoused the " large policy " of Lodge and Roosevelt knew precisely what use to make of the war with Spain. Their aims were partly patriotic or political: they would build up American sea power and claim for the United States its proper place among the nations of the world. But such a program was inseparable from economics. Sea power, as expounded by Mahan, was largely a matter of the control of world trade, and world trade, especially the trade of the Pacific, had figured largely in the various expansionist pronouncements which have been quoted in this study. Territorial expansion, in the minds of men like Lodge and Beveridge, found its justification largely in the control which it would give over markets and trade routes. It is pertinent, therefore, to enquire whether the war with Spain and the accompanying acquisition of insular possessions were, in reality, the results of economic pressure; whether, that is, business interests in the United States shared the aspirations of such intellectuals as Mahan, Lodge, Roosevelt, and Beveridge.

So reliable a scholar as Professor H. U. Faulkner has asserted that " the great cause for the war " with Spain is to be found in the fact that by 1898 the United States was " sufficiently advanced for financial imperialism," implying that the war was fought for markets and fields for investment.[8] This interpretation was directly contradicted by the late James Ford Rhodes, who declared quite as categorically that " the financial and business interests of the country were opposed to the war." [9] We may well enquire, there-

[8] H. U. Faulkner, *American Economic History*, pp. 624-625.
[9] J. F. Rhodes, *The McKinley and Roosevelt Administrations*, p. 55.

fore, what was, in reality, the attitude of American business both to the war (or to the intervention in Cuba, which brought on the war) and to the question of territorial expansion.[10]

We may begin with a generalization, the evidence for which will be presented as the chapter proceeds. American business, in general, had strongly opposed action that would lead to war with Spain. American business had been either opposed or indifferent to the expansionist philosophy which had arisen since 1890. But almost at the moment when the war began, a large section of American business had, for reasons that will become apparent, been converted to the belief that a program of territorial expansion would serve its purposes. Hence business, in the end, welcomed the " large policy " and exerted its share of pressure for the retention of the Spanish islands and such related policies as the annexation of Hawaii and the construction of an isthmian canal.

One public man to whom the welfare of American business was of so much concern that he may almost be considered its spokesman in the Senate, was McKinley's friend, Mark Hanna. No one was more unwilling than he to see the United States drift into war with Spain. To Hanna, in the words of his biographer, " the outbreak of war seemed to imperil the whole policy of domestic economic amelioration which he placed before every other object of political action." [11] Hanna's attitude appears to have

[10] The discussion which follows is adapted, with slight changes, from the writer's article, "American Business and the Spanish-American War," *Hispanic American Historical Review*, XIV, 163-201.

[11] Croly, *Marcus Alonzo Hanna*, p. 278.

been identical with that of leading business men. This conclusion is based not only upon the few published biographies of such men,[12] but also upon the study of a large number of financial and trade periodicals, of the proceedings of chambers of commerce and boards of trade, and of material in the *Miscellaneous Files* of the Department of State, containing numerous letters and petitions from business men and organizations.

That business sentiment, especially in the East, was strongly anti-war at the close of 1897 and in the opening months of 1898, is hardly open to doubt. Wall Street stocks turned downward whenever the day's news seemed to presage war and climbed again with information favorable to peace.[13] Bulls and bears on the market were those who anticipated, respectively, a peaceable and a warlike

[12] *Cf.* A. Carnegie, *Autobiography of Andrew Carnegie*, chap. xxviii; B. Alderson, *Andrew Carnegie: The Man and His Work*, pp. 101-102; C. Adler, *Jacob H. Schiff, His Life and Letters*, I, 308-309; J. G. Pyle, *Life of James J. Hill*, II, 77; G. Kennan, *E. H. Harriman*, I, 170; II, 1; H. A. Gibbons, *John Wanamaker*, I, 371-376. Carnegie, Schiff, and Hill were strongly anti-war and anti-imperialist. John Wanamaker supported the war and raised a regiment (which never saw service); there is no evidence in his biography that he was interested in annexations. Harriman's Union Pacific Railroad profited from American operations in the Philippines. It is not hinted that he foresaw this or worked for it. His business relations with the Far East did not begin till 1905. Biographies of Morgan, Rockefeller, Frick, Robert Bacon do not discuss the attitude of those men to the war or imperialism. For an apparently contradictory opinion of the attitude of business men, expressed by Thomas Beer, see *infra,* note 51.

[13] *Cf. Wall Street Journal,* December 3, 31, 1897; January 25, April 21, 1898; *Railway World,* XLII, 105, 217 (January 29, February 26, 1898).

solution of the Cuban question.[14] The " jingo," in Congress
or the press, was an object of intense dislike to the editors
of business and financial journals,[15] who sought to counter-
act his influence by anti-war editorials in their columns.[16]
Boards of trade and chambers of commerce added their
pleas for the maintenance of peace to those of the business
newspapers and magazines.[17] So marked, indeed, was the
anti-war solidarity of the financial interests and their spokesmen that the jingoes fell to charging Wall Street with want
of patriotism. Wall Street, declared the Sacramento *Evening Bee* (March 11, 1898), was "the colossal and aggre-
gate Benedict Arnold of the Union, and the syndicated

[14] *Wall Street Journal*, December 31, 1897; February 17, 1898.

[15] *Ibid.*, November 18, December 3, 1897; *Railway World, loc.
cit.*; *Banker and Tradesman*, XXVI, 78 (February 23, 1898);
American Banker, LXIII, 528 (March 30, 1898); *Journal of Commerce and Commercial Bulletin*, November 27, 1897; *Commercial
and Financial Chronicle*, LXV, 597 (October 2, 1897).

[16] *Journal of Commerce and Commercial Bulletin*, February 28,
1898; *Commercial and Financial Chronicle*, April 2, 1898; Boston
Journal of Commerce, LII, 40 (April 16, 1898); *Drugs, Oils and
Paints*, XIII, 401 (April, 1898); *Railway World*, XLII, 241-242
(March 5, 1898); *Banker and Tradesman, loc. cit.*; *Daily Com-
mercial News and Shipping List*, March 25, 1898.

[17] Chamber of Commerce of the State of New York, *Fortieth
Annual Report, 1897-1898*, p. 127; Boston Chamber of Commerce,
Thirteenth Annual Report, 1898, pp. 115-116; Baltimore Board of
Trade, *Report of President and Directors for Year Ending September
30, 1898*, p. 67; Philadelphia Board of Trade, *Sixty-Sixth Annual
Report*, pp. 50-51; Cleveland Chamber of Commerce, *Fiftieth Year*,
p. 66; Indianapolis Board of Trade, *Annual Report for Year Ending
June 1, 1898*, p. 20. Of the resolutions printed in these reports,
some spoke out strongly against war; others merely commended
President McKinley's conservative course in seeking a peaceful
solution of the Cuban question.

Judas Iscariot of humanity." Senator Thurston, of Nebraska, charged that opposition to war was found only
among the " money-changers," bringing from the editor of
The American Banker the reply that " there is not an intelligent, self-respecting and civilized American citizen anywhere who would not prefer to have the existing crisis cul-
minate in peaceful negotiations." [18]

This anti-war attitude on the part of several leading
financial journals continued up to the very beginning of
hostilities. The New York *Journal of Commerce and Commercial Bulletin* declared on February 28 that the only
possible excuses for war would be (1) a finding by the
naval board investigating the " Maine " disaster that the
ship had been destroyed by an official act of the Spanish
Government; or (2) a refusal by Spain to make reparation
if the board should hold that she had failed to exercise
due diligence in safeguarding the vessel. Either of these
events it held to be almost inconceivable. The *Commercial
and Financial Chronicle* expressed the belief on March 12
that the opposition of the financial interests would yet prevent war; and on April 2 the same journal branded as
" monstrous " the proposition to settle the Cuban and
" Maine " questions by war while the slightest chance remained for a peaceful solution. On April 16, after the
House of Representatives had passed the Cuban resolutions,
the Boston *Journal of Commerce* declared: " Sober second
thought had but little to do with the deliberations. . . .
The members were carried off their feet by the war fever

[18] *American Banker, loc. cit.*

that had been so persistently worked up since the Maine explosion. . . ." [19]

The reasons for this attitude on the part of business are not far to seek. Since the panic of 1893 American business had been in the doldrums. Tendencies toward industrial revival had been checked, first by the Venezuela war scare in December, 1895, and again by the free silver menace in 1896.[20] But in 1897 began a real revival, and before the end of the year signs of prosperity appeared on all sides. The New York *Commercial* conducted a survey of business conditions in a wide variety of trades and industries, from which it concluded that, " after three years of waiting and of false starts, the groundswell of demand has at last begun to rise with a steadiness which leaves little doubt that an era of prosperity has appeared." January, 1898, said the same article, is " a supreme moment in the period of transition from depression to comparative prosperity." [21] This note of optimism one meets at every turn, even in such a careful and conservative sheet as the *Commercial and Financial Chronicle*. As early as July, 1897, this paper remarked: " We appear to be on the eve of a revival in business "; and in December after remarking upon the healthy condition of the railroads and the iron industry, it concluded: " In brief, no one can study the industrial conditions of today in America without a feel-

[19] *Com. and Fin. Chron.*, LXVI, 641; Boston *Jour. of Com.*, LII, 40.

[20] G. H. Hull, *Industrial Depressions . . . or Iron the Barometer of Trade*, pp. 161-173.

[21] New York *Commercial*, January 3, 1898. The only flaw in the picture was continued depression in the cotton goods industry.

ing of elation. . . ." [22] The *Wall Street Journal* found only two " blue spots " in the entire country: Boston, which suffered from the depressed demand for cotton goods, and New York, where senseless rate cutting by certain railroads caused uneasiness. " Throughout the west, southwest and on the Pacific coast business has never been better, nor the people more hopeful." [23]

A potent cause for optimism was found in the striking expansion of the American export trade. A volume of exports far in excess of those of any recent year, a favorable balance of trade of $286,000,000, and an especially notable increase in exports of manufactures of iron, steel, and copper, convinced practically every business expert that the United States was on the point of capturing the markets of the world. " There is no question," said one journal, " that the world, generally, is looking more and more to the United States as the source of its supply for very many of the staple commodities of life." [24] Especially elated were spokesmen of the iron and steel industry. Cheaper materials and improved methods were enabling the American producer to undersell his British competitor in Europe and in the British possessions,[25] and Andrew Carnegie was talk-

[22] *Com. & Fin. Chron.*, LXV, 134, 1046 (July 24, December 4, 1897).

[23] *Wall Street Journal*, December 23, 1897.

[24] *Banker and Tradesman*, XXVI, 297 (April 20, 1898). *Cf. American Banker*, LXIII, 178 (February 2, 1898); *Age of Steel*, LXXXIII, No. 1, p. 57 (January 1, 1898); *Rand-McNally Bankers' Monthly*, XV, 19 (January, 1898); *Statistical Abstract of the U. S.*, 1931, p. 488.

[25] *Iron Age*, December 9, 1897, p. 22; *Banker and Tradesman, loc. cit.*; *Railway World*, XLI, 837 (August 21, 1897).

ing of a great shipbuilding yard near New York to take advantage of these low costs.[26] The *Iron Age,* in an editorial on " The Future of Business," foretold the abolition of the business cycle by means of a better planned economy, consolidation of railroads and industries, reduction of margins of profit, higher wages, and lower prices to consumers.[27]

To this fair prospect of a great business revival the threat of war was like a spectre at the feast. A foreign complication, thought the *Commercial and Financial Chronicle* in October, 1897, would quickly mar " the trade prosperity which all are enjoying." Six months later (April 2, 1898), after a discussion of the effect of war rumors on the stock exchange, it declared: ". . . Every influence has been, and even now is, tending strongly towards a term of decided prosperity, and that the Cuban disturbance, and it alone, has arrested the movement and checked enterprise." [28] The *Banker and Tradesman* saw in the Cuban complication the threat of a " material setback to the prosperous conditions which had just set in after five years of panic and depression." The same journal summarized a calculation made by the Boston *Transcript* showing that in February, 1898, the wave of prosperity had carried the average price of twenty-five leading stocks within $5\frac{1}{2}$ points of the high for the preceding ten years and 30 points above the low of 1896, and that the Cuban trouble had, in a little over two months, caused a loss of over ten points, or more than one-

---

[26] *Daily Commercial News and Shipping List,* March 7, 1898.
[27] *Iron Age,* December 23, 1897, pp. 19-20.
[28] *Com. & Fin. Chron.,* LXV, 597-599; LXVI, 636.

third of the recent gain.[29] " War would impede the march of prosperity and put the country back many years," said the *New Jersey Trade Review*.[30] The *Railway Age* was of the opinion that the country was coming out of a depression and needed peace to complete its recovery. " From a commercial and mercenary standpoint," it remarked, " it seems peculiarly bitter that this war should have come when the country had already suffered so much and so needed rest and peace." [31]

The idea that war could bring any substantial benefits to business was generally scouted. It would endanger our currency stability, interrupt our trade, and threaten our coasts and our commerce, thought the *Commercial and Financial Chronicle*. It would " incalculably increase the loss to business interests," said the *Banker's Magazine;* while the *United States Investor* held that war was " never beneficial from a material standpoint, that is, in the long run." [32] The *Railroad Gazette* predicted that war would result in " interruption of business enterprise of every kind, stopping new projects and diminution of the output of existing businesses and contraction of trade everywhere." Railroads would lose more than they would gain. Even arms manufacturers were not all agreed that war would be desirable.[33] Journals speaking for the iron and steel in-

[29] *Banker and Tradesman*, XXVI, 326 (April 27, 1898). *Cf. ibid,,* XXVI, 130 (March 9, 1898).

[30] *New Jersey Trade Review*, March 1, 1898.

[31] *Railway Age*, XXV, 215, 253 (April 1, 15, 1898).

[32] *Com. & Fin. Chron.*, LXVI, 308 (February 12, 1898) ; *Banker's Magazine*, LVI, 358 (March, 1898) ; *U. S. Investor*, IX, 529 (April 9, 1898).

[33] *Railroad Gazette*, XXX, 236 (April 1, 1898). As to the position of arms and ammunition manufacturers, it is interesting to

dustry also argued that war would injure business. It "would injure the iron and steel makers ten times as much as they would be benefited by the prevailing spurt in the manufacture of small arms, projectiles and steel plates for war ships," in the opinion of one of these.[34] The *American Wool and Cotton Reporter* of New York and the *Northwestern Miller* of Minneapolis agreed that war was never materially beneficial in the long run, while trade journals in Atlanta, Chattanooga, and Portland, Oregon, saw as fruits of the approaching conflict only destruction, debt, and depressed industry.[35]

Many conservative interests feared war for the specific reason that it might derange the currency and even revive the free-silver agitation, which had seemed happily dead. The subsidence of that agitation and the prospect of currency reform were among the hopeful factors at the close of 1897.[36] It was not uncommonly charged that the jin-

find a representative of a New York firm engaged in that trade writing to the Secretary of the Interior in March, 1898, in behalf of a peaceful settlement in Cuba. M. Hartley to C. N. Bliss, March 16, 17, 1898. *Miscellaneous Letters* (Dept. of State), March, 1898, II. Hartley represented Hartley and Graham, of New York, associated with the Union Metallic Cartridge Co. and Remington Arms Co.

[34] *Iron and Steel*, LXXII, No. 15, p. 10 (April 9, 1898). *Cf. Iron Age*, March 17, 1898, p. 21; *Age of Steel*, LXXXIII, No. 10 (March 5, 1898).

[35] *American Wool and Cotton Reporter*, XII, 439 (April 7, 1898); *Weekly Northwestern Miller*, XI., 667 (April 29, 1898); "*Dixie*," *A Monthly Journal Devoted to Southern Industrial Interests*, XIV, No. 5, pp. 21-23 (May, 1898); *Tradesman*, XXXIX, 60 (May 1, 1898); Portland (Ore.) *Board of Trade Journal*, XI, 6 (May, 1898).

[36] *Wall Street Journal*, November 18, December 31, 1897.

goes were animated in part by the expectation that war
would lead to inflation in paper or silver. The New York
Journal of Commerce, in an editorial on " The Breeding
Grounds of Jingoism," had called attention to the fact that
the jingoes were generally silverites, including in their number " the financiers who desire to force bankruptcy on the
country as a means of breaking down the gold standard,"
and had quoted with approval an editorial from another
paper charging that Senator Morgan's championship of the
Cuban insurgents was part of " his wild scheming in the
interest of the silver standard." [37] The *Commercial and
Financial Chronicle* endorsed this view, declaring that many
of the Cuban agitators " are only interested in the establishment of a free-silver standard, a plan which they think
war would advance." [38] Similar views were expressed by
the *American Banker* of New York, the *United States Investor* of Boston, and the *Rand-McNally Bankers' Monthly*
of Chicago. The last-named quoted from a speech of Secretary of the Treasury Gage, delivered in Chicago in February, 1898, in which he had declared that " it would be
scarcely possible for this nation to engage in war in its
present condition . . . without a suspension of specie pay-

[37] New York *Journal of Commerce and Commercial Bulletin,*
May 21, June 5, 1897. A. W. Dunn relates that Senator Pettigrew,
of South Dakota, said to him: " . . . I want a war with Spain,
because I believe it will put us on a silver basis." A. W. Dunn,
From Harrison to Harding, I, 232.

[38] *Com. & Fin. Chron.,* LXIV, 974; LXVI, 308 (May 22, 1897;
February 12, 1898). *Cf.* John D. Hicks, *The Populist Revolt,*
p. 390: " The voting of bond issues to aid in financing the war
drew fire from the Populists, who would have preferred issues of
treasury notes, . . . "

ments and a resort to further issues of Government notes."
A war of any duration, in the opinion of the *United States
Investor*, would certainly derange the currency and reduce
business to a gambling basis.[39]

Something of a freak among New York financial journals
was the *Financial Record*, which, in November, 1897, denounced " the cowardice of our Administration in refusing
the phenomenally brave Cubans the commonest rights of
belligerency " as " a disgrace to the United States," and
argued that war with Spain, far from depressing securities
or injuring business, " would vastly increase the net earn-
ing power of every security sold on our market today." [40]
The mystery of this jingo attitude is explained when we
discover that this journal had been a warm advocate of
the free coinage of silver.

Business opinion in the West, especially in the Mississippi Valley, appears to have been less opposed to war and
less apprehensive of its results than that of the Atlantic
coast. The Kansas City Board of Trade, at the beginning
of 1897, had urged recognition of Cuban independence.[41]

[39] *American Banker*, LXII, 912-913; LXIII, 394 (May 26, 1897;
March 9, 1898); *United States Investor*, IX, 368 (March 12,
1898); *Rand-McNally Bankers' Monthly*, XV, 294 (April, 1898).
T. S. Woolsey, in his *America's Foreign Policy*, pp. 13-14, remarked
that currency reform would be impeded by any unusual complication, such as a war, and added: " This, perhaps, will suggest a
certain subtle connection between Jingoism and the fiat money
advocates."

[40] *The Financial Record, An Investors' Manual*, November 4, 17,
1897.

[41] The proposal of the Kansas City Board of Trade was forwarded
with a request for endorsement, to the Philadelphia Board of Trade,
which rejected it. Philadelphia Board of Trade, *Sixty-Fourth Annual
Report*, p. 15.

The Cincinnati Chamber of Commerce, at a meeting on
March 29, 1898, adopted " amidst much enthusiasm " resolutions condemning Spain for cruelties to the Cubans and
the destruction of the " Maine " and calling for a " firm
and vigorous policy which will have for its purpose—
peacefully if we can, but with force if we must—the redress
of past wrongs, and the complete and unqualified independence of Cuba." [42] The Chicago *Economist* denied that
war would seriously hurt business or endanger the gold
standard and asserted that the liberation of Cuba, by peace
or war, would mean another star of glory for the United
States and would produce " results of the highest value to
mankind." [43] The *Rand-McNally Bankers' Monthly,* of
the same city, while opposing war, called attention to the
fact that while the war scare had demoralized the stock
market, " general business activity apparently received an
impetus." [44] Similarly the *Age of Steel* (St. Louis), while
much preferring peace, " when not secured at the price of
national honor," comforted its readers with the thought
that although foreign trade might suffer, home trade and
industries would be stimulated by war.[45] A St. Louis bank
president, Mr. Lackland, believed that war would " cause a
boom in many lines of business in this country . . . and
give employment to a large number of persons who are now
out of work." [46] The Chattanooga *Tradesman* stated on

[42] *Fiftieth Annual Report* of the Cincinnati Chamber of Commerce and Merchant's Exchange, p. 49.
[43] *The Economist, A Weekly Financial, Commercial and Real-
Estate Newspaper,* XIX, 233, 322 (February 26, March 19, 1898).
[44] *Rand-McNally Bankers' Monthly,* XV, 199-201 (March, 1898).
[45] *Age of Steel,* LXXXIII, Nos. 10, 11 (March 5, 12, 1898).
[46] St. Louis *Republic,* March 3, 1898.

March 1, 1898, that a " small prospect " of war had already
stimulated the iron trade in certain lines and had benefited
the railroads by hurrying forward shipments of grain
and other commodities in anticipation of war prices.[47]
The *Mining and Scientific Press,* of San Francisco, while
holding that, in general, war " lets loose havoc and waste,
and entails destructive expense," conceded that " to nearly
everything related to the mining industry the war will be
a stimulus." [48]

Even in New York, business men saw some rays of light
piercing the war clouds. Stock market operators, according
to the *Wall Street Journal,* just after the " Maine " explosion, " did not look for any great break in the market,
because actual war with Spain would be a very small affair
compared with the Venezuela complication with Great
Britain." Their expectation was for a drop in stocks at
the beginning of hostilities, followed by a resumption of
the recent advance. In fact, the first shock might well be
followed by a boom.[49] " The nation looks for peace,"
declared *Dun's Review,* March 5, " but knows that its
sources of prosperity are quite beyond the reach of any
attack that is possible." *Bradstreet's* contrasted the jumpi-
ness of Wall Street over war news with " the calm way
in which general business interests have regarded the cur-

[47] *The Tradesman,* XXXIX, 58 (March 1, 1898). The same
paper, however, in its May issues, denied that any permanent good
to business could result from war. *Supra,* p. 241.

[48] *Mining and Scientific Press,* LXXVI, 390 (April 9, 1898). In
the issue of April 23, it remarked that war between the two chief
copper-producing countries would occasion a boom in that metal.
Ibid., p. 438.

[49] *Wall Street Journal,* February 17, 24, 1898.

rent foreign complications," and *Dun's Review* of March 12 stated that no industry or branch of business showed any restriction, while some had been rapidly gaining, that railroads were increasing their profits while speculators sold their stocks, and that there was a growing demand for the products of all the great industries.[50]

Despite such expressions as these, there seems little reason to question the belief that an overwhelming preponderance of the vocal business interests of the country strongly desired peace. By the middle of March, however, many organs of business opinion were admitting that a war with Spain might bring no serious disaster, and there was a growing conviction that such a war was inevitable. In the Senate on March 17, Senator Redfield Proctor, of Vermont, described, from his own observation, the terrible sufferings of the Cuban " reconcentrados." Proctor was supposedly no sensationalist, and his speech carried great weight. The *Wall Street Journal* described its effect among the denizens of the Street. " Senator Proctor's speech," it said, " converted a great many people in Wall Street, who have heretofore taken the ground that the United States had no business to interfere in a revolution on Spanish soil. These men had been among the most prominent in deploring the whole Cuban matter, but there was no question about the accuracy of Senator Proctor's statements and as many of them expressed it, they made the blood boil." [51]

[50] *Dun's Review*, March 5, 12, 1898. *Bradstreet's*, XXVI, 161 (March 12, 1898). Similar views were expressed by the *Dry Goods Economist*, April 9, 1898.

[51] *Wall Street Journal*, March 19, 1898. It was at this time that W. C. Beer, attempting to estimate the strength of war sentiment for the life insurance companies, noted (in the words of Thomas

The *American Banker*, hitherto a firm opponent of intervention, remarked on March 23 that Proctor's speech
showed an intolerable state of things, in view of which it
could not understand " how any one with a grain of human
sympathy within him can dispute the propriety of a policy
of intervention, so only that this outraged people might
be set free! " It still hoped, however, for a peaceful solution, declaring that the United States ought to urge the
Cubans to accept the Spanish offer of autonomy.[52] That
this growing conviction that something must be done about
Cuba was by no means equivalent to a desire for war, was
clearly revealed a few days later. Rumors circulated to the
effect that Spain was willing to sell Cuba and that J. P.
Morgan's return from a trip abroad was connected with
plans to finance the purchase. " There is much satisfaction
expressed in Wall Street," said the *Wall Street Journal*,
" at the prospects of having Cuba free, because it is believed that this will take one of the most disturbing factors out of the situation. . . . Even if $200,000,000 is
the indemnity demanded it is a sum which the United States
could well afford to pay to get rid of the trouble." Even
$250,000,000, it was thought, would be insignificant in
comparison with the probable cost of a war.[53]

Beer) " that the solidarity of Wall Street was imperfect. John
Jacob Astor wore a buttonhole of red, white, and blue flowers.
John Gates, Thomas Fortune Ryan, Wm. Rockefeller and Stuyvesant
Fish all were sounded before March 24, and were found to be
feeling militant." Beer thought the only steady opponents of war
were the life insurance people and the small bankers. Thomas Beer,
Hanna, pp. 199-200.

[52] *American Banker*, LXIII, 489.

[53] *Wall Street Journal*, March 31, April 1, 1898.

It remains to examine the attitude of certain American business men and corporations having an immediate stake in Cuba, or otherwise liable to be directly affected by American intervention. Much American capital, as is well known, was invested in the Cuban sugar industry. Upon this industry the civil war fell with peculiarly devastating effect, not only cutting off profits on capital so invested, but also crippling a valuable carrying trade between Cuba and the United States. Naturally enough, some firms suffering under these conditions desired to see the United States intervene to end the war, though such intervention might lead to war between the United States and Spain. In May, 1897, a memorial on the subject bearing over three hundred signatures was presented to John Sherman, Secretary of State. The signers described themselves as " citizens of the United States, doing business as bankers, merchants, manufacturers, steamship owners and agents in the cities of Boston, New York, Philadelphia, Baltimore, Savannah, Charleston, Jacksonville, New Orleans, and other places, and also other citizens of the United States, who have been for many years engaged in the export and import trade with the Island of Cuba." They called attention to the serious losses to which their businesses had been subjected by the hostilities in Cuba and expressed the hope that, in order to prevent further loss, to reestablish American commerce, and also to secure " the blessings of peace for one and a half millions of residents of the Island of Cuba now enduring unspeakable distress and suffering," the United States Government might take steps to bring about an honorable reconciliation between the parties to the conflict.[54]

[54] *Miscellaneous Letters* (Dept. of State), May, 1897, II. The memorial is covered by a letter from Geo. R. Mosle (of Mosle Bros.,

Another memorial, signed by many of the same sub-scribers, was presented to President McKinley on February 9, 1898, by a committee of New York business men. It asserted that the Cuban war, which had now continued for three entire years, had caused an average loss of $100,000,000 a year, or a total loss of $300,000,000 in the import and export trade between Cuba and the United States, to which were to be added " heavy sums irretrievably lost by the destruction of American properties, or proper-ties supported by American capital in the Island itself, such as sugar factories, railways, tobacco plantations, mines and other industrial enterprises; the loss of the United States in trade and capital by means of this war being probably far greater and more serious than that of all the other parties concerned, not excepting Spain herself."

The sugar crop of 1897-1898, continued the memorial, appeared for the most part lost like its two predecessors, and unless peace could be established before May or June of the current year, the crop of 1898-1899, with all the business dependent upon it, would likewise be lost, since the rainy season of summer and fall would be required " to prepare for next winter's crop, by repairing damaged fields, machinery, lines of railways, &c." In view of the importance to the United States of the Cuban trade and of American participation " in the ownership or management of Cuban sugar factories, railways and other enterprises," the petitioners hoped that the President would deem the situation " of sufficient importance as to warrant prompt and

16 Exchange Place, New York) to Hon. John Sherman, May 17, 1897. The list of signers is headed by Lawrence Turnure & Co.; August Belmont & Co. appear near the top.

efficient measures by our Government, with the sole object of restoring peace . . . and with it restoring to us a most valuable commercial field." [55]

How much weight such pressure from special interests had with the administration there is no way of knowing. But it is to be noted that the pressure from parties directly interested was not all on one side. Mr. E. F. Atkins, an American citizen who divided his time between Boston and his sugar plantation of Soledad near Cienfuegos, Cuba, which he had developed at a cost of $1,400,000, had been able, through protection received from the Spanish Government and through a corps of guards organized and paid by himself, to continue operations throughout the period of the insurrection. He was frequently in Washington, where he had influential friends, during both the Cleveland and McKinley administrations and worked consistently against the adoption of any measures likely to provoke war.[56]

Unlike some of the sugar plantations, American-owned iron mines in Cuba continued to do active business despite the insurrection. Three American iron and manganese enterprises in the single province of Santiago claimed to have an investment of some $6,000,000 of purely American

[55] *Ibid.*, February, 1898, I. The memorial was signed by seventy persons or firms from New York and nearby cities; forty from Philadelphia; and sixty-four from Mobile. It was presented to the President on the morning of February 9, 1898, by George R. Mosle, Wm. Moore Carson, and George Turnure, and thereafter, at the President's suggestion, sent to Assistant Secretary Wm. R. Day. See accompanying letter from the committee to Mr. Day.

[56] E. F. Atkins, *Sixty Years in Cuba*, pp. 209, 212, 274, *et passim.* Atkins's attitude is illustrated by his query (p. 209) " whether the sentimental feeling of sympathy with the Cubans should outweigh the property interests amounting to some $30,000,000 of United States citizens in Cuba."

capital, a large proportion of which was in property which could easily be destroyed. " We are fully advised as to our status in case of war," wrote the representative of one company to the Assistant Secretary of State, " and that this property might be subject to confiscation or destruction by the Spanish Government." War between Spain and the United States, wrote the president of another company, " will very likely mean the destruction of our valuable plant and in any event untold loss to our Company and its American stockholders." [57] An American cork company with large interests in Spain; a New York merchant with trade in the Mediterranean and Black Sea; a Mobile firm which had chartered a Spanish ship to carry a cargo of timber—these are samples of American business interests which saw in war the threat of direct damage to themselves.[58] They are hardly offset by the high hopes of an enterprising gentleman of Norfolk, " representing a party of capitalists who are enthusiastic supporters of the Government," who applied to the State Department for a letter of marque " to enable us to lawfully capture Spanish merchant vessels and torpedo boats," adding: " We have secured option on a fine steam vessel, and on receipt of proper documents will put to sea forth with." [59]

[57] Juragua Iron Co., Ltd. (per Josiah Monroe, Secy. and Treas.) to Day, Philadelphia, April 14, 1898. *Miscellaneous Letters* (Dept. of State), April, 1898, II. Spanish-American Iron Co. (per C. F. Rand, Pres.) to Day, New York, April 8, 1898. *Ibid.,* April, 1898, I.

[58] Armstrong Cork Co. to Secretary Sherman, March 8, 1898. *Ibid.,* March, 1898, I. John Duer to Department of State (telegram), March 28, 1898; R. H. Clarke (Mobile) to Hon. J. Wheeler, March 26, 1898. *Ibid.,* March, 1898, III.

[59] C. R. Fowles to Secretary Alger, April 23, 1898. *Ibid.,* April, 1898, III.

It seems safe to conclude, from the evidence available, that the only important business interests (other than the business of sensational journalism) which clamored for intervention in Cuba were those directly or indirectly concerned in the Cuban sugar industry; that opposed to intervention were the influence of other parties (including at least one prominent sugar planter) whose business would suffer direct injury from war and also the overwhelming preponderance of general business opinion. After the middle of March, 1898, some conservative editors came to think intervention inevitable on humanitarian grounds, but many of the most influential business journals opposed it to the end.[60]

We can now turn to the question whether American business was imperialistic; whether, in other words, business opinion favored schemes for acquiring foreign territory to supply it with markets, fields for capital investment, or commercial and naval stations in distant parts of the world. American business men were not unaware of the struggle for colonies then raging among European nations. Did they feel that the United States ought to participate in that struggle?

We have seen above that the rising tide of prosperity was intimately connected with the increase in American exports, particularly of manufactured articles. That the future welfare of American industry was dependent upon the command of foreign markets was an opinion so common as to

[60] *Com. & Fin. Chron.*, LXVI, 732 (April 16, 1898); *Journal of Commerce and Commercial Bulletin*, April 23, 1898; Boston *Journal of Commerce*, April 16, 1898; *U. S. Investor*, IX, 529 (April 9, 1898).

appear almost universal. The New York *Journal of Commerce* pointed out, early in 1897, that the nation's industrial plant had been developed far beyond the needs of domestic consumption. In the wire nail industry there was said to be machinery to make four times as many nails as the American markets could consume. Rail mills, locomotive shops, and glass factories were in a similar situation. " Nature has thus destined this country for the industrial supremacy of the world," said the same paper later in the year.[61] When the National Association of Manufacturers met in New York for its annual convention in January, 1898, " the discussion of ways and means for extending this country's trade, and more particularly its export business, was, in fact, almost the single theme of the speakers," according to *Bradstreet's,* which added the comment: " Nothing is more significant of the changed attitude toward this country's foreign trade, manifested by the American manufacturer today as compared with a few years ago, than the almost single devotion which he pays to the subject of possible export-trade extension." [62]

But if business men believed, prior to the opening of the war with Spain, that foreign markets were to be secured

[61] *Journal of Commerce and Commercial Bulletin,* February 24, May 27, 1897.

[62] *Bradstreet's,* XXVI, 66 (January 29, 1898). *Cf. American Banker,* LXII, 817 (May 12, 1897); *U. S. Investor,* IX, 400-401 (March 19, 1898); *Dry Goods Economist,* January 1, 1898; *American Wool and Cotton Reporter,* XII, 380 (March 24, 1898); *Tradesman,* XXXIX, 52 (June 15, 1898). The National Board of Trade, at its annual meeting in Washington in December, 1897, recommended various measures for the further extension of export trade. *Proceedings of the 28th Annual Meeting* of the National Board of Trade, pp. 337-338.

through the acquisition of colonies, they were strangely silent about it. To the program of colonial expansion which for almost a decade had been urged by such men as Mahan, Albert Shaw, Lodge, Roosevelt, and Morgan, business had remained, to all appearances, either indifferent or antagonistic. To the business man, such a program was merely one form of dangerous jingoism. A large section of business opinion had, indeed, favored plans for the building of a Nicaraguan canal with governmental assistance,[63] and some spokesmen for business had favored annexation of the Hawaiian Islands.[64] But beyond these relatively modest projects few business men, apparently, wished to go.[65] Two

[63] The National Board of Trade, a federation of local boards of trade, chambers of commerce, etc., in all parts of the country, consistently urged construction of the canal. *Cf. Proceedings* of its 28th annual meeting, p. 335. *Cf.* also Indianapolis Board of Trade, *Annual Report for Year Ending June 1, 1898,* p. 18; Philadelphia Board of Trade, *65th Annual Report,* pp. 25-26; Merchant's Exchange of St. Louis, *Annual Statement of the Trade and Commerce of St. Louis for Year 1898,* p. 17; Chamber of Commerce of San Francisco, *48th Annual Report,* p. 18. The National Association of Manufacturers, at its January, 1897, meeting, took " strong ground in favor of the Nicaragua Canal." *Journal of Commerce and Commercial Bulletin,* January 25, 1897.

[64] *Cf. Bradstreet's* XXV, 386 (June 19, 1897); New York *Commercial,* April 30, 1898; San Francisco Chamber of Commerce, *48th Annual Report,* p. 18.

[65] Exceptions to this general rule were the *Financial Record,* which was pro-war (as shown above) and which also hailed the prospect of colonial responsibilities (June 23, 1897, March 23, 1898); and the New York *Commercial,* which thought the United States should not only annex Cuba and Puerto Rico but should also buy St. Thomas from Denmark for a naval station (March 31, April 8, 1898). The *American Banker,* in April, 1898, thought it would be good business to buy Cuba, pay for it in silver, and set

of the most important commercial journals, the New York *Journal of Commerce* and the *Commercial and Financial Chronicle,* had stoutly opposed both the canal scheme and Hawaiian annexation.[66] The former satirized the arguments of the proponents of both schemes. " We must certainly build the canal to defend the islands, and it is quite clear that we must acquire the islands . . . in order to defend the canal." The canal was not only unnecessary, but unless fortified at each end and patrolled by two fleets, it would be a positive misfortune. Such protection—" the price of jingoism "—might " easily cost us $25,000,000 a year, besides the lump sum that will be required for the original investment, and there is absolutely no excuse whatever in our commercial or our political interests for a single step in this long procession of expenses and of complications with foreign powers." [67] As for Hawaii and Cuba, neither was fit for self-government as a state,—and the American constitution provided no machinery for governing dependencies. The Hawaiian Islands would have no military value unless the United States were to build a great navy and take an aggressive attitude in the Pacific.[68] The *Com-*

---

it up as an American protectorate. It remarked: "A nation that borrows foreign capital, and in fact mortgages its resources to foreigners, must expect when it becomes unable to pay to be interfered with from without." *American Banker,* LVI, 517-520.

[66] *Com. & Fin. Chron.,* LXIV, 211-213, 1205-1207 (January 30, June 26, 1897) ; *Journal of Com. & Com. Bull.,* June 17, August 14, 1897.

[67] *Journal of Com. & Com. Bull.,* September 8, 1897.

[68] *Ibid.,* June 17, October 21, 1897. Similarly, the *U. S. Investor* regarded Hawaiian annexation as a " menace," and the *Banker and Tradesman* thought the people of Cuba were " incapable and unfit

mercial and Financial Chronicle saw in colonies only use-less outposts which must be protected at great expense, and the St. Louis *Age of Steel* warned lest the expansion of the export trade might " lead to territorial greed, as in the case of older nations, the price of which in armaments and militarism offsets the gain made by the spindle and the forge." [69]

Colonies were not only certain to bear a fruit of danger and expense; they were valueless from the commercial point of view. Did not the colonies of Great Britain afford us one of the most valuable of our export markets? [70] Did we not trade as advantageously with Guiana, a British colony, as with independent Venezuela? " Most of our ideas of the commercial value of conquests, the commercial uses of navies and the commercial advantages of political control," said the New York *Journal of Commerce,* dated back to times when colonial policies were designed to monopolize colonial trade for the mother country.[71] The *Commercial and Financial Chronicle* believed that the current European enthusiasm for colonies was based on false premises; for although trade often followed the flag, " the trade is not always with the home markets of the colonizer. England and the United States are quite as apt to slip in

---

for self-government. . . . This country does not want Cuba." *U. S. Investor,* IX, 48 (January 8, 1898) ; *Banker and Tradesman,* XXVI, 161 (March 16, 1898).

[69] *Com. & Fin. Chron.,* LXVI, 446-448 (March 5, 1898) ; *Age of Steel,* LXXXIII, No. 1, p. 57 (January 1, 1898).

[70] Baltimore Chamber of Commerce, *43rd Annual Report,* p. 11. Address of the president, Robert Ramsay, January 31, 1898.

[71] *Jour. of Com. & Com. Bull.,* January 24, 1896.

with their wares under the very Custom-House pennant of the French or German dependency." [72] Outright opposition, such as this, to the idea of colonial expansion is not common in the business periodicals examined; much more common is complete silence on the subject. Positive and negative evidence together seem to warrant the conclusion that American business in general, at the opening of 1898, was either indifferent to imperialism, or definitely opposed.

Confidence in the continued expansion of the export trade was based upon faith in the working of natural forces in a world given over largely to a system of free trade. American industry had reached a point where it could meet the world on more than even terms in both the price and the quality of its products. Given a fair chance, these products would make their own way. Government could aid them, not by acquiring colonial markets but by removing or lowering the barriers that restricted imports of raw materials and exchange commodities. To one who has in mind the subsequent tariff history of the United States, it is surprising to discover the amount of free-trade sentiment which found expression in these months of 1897-1898. The preoccupation of Congress with the raising of duties in the Dingley Act was disturbing to those interested in the export trade. " It is pitiful," said the *Journal of Commerce*, " to see the national legislature bending its whole force to readjusting the trammels of a system which can only obstruct, and closing its eyes to the manifest, though unconscious, struggling of industry for a freedom that will enable it to

[72] *Com. & Fin. Chron.*, LXV, 1147-1148 (December 18, 1897).

compete successfully in any market of the world." [73] The futility of expecting to increase exports while at the same time barring out imports was stressed by more than one writer for business journals,[74] and a change toward free trade in American policy was freely predicted. "We are gradually losing our fear of the bugaboo of cheap foreign labor," said the *Iron Age,* "and are slowly realizing that we hold the key of the position, since there are no indications that European manufacturers will ever displace us in the van of progress." The *American Machinist* declared that the recent growth in the export trade showed that in many lines the tariff was a dead letter, that goods which could be sold under the nose of the foreign producer no longer needed protection in the home market, and that the machinery interests would in all probability bring pressure to bear on Congress " toward action which will equalize these matters." [75] The Chattanooga *Tradesman* was convinced that the great development in the export of manufactures was certain to have upon tariff policy an effect " both broad and radical," and the president of the Balti-

[73] *Jour. of Com. & Com. Bull.,* May 27, 1897. Similar apprehension was expressed by the *American Banker,* LXII, 817 (May 12, 1897), and the *Railway World,* XLI, 572 (June 5, 1897).

[74] *American Banker,* LXII, 2328-2329 (December 1, 1897); *Dry Goods Economist,* January 15, 1898.

[75] *Iron Age,* December 23, 1897; *American Machinist,* quoted in *Daily Com. News & Shipping List,* September 17, 1898. *Cf. Drugs, Oils and Paints,* XIV, 88 (August, 1898), which argued that while protective tariffs might be useful, the proper object of such a tariff was to make itself unnecessary, and that many American industries which had hitherto been dependent upon protection had now reached a " stage where the tariff neither protects the industry nor profits the Government."

more Chamber of Commerce, speaking on the same theme to that body in December, 1897, predicted that " the day is not so far distant when free trade, in some measure, at least, will become part of our political faith." [76]

In a free-trade world, colonies would be of no importance. But if countries to which American producers looked for their markets should adopt restrictive policies, then a change in the American attitude might easily occur. Two events in the late fall of 1897 gave warning that the world at large might not continue hospitable to American products. The first was an address by Count Goluchowski, Austro-Hungarian Foreign Minister, to the Austro-Hungarian Delegations, in which he complained of the " destructive competition with transoceanic countries " and warned that the peoples of Europe " must fight shoulder to shoulder against the common danger, and must arm themselves for the struggle with all the means at their disposal." The twentieth century, he declared, would be a " period marked by a struggle for existence in the politico-commercial sphere," and " the European nations must close their ranks in order successfully to defend their existence." [77]

In the United States, the Austrian's pronouncement was generally interpreted as aimed principally at this country. It caused widespread comment but little serious alarm. Many papers doubted the possibility of any European co-operation to exclude American products, pointing out that a stoppage of trade would injure Europe more than the United States, since we provided Europe with necessities in

[76] *Tradesman*, XXXIX, 52 (June 15, 1898) ; Baltimore Chamber of Commerce, *43rd Annual Report*, p. 11.

[77] *Literary Digest*, XV, 964 (December 11, 1897).

return for commodities most of which were either luxuries
or articles that we could produce ourselves.[78] Even if
Europe should exclude our products, thought the New York
Commercial, we should find an outlet in those other markets
now cherished by Europe. This opinion was shared by the
Philadelphia *Ledger,* which believed that, though concerted
action in Europe might cripple our markets there, our trade
with South America and the Far East could not " be directly
disturbed through any European alliance." But the New
York *Journal of Commerce,* in a thoughtful editorial, took
a more serious view of the speech. In their determined
quest for markets, it said, the industrial nations of Europe
were following two courses: acquisition of colonies and
the enactment of discriminatory tariffs. Hitherto each country had worked alone, but now there were signs of the rise
of alliances or combinations in tariff policy. Since Austria-
Hungary had a trade of but $10,000,000 a year with the
United States, the idea put forward by Count Goluchowski
must have been initiated elsewhere, and the paper suggested
that a probable source was Russia, which had reason to
seek to restrict the markets for American staples in both
Europe and Asia.[79]

The suspicion voiced by the *Journal of Commerce* that
behind the Austrian's speech might lie concealed a threat
to the American market in the Far East seemed partially
confirmed within a few days, with the coming of news
of European aggressions in China. Under the color of re-

[78] Atlanta *Constitution,* Philadelphia *Ledger,* Houston *Post,* in
ibid., XV, 965; New York *Commercial,* January 27, 1898; *Com. &
Fin. Chron.,* LXV, 1147-1148 (December 18, 1897).

[79] *Jour. of Com. & Com. Bull.,* November 30, 1897.

taliation for the death of two German missionaries, a German force, on November 14, expelled the Chinese garrison at Tsingtau, at the mouth of Kiaochow Bay, seized the forts and occupied the port. Eight days later the German Government presented its formal demands, which included a naval station on Kiaochow Bay and the grant of the sole right to build railways and open coal mines in Shantung. By early in January, 1898, China had yielded all, and a convention to that effect was signed March 6. Meanwhile, within a week after the occupation of Tsingtau, Russian warships arrived at Port Arthur, and by May, 1898, China had agreed to the lease to Russia for twenty-five years of Port Arthur, Dalny, and other territory in the Liaotung peninsula. Compensating advantages were demanded and received by Great Britain and France, and by July 1, 1898, the partition of China had to all appearances begun.[80]

Here were deeds more ominous than any words could be. They touched American business sentiment in a particularly sensitive spot, for though American trade with China was, in 1897, less than two per cent of its total foreign trade, exports to China in that year were almost double those of 1896, and there was a widespread belief that China was to provide an exceedingly important market for the surplus products of the United States.[81] While some

[80] H. B. Morse, *The International Relations of the Chinese Empire*, III, 105-127; J. Van A. MacMurray, *Treaties and Agreements with and concerning China, 1894-1919*, I, 112-116, 119-121, 128-130, 152-153; P. Joseph, *Foreign Diplomacy in China, 1894-1900*, chaps. ix-xiv.

[81] Tyler Dennett, *Americans in Eastern Asia*, pp. 579-582; *Jour. of Com. & Com. Bull.*, May 15, 1896, February 22, December 23,

papers made light of the danger to American business presented by the Chinese crisis,[82] and others professed to see positive advantage to the United States in the development of China under European direction,[83] the less optimistic saw a probability that American trade would find itself discriminated against or excluded altogether by the partitioning powers. Mr. Charles Denby, former Minister to China, in a note published in the *American Banker,* warned that with the seizure of territory, American commercial treaties with China " fall to the ground, and spheres of influence hostile to American commerce spring into existence." [84] Similar alarm was voiced by numerous papers in all parts of the country,[85] by none more vehemently than the New York *Journal of Commerce.* This paper, whose attitude hitherto might be characterized as pacifist, anti-imperialist, and devoted to the development of commerce in a free-trade world, saw the foundation of its faith crumbling as a result of the threatened partition of China. Declaring that free access to the markets of China, with her 400,000,000 people, would largely solve the problem of the disposal of

1897, January 8, 1898. Of all markets for American manufactures, said the paper on the last date, " China is incomparably the greatest."

[82] San Francisco *Bulletin,* January 4, 1898; *Financial Record,* December 29, 1897.

[83] *American Banker,* LXIII, 9 (January 5, 1898); New York *Commercial,* January 5, 22, 1898; Baltimore *Sun,* Kansas City *Journal,* in *Literary Digest,* XVI, 31-33 (January 8, 1898); *Com. & Fin. Chron.,* LXVI, 106-107 (January 15, 1898).

[84] *American Banker,* LXII, 2489 (December 29, 1897).

[85] New Orleans *Picayune,* in *Literary Digest, loc. cit.; Age of Steel,* January 8, 29, 1898; *U. S. Investor,* IX, 48 (January 8, 1898); Birmingham *Age-Herald,* March 25, 1898; *Nation* (New York), LXVI, 122-123 (February 17, 1898).

our surplus manufactures, the *Journal* came out not only for
a stern insistence upon complete equality of rights in China,
but unreservedly also for an isthmian canal, the acquisition
of Hawaii, and a material increase in the navy—three measures which it had hitherto strenuously opposed.[86] Nothing could be more significant than the manner in which
this paper was converted in a few weeks, justifying its
change on each point by the needs of the hour in the Far
East.

Finding the Department of State, under Secretary Sherman, quite unimpressed by the seriousness of the Chinese
situation,[87] the *Journal of Commerce* itself initiated a movement to arouse the Executive to a defense of American interests. At the paper's suggestion, a Committee on American Interests in China was organized in New York to work
for concerted action by chambers of commerce in important
cities. As a direct result of this propaganda, a committee of
the Chamber of Commerce of the State of New York laid
before that body on February 3, 1898, a report on "American Treaty Rights in China " and a memorial to the Presi-

[86] *Jour. of Com. & Com. Bull.*, December 28, 1897, January 7,
1898.

[87] *Ibid.*, January 5, 1898. Secretary Sherman had been inter-
viewed by the Philadelphia *Press* and was quoted as saying that
if the Powers should partition China, it would not interest us
materially, " as the powers would gladly seize the opportunity to
trade with us. Our commercial interests would not suffer, as far
as I can see, in the least—quite the contrary." Such remarks seemed
to the editor of the *Journal of Commerce* to suggest " serious intellectual limitations." For confirmation of Secretary Sherman's indifference to the partitioning of China, see L. M. Sears, *John
Sherman*, in Bemis (ed.), *American Secretaries of State*, IX, 15,
18, 122.

dent of the United States. The report summarized the history of the acquisition of commercial rights through treaties with the Chinese Government and argued that those rights were seriously endangered by the recent aggressions of European powers. American products, it pointed out, were already virtually excluded from French Cochin China—an omen of what was to be expected elsewhere if France and other powers made good their positions on Chinese soil. " The Administration at Washington," the report continued, " seems to be supine about the present menace to those important interests of our citizens in China. . . . Under these circumstances it would seem that unless those concerned in our export trade take steps to agitate the matter and to have their interests safeguarded, nobody else will do it." The memorial to the President, which was promptly adopted by the Chamber, pictured the growing importance of American trade with China and the new dangers threatening it and respectfully urged that steps be taken " for the prompt and energetic defense of the existing treaty rights of our citizens in China, and for the preservation and protection of their important commercial interests in that Empire." [88]

[88] These documents were printed in a small pamphlet entitled " Commercial Rights of the United States in China," a copy of which is in Department of State, *Miscellaneous Letters,* June, 1898, II, accompanying a letter of E. Frazar to Secretary Day, June 17, 1898. Another document there printed is a communication from about seventy mercantile and manufacturing firms and individuals in New York, Philadelphia, Pittsburgh, Paterson, etc., urging the New York Chamber to bring the situation in China to the attention of the Department of State. The original of the memorial to the President is in *Misc. Letters,* February, 1898, I. The part played by the *Journal of Commerce* is related in the issue of June 18, 1898.

Within a few weeks similar action was taken by the Chambers of Commerce or Boards of Trade of Philadelphia, San Francisco, Baltimore, Boston, and Seattle.[89] Not content with this action, a group of merchants interested in the Eastern trade held a meeting on March 3, at 59 Wall Street, New York, to form a permanent organization for the protection of that trade. A few days later, with the cooperation of the New York Chamber of Commerce, they took steps to organize the American China and Japan Association, to foster and safeguard the interests of citizens of the United States and others concerned in the trade with those empires and to secure and disseminate information relating thereto. The organization was not perfected until June 16. By that time the battle of Manila Bay had broadened the American outlook in the Orient, and the organization followed suit, changing its title to the American Asiatic Association and including in its field of interest American trade not only in China and Japan, but also in " the Philippine Islands, and elsewhere in Asia and Oceania." Promptly upon its organization, the Association put itself into communication with the Department of State, offering its services for consultation or cooperation.[90]

[89] Philadelphia Board of Trade to the President, February 25, 1898; San Francisco Chamber of Commerce to same, March 8, 1898; Baltimore Chamber of Commerce to Secretary Sherman, March 17, 1898; Boston Chamber of Commerce to the President, March 30, 1898; Seattle Chamber of Commerce to same, April 14, 1898. Dept. of State, *Misc. Letters,* February-April, 1898.

[90] E. Frazar to Day, June 17, 1898. Dept. of State, *Misc. Letters,* June, 1898, II. Accompanying the letter is a printed constitution of the Association. *Cf.* for first steps New York *Commercial,* March 10, 1898.

In the light of this widespread and intense interest in the preservation of the Chinese market, we can perhaps understand why American business, which had been, to all appearances, anti-war and anti-imperialist, was filled with sudden enthusiasm at the news of Dewey's victory at Manila Bay. Not only did the news dissipate all fears of a long and costly war and send stock prices rapidly upward;[91] still more important, it seemed to place in American hands, all unexpectedly, the key to the trade of the Orient. The attack on the Spanish fleet at Manila had been anticipated for months and well advertised by the American press.[92] Some papers had speculated upon the value of the islands as an American colony and had foreseen that a victory there might greatly alter our relation to the imbroglio in China.[93] But for most, this thought did not occur until arrival of the news that the Spanish fleet was destroyed and Dewey safely in possession of Manila Bay. Then, at last, business men

[91] *Dun's Review,* May 7, 1898, said railway stocks had advanced on the average of $2.79 per share since the news, adding: " One day's work by the officers and men at Manila has given many days' work to thousands of people at home . . . and has placed all American industries and interests on a stronger footing for any conceivable future." *Cf. Jour. of Com. & Com. Bull.,* May 3, 1898; *Com. & Fin. Chron.,* LXVI, 874 (May 7, 1898).

[92] New York *Sun,* November 8, 1897, March 13, 1898.

[93] The *U. S. Investor,* IX, 624 (April 30, 1898) thought that such a victory, even if we did not retain the islands, " might pave the way for future interventions on the part of the United States in the affairs of the East." The *Financial Record,* May 5, 1898 (in an editorial written before receipt of the news of the battle), thought the Philippines " would be good trading material for getting our share of what is going in Asia." *Cf.* New York *Commercial,* April 27, 1898; New York *Sun,* April 29, 1898.

joined the jingoes in their acclaim of imperial conquests.
Senator Lodge's exclamation—" We hold the other side of
the Pacific, and the value to this country is almost beyond
recognition "—was matched by many a formerly conservative business journal. It was not the intrinsic value of the
Philippines or their trade that most impressed American
writers, though this angle of the subject was not over-
looked.[94] Rather, their importance appeared to lie in their
position as a gateway to the markets of Eastern Asia.

It has been shown that the aggressions of the European
powers in China had converted the New York *Journal of
Commerce* to the belief that the United States must dig
an isthmian canal, acquire Hawaii, and enlarge its navy.[95]
The same paper now took the lead in insisting that the
newly won vantage point in the Philippines be retained and
utilized to uphold American rights in China. However dis-
concerting might be our possession of Manila to European
plans in the Far East, we must deal with it as a " factor
in the protection of our interests in that part of the world."
Hitherto we had " allowed Great Britain to fight our battle

[94] The New York *Commercial,* May 7, 1898, declared the Philippines were " treasure islands "—" the richest islands in the world."
Their development by American capital, it said (June 7), would
stimulate the trade of the Pacific Coast and promote the establishment of new industries in the West. The *Daily Commercial News
and Shipping List* of San Francisco also saw great possibilities of
trade with the islands (May 13) and hailed the prospect of " Gold
in the Philippines " (June 17). *Cf.* Chattanooga *Tradesman,* May
15, 1898.

[95] Subsequently the paper had reverted at least partially to its
earlier opposition to the canal and Hawaiian annexation. Issues of
April 2 and June 25, 1898. But on May 31 it urged that control
of the Hawaiian islands was " imperative."

for an open market in China: with our flag floating within 500 miles of Hong Kong we shall be able to give that policy something more than merely moral support in the future." There was thus " introduced a most formidable element of resistance to all that France and Russia at least seem to be working for in Asia." To return the islands to Spain or to dispose of them to England or any other power, said the same paper a few days later, " would be an act of inconceivable folly in the face of our imperative future necessities for a basis of naval and military force on the Western shores of the Pacific." [96]

Endorsement of these views came rapidly from all sides. " Some broad-minded men," said the *Wall Street Journal,* May 5, " believe that the United States should retain enough interest in the Philippines to be sure of a coaling station and a naval base in Asiatic waters, under belief that the breaking up of China will make it necessary for this country to be in a position to protect, not only the existing trade with the far east, but the enormously greater trade likely to be developed in the next 25 years." The *American Banker,* of May 11, while absolving the United States from entering the war for any selfish purpose, declared that it could not relinquish the territories which it had been forced to seize, with the result that its diplomacy would no longer be a negative quantity in European counsels, " particularly

[96] *Jour. of Com. & Com. Bull.,* May 3, 4, 11, 1898. The paper held consistently to this position. August 24, 1898, it said: " We can establish ourselves as one of the Oriental powers by acquiring a really important stake in the Philippines, or we may resign ourselves to seeing the open door shut gradually in our faces." *Cf ibid.,* February 1, 1899.

not as respects the inevitable partition of the Chinese Empire. That a war with Spain," it added, " should have transpired at precisely this time, when Europe is tending to divide a considerable section of the inhabited earth, is a coincidence which has a providential air." [97] The *Banker and Tradesman* likewise discerned the hand of Providence in bestowing the Philippines upon the United States at a time when Russia, France, and Germany were threatening American trade in China, and asked whether we could rightly throw away " a possession which would be of such great advantage to us in maintaining and defending our interests in this part of the globe." It asserted later that the answer to the question of the open door in China " was given, as European nations very well know, when Dewey entered Manilla Bay and won his glorious victory." [98] Similar views appeared in the *Age of Steel*, the *Iron Age*, the *United States Investor*, and the *Financial Record*. *Bradstreet's* thought the possession of Manila would greatly accelerate the growth of American trade in Asia and predicted that that city " might in time even rival Hong Kong as a distributive trade center." The New York *Commercial*, using figures supplied by the Bureau of Statistics in Washington, pointed out that countries closely adjacent to the Philippines contained 850,000,000 people and purchased over one billion dollars worth of goods a year, mostly articles which might be grown or manufactured in the United States. " With the Philippines as a three-quarter way house, forming a superb trading station, the bulk of this trade

[97] *American Banker*, LXIII, 785.
[98] *Banker and Tradesman*, XXVI, 456, 776 (June 1, August 24, 1898).

should come to this country." [99] The New York Chamber
of Commerce, in a report on "American Interests in China,"
argued that, in face of the prospect that European spheres
of influence in China might become permanent territorial
acquisitions, the only course by which the United States
could protect her interests appeared to be active participation in politics on the " dangerous ground of the Far East "
—a participation which might be " hastened and material-
ized through our possible occupation of the Philippine
Islands." [100]

The insistence that the Philippines be retained, for the
sake of their own trade and as a gateway to Asiatic markets, was confined to no one section of the country. In
the South, business men saw in possession of the islands
assurance of the continued growth of the marketing of
American cotton goods in China.[101] The Pacific Coast, very
naturally, displayed a lively interest. In Dewey's victory,
the *Mining and Scientific Press* saw an earnest that the
coast cities would be transformed from the back door to
the front door of civilization. " The guns that destroyed
the Spanish fleet in Manila Bay thundered a warning to
the nations of our approaching commercial supremacy in
the Orient." The *Commercial Bulletin of Southern California* believed acquisition of the Philippines would greatly

[99] *Age of Steel,* May 21, 1898; *Iron Age,* June 23, 1898; *U. S.
Investor,* IX, 953, 1017 (July 2, 16, 1898) ; *Financial Record,* June
15, 1898; *Bradstreet's,* XXVI, 356 (June 4, 1898) ; New York
Commercial, June 1, 1898.

[100] *Jour. of Com. & Com. Bull.,* June 17, 1898.

[101] *Tradesman,* June 15, September 1, 1898; *"Dixie,"* XIV,
No. 6, p. 27 (June, 1898). *Cf.* New Orleans *Picayune,* quoted in
New York *Jour. of Com. & Com. Bull.,* May 18, 1898.

hasten the growth of trans-Pacific trade and asserted it was with this expectation that " Pacific Coast people so generally favor territorial expansion." The *Daily Commercial News and Shipping List,* of San Francisco, thought the coast people would make determined efforts for the retention of the Philippines.[102] The Chamber of Commerce of Seattle and the Chamber of Commerce, Merchants' Association, and Manufacturers' and Producers' Association of San Francisco petitioned the President to retain not only the Philippines, but the Caroline and Ladrone Islands, " and all other lands which are now, or may hereafter be acquired in the present war with Spain," in the interests of humanity and the Oriental trade of the United States.[103] Even James J. Hill, who had been a strong opponent of the war, stated to a newspaper reporter that if it rested with him, he would retain the Philippines. " If you go back in the commercial history of the world," he was reported as saying, " you will find that the people who controlled the trade of the Orient have been the people who held the purse strings of nations." [104]

[102] *Mining and Scientific Press,* LXXVI, 534, 643 (May 21, June 18, 1898) ; *Com. Bull. of Sou. Cal.,* June 17, December 23, 1898; *Daily Com. News & Shipping List,* August 10, 1898.

[103] Seattle *Post-Intelligencer,* August 8, 1898. Chamber of Commerce of San Francisco, *49th Annual Report,* pp. 23-24. The quotation is from resolutions adopted July 29, 1898, by the San Francisco Chamber of Commerce in conjunction with the other bodies named above. On the other hand, the Los Angeles Chamber of Commerce, at its meeting on August 4, 1898, voted strongly against annexing the Philippines. *Daily Com. News & Shipping List,* August 6, 1898.

[104] Seattle *Post-Intelligencer,* June 1, 1898. *Cf.* Pyle, *op. cit.,* II, 77.

It must not be inferred that business opinion was unanimous in favor of retaining the Philippines. There was an undercurrent of opposition or indifference. The New York *Journal of Commerce,* just before the signing of the peace protocol, deplored the fact that timid people were shrinking from imperialism and that " the business men of the country are maintaining a deathlike silence." [105] The *Commercial and Financial Chronicle* was cautious, pointing out that Spain's distant possessions had proved her most vulnerable point—a fact from which the United States might learn a lesson—and hoping that the United States might yet find a way to avoid such a dangerous responsibility. The Baltimore *Journal of Commerce* was, in July, strongly opposed to annexation, and two months later held that no one yet knew whether " our position as wetnurse to Cuba, proprietors of Porto Rico and pantata to the Philippines is likely to bring us profit or loss." The *Iron Age,* which early in the summer had been strongly for expansion was by September harboring qualms as to the real value of colonies to the business man.[106] Everett Frazar, president of the American Asiatic Association, was personally a warm supporter of annexation, but the Association held upon its table for months without action a resolution on the subject.[107] The

[105] *Jour. of Com. & Com. Bull.,* August 11, 1898.

[106] *Com. & Fin. Chron.,* LXVI, 876-878, 922-924 (May 7, 14, 1898) ; Baltimore *Journal of Commerce,* July 16, September 10, 1898; *Iron Age,* September 29, November 24, 1898. By August, the *Chronicle* had come to regard annexation as inevitable. (LXVII, 401, August 27, 1898.)

[107] Everett Frazar to Pres. McKinley, November 11, 1898. Dept. of State, *Misc. Letters,* November, 1898, I. Other business men wrote McKinley opposing annexation of the Philippines. T. G.

San Francisco *Call,* representing the California and Hawaiian sugar interests of the Spreckels family, was strongly opposed to annexation, arguing not only that Anglo Saxons had no aptitude for tropical colonization, but also frankly warning Californian sugar-beet growers of the danger of competition from Philippine cane-sugar.[108]

There is no way of measuring accurately the strength of business opinion for and against the retention of the Philippines. Judging opinion as best we can from the available expressions of it, it seems safe to conclude that after the battle of Manila Bay American business became definitely imperialistic—that is, if a wish to retain the Philippines is an evidence of an imperialistic attitude. It seems certain, too, from the prominence given to the Chinese situation in nearly every discussion of the value of the islands, that the conversion of business opinion was accomplished by the combination of a European threat against the freedom of the American market in China, present and prospective, with the dramatic coup of the American fleet in a fine harbor so near the Chinese coast. In one paper, the New York *Journal of Commerce,* there appears with beautiful clarity the shift of position induced by the action of the European Powers in China. In November, 1897, against all schemes of colonial or naval expansion; in December, for

---

Bush, president of the Mobile and Birmingham Railroad Co., thought all we needed was a coaling and naval station in the Philippines. Wharton Barker, of Philadelphia, thought trade could best be built up by reciprocity with the Americas, not by expansion in the Far East. Bush to McKinley, July 30, 1898. *Ibid.,* July, 1898, III. Barker to McKinley, August 25, 1898. *Misc. Letters Sent to the Pres. & the Secretary of State, Paris Peace Commission, 1898.*

[108] San Francisco *Call,* September 10, 17, December 15, 1898.

a canal, Hawaii annexation, and a big navy; in May and thereafter, for retention of the entire Philippine archipelago and aggressive assertion of American rights in China— the *Journal* reveals a process of thought which perhaps occurred less clearly and consciously in the minds of many business men.

Having concluded that the Philippines were wholesome and digestible, business was disposed to treat itself to more of the same diet. The venture in the Philippines strengthened immeasurably the demand for the annexation of Hawaii. " The battle of Manila Bay," said the *Journal of Commerce*, May 31, " makes it imperative that we should establish permanent arrangements which will make the [Hawaiian] islands a half-way house on the road to the Philippines." But there were other Pacific islands that beckoned. " Bridge the Pacific! " cried the Philadelphia *Press*. " With the Philippines go the Carolines, a Spanish possession, Samoa and the Hawaiian Islands complete the chain." [109] The war in the Pacific, the prospect of new possessions there, and the voyage of the " Oregon " also gave new force to the demand for an isthmian canal.[110] In the Caribbean, business interests not only insisted that the United States needed Puerto Rico for its strategic and commercial value,[111] but suggested that it might prove im-

[109] Quoted in New York *Commercial*, May 13, 1898.

[110] *Cf.* resolutions of San Francisco Chamber of Commerce, May 4, 1898, in *Daily Commercial News and Shipping List,* May 6, 1898.

[111] The New York *Journal of Commerce* (May 11, 1898) thought either Puerto Rico or Cuba was necessary for reasons similar to those dictating the retention of the Philippines. " We want no

possible to adhere to the Teller Amendment, which had pledged the United States not to annex Cuba. The New York *Journal of Commerce*, voicing skepticism as to the capacity of the Cubans for orderly government, declared: " The Teller amendment . . . must be interpreted in a sense somewhat different from that which its author intended it to bear." The American flag must float over Cuba until law and order were assured.[112] American covetousness in the Caribbean was not limited to the Spanish islands. The New York *Commercial*, which in March had commended Lodge's proposal for the purchase of the Danish Islands,[113] now saw signs that the British West Indies might be interested in coming under the American flag and urged that the Bahamas, Jamaica, and Bermuda be not lost sight of during the war. The *Journal of Commerce*, endorsing the same idea, remarked: " Our people are now in an expansive mood and there is a deep and strong American senti-

---

acquisitions other than those needful for strategic purposes, but whatever territory of that nature falls into our hands must never be parted with." Letters from business men to the Department of State urged the annexation of Puerto Rico as a " garden spot," capable of contributing greatly to American commerce. J. H. Hamlin & Son, Portland, Me., to McKinley, May 11, 1898. Dept. of State, *Misc. Letters*, May, 1898, II. T. G. Bush, Anniston, Ala., to McKinley, July 30, 1898. *Ibid.*, July, 1898, III.

[112] *Jour. of Com. & Com. Bull.*, May 24, 1898. Similarly, the *American Banker* (LXIII, 986, June 8, 1898) thought conditions in Cuba might force the United States to abandon its pledge as to the independence of the island; and the *Banker and Tradesman* (XXVI, 688, July 27, 1898) believed it might be necessary to " take absolute possession of the island, and put down the insurgents." Similar views were expressed by T. G. Bush (above, note 111), and by the *Wall Street Journal*, May 5, 1898.

[113] New York *Commercial*, March 31, 1898.

ment that would rejoice to see the British flag, as well as the Spanish flag, out of the West Indies." [114]

Merchants and manufacturers now saw in the acquisition of colonies a partial solution of the disposal of surplus American products. European countries, prejudiced against our goods, said the New York *Commercial* (evidently recalling Count Goluchowski's speech), had acquired colonial markets while we had none; but the acquisition of the Spanish islands would supply the lack; their development by American capital would stimulate the demand for the products of our fields and factories. We should regulate their customs in a manner to favor our own industries and shipping and discourage those of other countries.[115] This proposed procedure was condemned by the *Journal of Commerce,* the *Commercial and Financial Chronicle,* and other journals and organizations, which insisted that after urging the " open door " in China we must adhere to the same principle in our new possessions.[116] But whether the door was to be open or closed to the rest of the world, an active and lucrative trade with the new possessions was

[114] *Ibid.,* May 12, 1898; *Jour. of Com. & Com. Bull.,* August 25, 1898.

[115] New York *Commercial,* May 9, June 8, August 4, 1898.

[116] *Jour. of Com. & Com. Bull.,* May 31, July 13, 1898; January 6, February 1, 1899; *Com. & Fin. Chron.,* LXVI, 922-924, LXVII, 290, 401, 1082-1083 (May 14, August 13, 27, November 26, 1898; *U. S. Investor,* IX, 1704-1705 (November 26, 1898); *Rand-McNally Bankers' Monthly,* XVI, 464 (December, 1898). The American Asiatic Association, in a set of resolutions adopted January 5, 1899, called for the application of the " open door " policy in the Philippines. American Asiatic Association to Secretary Hay, January 7, 1899. Dept. of State, *Misc. Letters,* January, 1899, I.

widely anticipated. " One way of opening a market is to conquer it . . . ," said the *Railway World* in August. "Already our enterprising merchants are beginning to organize to take possession of the markets which our army and navy have opened to them." The Chicago *Inter-Ocean,* in a series of interviews with merchants and manufacturers in several cities, found them " very generally waking up to the opportunities which the war has brought at a moment when the immense increase of our manufacturing capacity has rendered foreign outlets absolutely necessary to us." The Bureau of Statistics reported large numbers of inquiries from all parts of the country, but chiefly from the great producing and business centers, as to the imports of Cuba and Puerto Rico.[117] Not only the trade prospects but also the opportunities for American capital and skill to develop the resources of the islands excited enthusiasm. A national bank for Hawaii was organized immediately after passage of the annexation resolution. Similar plans were afoot for Puerto Rico and Cuba, and enterprising Americans were studying financial conditions in the Philippines. " Railroad building may be expected to boom in all the islands which may fall under the influence of the United States," said *Rand-McNally Bankers' Monthly.* Cane sugar and tobacco growing would receive an impetus. " The forests may also be made to yield handsome returns, . . . and in fact every

[117] *Railway World,* XLII, 861 (August 6, 1898) ; Chicago *Inter-Ocean* quoted in Portland *Morning Oregonian,* September 14, 1898; *Rand-McNally Bankers' Monthly,* XVI, 199 (September, 1898), for Bureau of Statistics. Similar enthusiasm for the markets offered by the new possessions is found in the *American Exporter,* XLIII, No. 1, p. 10 (December, 1898), and *ibid.,* No. 2, p. 10 (January, 1899), and in the *Financial Record,* December 21, 1898.

industry, so long under the blighting rule of Spain, will be exploited and made to show the advantages accruing from better government and wider enterprise." [118]

American business had yielded reluctantly to the necessity of a war with Spain, forced upon the United States by popular reaction to the distressing situation in Cuba. It had not foreseen, or if it foresaw had feared, the colonial responsibilities to which such a war might lead. But when Dewey's dramatic victory on the first of May offered a Far Eastern base from which the threatened markets in China might be defended, it had gladly accepted the result, and long before the conclusion of peace with Spain, it was building high hopes upon the supposed opportunities for trade and exploitation in a string of dependencies stretching from the Philippines to Puerto Rico.

[118] *Bankers' Magazine*, LVII, 171-173 (August, 1898); *Rand-McNally Bankers' Monthly*, XVI, 107-108 (August, 1898); *cf.* also *Tradesman*, November 15, 1898, pp. 60-61.

VIII

"THE IMPERIALISM OF RIGHTEOUSNESS"

In the last chapter, an attempt was made to analyze the attitude of economic interests in the United States toward the war with Spain and the acquisition of a colonial empire. One other aspect of American life had its organized bodies, its periodical publications, and its recognized spokesmen. I refer to organized religion. What was the attitude of the churches in the United States toward the war and toward the assumption of colonial responsibilities and a larger place in world affairs?

It may be noted, at the start, that American religious thought—at least, Protestant thought—in the 1890's was imbued with something of the same spirit of self-assertiveness which we observed in the deliberations of Congress in the two years preceding the war. In an earlier chapter we noticed the contributions to " the new manifest destiny " of that widely read clergyman, the Rev. Josiah Strong, author, as one religious periodical remarked in 1898, " of that marvelous book, ' Our Country.' " [1] In that volume, it will be recalled, Dr. Strong had predicted that the Anglo-Saxon race, through the possession, along with other valuable traits, of " a pure spiritual Christianity," and under sure marks of divine favor, would within a century or so have "Anglo-Saxonized mankind." [2] Strong was no doubt an

[1] *Religious Telescope,* LXIV, 1548 (December 7, 1898).
[2] Strong, *Our Country,* pp. 208-227. *Cf. supra,* pp. 5-6.

extremist, but more sober thinkers agreed with him in the belief that the United States, as a powerful Christian nation, should stand aggressively for Christianity and the uplifting of mankind the world over. The Episcopalian *Churchman,* in an editorial on Armenia, in 1897, declared that the distressing situation there was of peculiar concern to Great Britain and the United States.

> Great peoples have great responsibilities. They can have no wars for self-aggrandizement. They must—or be recreant to all that makes them grand or free or worth dying for—stand by the weak and defend the helpless, and advance the banner of mercy and justice over the world.[3]

There was a widespread feeling that the time was ripe for a great Christian advance. The Baptist *Standard,* while conservative as to American policy—opposing the annexation of Hawaii and political entanglement in the affairs of China[4]—nevertheless saw doors opening to Christianity in distant lands. Predicting that Egypt would presently fall under either French or British domination and that " the gaudy formalism of the Moslem code " would there receive its death blow, the paper announced: " In what the future holds for north Africa, Christianity finds a breach through which to besiege Islam decisively. Shall not the breach be entered? "[5] A publication which held such an opinion of European missionary responsibility in the Near East could not consistently repudiate a similar responsibility for America in the Far East.[6]

[3] *Churchman,* LXXVI, 268 (September 4, 1897).

[4] *Standard,* XLV, 418-419 (January 29, 1898).

[5] *Ibid.,* pp. 458-459 (February 12, 1898).

[6] For the *Standard's* acceptance of this responsibility for the Philippines, see *infra,* pp. 293-294.

The impending collapse of the old order of things in China presented to American Christians, in the opinion of the Presbyterian *Interior*, " a supreme missionary opportunity." In it was to be heard " the ringing of the bell of Divine Providence calling upon those who have the gospel of the world's salvation to see, and to seize this new, this august opportunity for preaching it in a world-empire that has so long been waiting for it." [7] The Rev. J. H. Barrows, in a series of lectures on " The Christian Conquest of Asia " delivered at Union Theological Seminary in the winter and spring of 1898, suggested that American commerce and American Christianity would go hand in hand across the Pacific.

God has placed us like Israel of old, in the center of the nations, . . . while to west of us is that Asiatic world of immeasurable greatness which when awakened out of sleep, will combine with America to make the Pacific ocean the chief highway of the world's commerce . . . and wherever on pagan shores the voice of the American missionary and teacher is heard, there is fulfilled the manifest destiny of the Christian Republic; . . .[8]

In this approaching conquest of Asia, the Hawaiian Islands would be of strategic importance in a religious no less than in a commercial or military sense. They constituted, said John R. Mott,

a veritable cross-roads of the nations. This fact has added meaning in our generation in which the Pacific is becoming increasingly the theatre of some of the largest activities of the world. . . . God has not worked here in vain. He has built up a strong Christian community. He recognized

---

[7] *Interior*, XXIX, 323-324 (March 17, 1898).

[8] J. H. Barrows, *The Christian Conquest of Asia*, pp. 237-239, 248-249.

before men did the great importance of this cluster of islands in the central Pacific, and caused to be planted there a Christian nation which is at the same time a great lighthouse and a base of operations for the enterprise of universal evangelization.[9]

From such quotations as these we may infer that the missionary-minded among religious people in the United States were quite as eager to discover foreign outlets for their energy as were commercial people. This spirit had its obvious bearing upon the Cuban situation and would bear similarly, in due time, upon the question of retaining the Philippines and other Spanish islands. Had not the United States a moral and religious responsibility in Cuba? And might not the Philippines be a portal to religious activity, as well as to trade, in Asia?

Viewing the Cuban problem as a moral one, organized religion was much less opposed than was business to intervention and the coming of war. " Should we now go to war," wrote the editor of one Methodist paper, " our cause will be just, and Methodism will be ready to do its full duty. Every Methodist preacher will be a recruiting officer." [10]   The Catholic *Ave Maria,* soon after the war began, took occasion to comment upon the belligerency of the Protestant clergy.

The pulpits of the country resound with war-cries and calumnies against our foes. Many of the pious men who occupy them preferred war to peace, and war at any cost rather than peace as a result of the Holy Father's arbitration.[11]

[9] John R. Mott, *Strategic Points in the World's Conquest,* pp. 206-207.
[10] *Northern Christian Advocate,* LVIII, 232 (April 13, 1898).
[11] *Ave Maria,* XLVI, 596 (May 7, 1898).

The editor thought it might be a good idea for these Protestant clergymen to go to war in a body,

> were it not for the sane, sincere, gentle-souled among them, —men like the Rev. Dr. Parker, of Hartford, who in a public address used these words: " Would to God that the leaders of the churches other than the Roman Church had spoken and acted as the Pope did." [12]

The *Ave Maria* itself had advocated arbitration of the controversy with Spain by the Holy See.[13] Its charge that the Protestant bodies had preferred war is borne out by the expressions of certain of their publications. The *Interior,* for example, had doubted whether disinterested and impartial arbitrators could be agreed upon, and had felt that even if that difficulty could be surmounted, " much precious time would be wasted. . . . Over this Cuban business far too much time has been wasted already. Shall thousands of starving and dying Cubans appeal to the humane people of this republic in vain? " [14] Bishop Whitaker, of the Episcopal diocese of Pennsylvania, believed that the only way to enforce the President's " humane and righteous determination was by the force of arms; and that means war." [15] Some representatives of Christianity were ready to fight not only to save " starving and dying Cubans," but to avenge alleged insults and injuries to the United States. The *Religious Telescope,* " weekly organ of the United Brethren in Christ," thought De Lome's famous letter criticizing McKinley sufficient ground for recalling the Ameri-

[12] *Ibid.,* p. 692 (May 28, 1898).
[13] *Ibid.,* p. 371 (March 19, 1898).
[14] *Interior,* XXIX, 353 (March 24, 1898).
[15] *Church Standard,* LXXV, 40-41 (May 14, 1898).

can minister in Madrid and recognizing the independence of Cuba, even should these steps lead to war, for " there are some things worse than war." [16] The *Christian and Missionary Alliance* was sure that the " Maine " had been destroyed as the result of a Spanish plot and hinted that war was the proper remedy.[17]

Upon less warlike journals Senator Proctor's speech on March 17 apparently produced an effect similar to that upon wavering business men. The Congregational *Advance,* which had denounced the sensationalism of the yellow journals and as late as March 10 had declared that the great, conservative body of the nation were as yet opposed to intervention, accepted Proctor's speech as bearing out all the newspapers had said and came out strongly for Cuban independence.[18] Similarly with the Baptist *Standard:*

Senator Proctor [it said] is perhaps the first prominent man, well known to be fair and discriminating, who has visited Cuba from the United States in an unofficial capacity during the past few months. . . . The feeling is growing that the crisis in the Cuban problem is very near at hand.[19]

Combined with the sense that the United States was about to perform a noble humanitarian service was the satisfying faith that this would be but carrying out the judgment of

[16] *Religious Telescope,* LXV, 196 (February 16, 1898).

[17] *Christian and Missionary Alliance,* XX, 204 (March 2, 1898). This periodical was published by the organization of the same name, a non-sectarian body formed in 1887 and devoted especially to missionary work in neglected fields. See *New Schaff-Herzog Encyclopedia of Religious Knowledge,* III, 41.

[18] *Advance,* XXXV, 315, 382-383 (March 10, 24, 1898).

[19] *Standard,* XLV, 579 (March 26, 1898). *Cf. Congregationalist,* LXXXIII, 411 (March 24, 1898) ; *California Christian Advocate,* March 23, 1898.

God. In an abusive article entitled " The Spaniard's Trail,"
the editors of the *Advance* described the trail of blood and
tears everywhere left by the Spanish conqueror. But Providence had been " working against the relentless invader and
conqueror in the New World," and

the Providence which has worked to weaken this relentless
power will work until its cruel grasp upon its last victim
has been unloosed. . . . The Fatherhood of God which
broods over the great nations, nurturing and cherishing all
good hope and progress, also broods over the islands of
the sea, and has an ear open to the cry of their sorrows
and a hand to help in their needs.[20]

" In the name of humanity," said the *Interior,* " and of
Christian civilization, a day of the Lord, a judgment day,
is at hand. . . . The blowing up of the *Maine* in the Havana harbor—let it remain in history as the fitting punctua-
tion mark at the end of Spanish misrule." [21]

In like tone, the *Evangelist,* also Presbyterian, declared:
"And if it be the will of Almighty God, that by war the
last trace of this inhumanity of man to man shall be swept
away from this Western hemisphere, let it come!" [22] The
Christian and Missionary Alliance saw in war not only the
scourge used by God for sinful nations:

It has often been also the ploughshare as well as the sword,
opening up the world to the Gospel, preparing for the seed
of the kingdom. It is a time for those who are looking for
His coming to watch and pray.[23]

[20] *Advance,* XXXV, 453 (April 7, 1898). Yet a week later
(*ibid.,* p. 490) the same paper quoted with apparent approval
former Senator Edmunds's demonstration that there was no ground
for going to war.

[21] *Interior,* XXIX, 459 (April 14, 1898).

[22] *Evangelist,* March 31, 1898, pp. 6-7.

[23] *Christian and Missionary Alliance,* XX, 204 (March 2, 1898).

The Episcopalian *Churchman,* which in the fall of 1897 had spoken strongly for the maintenance of peace, now remarked that if war should come it would be the doing of no one man or party—a state of affairs which showed that no human agency could control the force of events. " God alone knows the issues of life and death, of peace and war." Individuals, it said, should continue to do what they could for peace, but should remember that peace might " be secured at a price no true people can afford to pay—at the cost of honor and self-respect." [24]

When war was actually declared, the churches found no difficulty in justifying it. It was a war for humanity, said the Episcopal *Church Standard;* history had declared against Spain as a colonial power.[25] In an editorial on " The Church in the War," the *Outlook* asserted that the churches almost unanimously recognized the fact that " the Nation had been moved to battle by the demand of awakened conscience answering to the call of outraged humanity." [26] The *Standard,* while holding that war had been hastened by a " combination of jaundiced activities "—evidently the yellow press—nevertheless confessed that it was a " righteous war," which we had entered not for revenge, conquest, greed of territory, or martial glory. The United States, it said, would go to Cuba

with a loaf of bread at the end of its bayonet, with its warships laden with flour and shot. Its banners have been preceded by the Red Cross flag, and will be followed by

[24] *Churchman,* LXXVII, 414 (March 19, 1898).
[25] *Church Standard,* LXXIV, 857-858 (April 30, 1898).
[26] *Outlook,* LIX, 157 (May 21, 1898).

school books and Bibles. . . . Christian citizens will uphold the president and stand by the flag.[27]

Similarly, the *Baptist Union,* though deploring the evils of
war, found satisfaction in the belief that this war was being
waged for unselfish and righteous ends;[28] while the
Christian and Missionary Alliance believed, not only that
it was a war for humanity, but that it was God's instrument
for striking another blow " at that system of iniquity, the
papacy."

This editorial, published in the issue of April 27, before
the battle of Manila Bay, is noteworthy as displaying an early
interest in the Philippines, which, in the writer's opinion,
would, along with Cuba and Puerto Rico, be freed " from
the intolerable yoke of Spanish oppression " and opened
" to the Gospel of the Lord Jesus Christ. . . . God is beat-
ing down the long-closed doors." The writer referred to a
European paper which had said that the Catholic powers of
Europe would never permit the United States to control the
Catholic Philippines. He mentioned the idea merely to
scoff at it.

But God is stronger than either the Romish Church or the
Catholic powers of Europe. We should pray not only that
Cuba be free, but that these fair Eastern isles shall also become the scenes of Gospel triumphs and the salvation of
countless souls.[29]

American Catholics refused to concede a monopoly of
patriotism to their Protestant rivals. The *Catholic Herald*
had opposed the early demands for intervention in Cuba

[27] *Standard,* XLV, 661 (April 23, 1898).
[28] *Baptist Union,* VIII, 322 (May 7, 1898).
[29] *Christian and Missionary Alliance,* XX, 393 (April 27, 1898).

and had advocated papal arbitration between Spain and the Cubans.[30] It had some sarcasm for the "bloodthirsty preachers" of the Protestant churches.[31] But it announced on April 9 that if war came, American Catholics would be patriotic citizens; it supported intervention when that became a reality; and in May rejoiced that:

In a few weeks the chains forged by Spain will be loosed by American bravery, and the world will wonder why the United States tolerated them so long.[32]

The *Catholic News* asserted that the United States had entered the war purely from a sense of duty, and that "the spectacle we present today is a truly inspiring one."[33] In order, as one Protestant journal remarked, to extricate American Catholics from the difficult position in which they had been placed by the Pope's Spanish sympathies, the American archbishops issued a circular to be read in all the churches, declaring that whatever had been the opinions of individuals before the opening of hostilities, there could "now be no two opinions as to the duty of every loyal American citizen," and that American Catholics were loyal to their flag and country and obedient to the supreme authority of the nation. The same circular directed priests to pray for American victory.[34]

From the evidence examined, it would seem that almost the only Christian denominations that were genuinely and thoroughly opposed to war were the Friends and Unitarians.

[30] *Catholic Herald,* March 12, April 2, 1898.
[31] *Ibid.,* May 7, 1898.
[32] *Ibid.,* April 9, 30, May 28, 1898.
[33] *Catholic News,* April 23, 1898.
[34] *Northern Christian Advocate,* LVIII, 305 (May 18, 1898).

The Unitarian *Christian Register* plead for patience with Spain and denied that war could bring any benefit to the United States—that it could vindicate national honor, win commercial advantages, or enhance the nation's civilizing influence.[35] The *Friend*, a Quaker publication, counselled forbearance toward Spain and recommended arbitration of the pending questions,[36] and the Society of Friends, early in April, sent to the President and Congress a memorial urging a peaceful settlement and declaring: "We hold there can be no differences between nations that cannot be more advantageously settled by peaceful negotiations." [37] But such instances of pressure against war from the religious organizations appear to have been negligible. "I came not to bring peace but a sword" may well have been the favorite text of Protestant ministers.

The faith that America's intervention in Cuba and her attack upon Spanish dominion elsewhere had the approval of Divine Providence was confirmed by the early and complete triumphs of American arms. The story of Dewey's victory seemed to one editor to "read almost like the stories of the ancient battles of the Lord in the times of Joshua, David, and Jehoshophat." [38] "The magnificent

[35] *Christian Register*, LXXVII, 5, 262 (January 6, March 10, 1898).

[36] *Friend*, LXXI, 255, 271 (February 26, March 12, 1898).

[37] *Ibid.*, p. 294 (April 2, 1898).

[38] *Christian and Missionary Alliance*, XX, 468 (May 18, 1898). The same paper found in the events of the war an explanation and a fulfillment of the prophecy in the eighteenth chapter of *Isaiah:* "In that time shall the present be brought unto the Lord of hosts of a people scattered and peeled, and from a people terrible from their beginning hitherto." *Ibid.*, XXI, 13 (August 10, 1898).

fleets of Spain," said another writer, "have gone down as marvelously, I had almost said, as miraculously, as the walls of Jericho went down." [39]

The meaning of such manifestations of divine favor was obvious. "God's mighty hand," said the *Christian and Missionary Alliance*, "is leading on, and opening the way for an immediate evangelization of the world and signalizing his people to follow up the providential openings with prompt coöperation and obedience." [40] Spanish rule had driven American missionaries from the Caroline Islands and excluded them from the Philippines, "but God has interposed, and a brighter dawn has come." [41]

The publications which had been readiest in welcoming the war were among the most emphatic in urging acceptance of the responsibilities which the war, as it seemed by providential decree, had laid at the doors of the United States. For this nation to decline to take the Philippines, thought the *Religious Telescope*, would be "to refuse, for selfish reasons, to assume the duty and the responsibility which a gracious Providence has thrust upon it." In fact, we might properly go much further.

The acquiring of the Ladrone, the Caroline, and the Philippine islands, and even Cuba, Porto Rico, and the Canaries, *as the result of the war into which Spain, by her barbarities in Cuba, forced us*, will be no violation of the spirit of isolation. . . . [To refuse such responsibilities] would be to render the nation guilty of a great crime in the sight

---

[39] Alexander Blackburn, in the *Standard*, XLV, 913 (August 6, 1898).

[40] *Christian and Missionary Alliance*, XXI, 98-100 (July 27, 1898).

[41] *Ibid.*, XX, 564 (June 15, 1898).

of high Heaven. The times are ripe for us to extend the blessings of free government to all those portions of the earth which God and the fortunes of war render it reasonably obligatory upon us to extend them to.[42]

We may infer that the religious groups represented by the papers just quoted—the United Brethren and the Christian and Missionary Alliance—accepted the expansionist program with a devout enthusiasm quite as striking as the more worldly fervor which marked the attitude of the spokesmen for American business. Of the larger Protestant denominations, while some showed signs of wavering at first, nearly all (if we can judge their attitude from their official publications) came rather early to the conclusion that Providence had opened doors for humanitarian and evangelizing enterprise upon which the American people could not rightly turn their backs.

We may glance first at the Baptists. In an editorial entitled "A New Policy," the *Baptist Union,* on May 14, declared that the war marked a departure from our traditional policy of non-intervention and isolation.

In the divine administration the election and separation of a people to peculiar privilege has always been with a view to the wider diffusion of blessing. . . . May not this principle be about to find fresh illustration in the history of the American nation, and the gathered force of the years be directed to the liberation and uplifting of others? [43]

Declaring, later in the year, that "the responsibility of success" imposed upon the United States the obligation of giving to the people of the conquered islands stable

[42] *Religious Telescope,* LXIV, 931 (July 27, 1898). *Cf. Christian and Missionary Alliance,* XXI, 108 (August 3, 1898).
[43] *Baptist Union,* VIII, 338.

government and salvation from anarchy and barbarism, the same journal added:

A still higher obligation rests upon us. We must give to these islands which we have delivered the Gospel whose principles are the only true foundation and guarantee of liberty. The conquest by force of arms must be followed up by conquest for Christ.[44]

Some Baptist publications were more cautious. The *Watchman* suggested that the history of our dealing with the Indians cast grave doubt upon our fitness for bestowing benevolent government upon the Filipinos.[45] If we were to govern alien races successfully, we must first clean up our government at home.[46]. It was, indeed, our responsibility to deliver the Filipinos from oppression and ,open their islands to civilization, but this could be accomplished through guarantees in the peace treaty; annexation was unnecessary.[47] If we should, nevertheless, assume the government of the Philippines, we must do so as trustees, not as exploiters.[48] Yet even the conservative editor of this magazine could write with some enthusiasm of the strategic value of the Philippines in the impending struggle between Christianity and Orientalism, and of the new part which

[44] *Ibid.,* p. 631 (August 27, 1898).

[45] *Watchman,* August 11, 1898. This argument was contested by another Baptist periodical, the *Journal and Messenger,* August 18, 1898, which saw no reason to fear American government in the Philippines because of mistakes in the Indian administration. The eyes of the world, it believed, would be upon us, and competent men would be sent to the Philippines.

[46] *Watchman,* September 15, December 1, 1898.

[47] *Ibid.,* August 25, 1898.

[48] *Ibid.,* September 22, 1898.

the United States was about to play in the task of civilizing the world.[49]

The *Standard,* representing the same denomination, was a hesitant convert to the expansionist program. In May, it still opposed annexing Hawaii and feared that, " with four baby republics on our hands,"—Hawaii, Cuba, Puerto Rico, and the Philippines—we might find it difficult to deal adequately with problems nearer home.[50] It complained that a new spirit of self-aggrandizement was becoming apparent in the American people, and that there was danger of the war's being diverted from its original altruistic purpose.[51] Yet it was soon publishing articles from contributors who asserted that the nation had a new duty " to throw its strong protecting arms around the West India Islands in the East and the Philippine Islands in the West," [52] and to practise an " imperialism of righteousness." [53] In August it was expressing gratification at the missionary opportunities which would be afforded in the conquered islands and was ready to admit that the United States should assume control of the Philippines if such a course were not opposed by the Filipinos or the European powers.[54] Hailing a contemporary Anglo-Saxon triumph—Kitchener's victory at Omdurman—as meaning that " one more of the dark places of the earth " had been " claimed by civilization, and by

[49] *Ibid.,* September 29, October 27, 1898.

[50] *Standard,* XLV, 715 (May 14, 1898).

[51] *Ibid.,* XLV, 783 (June 11, 1898).

[52] Thos. J. Morgan, " The New Republic and Its New Duties," *ibid.,* XLV, 882 (July 23, 1898).

[53] Alexander Blackburn, " The Imperialism of Righteousness," *ibid.,* p. 913 (August 6, 1898).

[54] *Ibid.,* pp. 945, 960-961 (August 20, 27, 1898).

Christianity," [55] it challenged American Baptists to rise to their new opportunities in those other dark places opened by Dewey and by Shafter. "The opportunity is ours; the divine agencies are available; and Christ's leadership is apparently assured." [56]

Other Baptist publications were enthusiastic over the new opportunities for missionary work. "With startling suddenness," remarked the *Baptist Missionary Magazine,* "our religious and moral responsibilities have in a new and weightier sense become worldwide"; and it proceeded to map out the new possessions for missionary work.[57] "To give to the world the life more abundant both for here and hereafter," said a writer in the *Baptist Missionary Review,* "is the duty of the American people by virtue of the call of God. This call is very plain. The hand of God in history has ever been plain." [58]

A similar spirit, apparently, animated the majority of the Methodist group. The *Christian Advocate* of Nashville and the *Christian Advocate* of New York were anti-imperialist,

[55] *Ibid.,* XLVI, 34 (September 17, 1898).

[56] *Ibid.,* pp. 106-107 (October 15, 1898). The *Standard,* however, maintained before and after ratification of the peace treaty that our occupation of the Philippines should be regarded as temporary and should be terminated upon the fulfillment of our civilizing mission. *Ibid.,* pp. 206, 436, 467 (November 19, 1898, February 4, 11, 1899).

[57] *Baptist Missionary Magazine,* LXXVIII, 483 (August, 1898). "With its motto 'North America for Christ' the Home Mission Society will assume the work in Cuba and Porto Rico, but the Missionary Union is called upon to care for the Pacific Island additions to our territory."

[58] Rev. S. A. Perrine, "A Case of Manifest Destiny," *Baptist Missionary Review,* IV, 424-428.

though the latter paper in the end admitted that good might
result from American rule in the Philippines and characterized the ratification of the peace treaty as the lesser of two
evils.[59] On the other hand, Methodist papers published in
Syracuse, Chicago, St. Louis, and San Francisco welcomed
the opportunities and responsibilities incidental to the retention of the Philippines.[60] The *Methodist Review* of
Nashville rejoiced that the war would " open up Cuba,
Porto Rico, and the Philippines to the distribution and
proclamation of the pure word of God " and teach Americans that their nation had a duty as one of the great powers;
it must stand shoulder to shoulder with Great Britain as
champion of the oppressed, defender of liberty, and protector of Christian preachers.[61] The *Methodist Review* of
New York spoke of expansion with approval in July, and
later in the year expressed the belief that if, " by the direction of divine Providence," the United States should adopt
a policy of foreign colonization, it would be found that
the " foreign policy of the United States is foreign missions." [62] The Methodist Episcopal Church Conference for
Central New York, in its report for 1898, declared that
while Christian citizens might differ upon the question of

[59] *Christian Advocate* (Nashville), July 7, August 11, December
15, 1898; January 19, February 23, 1899. *Christian Advocate* (New
York), May 26, November 10, 1898; January 19, February 9, 1899.

[60] *Northern Christian Advocate*, May 11, August 17, 31, 1898.
Northwestern Christian Advocate, May 8, 1898; January 4, February
15, 1899. *Central Christian Advocate*, January 4, 1899. *California
Christian Advocate*, May 11, 18, December 28, 1898.

[61] *Methodist Review* (Nashville), XLVII, 446-447 (July-August,
1898).

[62] *Methodist Review* (New York), LXXX, 513-523, 824 (July,
1898, September-October, 1898).

retaining the conquered islands, " we are one in the conviction that the church must not fail to enter any door that is opened for the free propagation of the Gospel of Christ." [63] The Central Illinois Conference was equally explicit, declaring:

In view of the gracious providence of God which has guided and guarded the church during the past years, giving victories, throughout the earth, there is occasion for sincere gratitude and praise. Never was the image of the angel flying in the midst of heaven cleaving the air with its mighty wings, bearing the everlasting gospel to every kindred, tongue and people, more clearly defined than now.[64]

Presbyterians were by no means to be outdone by Methodists and Baptists. The *Church at Home and Abroad,* official publication of the Presbyterian Church in the United States of America, remarked upon the idealistic purposes of the war and predicted that: " The Great Ruler of the nations is able to use this conflict for the furtherance of his purposes, so that the ultimate issue may be the progress of his kingdom." [65] " The Lord of Hosts has given us victories on land and sea," said the *Presbyterian Banner.* Spain's power to oppress the people of Cuba, Puerto Rico, and the Philippines was broken by the force of our arms.

[63] *Report* of M. E. Church Conference, Central New York, for 1898, p. 121.

[64] *Minutes,* M. E. Church Conference, Central Illinois, 1898, p. 60.

[65] *Church at Home and Abroad,* XXIII, 471 (June, 1898). In a similar vein, the *Associate Reform Presbyterian* remarked, May 18, 1898: " We believe that the interests of Christ's Kingdom will be advanced in the outcome of this struggle. It may be that we are on the eve of great changes."

But victories had brought responsibilities. If the people of the islands were to have real freedom, to become capable of self-government, they must have Christian truth. Would the churches meet their obligation as successfully as the government had done? [66] The *Interior* at first viewed with misgiving the possibility that the United States might retain the Philippines—" one of the most difficult problems," it thought, " the war with Spain will bequeath to the American people." [67] But a month later it had come to regard retention of the islands as an inescapable duty. Denouncing the insinuation that we were on the road to becoming conquerors and oppressors as " an insult to the American people," it declared:

By no possibility can we become oppressors. The work of emancipation has providentially been thrust upon us. . . . The question is, shall we back out of, and back down from, our responsibility and duty, and selfishly abandon peoples who are holding up their manacled hands to us and praying us not to desert them?

Against such a policy of abandonment, said the writer, " the churches will stand solidly." [68] The religious press, he remarked, was practically unanimous " as to the desirability of America's retaining the Philippines as a duty in the interest of human freedom and Christian progress." [69]

Calling the churches to face their new responsibilities and to demand that the " shiftless and treacherous policy of everlasting ' retrenchment ' along all our missionary lines

[66] *Presbyterian Banner*, August 18, 1898.
[67] *Interior*, XXIX, 616 (May 19, 1898).
[68] *Ibid.*, p. 779 (June 23, 1898).
[69] *Ibid.*, p. 1040 (August 25, 1898).

shall be ended," this paper indicated the expanding outlines of the field that lay ahead:

Instantly the issues of the war shall have opened the way
for it, there will be in Cuba and in the Philippines a
new field for missions, and Christian education, of the
most inspiring opportunity. Then, too, great China, as
every one perceives, is on the eve of the most fateful
crisis. . . .[70]

Thus, like so many of the commercial people, the editor of
this church paper saw the Philippines as a gateway to the
Asiatic mainland. The thought was developed more at
length in a later issue. With China in collapse, the time
had come to do for her what England had done for India.
The United States, from its great power and its unselfish
purposes, was the logical instrument for the fulfillment of
this work. Its influence on the side of right and humanity
might be "the means chosen by Providence to effect what
might otherwise have to be accomplished much more slowly
and at much vaster expense to the human race." [71] A con-
tributor to the same publication linked the United States
and Great Britain as partners in shaping the religious future
of China. "We have been morally compelled to become
an Asiatic power," wrote Dr. J. H. Barrows. ". . . Every
American missionary in Asia from whom I have heard in
recent months, has thanked God that the American flag has
entered the Far East. . . . America and Great Britain will
see to it that China is not Russianized." [72]

The *Evangelist*, another Presbyterian weekly, had qualms
about annexing the Philippines and adopting millions of

[70] *Ibid.*, p. 808 (June 30, 1898).
[71] *Ibid.*, pp. 1040-1041 (August 25, 1898).
[72] John Henry Barrows, D. D., " God's Hand in Recent American
History," *ibid.*, XXIX, 1441-1442 (November 24, 1898).

" dusky Asiatics " as American citizens,[73] but it recognized that the United States had a duty which it must perform, either through annexation or by means of a protectorate. and a similar duty in Cuba and Puerto Rico.[74] The policy of isolation, however wise in Washington's time, must yield to the force of circumstances, and the United States must exert its influence in the interest of the oppressed everywhere.[75]

The Presbyterian Church took the lead in preparing for active missionary work in the new possessions. At the invitation of the Presbyterian Board of Foreign Missions, an interdenominational conference was held in New York on July 13, 1898, at which the Philippine Islands were designated as a field sufficiently large for Presbyterians, Baptists, and Methodists. At an October meeting the Presbyterian Board resolved that, " in view of the indications of the Divine Providence in opening fields for missionary effort in the new possessions," its officers should be authorized to accept contributions to finance the work, and a month later it instituted a search for suitable persons to begin operations in the new field.[76] In reporting this action, the *Church at Home and Abroad* remarked:

[73] *Evangelist*, August 4, 1898, p. 4. Similar doubts were expressed by the *Associate Reform Presbyterian* (December 21, 1898), which feared that by annexing the Philippines the United States would lose its moral vantage-ground. We should seek glory as helpers of the weak and oppressed, not as conquerors.

[74] *Evangelist*, August 18, 1898, p 6; October 27, 1898, pp. 6-7.
[75] *Ibid.*, July 7, 1898, p. 6.

[76] *Sixty-second Annual Report of the Board of Foreign Missions of the Presbyterian Church in the United States.* In the *Sixty-third Annual Report,* a year later, it was reported that three clergymen, two of them with their wives, and one medical missionary with his wife were in the Philippines.

In the coming years our missionary influence will more
and more lie westward from our Pacific coast. . . . So
we are brought to the front of Christendom over against
the front of Asiatic heathendom. Let not a mistaken judgment or a political prejudice or a fear of national expendi-
ture close it against us.[77]

The Congregational Church had long been active in missionary work and it was not to be expected that it would
look coldly upon the new opportunities. Spokesmen for
that denomination were, as a matter of fact, among the
most enthusiastic in accepting the moral responsibilities
created by the war. Cuba was near at hand and offered a
promising field. Catholicism, said the *Advance,* had done
little for the Cubans.

Will Protestantism enter Cuba and show a different spirit?
Will it go there with material help in one hand and spiritual
help in the other? . . . The churchmen of our land should
be prepared to invade Cuba as soon as the army and navy
open the way, to invade Cuba in a friendly, loving Christian
spirit, with bread in one hand and the Bible in the other,
and win the people to Christ by Christ-like service. Here
is a new mission field right at our doors which will soon
be open. Shall we not enter it?[78]

Destiny, thought the *Congregationalist* had thrust upon the
United States responsibility for Cuba and the Philippines.
In the spirit of the Teller Resolution, we should give them
a chance at self-government. If they proved incompetent
for the task, we could annex them for their own good.[79]

The *American Missionary,* organ of the American Missionary Association—a Congregational body sponsoring

[77] *Church at Home and Abroad,* XXIV, 392-393 (November,
1898).
[78] *Advance,* XXXV, 657 (May 19, 1898).
[79] *Congregationalist,* LXXXIII, 683 (May 12, 1898).

missionary work among colored populations—reported encouragement from various quarters for a missionary campaign in Cuba The Alumni Association of Oberlin Theological Seminary favored such a campaign. A triennial council of Congregational Churches at Portland, Oregon, " greeted with enthusiastic applause " a reference to the need of Christian educational work in Cuba. Letters came in from volunteers for such work in both Cuba and Puerto Rico. The *American Missionary* sent out an appeal for the necessary " sinews of war." [80]

As to the more distant Philippines, the *Advance* doubted at first whether the United States was called upon to accept such a weighty responsibility,[81] but it soon came to regard those islands as presenting not only " a market and a gate of opportunity to Oriental trade," but also a fair field for religious work.

Morally and religiously, we should not shun an opportunity to lift up a barbarous people. . . . Who knows but that this is a plan of Providence to bring the land favored of God and flowing with religious speech into touch with a land in need of the Gospel? [82]

Admitting that expansion would present dangers and problems, it concluded: " However, no nation which takes council [*sic*] of its fears rather than of its hopes can occupy a commanding position in the affairs of the world." [83]

Similarly, the *Congregationalist*, while admitting that every extension of dominion would involve new burdens

[80] " Shall Cuba Be Taken for Christ? " *American Missionary*, LII, 106 (September, 1898).

[81] *Advance*, XXXV, 626 (May 12, 1898).

[82] *Ibid.*, p. 658 (May 19, 1898).

[83] *Ibid.*, p. 859 (June 30, 1898).

and perils, saw no way of escape from such responsibilities. The war over, we should have on our hands Cuba, Puerto Rico, Hawaii, and probably some portion of the Philippines, in each of which a large majority of the population were unfit for citizenship.

But [it continued] if we are determined to follow where God in his providence leads we shall walk safely, and for this guidance every Christian will pray earnestly. Then we shall face our responsibility as a nation must which believes that the purpose of its government is to exalt mankind, and we shall ennoble our own citizens by honest efforts to give the blessings of freedom to other lands.[84]

Repudiating the Springfield *Republican's* charge that the religious press had been seized by a " delirium of jingoism," the editors of the *Independent* declared: " There is no delirium, no jingoism, in the acceptance by our religious people of the responsibilities put upon us by the war." [85] We are not pessimists but " possumists," they said, " in the matter of the nation's ability to grapple with the problems of annexation." [86]

Of special interest to Congregationalists, because of the work of the American Board of Commissioners for Foreign Missions, were the Caroline Islands. Missionary efforts had begun there, on Ponape and Kusaie, in 1852, and in the course of years many natives had been converted. But as the result of an international dispute over the ownership of these and other islands, which was referred to the

[84] *Congregationalist,* LXXXIII, 206 (August 18, 1898). It is noteworthy that this periodical was published in Boston, the hotbed of anti-imperialism.

[85] *Independent,* L, 1137 (October 20, 1898).

[86] *Ibid.,* pp. 994-995 (October 6, 1898).

Pope for arbitration, the Carolines were in 1885 assigned to Spain. A rebellion of the natives of Ponape against Spanish rule led to the expulsion of the Protestant missionaries and a complete suspension of their work.[87] The war seemed to offer an opportunity for the return of the missionaries to the Carolines. Declaring that Spain had repeated in the Carolines " her outrageous performances in other parts of the world," one paper, even before Dewey's victory, demanded that they " be taken from her, along with Cuba and Porto Rico." [88] The *Advance* voiced a similar opinion in June.[89] The *Missionary Herald*, official publication of the American Board, stated that while the Board made it a rule to take no part in political discussion and had nothing to say about the question of territorial acquisitions by the United States, it nevertheless deemed it proper to ask that guarantees of perfect religious toleration in the Carolines should be secured.[90] At its annual meeting in October, 1898, the American Board received a report from one of its committees announcing that the war had

opened the door wide for the prosecution of missionary effort in our Micronesian field. With religious liberty restored in the Carolines, and " the American flag floating over the Ladrones," our missionaries may work unterrified by papal interference and Spanish treachery. . . . This is the Lord's doing, and it is marvelous in our eyes.[91]

[87] " The Caroline Islands and Religious Liberty " (unsigned), *Missionary Herald*, XCIV, 261-263 (July, 1898).

[88] Toledo *Blade*, quoted in New York *Commercial*, April 27, 1898.

[89] *Advance*, XXXV, 794 (June 16, 1898).

[90] *Missionary Herald*, XCIV, 253 (July, 1898).

[91] *Eighty-eighth Annual Report of American Board of Commissioners for Foreign Missions*, presented at the Annual Meeting at Grand Rapids, Mich., October 4-7, 1898, pp. xxv, 115.

A vigorous propaganda for the annexation of the Carolines was carried on by Mr. Edward Van Dyke Robinson,
who wrote to an adviser to the American Peace Commission that the feeling on this subject among religious people,
business men, and scholars was so strong that if the treaty
should leave these islands in the hands of Spain, it would
" prove the political destruction of all connected with it." [92]

The Episcopal Church in the United States was apparently as willing as any other to accept the new responsibilities
created by the war. Two weeks after the battle of Manila
Bay, the *Church Standard* hailed " the opening up to the
special care of American Christianity of two populous regions "—Cuba and the Philippines.[93] In June the *Church
Eclectic,* an Anglo-Catholic magazine, foresaw new questions of great seriousness arising from the conflict. The
future of the Philippines, of Cuba, perhaps of Puerto Rico
and even the Canary Islands, would be in the hands of

[92] E. Van D. Robinson to Capt. Bradford, Ann Arbor, Mich.,
September 27, 1898. *Miscellaneous Letters Sent to Members of the
Peace Commission, 1898* (MSS, Dept. of State). *Cf.* Robinson's ar-
ticle, " The Caroline Islands and the Terms of Peace," *Independent,*
L, 1046-1048 (October 13, 1898). Robinson continued his propa-
ganda even after the signing of the peace treaty. *Cf.* his letter to
Congressman R. R. Hitt, Rock Island, Ill., December 20, 1898, in
Miscellaneous Letters, 1898, December, enclosing a petition urging a
supplementary treaty for the purchase of the Caroline, Pelew, and
Ladrone groups. The *Miscellaneous Letters* for 1898 contain much
material on the Spanish treatment of American missionaries in the
Carolines.

The Carolines were subsequently sold by Spain to Germany. *Cf.
infra,* pp. 342-344. The *Missionary Herald* (XCV, 272-274,
July, 1899) found reason to be satisfied with prospects for missionary work under German rule.

[93] *Church Standard,* LXXV, 42 (May 14, 1898)

the American Congress. Would it be possible to make good our disavowal of all desire to add to our territory by conquest?

Certainly we ought not to be expected to fight to free one island from Spanish rule and then return to Spain other islands which may be ours by conquest.[94]

In September, the same periodical was urging the organization of missions throughout South America and the West Indies, on the ground of the alleged degeneracy of the Catholic Church in those areas.

Never before [it said] has the Church in this country been confronted so suddenly with new foreign relations requiring new policies as at the present time. The raising of the American flag over the Hawaiian Islands, the acquisition of Porto Rico and the lesser Antilles [sic], the temporary, if not permanent, ascendancy of the United States to a greater or less extent over Cuba and the Philippine Islands, . . . all combine to make the present a turning point in the treatment of problems relating to lands outside the present borders of the United States.[95]

The Churchman believed, in June, that the country was " being led through a profound educational process " and that those who clung blindly to the traditions of the past were perhaps " resisting a higher purpose than that of their fellows. . . . If God has brought us to the parting of the ways, we cannot hold back without rejecting divine leadership." [96] In August, it was arguing that outright annexation of Cuba, with the consent of the inhabitants " would save

[94] The Church Eclectic: an Anglo-Catholic Magazine of Church Literature, XXVI, 263 (June, 1898).
[95] Ibid., pp. 542-543 (September, 1898).
[96] Churchman, LXXVII, 806 (June 4, 1898).

the Cubans years of turmoil." [97] In November, in a long
editorial, it took issue with Bishop Potter, of New York,
who had delivered an anti-imperialist address. Said the
editor:

Woe to any nation brought to a pass where it is called
to guide a weaker people's future which hesitates for fear
its own interests will be entangled and its own future im-
perilled by the full discharge of an unmistakable duty.
. . . The power and wealth, the intelligence and the wisdom of the United States, are a solemn trust for the upbuilding and civilization of the world.[98]

Bishop Potter's attack upon imperialism [99] apparently
found little favor among other dignitaries of the Episcopal
Church. Bishop Hall, of Vermont, was convinced that the
nation had been " used by Almighty God as an instrument
for putting an end to a selfish system of misgovernment,"
and that it must now face the responsibility of " establishing a righteous and a stable rule in the place of that which
we have overthrown." [100] The *Spirit of Missions,* published
by the Domestic and Foreign Missionary Society of the
Protestant Episcopal Church, printed extracts from a ser-
mon preached by the Bishop of Missouri at the General
Convention of the Church in October, 1898. The ear of
faith, he said, could now easily catch the message:

Speak unto the children of the Church that they go forward,
. . . Hawaii, Porto Rico—go forward and possess the land.

[97] *Ibid.,* LXXVIII, 274 (August 27, 1898).

[98] *Ibid.,* pp. 727-728 (November 19, 1898).

[99] Bishop Potter's address is printed in the *Church Standard,*
LXXV, 636-637.

[100] *Ibid.,* p. 639 (October 1, 1898). Bishop Hall's statement
received the endorsement of the editor of the *Church Standard.*
Ibid., p. 635.

The Philippines—if the flag we honor and love is to float
sovereign there, go ye in there also. And if the forceful
logic of events that we wot of lift the flag in unfurled
permanence over other regions yet, go ye there, too, to
bide and work and help and save.[101]

The same spirit was exemplified in a report of a committee
of the Board of Missions, which declared:

American civilization and American ideals and institutions,
with American power to uphold and extend them, have
moved on, in the providence of God, to the islands of the
Pacific; aye! onward to the kingdoms and peoples of the
far East, and soon we shall have no more talk of *foreign*
missions, for every Christian man, in every land, will realize
that humanity is one, as Christ is one. . . .[102]

Spokesmen for the Disciples of Christ clearly saw God's
hand in the events of the war. To President Butler, of
Butler College, the guns at Manila were " God's own
trumpet-tones summoning his people out of their isolation
into the broad arena of the world's great life." [103] The
editor of the *Christian-Evangelist* believed that " a great and
effectual door is being opened before American Christians
for aggressive evangelistic work." [104] To another editor of
the same denomination it appeared that the period had
providentially arrived " to crack the Monroe Doctrine like
a shell, and to introduce the nation to an enlarged mission.
. . . The Lord has not raised up this mighty people to

[101] *Spirit of Missions,* LXIII, 523 (November, 1898).
[102] *Church Standard,* LXXV, 792 (October 29, 1898).
[103] *Christian-Evangelist,* XXXV, 13 (July 7, 1898).
[104] *Ibid.,* pp. 66-67 (July 21, 1898).

dwell in selfish contentment, indifferent to the wrongs and oppressions of other lands." [105]

The attitude of these Protestant churches to the war and its results was well summed up some months later by the *Churchman* in some remarks upon the celebration in honor of Admiral Dewey in the fall of 1899. To no admiral since the days of Drake, thought the writer, had it been given " so clearly to point his nation to a more unexpected or nobler goal than that to which he called us by the morning guns of that great first of May." The shouts in his honor evidenced no love of war or conquest, but rather

a joy that we should have been called through him to emancipate, to educate and in the highest sense to free races long held in bondage, political, mental and moral, to free them even at our own cost for the sake of the righteousness that exalts the nation by enlarging the hope of the human race.[106]

The inhabitants of the former Spanish islands, which were thought to be such promising fields for missionary work, were for the most part Catholic Christians—in Cuba and Puerto Rico, almost solidly so; in the Philippines, all but the relatively small number of Mohammedan Moros in the south and " wild tribes " in the mountain regions. The Philippine Islands, in fact, were the single flourishing outpost of Christianity in the Far East. The missionary enthusiasm of the Protestant churches, therefore, in so far as it was not based upon ignorance of the facts, contemplated a proselytizing assault upon these citadels of Catholicism. Hence one would hardly expect to find in American

[105] *Christian Standard*, XXXIV, 1090 (August 20, 1898).
[106] *Churchman*, LXXX, 407 (October 7, 1899).

Catholics the same religious zeal for expansion that flourished among their Protestant brethren.

We have already observed that certain Catholic publications were inclined to criticize the Protestant clergy for their warlike spirit. Not unexpectedly we find a similar attitude displayed toward Protestant missionary fervor. The *Ave Maria,* which had opposed the war, was skeptical of the beneficence of its results. Of McKinley's annual message in December, 1898, it said:

It is a labored effort to justify a war that every sane man must sooner or later regard as unjustifiable, and to shift the responsibility of its inevitably disastrous consequences. . . . We shall have to fight the gentle savages of the Philippines yet; and those who were so eager to arm them will not be so ready to fight them.[107]

The same paper warned the Filipinos of the impending invasion of Protestant missionaries. Recalling how, in Hawaii, the result of missionary rule had been to rob a poor "widow woman" of lands and throne, it prophesied:

The unfortunate people of Manila will remember Dewey's bombardment as a restful holiday compared with the times that will come if the preachers ever invade the Philippines, bringing divorce and sundry other things with them.[108]

It would be a mistake, however, to assume that American Catholics, in general, opposed the expansionist policy. The *Catholic World,* for example, while it saw danger in "our

[107] *Ave Maria,* XLVII, 789 (December 17, 1898).

[108] *Ibid.,* p. 23 (July 2, 1898). *Cf. ibid.,* p. 312 (September 3, 1898): "It was an ill day for Hawaii when sectarian missionaries set foot on their shores. . . . The end of a century of high civilization has been signalized by national crimes without parallel in modern history. The seizure of Hawaii is one of them."

racial thirst for globe conquest," felt that the great events impending in the Pacific made it imperative that the United States should have " a coaling station, a harbor of defence, and a store-house of ammunition in the midst of these activities." The American flag must wave over Honolulu, if not also over Manila.[109] It ridiculed Protestant talk about the " evangelization of the Philippines," wondering whether the " pure religion " now to be carried thither would " have the same fatal results there as it had in the Sandwich Islands," [110] but it did not regard this danger seriously. Attempts to proselytize the Catholics of Cuba and the Philippines, it predicted, would be as futile as similar efforts in the Latin countries of the old world or in South America.

Spanish America may be wicked and irreligious, but it will never be Protestant. The efforts of the Missionary Societies to send a bevy of missionaries to our newly acquired possessions will result only in discrediting Americanism among the people.

The better course would be to send some accredited American priests.[111]

Some Catholic clergymen, like their Protestant counterparts, saw the hand of Providence in the war. American rule would not endanger the religious welfare of the people of the new possessions, while it would bring them the blessings of American political institutions. " We cannot," wrote Rev. H. E. O'Keeffe, " leave the Antilles and the Philippines to be fought over and gobbled up by European

[109] *Catholic World*, LXVII, 426 (June, 1898).
[110] *Ibid.*, p. 563 (July, 1898).
[111] *Ibid.*, p. 854 (September, 1898).

kingdoms. Our love of those historic realities—liberty, progress, democracy—will not permit it." The same writer had no fear of the influence of Protestant boards of missions in the islands, for—

Wealth is the weakest power in missionary tactics. The warmth and glow and strength of Catholicism, so fitly represented in America, will as easily conquer not only those who are Catholic to the marrow of their bones, but likewise the Mongolian, the Negro, and the Malay.[112]

Rev. A. P. Doyle thought the coming of the Americans to the Philippines providential, but all would depend upon how the situation was handled. Protestant missionaries should be persuaded to stay away. He would " select the most thorough Americans among the Catholic priests of the country and establish an *entente cordiale* between them and the civil authorities." A broad-minded military man— not necessarily a Catholic, but one who had no antipathy to the Church—should be made governor-general. He should establish courts, introduce modern sanitation, suppress vice, and leave religion alone. By such tactics, said Father Doyle, we should win the Filipinos to our ways and before many years should " have planted among the Orientals the seeds of the freest and best government on the face of the earth." [113]

[112] Rev. H. E. O'Keeffe, C. S. P., " A Word on the Church in the New Possessions," *ibid.*, LXVIII, 319-322 (December, 1898).

[113] Rev. A. P. Doyle, C. S. P. ," Religious Problem of the Philippines," *ibid.*, pp. 119-124 (October, 1898). It is to be noted that the Episcopal *Church Standard* (LXXV, 295) commented favorably upon the departure of Rev. Francis B. Doherty, a Paulist missionary, for the Philippines, and expressed the hope " that the Roman Catholic Church in America will contribute its share toward Christianizing the natives of the Philippines."

Thus Catholics joined with Protestants—though in an atmosphere beclouded with mutual suspicion—in hailing the civilizing mission of the United States in its newly won possessions. Even the *Ave Maria,* anti-imperialist though it was, did not close its eyes to possible benefits of the new policy. If Cuba and Puerto Rico were to become parts of the United States, it remarked, three million Catholics would be added to the census figures, and three new sees— " one of them, Santiago de Cuba, is the oldest in the Western hemisphere—will most probably, though not necessarily, be attached to the hierarchy of the United States." [114] The *Catholic Herald* foresaw benefits from American control for Catholics in the Philippines. Referring to reports of Filipino atrocities against the Dominicans, it remarked that American rule would soon put a stop to such outrages, that the Catholic Church would be treated in the Philippines as in the United States, and that religion would flourish.[115] American law would reign in the Philippines until England should consent to exchange Canada for them.[116]

It would appear that the only religious bodies that offered any serious opposition to expansion were those which had opposed the war; namely, Quakers and Unitarians.[117] The

[114] *Ave Maria,* XLVII, 183 (August 6, 1898).

[115] *Catholic Herald,* November 28, 1898.

[116] *Ibid.,* December 5, 1898.

[117] From such rather unexpected quarters as Mormon and Theosophist publications came endorsements of the expansionist policy. The Mormon *Improvement Era,* in April, 1898, remarked " that a divine Providence watches over the affairs of nations, guides their destiny and appoints to each its mission," and went on to point out that Spain's failure in colonial administration was about to be

Friend deplored the rise of the ideas of imperialism and manifest destiny, fearing that the war would have turned men's minds from a humanitarian view to a glorification of the nation's rôle in world affairs.[118] The *Christian Register,* which lamented that millions of dollars had already been wasted on foreign missions,[119] regretted to hear talk of buying and selling a nation of seven million people and of exploiting the people of Cuba, Hawaii, and the Philippines " for the benefit of our manufactures and our commerce. The very conception," it added, " is un-American. It belongs to a ' strong government.' " Let Cincinnatus return to his plow!

There is nothing which would so ennoble our own people, nothing which would so increase our influence among the nations, as such a spectacle of self-control. As Washington refused to be king, so must America refuse to join the partnership of the giants, who are dividing among themselves the spoils of the half-civilized world.[120]

This paper reported sympathetically an anti-imperialist mass-meeting in Boston in June.[121] In October it still believed that the better part of the American people were opposed to expansion. [122] It was unconverted by a corres-

rewarded with the loss of her last colonial possessions. The United States, by the same token, was destined to receive wider responsibilities. *Improvement Era,* I, 450-455, 694-695 (April, July, 1898). The *New Century,* a Theosophist publication, saw in the contest with Spain a part of "the great drama of LIGHT and DARKNESS," and remarked that the duty of the United States was plain, even in the Philippines. *New Century,* April 16, August 20, 1898.

[118] *Friend,* LXXII, 177 (12th Mo. 17, 1898).
[119] *Christian Register,* LXXVIII, 312 (March 23, 1899).
[120] *Ibid.,* LXXVII, 514-515 (May 12, 1898).
[121] *Ibid.,* p. 720 (June 23, 1898).
[122] *Ibid.,* p. 1116 (October 6, 1898).

pondent from Fall River, who predicted that if the Philippines were taken they would provide such an excellent
market for American cloth that " the Fall River factories
will be running day and night, to clothe the heathen in the
far-away Pacific, and the Unitarian Church at Fall River
will become prosperous, and contributions will pour into
the treasury of the A. U. A." [123]

We may conclude that the great preponderance of vocal
religious sentiment, in the summer and fall of 1898, was in
favor of retaining the Philippines and the other Spanish
islands which had yielded to American arms. President
McKinley, with whom the decision rested, was neither unaware of this sentiment nor indifferent to it. In fact, he
was well informed. Senator Platt, of Connecticut, after a
tour of his state, reported to McKinley in August that in
his opinion nine-tenths of the people of Connecticut had
an intense feeling that the United States should insist upon
the cession of all the Philippine Islands.

Those who believe in Providence [he wrote] see, or think
they see, that God has placed upon this Government the
solemn duty of providing for the people of these islands a
government based upon the principle of liberty no matter
how many difficulties the problem may present. They feel
that it is our duty to attempt its solution. Among Christian,
thoughtful people the sentiment is akin to that which has
maintained the missionary work of the last century in
foreign lands. . . . If in the negotiations for peace Spain
is permitted to retain any portion of the Philippines it
will be regarded as a failure on the part of this nation to
discharge the greatest moral obligation which could be
conceived." [124]

[123] *Ibid.*, p. 1408 (December 15, 1898).
[124] L. A. Coolidge, *An Old-Fashioned Senator, Orville H. Platt
of Connecticut,* pp. 287-288.

Nor were the clergy idle in bringing this aspect of the matter to the President's attention. On September 23, Rev. D. W. LeLacheur, Superintendent of Missions of the Christian and Missionary Alliance in China and Malaysia, called at the Department of State. He bore a letter from the president and secretary of the organization, praying that every effort be made to keep open the doors for missionary work in the Philippines, and a resolution passed by a large gathering at Old Orchard Beach, Maine, urging that those islands should not be permitted " to pass again under the blighting influence of Spanish rule." [125] The purpose of this clergyman's visit was thus stated in the official organ of the body which he represented:

Our dear brother Rev. D. W. LeLacheur is visiting Washington this week for the purpose of interviewing the President and Secretary of State with reference to the conditions and needs in China and the Asiatic islands. One special object of Mr. LeLacheur's visit is to impress upon the administration from his own personal knowledge the importance of securing an open door for missions in the Philippine Islands and holding the advantage which God has given to the American government in the interests of religious liberty and Christian evangelization in this important region. . . . We trust the prayers of our people will accompany him and give him favor with those in authority so that the new force may be called to the pressure already brought to bear upon the Government and Peace Commissioners in favor of the retention of these valuable and down trodden islands.[126]

[125] Adee to Day, September 23, 1898 (copy), enclosing copy of letter from A. B. Simpson and A. E. Funk to Secretary of State, September 21, 1898. The former is in *Special Missions*, IV, 274; the latter in *Paris Peace Commission, 1898*, II, Dept. of State.

[126] *Christian and Missionary Alliance*, XXI, 300 (September 28, 1898).

Similar ideas existed in the President's own household. Mr. W. C. Beer, who visited the White House in October, found Mrs. McKinley much preoccupied with the prospect of " converting the Igorrotes." [127] McKinley's own account of the religious experience which led to his decision to keep the Philippines is well known. He had, he said, sought counsel from all sides and got little help. He had paced the floor of the White House till midnight, night after night. Finally, he had prayed for guidance, and the answer had come that " there was nothing left for us to do but to take them all, and to educate the Filipinos, and uplift and civilize and Christianize them, and by God's grace do the very best we could by them as our fellow-men for whom Christ also died." [128] The answer that thus seemed to McKinley to have come to him from above may easily have grown from seed planted in his mind by the clergy and the religious press.

[127] W. C. Beer to Thos. Beer, October 23, 1898. " Mrs. McK. talked ten to the minute about converting the Igorrotes. . . . Anyhow she wants you and Alice to pray for the Igorrotes. . . . " Beer, *Hanna,* p. 211, note.

[128] C. S. Olcott, *The Life of William McKinley,* II, 109-111.

IX

CONSUMMATION

In the early summer of 1898, while the organs of business and religion were exerting their best efforts to bring about the annexation of the Spanish Islands, the expansionist policy achieved its first triumph. A joint resolution annexing the Hawaiian Islands to the United States passed the House of Representatives on June 15, the Senate on July 6, and received the President's signature on July 7.[1] On August 12, the islands passed formally under the sovereignty of the United States.

The annexation of Hawaii was a by-product of the war with Spain. With no hope for the ratification of the treaty of annexation by the Senate, and with the powerful opposition of Speaker Thomas B. Reed in the House blocking action by joint resolution, the chances of annexation had seemed, in the early spring, desperately low.[2] To Minister Hatch, in Washington, the situation seemed to threaten not only the failure of annexation but the eventual loss of reciprocity as well.[3] Hatch had felt, as we have seen,

[1] *Stat. L.*, XXX, 750-751.

[2] Professor Thomas A. Bailey, after a careful study of the situation in Washington and Honolulu in the spring of 1898 (" The United States and Hawaii during the Spanish-American War," *American Historical Review*, XXXVI, 552-560), concludes that " if the war had not come when it did and if Dewey had not fought successfully at Manila, Hawaii would not have been annexed for some years to come, if ever " (p. 560).

[3] Hatch to Cooper, April 14, 1898. Spaulding Collection.

that war with Spain would greatly improve the chances of annexation,[4] and when war became certain, he made every effort to see that it was utilized for that purpose. Anticipating, upon the advice of friends in the Senate, that the President might find it convenient to take possession of Hawaii by executive act, as a war measure, without awaiting action by Congress, Hatch urged that the Hawaiian legislature give its consent in advance to such procedure.[5] The Hawaiian Government declined to follow this suggestion, but despite the demands of foreign and royalist groups that it adopt a position of neutrality, it proffered full assistance and support to the United States, even to the extent of suggesting a formal alliance.[6] It facilitated the purchase and storing of coal in Honolulu by the Navy Department and permitted the free use of Honolulu harbor by the expeditions sent to reenforce Dewey at Manila.[7] By thus making itself virtually an ally of the United States and thereby taking the risk of possible Spanish reprisal, the Hawaiian Government provided the annexationists in Washington with a telling argument. How, it was asked, could the United States refuse to extend its full protection over

that steadfast body of men [who], pressed and menaced by the influence of so many empires and kingdoms, threatening them with the danger that would follow if they permitted

[4] *Supra*, p. 225.

[5] From Hatch's letter to Cooper of April 14, cited above, it is evident that he had proposed this course in a letter of March 16, which is not in the Spaulding Collection. *Cf.* Bailey, *op. cit.*, pp. 553-554.

[6] *Ibid.*, pp. 554-555.

[7] *Ibid.*, pp. 555-556.

the American flag to stay in their harbor, remained constant in their devotion to the colors they loved and the people they always trusted? [8]

Inevitably, Dewey's victory at Manila turned American eyes to the Pacific as never before. To the lay mind, at least, it appeared that Honolulu was a way-station on the route to Manila, essential to safeguard communications with Dewey.[9] Although this argument for taking Hawaii was not altogether sound—since the United States possessed, at Kiska in the Aleutian Islands, a harbor much nearer than Honolulu to the great circle route to Manila [10]—it had its effect. In addition, the annexationists brought forward the testimony of military and naval experts—Captain Mahan, General Schofield, and Chief Engineer Melville of the Navy—to prove that the possession of Hawaii was essential for the defense of the Pacific coast.[11] It is interesting to note that the supposed British menace of a few years before had now given place to a Japanese menace. Both the Foreign Relations Committee of the Senate and the Foreign Affairs Committee of the House referred ominously to the rapidly growing Japanese population in the

[8] *Cong. Rec.*, 55th Cong., 2d sess., p. 5773. From speech of Hitt, of Illinois, in the House of Representatives, June 11, 1898. This was, wrote Hatch, " the point of Mr. Hitt's speech which drew out the greatest applause." Hatch to Cooper, June 12, 1898. Spaulding Collection.

[9] *Supra*, p. 274.

[10] *Cong. Rec.*, 55th Cong., 2d sess., pp. 5779-5780. Dinsmore, of Arkansas, asserted that the distance from San Francisco to Manila via Kiska and Yokohama was 803 miles shorter' than by Honolulu. *Cf.* Bailey, *op. cit.*, p. 558.

[11] *Senate Documents* Nos. 62, 188, 315; *Senate Report* No. 681, p. 99; *House Report* No. 1355, pp. 8-20—all 55th Cong., 2d sess.

islands and the still pending controversy which had arisen
out of Hawaii's attempt to check Japanese immigration; and
both contended that only annexation by the United States
would save the islands from incorporation in the growing
Empire of Japan. Said the Senate Committee:

> The present Hawaiian-Japanese controversy is the pre-
> liminary skirmish in the great coming struggle between the
> civilization and the awakening forces of the East and the
> civilization of the West. The issue is whether, in that
> inevitable struggle, Asia or America shall have the vantage
> ground of the control of the naval "Key of the Pacific,"
> the commercial "Crossroads of the Pacific." [12]

The joint resolution of annexation which the Committee
on Foreign Relations had brought into the Senate on March
16, 1898,[13] languished there for months. On May 4, three
days after Dewey's victory, a similar resolution was introduced in the House.[14] It was referred to the Committee
on Foreign Affairs, whence, on May 17, Chairman Hitt reported it back to the House with the endorsement of a
majority of the committee.[15] It was known that the resolution would easily pass the House if it could be brought
to a vote. The one obstacle was Speaker Reed, implacable

[12] *Senate Report* No. 681, 55th Cong., 2d sess., pp. 30-31. *Cf.*
House Report No. 1355, 55th Cong., 2d sess., pp. 4-5. McKinley,
in a conversation with Senator Hoar, urged the Japanese menace as
the principal reason for annexation. Hoar, *Autobiography of
Seventy Years,* II, 307-308. *Cf.* Dennett, *Americans in Eastern Asia,*
pp. 612-615.

[13] *Supra,* p. 225.

[14] *Cong. Rec.,* 55th Cong., 2d sess., p. 4600.

[15] *Ibid.,* p. 4989. *House Report* No. 1355, 55th Cong., 2d sess.
The report of the Democratic minority opposing the resolution is
included as Part II in the same report.

opponent of annexation, who as chairman of the Committee on Rules could prevent the consideration of the resolution. For three weeks he held out against pressure from the
Administration and his fellow-Republicans in Congress,
but there was a limit beyond which even he would not go
in opposing the wishes of his party, and he finally gave his
consent to tactics which would bring the resolution before
the House without a special rule.[16] On June 10, the resolution was made the special order of business to be voted
upon on June 15.[17] All was now plain sailing, as far as the
House was concerned. As the outcome was known in advance, the debate was a formality. Champ Clark, who made
one of the chief speeches in opposition,[18] sought to do little
more than entertain the House with his ridicule of the
project. Why this sudden need for an island? he asked.
Had we not defeated Great Britain in two wars without an
island? Had Andrew Jackson needed an island at New
Orleans? Evidently Mahan's teachings had been lost upon
Clark. More seriously he warned that if we took Hawaii
we should not stop there. "All history proves that the
passion for acquiring territory grows with what it feeds
on." Already Senator Henry Cabot Lodge, " that preeminent twister of the British lion's caudal appendage," was
preparing to purchase the islands of St. Thomas, St. John,
and St. Croix, and many in Congress were talking of annexing Puerto Rico, the Philippines, the Canaries and Carolines. " The jingo bacillus is indefatigable in its work."

[16] Wm. A. Robinson, *Thomas B. Reed, Parliamentarian*, pp. 366-
367. Dunn, *From Harrison to Harding*, I, 290-291.
[17] *Cong. Rec.*, 55th Cong., 2d sess., p. 5766.
[18] *Ibid.*, pp. 5788-5795.

Annex Hawaii, said Clark, and it would soon be a state—a pocket borough.

How can we endure our shame when a Chinese Senator from Hawaii, with his pigtail hanging down his back, with his pagan joss in his hand, shall rise from his curule chair and in pigeon English proceed to chop logic with George Frisbie Hoar or Henry Cabot Lodge? O tempora! O mores!

Neither Clark's ridicule nor the more serious arguments of his colleagues [19] could affect the outcome. The resolution passed the House on June 15, by a vote of 209 to 91,[20] divided for the most part on party lines.

The fight now shifted to the Senate, where the result was by no means a foregone conclusion. Minister Hatch considered the chances excellent, but he complained of the disposition of the opposing Senators to hunt up all possible technicalities against annexation by joint resolution, and saw a danger that a quorum might not be held until the end of the debate.[21] Senator Lodge did not expect the Senate opposition to hold out very long, for as he wrote, " the President has been very firm about it and means to annex the Islands any way." [22]

[19] Cf. speeches of Alexander (N. Y.), Walker (Mass.), Newlands (Nev.), for the resolution; Dinsmore (Ark.), Bell (Colorado), Meyer (La.), against it. Ibid., pp. 5785-5788, 5795, 5828-5832, 5779-5780, 5832-5834, 5984.

[20] Ibid., p. 6019.

[21] Hatch to Cooper, June 22, 1898. Spaulding Collection.

[22] Lodge to Roosevelt, June 15, 1898. Lodge, Selections from the Correspondence of Theodore Roosevelt and Henry Cabot Lodge, I, 311. It was possibly with a view to annexation by executive act, if the resolution should fail of passage, that John Bassett Moore inquired of Hatch whether the Hawaiian Government had signified its consent to the cession of its territory and sovereignty to the

The joint resolution from the House was introduced in the Senate on June 16 and referred to the Committee on Foreign Relations, which reported it without amendment on the following day.[23] In the debate, which opened on June 20 and continued until July 6, when the vote was taken,[24] the friends of annexation, for the most part, remained silent, giving to the opposition Senators ample time in which to state their objections. These may be briefly summarized. The existing Hawaiian Government, it was argued, owed its existence to the illegal action of Minister Stevens in 1893; it had no right to speak for the Hawaiian people.[25] The islands had no military or other value to the United States.[26] Annexation by joint resolution was unconstitutional.[27] Hawaii, if annexed, would in all probability become a state with two Senators. In view of this unwelcome possibility, Senator Morrill announced that he was opposed to annexation " whether by treaty, by joint resolution, by flagrant Executive usurpation, or in any manner which leaves an open door for their admission into the

United States in any other way than by its ratification of the treaty of the preceding year. Moore to Hatch, June 29, 1898, copy, enclosed in Hatch to Cooper, July 1, 1898. Spaulding Collection. Hatch felt that his government had made a mistake in failing to authorize annexation by congressional resolution or executive act, as he had advised in March. Such action, he thought, would have removed one objection to the resolution in the Senate, as well as providing still another alternative. Hatch to Cooper, June 9, June 22, 1898. Ibid.

23 Cong. Rec., 55th Cong., 2d sess., pp. 6022, 6062.

24 Ibid., pp. 6141-6708, passim.

25 Ibid., pp. 6409-6418, 6465-6488, 6693-6702.

26 Ibid., pp. 6141-6145, 6188-6191, 6260-6268.

27 Ibid., pp. 6145-6156, 6308-6312.

Union as a state." [28] But if the islands were not to become
a state, the case was no better, for the United States was
unsuited for a colonial policy.[29] Yet it was the inauguration of an ambitious and dangerous scheme of colonial expansion that some Senators detected in the proposal to
annex Hawaii.

Is not this but the opening of a grand avenue of conquest
and of power? The Philippines next. Part of Asia next.
Where will be the limits? . . . This Hawaiian scheme
is but the entering wedge that cleaves a way open for
empire.[30]

One supporter of the resolution rose to repudiate all
such grandiose designs and to argue that the United States
could annex Hawaii without committing itself to a further
extension of its sovereignty. Senator Hoar, of Massachusetts, had long been in favor of Hawaiian annexation. But
he had been alarmed, in recent months, by the widespread
talk of colonial empire and had hesitated to vote for the
Hawaiian treaty or resolution in the fear that it might be
but the first step toward an unwholesome imperialism. He
had expressed these misgivings to President McKinley and
had received an emphatic assurance of the President's opposition to schemes of empire.[31] Now, supporting the
Hawaiian resolution in the Senate, Hoar attempted to
draw a sharp distinction between the type of expansion

[28] *Ibid.*, p. 6141.

[29] *Ibid.*, pp. 6268-6271.

[30] *Ibid.*, p. 6483. Speech of Senator Caffery, of Louisiana. *Cf.*
ibid., pp. 6350-6355.

[31] Hoar, *loc. cit.* Hoar stated: " I never, at any time during the
discussion of the Philippine question, expressed a more emphatic
disapproval of the acquisition of dependencies or Oriental Empire
by military strength than he [McKinley] expressed on that occasion."

which it represented—an invitation, as he said, " to willing and capable people to share with us our freedom, our self-government, our equality, our education, and the trans-cendant sweets of civil and religious liberty "—and the type " held out to us in the far East and in the West Indies as the result of military conquest,"—the type which had been " the ruin of the empires and republics of former times." The latter type, " dominion over subject people, and the rule over vassal states," was " forbidden to us by our Constitution, by our political principles, by every lesson of our own history and of all history." Our rule, said Hoar, should be to acquire no territory " except where we can reasonably expect that the people we acquire will, in due time and on suitable conditions, be annexed to the United States as an equal part of a self-governing Republic." [32]

It was in vain that Hoar sought to enforce the distinc-tion, as he himself was presently to learn. Already his col-league from Massachusetts was rejoicing that the Adminis-tration was committed to a " large policy," [33] while another Senator, the author of the Teller Resolution, was proclaim-ing that wherever the American flag should fly, " by right of conquest or by the consent of the people," there it should remain;

and the party or the men who propose to take it down will reckon with the great body of the American people, who believe that it is the best flag and the best Government, better calculated to bring peace and prosperity to men than any other flag and Government under the sky.[34]

When the Senate, on July 6, passed the joint resolution

[32] *Cong. Rec.*, 55th Cong., 2d sess., pp. 6660-6665.
[33] Lodge, *op. cit.*, I, 300.
[34] *Cong. Rec.*, 55th Cong., 2d sess., p. 6157.

by a vote of 42 to 21,[35] it took the road which led logically to the possession of Puerto Rico and the Philippines, Guam and Samoa.

William McKinley was not, by temperament or inclination, an imperialist. In common with Mark Hanna, he had looked forward to his term of office as a period of "domestic economic amelioration." There is no reason to doubt his sincerity when he told Schurz, at the beginning of his administration, that he had no plan for annexing Hawaii; or when, in his first annual message, he said: "Forcible annexation . . . cannot be thought of. That by our code of morality would be criminal aggression"; [36] or when, later on, he assured Hoar of his opposition to "Oriental Empire." McKinley did not foresee, as Lodge, Roosevelt, and Beveridge foresaw, the destination to which the war with Spain was to lead. When he learned of Dewey's victory at Manila, he had to look up its location on a globe. "I could not have told," Kohlsaat remembered him as saying, "where those darned islands were within 2,000 miles!" [37]

Nor was Judge Day, McKinley's Secretary of State, privy to the "large policy" of the expansionists. "Unfortunately there is nothing we can do but give those islands back to

[35] *Ibid.*, p. 6712. Most Republicans voted for, most Democrats against, the resolution, but Morrill, of Vermont, was with the "Noes" and Gorman, of Maryland, and Morgan and Pettus, of Alabama, with the "Ayes."

[36] *Ibid.*, p. 4.

[37] H. H. Kohlsaat, *From McKinley to Harding*, p. 68. Kohlsaat related that McKinley said to him some months later: "If old Dewey had just sailed away when he smashed that Spanish fleet, what a lot of trouble he would have saved us." *Ibid.*

Spain," Day is reported to have remarked when he was first informed of Dewey's victory.[38] In an outline of the President's probable peace terms drafted on June 3, 1898, Day stated that Spain would be permitted to retain the Philippine Islands, "except a port and necessary appurtenances." [39]

But both McKinley and Day were at the mercy of circumstances, and McKinley, as earlier in the Hawaiian episode, was now clay in the hands of the little group of men who knew all too well what use to make of the war. "We see already the beginnings of an 'Imperial' party here," wrote Walter Hines Page on May 9.[40] The influence of the "Imperial Party" upon McKinley was soon apparent. On June 14, Day cabled to John Hay in London that the proposal to return the Philippines to Spain would probably have to be modified—that it was now impossible to determine what disposition would be made of the islands.[41] Ten days later Senator Lodge made a report to his friend Theodore Roosevelt, who from Cuba had been writing urgent letters about the necessity of securing Puerto Rico, the Philippines, and Hawaii.[42] Lodge had seen Day and had been assured that there was no question in any one's mind about Puerto Rico. Furthermore:

He [Day] dined with me the other night and Mahan and I talked the Philippines with him for two hours. He

[38] T. B. Mott, *Myron T. Herrick, Friend of France*, p. 325. This was the recollection of Herrick, at whose house Day was staying at the time. Day had succeeded John Sherman as Secretary of State April 28, 1898.

[39] Tyler Dennett, *John Hay*, p. 190. Day to John Hay, June 3, 1898.

[40] B. J. Hendrick, *The Training of an American; The Earlier Life and Letters of Walter H. Page*, pp. 264-265.

[41] Dennett, *John Hay*, p. 191.

[42] Lodge, *op. cit.*, I, 299, 309.

said at the end that he thought we could not escape our destiny there.[43]

The report of Day's conversion was premature, but undoubtedly the " large policy " was making progress.

, The naval battle off Santiago on July 3 completed the destruction of Spain's naval power. On July 15, the military commander of Santiago agreed to surrender the city and the defending army to the besieging force under General Shafter. Ten days later, an American expeditionary force landed at Guanica, Puerto Rico, and began, almost unresisted, the conquest of that island. Meanwhile, an army of over ten thousand regulars and volunteers had sailed in three expeditions from San Francisco for the Philippines, and by July 24 the last of them were in position before Manila.[44] Nothing, unless a speedy move for peace, could save for Spain any remnant of her colonial empire.

Accordingly, on July 18, the Spanish Government undertook, through the French Government and the French Ambassador in Washington, M. Cambon, to approach President McKinley on the subject of peace. Because of delays in Paris and elsewhere, M. Cambon was not able to present the Spanish communication until July 26.[45] The note intimated that Spain was ready to part with Cuba and invited the President to suggest a political status for the island which might result in the termination of hostilities. Since Spain had not provoked the war—so wrote the Spanish

[43] *Ibid.*, p. 313.

[44] F. E. Chadwick, *The Relations of the United States and Spain: The Spanish-American War*, II, 362-396, *passim.*

[45] *Ibid.*, pp. 427-429. The Spanish note of July 22 is in *U. S. For. Rel., 1898*, pp. 819-820.

Minister of State to Cambon—the Spanish Government understood " that the conqueror should not be arbiter of territories foreign to Cuba which have been attacked by the United States." [46] Might not Puerto Rico and the Philippines yet be saved for Spain?

Of saving Puerto Rico there was not the slightest chance. Its fate was already settled in the minds of McKinley and his advisers. Not so with the Philippines. The United States must, indeed, retain a harbor there to serve as a naval base in the Far East, but the draft of a reply to the Spanish note first submitted to the President and Cabinet by Secretary Day called for no more than this.[47] The remainder of the archipelago might be relinquished to Spain. Upon this question the Cabinet divided sharply. Secretaries Gage and Long believed, with Day, that the retention of a naval base was all that need be asked, but the voices of business and of religion were heard arguing for the taking of the entire group of islands. Secretary Wilson " was strong for evangelizing the islands and favored keeping the whole group," while Secretary Bliss and Attorney-General Griggs " saw great commercial opportunities " in the same policy.[48] After several days of discussion during which there came a significant dispatch from John Hay in London saying that the British Government would look favorably upon the retention of the Philippines by the United States,[49] it was agreed to keep the question open

[46] Chadwick, op. cit., II, 431. Spanish Diplomatic Correspondence and Documents, 1896-1900, p. 209. Almodovar to Cambon, July 28, 1898.

[47] Olcott, The Life of William McKinley, II, 61.

[48] Ibid., pp. 62, 63.

[49] Dennett, John Hay, p. 191.

until more information could be obtained, leaving its final determination to the peace commissioners.

The American reply handed to Ambassador Cambon on July 30 required that Spain relinquish " all claim of sovereignty over or title to Cuba "; that, in lieu of pecuniary indemnity, which the President, " desirous of exhibiting signal generosity," would not claim, she cede to the United States Puerto Rico and other West Indian islands under her sovereignty and " an island in the Ladrones to be selected by the United States "; and that, " on similar grounds," she consent that the United States occupy and hold " the city, bay, and harbor of Manila pending the conclusion of a treaty of peace which shall determine the control, disposition, and government of the Philippines." [50] Efforts of the Spanish Government to secure an interpretation of the last clause which would protect Spanish sovereignty in the Philippines and make it appear that only administrative reforms were contemplated, were fruitless.[51] McKinley did consent to the substitution of " disposition " for " possession," which had at first appeared in the draft of the reply,[52] and assured Cambon that the Philippine question had not been " prejudged," [53] but he refused to accept the Spanish interpretation of the proposed terms and insisted upon the signature of a protocol embodying the American terms in black and white.[54] The protocol, which

[50] U. S. For. Rel., 1898, pp. 820-821.

[51] Ibid., pp. 822-823. Span. Dipl. Corr. & Documents, pp. 213, 214.

[52] Ibid., p. 214.

[53] Senate Document No. 148, 56th Cong., 2d sess., p. 55.

[54] U. S. For. Rel., 1898, pp. 823-824. Span. Dipl. Corr. & Documents, p. 220.

in addition to the terms already mentioned contained provision for the evacuation of Cuba and Puerto Rico and for
the assembling of peace commissioners in Paris not later
than October 1, was signed on August 12 by Secretary Day
and Ambassador Cambon.[55]   Immediately thereafter the
President issued a proclamation suspending hostilities.[56]
Since cable communication with Manila was broken, the
news did not arrive there until August 16.   Meanwhile,
on the fourteenth, the city of Manila had been surrendered
to the American army under General Merritt.[57]

Three days after the signing of the protocol Senator
Lodge reported upon the situation to his friend Roosevelt.

The war is over and so far as the West Indies is concerned all is right. The administration seems to be hesi-
tating about the Philippines, but I hope they will at least
keep Manila, which is the great prize, and the thing which
will give us the Eastern trade. Everything will depend
upon the character of the Peace Commission. A great many
names are suggested which would not be fortunate selections, but if Davis goes, as reported this morning, all will
be well.[58]

The personnel of the commission, as finally determined
upon, must have been very satisfactory to Senator Lodge.
Senator Gray, of Delaware, for years the chief defender of

[55] U. S. For. Rel., 1898, pp. 828-830.
[56] Ibid., p. 830.
[57] Chadwick, op. cit., II, 421-422, 441.
[58] Lodge, op. cit., I, 337. A few days before this Lodge had suggested to Secretary Day that the United States receive from Spain
the entire Philippine archipelago, retain Luzon, and trade the remainder to England " in exchange for the Bahamas and Jamaica and
the Danish Islands, which I think we should be entitled to ask
her to buy and turn over to us." Lodge to Day, August 11, 1898.
Dept. of State, Misc. Letters, 1898, August, II.

Cleveland's "little America" policy, represented the anti-imperialists and the Democrats. Secretary Day, not wholly converted by the efforts of Lodge and Mahan, represented the moderates. These men were the minority. With them went Senator C. K. Davis, of Minnesota, whose presence, Lodge thought, would make all well; Senator Frye, of Maine, long an advocate of Hawaiian annexation; and Whitelaw Reid, of the New York *Tribune*. Thus three of the five commissioners were trustworthy expansionists. Their leader was Reid, if we may credit his later account. When the President called the five into consultation and asked their opinions about keeping the Philippines, it was Reid alone who spoke out boldly for holding the entire group. Davis and Frye talked of dividing the archipelago, keeping Luzon and other northern islands and perhaps turning the remainder over to Holland. Day wished to keep nothing "unless possibly a coaling station, and on even that he had some doubts," while "Gray was even stronger than Day." Reid, on the other hand, argued that "having broken down the power in control of them, we could not honorably desert them and should be extremely unwise to turn over the task of controlling them to any other power." [59] Subsequently, in Paris, Davis and Frye joined with Reid in urging the retention of all the islands. Their argument, written by Reid and signed by all three, may very likely have influenced McKinley's decision. [60]

[59] Cortissoz, *Life of Whitelaw Reid,* II, 247-248.

[60] *Senate Doc.* No. 148, 56th Cong., 2d sess., pp. 32-33; Olcott, *op. cit.,* II, 125-128. The opinions of the commissioners were telegraphed to Hay in Washington October 25, 1898. On the following day, Hay cabled instructions to demand cession of the entire archipelago. *Senate Doc.* No. 148, 56th Cong., 2d sess., p. 35. Hay replaced Day as Secretary of State, September 30, 1898.

The decision, however, was McKinley's, not the commissioners', and their advice was but one of the factors that determined it. It seems evident that from the signing of the protocol on August 12 to October 26, McKinley was suspending judgment and meanwhile listening to the voices that reached him from the country and from abroad. To the British wish that the United States retain the Philippines was now added a similar expression on the part of Japan. In a note of September 8, the Japanese Government made known its belief that Spain was incapable of suppressing the existing insurrection or of maintaining order in the islands and that a native government would, through intrigue and disorder, present an invitation to seizure by other powers. In the interest of peace in the Far East, the Japanese Government would be willing either to see the United States assume alone the task of governing the islands, or to join with the United States and possibly with a third power in establishing a protectorate over them.[61]

Such expressions of opinion from foreign powers must have had weight with McKinley. The impression that neither the Spanish nor the Filipinos would be able to establish stable government in the islands was strengthened by reports of American officers and others who were or had been on the scene.[62] The extent to which the President

[61] A. L. P. Dennis, *John Hay*, in Bemis, *American Secretaries of State*, IX, 26.

[62] *Senate Doc.* No. 148, 56th Cong., 3d sess., pp. 18-21, 24-26. Even Admiral Dewey, who had formerly expressed the belief that the Filipinos were more capable of self-government than the Cubans, cabled in October: "The natives appear unable to govern." *Ibid.*, p. 27. *Cf. Senate Doc.* No. 62, 55th Cong., 3d sess., p. 383.

was subjected to pressure from business and religious groups we can only infer. We have seen something of the desire of such groups, as expressed in their publications, for the retention of the Philippines. It was while the terms of peace were still undetermined that Abram S. Hewitt, of New York, wrote to call McKinley's attention to the chapter on the control of the tropics in Kidd's *Social Evolution*,[63] and to say that he agreed with Kidd that, while Americans would never colonize tropical islands, they might supply the necessary control.[64] It was in September that "dear Brother" Le Lacheur was in Washington to persuade the President and Secretary of State of the need of retaining "those valuable and down trodden islands."[65] It was in October, while McKinley still hesitated whether to take all the islands, that a visitor at the White House found Mrs. McKinley talking "ten to the minute about converting the Igorrotes."[66] These few hints of the influences at work, together with McKinley's own account of his prayerful approach to the problem,[67] suggest the process by which his decision was reached.

[63] *Supra*, p. 18.

[64] A. Nevins, *Abram S. Hewitt, with Some Account of Peter Cooper*, pp. 590-591.

[65] *Supra*, p. 315.

[66] *Ibid.*

[67] Olcott, *op. cit.*, II, 110-111. McKinley's full account of the answer that somehow came to his prayer is suggestive of the varied arguments that had been at work in his mind: "(1) That we could not give them back to Spain—that would be cowardly and dishonorable; (2) that we could not turn them over to France or Germany—our commercial rivals in the Orient—that would be bad business and discreditable; (3) that we could not leave them to

By September 16, he had resolved to demand the cession of Luzon, the island which offered the greatest commercial opportunities and in which the native revolt against Spanish authority had made greatest headway. His initial instructions to the peace commissioners, of that date, were highly successful in combining a profession of high ideals and generous purposes with a demand for the brightest jewel in Spain's eastern crown. Reminding the commissioners that the United States had taken up arms " only in obedience to the dictates of humanity and in the fulfillment of high public and moral obligations," the President expressed the wish that the peace might be made in the same spirit.

The luster and the moral strength attaching to a cause which can be confidently rested upon the considerate judgment of the world should not under any illusion of the hour be dimmed by ulterior designs which might tempt us into excessive demands or into an adventurous departure on untried paths.

We should crown our signal triumph in war with an example " of moderation, restraint, and reason in victory."

Nevertheless, " the march of events rules and overrules human action," and " without any desire or design on our part," the success of our arms at Manila had " brought us new duties and responsibilities which we must meet and discharge as becomes a great nation on whose growth and career from the beginning the Ruler of Nations

themselves—they were unfit for self-government—and they would soon have anarchy and misrule over there worse than Spain's was; and (4) that there was nothing left for us to do but to take them all, and to educate the Filipinos, and uplift and civilize and Christianize them, and by God's grace do the very best we could by them, as our fellow-men for whom Christ also died."

has plainly written the high command and pledge of civilization." As a result of this unsought responsibility and, as incidental thereto, " the commercial opportunity to which American statesmanship can not be indifferent," McKinley believed that " the United States cannot accept less than the cession in full right and sovereignty of the island of Luzon." [68]

For more than a month after these instructions were sent, McKinley remained in doubt whether to demand more than Luzon. The reports which came to him during that period emphasized the interdependency of the islands. General Merritt, who went from Manila to Paris to lay his opinion before the commissioners, stated at first that it would be feasible to hold Luzon alone, but under questioning by Messrs. Davis, Frye, and Reid admitted that inconvenient complications might arise if the islands were divided. Manila, he said, owed its prosperity to its position as capital of the Archipelago. If the trade of the southern islands were deflected elsewhere, Manila would suffer, while if disorders broke out in the other islands, " the effect upon our possessions in Luzon would be disastrous." [69] Similar statements were made by a Mr. Foreman, who had resided eleven years in the Philippines.[70]

On the basis of this and other information, the commissioners, on October 25, cabled their opinions at length to Secretary Hay. Day was still cautious, proposing that the United States take Luzon and provide by the treaty with Spain against the alienation of other islands without

[68] *Senate Doc.* No. 148, 56th Cong., 2d sess., pp. 3-8.
[69] *Ibid.,* pp. 18-21.
[70] *Ibid.,* pp. 24-26.

our consent. Gray opposed taking anything at all. But Frye, Davis, and Reid, in the statement written by the last named, presented a strong argument for annexing the entire group.[71]

Probably this report confirmed McKinley in a decision which he had already virtually made. On the day on which this telegram was sent, and evidently before having seen it, he wrote Day that there was a very general feeling

that the United States, whatever it might prefer as to the Philippines, is in a situation where it cannot let go. The interdependency of the several islands, their close relation with Luzon, the very grave problem of what will become of the part we do not take, are receiving the thoughtful consideration of the people, and it is my judgment that the well-considered opinion of the majority would be that duty requires we should take the archipelago.[72]

McKinley had just returned from a trip to Omaha, Chicago, and other points in the middle West, in the course of which, according to A. W. Dunn, he had sounded public opinion by noting the applause that greeted references in his speeches to the duty of assuming colonial burdens.[73] A reading of the President's chief speeches on that trip, with their many references to " destiny," " duty," " humanity," and " the hand of Almighty God," makes the

[71] *Ibid.*, pp. 32-35.

[72] Olcott, *op. cit.*, II, 107-108. Since McKinley begins by asking that when the commissioners reach the Philippine question they inform him of their points of view, it seems evident that he had not received the cablegram of the same date. The latter was noted as received at the Department of State in part at 5:16 p. m., October 25 and the remainder on the morning of October 26, *Paris Peace Commission, 1898*, III.

[73] Dunn, *From Harrison to Harding*, II, 279.

theory seem plausible.[74] The impressions received on that trip were perhaps, in part, the basis of his interpretation of public opinion in the letter to Day.

Then came the argument of Davis, Frye, and Reid. On October 26, Secretary Hay cabled the commission that information received since their departure had convinced the President that the acceptance of the cession of Luzon alone,

leaving the rest of the islands subject to Spanish rule, or to be the subject of future contention, can not be justified on political, commercial, or humanitarian grounds. The cession must be of the whole archipelago or none. The latter is wholly inadmissible and the former must therefore be required.[75]

Having made this decision, McKinley adhered to it without wavering, even when the commissioners at Paris advised compromise.[76] Impressed with the warnings of the Spanish

[74] E. g., at Omaha: " The faith of a Christian nation recognizes the hand of Almighty God in the ordeal through which we have passed. Divine favor seemed manifest everywhere. In fighting for humanity's sake we have been signally blessed. . . . Now, as then, we will do our duty, . . . " Buffalo Express, October 13, 1898.

At Chicago: " My countrymen, the currents of destiny flow through the hearts of the people. Who will check them, then; who will divert them, who will stop them? And the movements of men, planned and designed by the Master of men, will never be interrupted by the American people." Ibid., October 19, 1898.

[75] Senate Doc. No. 148, 56th Cong., 2d sess., p. 35.

[76] The telegraphic correspondence between the Department of State and the commissioners at Paris is printed in Senate Document No. 148, 56th Cong., 2d sess., and in U. S. Foreign Relations, 1898. The protocols of the Paris conferences are printed in Senate Document No. 62, 55th Cong., 3d sess., Part II. The student of this material cannot fail to be impressed with the advantage that resulted from retaining ultimate control of the negotiations at Washingon,

commissioners that the demand for all of the Philippines, added to the insistence that Spain assume entire responsibility for the Cuban debt, would compel them to break off negotiations,[77] even Reid and Frye joined with Day in proposing that, in order to avoid a resumption of hostilities, Spain be permitted to retain the southern islands of Mindanao and Sulu.[78] To these proposals Secretary Hay replied that since the United States had a just claim against Spain for war indemnity, which could be satisfied only by the cession of the Philippines—and not wholly in that way, even were the Carolines added—and since obligation to the people of the Philippines forbade returning them to Spanish rule, the President saw no course but to insist upon the cession of all the islands.

The trade and commercial side, as well as the indemnity for the cost of the war, are questions we might yield. They might be waived or compromised, but the questions of duty and humanity appeal to the President so strongly that he can find no appropriate answer but the one he has here marked out.

The commissioners had previously been authorized [79] to

exempt from the persuasive personal influences that surrounded the commissioners at Paris—the advantage which President Wilson surrendered when he went to Paris in person.

[77] There is a good summary of these negotiations, especially in regard to the Cuban debt, in E. J. Benton, *International Law and Diplomacy of the Spanish-American War.*

[78] *Senate Doc.* No. 148, 56th Cong., 2d sess., pp. 45-48. These proposals were made November 11, at a crucial period in the negotiations. Davis opposed all concessions. Gray was now in favor of making reasonable financial concessions which would induce Spain to cede the islands, since he foresaw that a breaking off of negotiations would be followed by forcible seizure.

[79] *Ibid.,* p. 38.

offer a cash payment for public works and improvements of a pacific character in the islands, and Hay now directed that if necessary they might agree to pay from ten to twenty million dollars on this score, and more if Spain would cede a naval and telegraph station in the Carolines, but beyond this the President would yield nothing.[80]

An ultimatum embodying these terms—cession by Spain of the entire Philippine archipelago, payment by the United States of $20,000,000, with the admission, for ten years, of Spanish ships to the ports of the Philippines upon the same terms as American ships—was handed to the Spanish commissioners on November 21.[81] A final effort by the Spaniards to save something more from the wreck—through retention of the southern islands, through a larger cash payment by the United States, or through submitting to arbitration the question of responsibility for colonial debts —was summarily rejected in Washington, and on November 28 the Spanish commissioners accepted the American proposal.[82]

There remained the question of the Caroline Islands, in which, it will be recalled, certain missionary groups in the United States had felt a keen interest, and where it was hoped something might be done for the cause of missions.

[80] *Ibid.*, pp. 48-49. Hay to Day, November 13, 1898. Officially, the claim to the Philippines rested upon the ground of war indemnity only. There had been some disposition to claim them by right of conquest, but this position was regarded by a majority of the commissioners as untenable. *Ibid.*, p. 40. Olcott, *op. cit.*, II, 113-118.

[81] *Senate Doc.* No. 62, 55th Cong., 3d sess., Part II, pp. 210-211.

[82] *Ibid.*, pp. 211-215. *Senate Doc.* No. 148, 56th Cong., 2d sess., pp. 58-61.

either by the acquisition of the islands or at least by exacting from Spain a guarantee of full religious liberty therein. But since the Carolines had been neither touched by the war nor mentioned in the protocol of August 12, the only hope for accomplishing anything there lay in purchasing cession or rights for cash or through concessions elsewhere.

Neither the commissioners in Paris nor the President and Secretary of State in Washington were unmindful of American interests in the Carolines. Senator Frye thought those islands " infinitely more valuable than the Ladrones," and Reid thought the United States ought to have them—" the inhabitants being English-speaking Protestant Christians." Both advised that if the negotiations should be broken off Dewey should be instructed to seize the Carolines forthwith.[83] In Washington, the missionary argument seemingly had less weight than certain more material considerations. On November 1, Hay wrote the commissioners that American capitalists who were planning to lay a cable between Hawaii and Manila were anxious to acquire for that purpose the island in the Caroline group variously known as Kusaie, Ualan, and Strong Island, and that the President was disposed to recommend that an effort be made to purchase it before the peace negotiations were concluded.[84] Ten days later, Day, Frye, and Reid made the suggestion that Spain be permitted to retain Mindanao and the Sulu archipelago,

[83] *Ibid.*, p. 39. Olcott, *op. cit.*, II, 105-106.

[84] Hay to Day, November 1, 1898. *Paris Peace Commission, 1898*, II. This instruction was sent by mail. The reply to it, also in the form of a letter, was dated November 15. Moore to Hay, November 15, 1898. *Special Agents, 1898-1905.*

ceding instead one or more islands in the Carolines and granting religious freedom in all.[85] McKinley and Hay, while declining this proposal, were willing to pay for such concessions in the Carolines if they could be had in addition to the surrender of all the Philippines.[86] Accordingly, the commissioners, in presenting their ultimatum on November 21, stated that after acceptance by Spain of their demand for cession of the Philippines, they would like to proceed to discussion of such further matters as the purchase of Kusaie and the restoration of religious liberty in the Carolines.[87]

American designs upon the Carolines, however, ran athwart the colonial ambitions of Germany. That power had formerly asserted a claim to the Caroline and Pelew Islands, and after the papal arbitration of 1885 had assigned them to Spain, it had retained the right to establish at some undetermined place therein a coaling and naval station for the Imperial Navy.[88] In July, 1898, the German Under-Secretary for Foreign Affairs had called upon Ambassador White to discuss the relation between German and American aspirations in the Pacific and had received from White an intimation (unauthorized from Washington) that the United States would be sympathetic to the acquisition by Germany of the Carolines and possibly yet other Pacific islands.[89] In August, accordingly, the German Govern-

[85] *Senate Doc.* No. 148, 56th Cong., 2d sess., pp. 45-48.

[86] *Ibid.,* pp. 48-49, 60.

[87] *Senate Doc.* No. 62, 55th Cong., 3d sess., Part II, pp. 210-211.

[88] The German-Spanish protocol of December 17, 1885, is printed in *U. S. For. Rel., 1886,* pp. 776-778.

[89] White to Day (telegram and letter), July 12, 1898; White to Day (letter), July 30, 1898. *Dispatches, Germany,* LXVI. *Cf.*

ment opened negotiations with Spain which led to a secret
accord of September 10 by which Spain agreed to sell to
Germany the islands of Kusaie, Ponape, and Yap in the
Caroline archipelago, the definitive agreement to be delayed, however, until the Paris Conference should have
determined upon the disposition of the Philippine Islands.[90]
Apparently the Spanish Government did not feel altogether
bound by this preliminary agreement, for on December 4
the Minister of State wrote to the president of the commission in Paris that concessions in the Carolines might
be granted to the United States in exchange for commercial
privileges in Cuba and Puerto Rico.[91]

In the meantime, the German Government had become
alarmed at the news that the United States was seeking to
obtain Kusaie, and had protested vigorously through the
American chargé in Berlin, through the German Embassy
in Washington, and through the German Ambassador in
Paris, who was instructed to make known to the American
peace commissioners the strong interest of Germany in
Kusaie and other islands of the Caroline group, and to say
that Germany, if she took possession of the islands, would
be glad to extend to the United States the privilege of lay-

Richthofen's memorandum in *Die. Grosse Politik*, XV, 54-59. See
also L. B. Shippee, " Germany and the Spanish-American War,"
American Historical Review, XXX, 754-777.

[90] *Die Grosse Politik*, XV, 74-77.

[91] *Span. Dipl. Corr. & Documents*, pp. 353-354. Such an arrangement was refused by McKinley. *Senate Doc.* No. 148, 56th
Cong., 2d sess., p. 63. The Spanish commissioners in Paris, who
were apparently not informed of the agreement with Germany,
had previously proposed to cede Kusaie and to grant cable privileges
elsewhere in the Carolines or Ladrones instead of surrendering Mindanao and Sulu—a proposal which was likewise rejected in Washington. *Ibid.*, pp. 58-60.

ing a cable and erecting a telegraph station at a suitable point.[92] Undeterred by the German protests, the American peace commissioners continued to press their Spanish antagonists for the cession of Kusaie and for a guarantee of religious liberty in the other islands of the Caroline group.[93] But in the meantime German pressure at Madrid had exacted a promise that Kusaie would not be sold to the United States,[94] and the Spanish commissioners finally replied to the American proposals by saying that the cession of Kusaie and the question of religious liberty were outside the scope of the treaty and beyond their authority.[95]

[92] *Die Grosse Politik*, XV, 82-83. Münster, in Paris, talked with Reid on November 21. His account of the interview (*ibid.*, pp. 83-85) suggests a more yielding attitude on Reid's part than is conveyed by Day's version of the same conversation as sent to Washington. Day to Hay, November 22, 1898, and November 26, 1898 (reporting a later conversation), *Paris Peace Commission, 1898*, III. Reid, as reported by Day, refused to concede that Germany had prior rights in Kusaie. Following the conversations between Münster and Reid, Richthofen warned Hay through Jackson in Berlin and through Sternberg in Washington that German public opinion would be incensed if the United States took possession of Kusaie. Jackson to Hay, November 27, 1898. *Dispatches, Germany*, LXVII. *Die Grosse Politik*, XV, 86, note. Hay refused to be intimidated, wiring Day to observe any promises that the commissioners might have made to Münster, but otherwise leaving the matter to their discretion. Hay to Day, November 30, 1898. *Paris Peace Commission, 1898*, III. Day replied that the commissioners had made no promises to Münster, that they were unanimous in believing that Germany had no valid right to Kusaie, and that they would continue in their efforts to purchase it. Day to Hay, December 1, 1898. *Ibid.*

[93] *Senate Doc.* No. 148, 56th Cong., 2d sess., p. 64; *Senate Doc.* No. 62, 55th Cong., 3d sess., Part II, p. 251.

[94] *Die Grosse Politik*, XV, 87.

[95] *Senate Doc.* No. 62, 55th Cong., 3d sess., Part II, pp. 251-253. Some weeks after the signing of the peace treaty, Secretary Hay

The treaty of peace, by which Spain relinquished sovereignty over Cuba and ceded to the United States Puerto Rico, the Philippines, and Guam in the Ladrones, was signed in Paris December 10, 1898.[96] It was sent to the Senate January 4, 1899, and debated in executive session until February 6, when the Senate by a vote of 57 to 27 consented to ratification.[97]

The secret character of the proceedings prevented a public debate on the treaty proper, but a satisfactory substitute was found in discussion of several sets of resolutions relative to the acquisition of territory which were introduced and debated in open sessions of the Senate.[98] The first of these was introduced December 6, 1898, four days before

assured Ambassador Holleben that the United States would not oppose whatever arrangement Germany might make with Spain in regard to the Carolines. *Die Grosse Politik*, XV, 96-97. The German Government also had certain vague claims to rights in the Sulu archipelago, a part of the Philippines. That it refrained from pressing these claims was regarded in Berlin as a proper return for the surrender of American ambitions in the Carolines. *Ibid.*, pp. 84-85.

[96] *Stat. L.*, XXX, 1754-1762. In Article III (Philippines) it was stipulated that the United States would pay to Spain $20,000,000 within three months of the date of the exchange of ratifications of the treaty.

[97] *Journal of the Executive Proceedings of the Senate*, 55th Cong., pp. 1161-1284, *passim*.

[98] *Cf.* Senator Lodge's statement, January 24, 1899:

" The discussion of the treaty is being conducted, and to my mind properly conducted, behind closed doors, for there is much that must be said affecting other nations and other people which could not with propriety be said in public; but the treaty itself has been made public, and the debate upon these resolutions, taking a wide range, has covered, so far as could be fittingly done in open session, the broad question of policy involved in the ratification of the treaty." *Cong. Rec.*, 55th Cong., 3d sess., p. 959.

the signing of the treaty, by Senator Vest, of Missouri. It declared

That under the Constitution of the United States no power is given to the Federal Government to acquire territory to be held and governed permanently as colonies.

The colonial system of European nations can not be established under our present Constitution, but all territory acquired by the Government, except such small amount as may be necessary for coaling stations, must be acquired and governed with the purpose of ultimately organizing such territory into States suitable for admission into the Union.[99]

This was not only the earliest but the most sweeping of the resolutions which came before the Senate for discussion. Others, designed to commit the Senate, with varying degrees of finality, against the permanent retention of the Philippine Islands, were proposed by Senators Mason of Illinois, Bacon of Georgia, Sullivan of Mississippi, Lindsay of Kentucky, Allen of Nebraska, and McEnery of Louisiana—all except Mason, Democrats or Populists.[100] Of the McEnery Resolution, which was eventually adopted, more will be said later. It was the Vest Resolution which was longest before the Senate and constituted the official subject of most of the debate.

It was the provision for the acquisition of the Philippines which alone excited serious opposition. Opponents of the treaty made their first attack, as did the Vest Resolution, from the constitutional angle. The Constitution, Vest

[99] *Ibid.*, p. 20. For a recent discussion of the anti-imperialist movement in the United States see F. H. Harrington, "The Anti-Imperialist Movement in the United States, 1898-1900," *Mississippi Valley Historical Review*, XXII, 211-230.

[100] *Cong. Rec.*, 55th Cong., 3d sess., pp. 528, 561, 1342, 1348, 1445, 1479.

argued, conferred no power to acquire territory to be governed permanently as such; all acquisitions must be made with a view to the ultimate admission to statehood of the territory acquired. There was no place under our Constitution for the colonial system of Europe, based, as that system was, "upon the fundamental idea that the people of immense areas of territory can be held as subjects, never to become citizens." It was against that system that our Revolutionary War had been fought, and it was unthinkable that we should now reestablish it ourselves.[101] Other Democratic Senators supported Vest's contention,[102] but no Democrat made a more forceful argument on this score than the staunch Republican, Hoar, of Massachusetts. To annex foreign territory and govern it without the consent of its population, said Hoar, is utterly contrary to the sacred principles of the Declaration of Independence and is unconstitutional because promotive of no constitutional purpose. It had never occurred to the fathers of the Constitution that their descendants "would be beguiled from these sacred and awful verities that they might strut about in the cast-off clothing of pinchbeck emperors and pewter kings; that their descendants would be excited by the smell of gunpowder and the sound of the guns of a single victory as a small boy by a firecracker on some Fourth of July morning." [103] Almost alone among the Senators, Hoar

[101] *Ibid.,* pp. 93-96. Vest based his constitutional argument largely upon Taney's opinion in the Dred Scott case. In this point of the decision, Vest claimed, the entire Supreme Court had agreed with Taney.

[102] *Ibid.,* pp. 432-433 (Caffery, La.), 641 (McLaurin, S. C.), 783-784 (Turner, Wash.), 963-968 (Clay, Ga.), 1530 (Tillman, S. C.).

[103] *Ibid.,* p. 498. The speech occupies pp. 493-502.

declared that this principle forbade the taking not only of
the Philippines but of Puerto Rico.[104] Other opponents of
Philippine annexation argued that the Puerto Rican case
was different—that the people of that island were not
opposed to American rule, that they could properly be
incorporated in the American system, or that the annexation of the island was justified by considerations of national
safety.[105]

If the Philippine Islands were taken under American
sovereignty, argued Democratic Senators, the Constitution
in its full extent would at once become applicable. The
Filipinos would become citizens of the United States with
all the rights of other citizens; all taxes, duties, and imposts
must be applied to the islands equally with the continent.
American agriculture and American labor would be subjected to Oriental competition through the resulting elimination of barriers to immigration and importation.[106] The
same constitutional requirement that duties be uniform
would prevent the practise, in our Eastern possessions, of
the Open Door principle which we were demanding for
ourselves in China.[107]

But aside from these inconveniences and dangers to
which the incorporation of the Philippines would subject
the people of the United States, it could not be hoped that
American institutions, transplanted to the Asiatic islands,
would operate successfully. The Philippines were tenanted
by " a heterogeneous compound of inefficient Oriental

[104] *Ibid.*, p. 1384.
[105] *Ibid.*, pp. 1067, 1384.
[106] *Ibid.*, pp. 433, 1064-1067, 1430, 1447.
[107] *Ibid.*, p. 439.

humanity: " [108] The inhabitants differed from us in race, language, customs, and religion.[109] Such people were not suited to our institutions, nor ready for liberty as we understand it. " You can extend your power, but if you want to extend your nationality, extend your institutions, extend your liberty, you must do it with people of your own kind." [110] Why, asked Senator Tillman, reading some stanzas from Kipling's just published poem, " The White Man's Burden "—why should we mark their roads with our dead in a futile effort to call them from their " loved Egyptian night," to force upon them " a civilization not suited to them and which only means in their view degradation and a loss of self-respect? " [111]

But departure from the spirit of our republican institutions in the government of colonies would spell the destruction of those institutions at home. A large standing army, such as would be required for the government of subject peoples, was incompatible with democratic liberties. Roman liberties perished, said Senator Mallory, quoting the historian Froude,

only when Rome became the mistress of conquered races, to whom she was unable or unwilling to extend her privileges. . . . If there be one lesson which history clearly teaches, it is this, that free nations cannot govern subject provinces. If they are unable or unwilling to admit their dependencies to share their own constitution, the constitution itself will fall in pieces from mere incompetence for its duties.[112]

[108] *Ibid.*, p. 922.
[109] *Ibid.*, p. 1067.
[110] *Ibid.*, p. 438.
[111] *Ibid.*, p. 1532.
[112] *Ibid.*, p. 1070. *Cf. ibid.*, pp. 641, 930, 1445-1446.

Thus the argument slipped over from the question of constitutionality to that of expediency, or policy. Senator Chilton, of Texas, for example, was not opposed to expansion as such. He saw no objection to taking Cuba, Puerto Rico, or Guam. But to annex the Philippines, he thought, would not only endanger American institutions and the interests of American labor; it would inevitably draw the United States into the international broils of the Far East, where she would have to fight far from home and at a disadvantage; and it would deprive the American people of all moral right to uphold the Monroe Doctrine. If we entered the eastern hemisphere, what right had we to forbid the western to the powers of Europe? [113] Other speakers elaborated these same points. "The Monroe Doctrine is gone," lamented Hoar.[114] Even Senator Spooner, who felt compelled to vote for the treaty rather than see the islands returned to Spain, confessed to a fear that the possession of the Philippines might lead to embroilments with other powers over Asiatic questions.[115]

Having proved, to their own satisfaction, that the annexation of the Philippines was unconstitutional or impolitic or both, the opposing Senators turned to discount or ridicule the arguments advanced in favor of that policy. Possession of the Philippines would not help American trade, argued Senator Caffery. Nine-tenths of American exports went to Western Europe. Markets for our surplus products must be sought among people who could consume them. Tropical peoples have few wants and always export more than

[113] *Ibid.*, pp. 1445-1450.
[114] *Ibid.*, p. 501.
[115] *Ibid.*, pp. 1384-1388.

they import.[116] Senator White, of California, ridiculed the enthusiasm of boards of trade and chambers of commerce for " the riches which they seem to think will drop into their laps " if the Philippines were taken. The growing export figures for the years 1893 to 1898 seemed to him to disprove the need for colonies.[117] The trade of the Philippines, said McLaurin, was insignificant, even if we monopolized it, but England, Germany, and Spain all claimed shares of that trade. Even as a key to the Orient the possession of the islands was not essential to us.[118]

Nor was the opposition impressed by talk of destiny, duty, or religious opportunity. " Some of our worthy clergymen," said Senator Hoar, were " of late preaching from their pulpits the new commandment to do evil that good may come." [119] " In order to Christianize these savage people," said Caffery, " we must put the yoke of despotism upon their necks; . . . Sir, Christianity can not be advanced by force." [120] The real motive of the annexationists, he believed, was " lust for power and greed for land, veneered with the tawdriness of false humanity." The source of the expansionist movement seemed to some Southern and Western Senators to be in the same combinations of wealth that had elected McKinley in 1896. Now, " under the plea that the United States must have a wider and broader field for trade and commerce," the plutocracy was " pushing us to a line of action that threatens the very

[116] *Ibid.*, p. 438.
[117] *Ibid.*, pp. 924-925.
[118] *Ibid.*, pp. 638-642.
[119] *Ibid.*, p. 500.
[120] *Ibid.*, pp. 437-438.

foundations of the Republic." [121] Even lower motives than this were by some Senators attributed to the annexationists.

Do we want them [the Philippines] in order to send thither swarms of office-holders, carpetbaggers, to riot among them like slimy worms, eating out their substance? Ah! there is the rub. But for this, this perplexing problem would not to-day be seriously confronting the American people.[122]

Among the supporters of the treaty, the most effective constitutional argument was made by Senator Platt, of Connecticut. The right to acquire territory, said Platt, is a sovereign right, belonging to the United States by virtue of its national sovereignty. It is not confined to the treaty-making power or to the war power. And the right to acquire embraces the right to govern, to establish such government as the condition of the territory and the character of its population may require.

I deny [said Platt] that there is any constitutional or moral obligation to fit the territory for statehood or to ever admit it as a State. To claim that there is is to deny the inherent sovereign right of this people, this nation, to do what any nation may do anywhere. To do it is to deny that our nation has the same rights that other sovereign nations have.[123]

The right to govern territory is a sovereign right derived from the sovereign right to acquire. But if doubters sought the right to govern more specifically in the Constitution, said Platt, they could find it in ample measure, without limitation or qualification, in the clause empowering Congress to make all needful rules and regulations respecting

---

[121] *Ibid.*, p. 1297 (Berry, of Ark.). Similar language was used by McLaurin and Tillman, of S. C. *Ibid.*, pp. 641, 1532.

[122] *Ibid.*, p. 1347 (Rawlins, of Utah).

[123] *Ibid.*, p. 296. The whole speech is on pp. 287-297.

the territory of the United States. Here Platt anticipated the position later taken by the Supreme Court in the Insular Cases, suggesting a distinction between the " fundamental " and the " formal " provisions of the Constitution. He quoted the opinion of Mr. Justice Bradley in the case of the *Mormon Church* v. *United States:*

Doubtless Congress, in legislating for the Territories would be subject to those fundamental limitations in favor of personal rights which are formulated in the Constitution and its amendments; but these limitations would exist rather by inference and the general spirit of the Constitution, from which Congress derives all its powers, than by any express and direct application of its provisions.[124]

This definition of power was sufficiently elastic to permit the governing of the inhabitants of any territory in whatever condition of savagery, barbarism, or civilization. We must, said Platt,

provide for the people of any territory that we may acquire the most liberal, just, and beneficent government which they may be capable of enjoying, always with reference to their development and welfare and in the hope that they may be finally fitted for independent self-government. With this our obligation ceases. To hold that we should legislate otherwise is to hold that we are bound to perpetrate folly and invite disaster.[125]

There was no obligation to confer statehood upon a territory unsuited for it. There was no obligation to confer United States citizenship upon people unfit to be citizens. They might have to be treated for a while, said Senator Teller, as " subjects "—objectionable as that term was in

[124] *Ibid.*, p. 293. 136 *United States Reports*, 44.

[125] *Cong. Rec.*, 55th Cong., 3d sess., p. 295. To a question from Hoar whether he believed that governments derived their just powers from the consent of the governed, Platt replied: " From the consent of some of the governed." *Ibid.*, p. 297.

a republic.[126] Nor need it be anticipated that the United States would be flooded, against its will, with either the people or the products of the annexed territories. Platt interrupted the voicing of such predictions by Senator Chilton to say that after a thorough study of the subject he was convinced that neither the people nor the products of the Philippines could enter the United States without the consent of Congress.[127]

But if the Constitution imposed no restraints, did not the spirit of the Teller Resolution of the preceding April bind the United States in principle not to impose its government upon the Filipinos against their will? No one should have been better able than its author to interpret that resolution. In principle, said Teller, it was applicable to the other Spanish islands no less than to Cuba. Had the resolution been broadened to include them all, he was sure it would still have had unanimous consent in Congress. But the resolution could not be applied unconditionally. For the present we could do nothing but assume the government of Cuba, Puerto Rico, and the Philippines. Only when their people should show themselves capable of self-government should we regard them as entitled to it. For the present they must remain under the American flag and American sovereignty, receiving "that moral aid, that moral encouragement, which will enable them to take care of themselves." Eventually, they would become either independent nations or integral parts of the United States, with all the rights implied by that status. Teller suggested no time limit for the probationary period.[128]

[126] *Ibid.*, p. 969.
[127] *Ibid.*, p. 1447.
[128] *Ibid.*, pp. 325-330.

The gloomy forebodings of the opposition were scoffed at by the supporters of the treaty. What danger was there to the essential liberties of the Filipinos? Senator Foraker knew of no one who wished to keep or govern them indefinitely, against their will, by force.[129] The American people, said Nelson, " have no purpose to enslave or enthrall the people of the Philippine Islands. . . . We come as ministering angels, not as despots." [130] Senator Lodge was indignant that any one should fear for the welfare of the Filipinos under the blessings of American government. He himself was willing to trust life, property, honor, his children and his children's children to the control of the American people and the American Congress. Then why hesitate to entrust to them the government and welfare of the Filipinos? [131] As for the alleged danger to American liberties, had the liberties of the English people suffered as a result of British imperialism? Rather, asserted Nelson, those liberties had increased and broadened since England became a colonial power.[132]

Indeed, expansion might be the salvation rather than the death-knell of American liberties. In over a century of self-government, said Senator Wolcott, of Colorado, we had seen the growth of increasing bitterness over internal policy.

Who is to say that in the evolution of such a Republic as this the time has not come when the immense development of our internal resources and the marvelous growth of our domestic and foreign commerce and a realization of

[129] *Ibid.*, pp. 563-572.
[130] *Ibid.*, p. 838.
[131] *Ibid.*, pp. 958-960.
[132] *Ibid.*, p. 834.

our virile strength have not stimulated that Anglo-Saxon restlessness which beats with the blood of the race into an activity which will not be quenched until we have finally planted our standard in that far-off archipelago which inevitable destiny has intrusted to our hands?

It may well be that this people have found, through the outlet which the results of the war with Spain compelled us to take, the one course which shall lead to the perpetuity of our institutions and the safety and stability of the Republic.[133]

But after all—as the religious press had so often reiterated—was it not Providence that had placed upon the American people a responsibility which they could not reject? So, at any rate, thought Senator Orville H. Platt. The same force that had once guided Pilgrim sails to Plymouth Rock had impelled our ships at Manila and our army at Santiago. Upon us rested the duty of extending Christian civilization, of crushing despotism, of uplifting humanity and making the rights of man prevail. "Providence has put it upon us. We propose to execute it." [134]

The faithful servant would have his material reward. Of the economic advantages of annexation little was said by the supporters of the treaty. "The opponents of the treaty," said Senator Lodge, "have placed their opposition on such high and altruistic grounds that I have preferred to meet them there." For this reason, he said, he had preferred not to discuss

the enormous material benefits to our trade, our industries, and our labor dependent upon a right settlement of this question, both directly and indirectly. For this reason I have not touched upon the commercial advantages to the

[133] *Ibid.*, p. 1451.
[134] *Ibid.*, pp. 502-503.

country involved in the question of these islands, or the far greater question of the markets of China, of which we must have our share for the benefit of our working-men.[135]

Thus the debate on the various resolutions dragged on until February 6, the day set for the vote on the treaty. All efforts to secure action on the resolutions prior to action on the treaty failed. Meanwhile various forms of pressure and persuasion had been at work to secure the Democratic and Populist votes necessary for ratification. The whole weight of the Republican organization was exerted to this end. If we may believe Mr. A. W. Dunn and others, promises were made and pressure was applied to certain wavering Democratic Senators.[136] William Jennings Bryan came to Washington and urged ratification of the treaty on the ground that it was necessary to end the war and that Philippine independence might be more readily secured through action by the United States than through a renewal of negotiations with Spain.[137] As a result of these diverse influences,[138]

[135] *Ibid.*, p. 960.

[136] Dunn, *op. cit.*, I, 279-283. *Cf.* W. S. Holt, *Treaties Defeated by the Senate*, pp. 171-173.

[137] Paxton Hibben, *The Peerless Leader: William Jennings Bryan*, pp. 220-222. M. E. Curti, *Bryan and World Peace*, pp. 129-132. Bryan may also have argued, as was asserted by Senator Hoar, that it was politically expedient to let the Republicans have their treaty in order that the Democrats might have a new issue in 1900. Hoar, *op. cit.*, II, 322-323. Messrs. Hibben and Curti agree in ascribing higher motives to Bryan. There are numerous references in the debates to the partisan character of the controversy, and at least one to Bryan. *Cong. Rec.*, 55th Cong., 3d sess., pp. 1450, 1480-1484, 1530.

[138] On February 4, 1899, hostilities broke out between the Filipinos under Aguinaldo and the American forces before Manila. Whether this occurrence influenced the vote on the treaty it is

fifteen Democrats, Populists, and Independents joined the Republican majority. Hoar, of Massachusetts, and Hale, of Maine, on the Republican side, voted against ratification. The vote stood 57 to 27, or one vote above the necessary two-thirds majority.[139]

With the treaty disposed of, the Senate turned to the task of clarifying, by resolution, its intentions with regard to a permanent policy for the Philippines. On February 6, shortly before the vote on the treaty, Senator McEnery, of Louisiana, had introduced a resolution, the purport of which was merely to leave open the question of the status and the

impossible to say. Senators who declared against any compromise with men in rebellion against the United States would have voted for the treaty anyway. Opposition Senators asserted that passage of a resolution renouncing any idea of permanent possession of the Philippines would have prevented the outbreak. *Ibid.*, pp. 1485-1495, *passim*. Senator Lodge asserted positively that the fighting at Manila did not change the results. Lodge, *op. cit.*, I, 391-392.

[139] *Journal of the Executive Proceedings of the Senate,* 55th Cong., p. 1284. A classification of the Senators voting on the treaty based upon the *Biographical Directory of the American Congress, 1774-1927* shows the majority as composed of 42 Republicans, 11 Democrats, 2 Populists, and 2 Independents; the minority, of 22 Democrats, 2 Republicans, 1 Populist, 1 Silver Republican, and 1 Republican-Populist fusion Senator. Different figures are given by Holt, *op. cit.*, p. 169 and note 12. Several Senators were not easily classifiable.

Just before the final vote on ratification, the Senate defeated, 30 to 53, an amendment offered by Senator Gorman by which Spain, instead of ceding the Philippine Islands to the United States, would merely have relinquished sovereignty over them, as in the case of Cuba, and by which, furthermore, the United States would have assumed responsibility for their control only until the people of the islands should be enabled to establish a form of free government suitable to their condition. *Journal of the Executive Proceedings of the Senate,* 55th Cong., p. 1283.

ultimate disposition of the islands. This resolution came before the Senate again after the executive session and, with others, was debated from time to time until February 14. Anti-imperialist Senators, who wished something stronger than the McEnery Resolution, almost won their point when, on the last day of debate, an amendment offered by Bacon, of Georgia, expressly promising independence upon the establishment of a stable government in the Philippines, was defeated only by the casting vote of the Vice President.[140] Thereafter, the unamended McEnery Resolution, though denounced by Bacon and Hoar as an annexation resolution in disguise and as designed for no other purpose than to protect Louisiana sugar planters from Filipino competition,[141] was adopted by a vote of 26 to 22.[142] It read as follows:

That by the ratification of the treaty of peace with Spain it is not intended to incorporate the inhabitants of the Philippine Islands into citizenship of the United States, nor is it intended to permanently annex said islands as an integral part of the territory of the United States; but it is the intention of the United States to establish on said islands a government suitable to the wants and conditions of the inhabitants of said islands, to prepare them for local self-government, and in due time to make such disposition of said islands as will best promote the interests of the citizens of the United States and the inhabitants of said islands.[143]

Nominally a joint resolution, the McEnery Resolution was never passed by the House of Representatives. Thus

[140] *Cong. Rec.*, 55th Cong., 3d sess., pp. 1845-1846. The wording of the Bacon proposal followed closely that of the Teller Resolution in regard to Cuba.

[141] *Ibid.*, pp. 1835, 1840.

[142] *Ibid.*, p. 1847.

[143] *Ibid.*, p. 1830.

24

it had little significance other than as an expression of the opinion of twenty-six Senators—less than one-third of the full membership of the Senate. But even had it been a matured and official expression of both houses of Congress, it would have put no real restrictions upon the policy of the United States in the Philippines. In response to the urgings of destiny, duty, religion, commercial interests, and naval strategy, the United States had utilized the war with Spain to acquire an island empire in the Caribbean and the Pacific. It was now free, even if bound by the terms of the innocuous McEnery Resolution, to use its new power in whatever way would " best promote the interests of the citizens of the United States and the inhabitants of said islands "—and it is to be noted that the interests of the citizens of the United States were placed first.

BIBLIOGRAPHY

MANUSCRIPT SOURCES

The following unpublished materials in the archives of the Department of State have been utilized: correspondence with ministers and ambassadors abroad in *Dispatches, Germany,* Vols. 66 and 67; *Dispatches, Great Britain,* Vol. 173; *Dispatches, Hawaii,* Vol. 25; *Instructions, France,* Vol. 22; correspondence with the Hawaiian Legation in Washington in *Notes to Hawaii,* Vol. 1, and *Hawaii, Notes,* Vols. 3 and 4; papers pertaining to the peace negotiations of 1898 in a number of volumes; namely, *Paris Peace Commission, 1898,* Vols. 2 and 3; *Miscellaneous Letters Sent to Members of the Peace Commission, 1898; Miscellaneous Letters Sent to the President and the Secretary of State, Paris Peace Commission, 1898; Special Agents, 1898-1905;* and *Special Missions,* Vol. 4; letters from non-diplomatic sources in *Miscellaneous Letters,* 1892, 1893, 1897, 1898, 1899; notes of interviews in *Memoranda of Conversations with the Secretary of State, 1893-1898.*

The archives of the Navy Department have yielded some useful material in the unbound letters from squadron commanders and in two volumes of instructions entitled *Confidential Correspondence,* Vol. 2, and *Ciphers Sent,* Vol. 1. These volumes are in the Navy Department Library.

The Stephen Spaulding Memorial Collection, in the General Library, University of Michigan, contains a large number of photostatic copies of diplomatic correspondence from the Hawaiian Archives at Honolulu and typed transcripts of documents from the same source and from the files of the Department of State and Navy Department in Washington. These materials afford a fairly satisfactory view of the Hawaiian side of Hawaiian-American relations in the crucial periods, 1889-1893 and 1897-1898.

GOVERNMENTAL PUBLICATIONS

United States:

    Biographical Directory of the American Congress, 1774-1927. Washington, 1928.

    Congressional Record,
        50th Cong., 2d sess.
        51st Cong., 2d sess.
        52d Cong., 2d sess.
        53d Cong., 2d sess.
        53d Cong., 3d sess.
        54th Cong., 1st sess.
        54th Cong., 2d sess.
        55th Cong., 1st sess.
        55th Cong., 2d sess.
        55th Cong., 3d sess.
        58th Cong., 3d sess.

    Foreign Relations. See *Papers Relating to the Foreign Relations of the United States.*

    House Report No. 1466, 51st Cong., 1st sess. Report of Ways and Means Committee on tariff legislation, 1890.

    House Report No. 3422, 51st Cong., 2d sess. Report on safeguarding reciprocal trade relations with Hawaii, 1891.

    House Executive Document No. 1, Part III, 52d Cong., 2d sess. Report of Secretary of Navy, December, 1892.

    House Document No. 3, 54th Cong., 1st sess. Report of Secretary of Navy, November, 1895.

    House Report No. 1355, 55th Cong., 2d sess. Report of Committee on Foreign Affairs on joint resolution for annexation of Hawaii, May 17, 1898.

    Journal of the Executive Proceedings of the Senate of the United States of America, Washington, 1909.
        52d Cong.
        55th Cong.

    Malloy, W. M., *Treaties, Conventions, International Acts, Protocols, and Agreements between the United States of America and Other Powers, 1776-1909. Senate Document* No. 357, 61st Cong., 2d sess., 2 vols., Washington, 1910.

    Moore, John B., *Digest of International Law,* 8 vols., Washington, 1906.

Papers Relating to the Foreign Relations of the United States, 1881, Washington, 1882.

1886, Washington, 1887.

1894, Appendix I, Washington, 1895. Secretary Gresham's report on Samoa, 1894.

1894, Appendix II, Washington, 1895. Reprints, with continuous paging, a large number of separate documents bearing on Hawaiian relations.

1895, Washington, 1896.

1896, Washington, 1897.

1898, Washington, 1901.

Richardson, James D. (editor), *A Compilation of the Messages and Papers of the Presidents,* 10 vols., Washington, 1896-1899.

Senate Report No. 2332, 50th Cong., 1st sess. Report of Senate Finance Committee on tariff legislation, 1889.

Senate Report No. 1944, 51st Cong., 2d sess. Report of Senate Committee on Foreign Relations relative to Maritime Canal Company of Nicaragua.

Senate Report No. 227, 53d Cong., 2d sess. Report of Committee on Foreign Relations relative to Hawaiian matters, 1894. Contains a large quantity of testimony and affidavits in regard to the Hawaiian revolution of 1893.

Senate Executive Document No. 16, 53d Cong., 3d sess. Report of Rear-Admiral J. G. Walker on situation in Hawaii, 1894.

Senate Executive Document No. 31, 53d Cong., 3d sess. Special message urging consent to lease of Necker Island by the Hawaiian Government to Great Britain.

Senate Document No. 62, 55th Cong., 2d sess. Letter of Gen. J. M. Schofield relative to annexation of Hawaii.

Senate Document No. 188, 55th Cong., 2d sess. Statement on Pacific interests of the United States by G. W. Melville, Engineer-in-Chief, U. S. Navy.

Senate Document No. 315, 55th Cong., 2d sess. Letter of G. W. Melville relative to British interest in Hawaii.

Senate Report No. 681, 55th Cong., 2d sess. Report of Committee on Foreign Relations on joint resolution for Hawaiian annexation, March 16, 1898.

Senate Document No. 62, 55th Cong., 3d sess. *A Treaty of Peace between the United States and Spain.* Part II comprises the protocols of the conferences at Paris and related material.

Senate Document No. 148, 56th Cong., 2d sess. *Papers Relating to the Treaty with Spain.* Telegraphic correspondence between the Department of State and the commissioners in Paris, 1898.

Senate Executive Report No. 1, 57th Cong., 1st sess. Report by Committee on Foreign Relations on treaty for purchase of Danish West Indies, 1902. Contains as appendix, Lodge's report of 1898.

Statistical Abstract of the United States,
   1907, Washington, 1908.
   1925, Washington, 1926.
   1931, Washington, 1931.

Statutes at Large of the United States,
   Vol. XXV, Washington, 1889.
   Vol. XXVI, Washington, 1891.
   Vol. XXVII, Washington, 1893.
   Vol. XXX, Washington, 1899.

United States Reports. Cases Adjudged in the Supreme Court,
   Vol. CXXXVI, New York, 1890.

Germany:

Die Grosse Politik der Europaischen Kabinette, 1871-1914, 40 vols., Berlin, 1922-1927. Volume XV, *Rings um die Erste Haager Friedenskonferenz* (1924).

Hawaii:

Report of the Proceedings of the Committee on Foreign Relations to the Legislature of 1890, in regard to the Investigation of Treaty Matters, Honolulu, 1890.

Minority Report, Committee on Foreign Relations. Presented by Hon. H. P. Baldwin, June 14, 1890. [Honolulu, 1890.]

Reply of Minister Austin to the Majority Report of Committee on Foreign Relations, in the Legislative Assembly, June 13, 1890. [Honolulu, 1890.]

Spain:

Spanish Diplomatic Correspondence and Documents, 1896-1900. Presented to the Cortes by the Minister of State. [Translation.] Washington, 1905.

NON-GOVERNMENTAL SOURCE MATERIALS

Contemporary Books and Articles, Reminiscences, etc.:

Atkins, E. F., *Sixty Years in Cuba,* Cambridge, 1926.

Barrows, J. H., *The Christian Conquest of Asia,* New York, 1899.

———, "God's Hand in Recent American History," *The Interior,* XXIX, 1441-1442, November 24, 1898.

Bates, G. H., "Some Aspects of the Samoan Question," *Century Magazine,* XV, 945-949, April, 1889.

Bishop, Sereno E., "The Hawaiian Queen and Her Kingdom," *Review of Reviews,* IV, 147-163, September, 1891.

Blackburn, Alexander, "The Imperialism of Righteousness," *The Standard,* XLV, 913, August 6, 1898.

Burgess, John W., *The Foundations of Political Science,* New York, 1933. A reprinting of certain chapters from *Political Science and Comparative Constitutional Law,* with a "Foreword" by Nicholas Murray Butler.

———, *Political Science and Comparative Constitutional Law,* 2 vols., Boston and London, 1890.

———, *Reminiscences of an American Scholar,* New York, 1934.

Carnegie, Andrew, *Autobiography of Andrew Carnegie,* Boston and New York, 1920.

Cooley, T. M., "Grave Obstacles to Hawaiian Annexation," *Forum,* XV, 389-406, June, 1893.

Darwin, Charles, *The Descent of Man, and Selection in Relation to Sex,* 2 vols., London, 1871.

Dole, Sanford B., *Memoirs of the Hawaiian Revolution,* edited by Andrew Farrell, Honolulu, 1936.

Douglass, Frederick, "Haiti and the United States: Inside History of the Negotiations for the Môle St. Nicholas," *North American Review,* CLIII, 337-345, 450-459, September, October, 1891.

Doyle, A. P., "Religious Problem of the Philippines," *Catholic World,* LXVIII, 119-124, October, 1898.

Dunn, A. W., *From Harrison to Harding,* 2 vols., New York and London, 1922.

Eddy, U. S., "Our Chance for Commercial Supremacy," *Forum,* XI, 419-428, June, 1891.

Fiske, John, *American Political Ideas Viewed from the Standpoint of Universal History,* New York, 1885.

———, "Manifest Destiny," *Harper's New Monthly Magazine,* LXX, 578-590, March, 1885.

Ford, W. C. (ed.), *The Letters of Henry Adams,* Boston and New York, 1930.

Foster, John W., *Diplomatic Memoirs,* 2 vols., Boston and New York, 1909.

Gobineau, Joseph Arthur, Count of, *Moral and Intellectual Diversity of Races* [Translation], Philadelphia, 1856.

Hoar, George F., *Autobiography of Seventy Years,* 2 vols., New York, 1903.

Kidd, Benjamin, *The Control of the Tropics,* New York, 1898.

———, *Social Evolution,* new ed., New York and London, 1894.

Kohlsaat, H. H., *From McKinley to Harding,* New York and London, 1923.

Liliuokalani, *Hawaii's Story by Hawaii's Queen,* Boston, 1898.

Lodge, H. C., "Our Blundering Foreign Policy," *Forum,* XIX, 8-17, March, 1895.

——— (editor), *Selections from the Correspondence of Theodore Roosevelt and Henry Cabot Lodge,* 2 vols., New York and London, 1925.

MacMurray, J. Van A., *Treaties and Agreements with and Concerning China, 1894-1919,* 2 vols., New York, 1921.

Madden, H. M. (ed.), "Letters of Sanford B. Dole and John W. Burgess," *Pacific Historical Review,* V, 71-75, March, 1936.

Mahan, A. T., *The Influence of Sea Power upon History, 1660-1783,* Boston, 1890.

———, *The Interest of America in Sea Power, Present and Future,* Boston, 1897.

———, *Lessons of the War with Spain,* Boston, 1899.

Melville, G. W., "Our Future in the Pacific—What We Have There to Hold and Win," *North American Review,* CLXVI, 281-296, March, 1898.

Morgan, T. J., "The New Republic and Its New Duties," *The Standard,* XLV, 882, July 23, 1898.

Mott, John R., *Strategic Points in the World's Conquest,* New York, Chicago, and Toronto, 1897.

Nevins, Allan (ed.), *Letters of Grover Cleveland, 1850-1908,* Boston and New York, 1933.

O'Keeffe, H. E., "A Word on the Church in the New Possessions," *Catholic World,* LXVIII, 319-322, December, 1898.

Palmer, Julius A., Jr., *Again in Hawaii.* Boston, 1895. Special correspondence to the New York *Evening Post,* 1895.

———, *Memories of Hawaii and Hawaiian Correspondence,* Boston, 1894. Contains special correspondence to the Boston *Transcript,* 1894.

Patten, Simon N., *The Theory of Social Forces.* Supplement to *Annals* of the American Academy of Political and Social Science, VII, Philadelphia, 1896.

Perrine, S. A., "A Case of Manifest Destiny," *Baptist Missionary Review* (Cuttack, India), IV, 424-428, November, 1898.

Procter, John R., "Hawaii and the Changing Front of the World," *Forum,* XXIV, 34-45, September, 1897.

Robinson, E. Van D., "The Caroline Islands and the Terms of Peace," *Independent,* L, 1046-1048, October 13, 1898.

Schofield, J. M. and Alexander, B. S., "Report on Pearl Harbor, 1873," *American Historical Review,* XXX, 561-565, April, 1925.

Schurz, Carl, "Manifest Destiny," *Harper's New Monthly Magazine,* LXXXVII, 737-746, October, 1893.

Strong, Josiah, *Our Country: Its Possible Future and Its Present Crisis,* revised ed., New York, 1891. The first edition was copyrighted in 1885.

Thurston, Lorrin A., *Memoirs of the Hawaiian Revolution,* edited by Andrew Farrell, Honolulu, 1936.

Woolsey, T. S., *America's Foreign Policy,* New York, 1898.

Young, Lucien, *The Boston at Hawaii,* Washington, 1898.

Zincke, F. B., *Last Winter in the United States,* London, 1868.

Business and Trade Journals:

Age of Steel (St. Louis), 1898.

American Banker (New York), 1898.

American Exporter (New York), 1898.

American Wool and Cotton Reporter (New York), 1898.

Banker and Tradesman (Boston), 1898.

Banker's Magazine (New York), 1898.

Bradstreet's, A Journal of Trade, Finance, and Public Economy (New York), 1898.

Commercial and Financial Chronicle (New York), 1897, 1898.

Commercial Bulletin of Southern California (Los Angeles), 1898.

Daily Commercial News and Shipping List (San Francisco), 1898.

"Dixie," A Monthly Journal Devoted to Southern Industrial Interests (Atlanta), 1898.

Dry Goods Economist (New York), 1898.

Drugs, Oils, and Paints (Philadelphia), 1898.

Dun's Review, A Weekly Review of Business and Finance (New York), 1898.

The Economist, A Weekly Financial, Commercial, and Real-Estate Newspaper (Chicago), 1898.

The Financial Record, An Investors' Manual (New York), 1897, 1898.

The Iron Age (New York), 1897, 1898.

Iron and Steel (Chicago), 1898.

Journal of Commerce (Boston), 1898.

Journal of Commerce and Commercial Bulletin (New York), 1893, 1896, 1897, 1898.

Journal of Finance (New York), 1893.

Mining and Scientific Press (San Francisco), 1898.

New Jersey Trade Review (Newark), 1898.

New York *Commercial,* 1898.

Railroad Gazette (New York), 1898.

Railway Age (Chicago), 1898.

Railway World (Philadelphia), 1898.

Rand-McNally Bankers' Monthly (Chicago), 1898.

The Tradesman (Chattanooga), 1898.

United States Investor (Boston), 1898.

Wall Street Journal (New York), 1897, 1898.

Weekly Northwestern Miller (Minneapolis), 1898.

Reports of Boards of Trade and Chambers of Commerce:

Baltimore Board of Trade, *Report of President and Directors for Year Ending Sept. 30, 1898,* Baltimore, 1898.

Baltimore Chamber of Commerce, *Forty-third Annual Report,* Baltimore, 1898.

Boston Chamber of Commerce, *Thirteenth Annual Report,* Boston, 1899.

Cincinnati Chamber of Commerce, *Fiftieth Annual Report,* Cincinnati, 1899.

Cleveland Chamber of Commerce, *Fiftieth Year,* Cleveland, 1898.

Indianapolis Board of Trade, *Annual Report for Year Ending June 1, 1898,* Indianapolis, 1898.

Chamber of Commerce of the State of New York, *Fortieth Annual Report, 1897-1898,* New York, 1898.

Philadelphia Board of Trade, *Sixty-Fourth Annual Report,* Philadelphia, 1897. *Sixty-Fifth Annual Report,* Philadelphia, 1898. *Sixty-Sixth Annual Report,* Philadelphia, 1899.

Portland (Oregon) *Board of Trade Journal,* Portland, 1898.

Chamber of Commerce of San Francisco, *Forty-Eighth Annual Report,* San Francisco, 1898. *Forty-Ninth Annual Report,* San Francisco, 1899.

Merchants' Exchange of St. Louis, *Annual Statement of the Trade and Commerce of St. Louis for Year 1898,* St. Louis, 1899.

National Board of Trade, *Proceedings of the 28th Annual Meeting,* Philadelphia, 1898.

Religious periodicals:

Baptist:

Baptist Missionary Magazine (Boston), 1898.

The Baptist Union (Chicago), 1898.

The Journal and Messenger (Cincinnati), 1898.

The Standard, A Baptist Newspaper (Chicago), 1898.

The Watchman (Boston), 1898.

Congregational:

The Advance (Chicago), 1898.

The American Missionary. Published by the American Missionary Association (New York), 1898.

The Congregationalist (Boston), 1898.

The Independent (New York), 1893, 1894, 1898.

Missionary Herald. Published by the American Board of Commissioners for Foreign Missions (Boston), 1898.

American Board of Commissioners for Foreign Missions, *Eighty-eighth Annual Report,* Grand Rapids, 1898.

Disciples of Christ:
> *The Christian-Evangelist* (St. Louis), 1898.
> *The Christian Standard* (Cincinnati), 1898.

Episcopal:
> *The Church Eclectic: an Anglo-Catholic Magazine of Church Literature* (Milwaukee), 1898.
> *The Churchman: An Illustrated Weekly News Magazine* (New York), 1897, 1898.
> *The Church Standard* (Philadelphia), 1898.
> *The Spirit of Missions.* Published by the Domestic and Foreign Missionary Society of the Protestant Episcopal Church in the U. S. A. (New York), 1898.

Methodist:
> *The Christian Advocate* (New York), 1898.
> *Christian Advocate,* General Organ of the M. E. Church, South (Nashville), 1898.
> *California Christian Advocate* (San Francisco), 1898.
> *Central Christian Advocate* (St. Louis), 1899.
> *Northern Christian Advocate* (Syracuse), 1898.
> *Northwestern Christian Advocate* (Chicago), 1898.
> *The Methodist Review* (Nashville), 1898.
> *The Methodist Review* (New York and Cincinnati), 1898.
> Methodist Episcopal Church Conference, Central Illinois, 1898, *Minutes,* Galesburg, 1898.
> Methodist Episcopal Church Conference, Central New York, 1898, *Report,* Syracuse, 1898.

Presbyterian:
> *Associate Reform Presbyterian* (Due West, S. C.), 1898.
> *The Church at Home and Abroad* (Philadelphia), 1898.
> *Evangelist* (New York), 1898.
> *The Interior* (Chicago), 1898.
> *Presbyterian Banner* (Pittsburgh), 1898.
> Board of Foreign Missions of the Presbyterian Church in the United States, *Sixty-Second Annual Report,* New York, 1899. *Sixty-third Annual Report,* New York, 1900.

Roman Catholic:
> *The Ave Maria* (Notre Dame, Ind.), 1898.
> *The Catholic Herald* (New York), 1898.
> *The Catholic News* (New York), 1898.
> *The Catholic World* (New York), 1898.

Miscellaneous:
 The Christian and Missionary Alliance. Published by the organization of the same name (Nyack, N. Y.), 1898.
 The Christian Register (Unitarian, Boston), 1898.
 The Friend (Quaker, Philadelphia), 1898.
 Improvement Era (Mormon, Salt Lake City), 1898.
 The New Century (Theosophist, New York), 1898.
 The Religious Telescope, Weekly Organ of the United Brethren in Christ (Dayton, Ohio), 1898.

General magazines:
 Blackwood's Edinburgh Magazine (Edinburgh), CLXIII, 1898.
 Harper's New Monthly Magazine (New York), LXXXVII, 1893.
 Literary Digest (New York), VI-XVI, 1893-1898.
 Literary World (Boston), XXI, 1890.
 The Nation (New York), LIII, 1891; LVII, 1893; LIX, 1894.
 North American Review (New York), CLVI-CLVII, 1893; CLXVI, 1898.
 Open Court (Chicago), VII, 1893.
 The Outlook (New York), LIX, 1898.
 Overland Monthly (San Francisco), XXIII, 1894; XXXI, 1898.
 Political Science Quarterly (New York, Boston, Chicago), IX, 1894.
 Review of Reviews (New York), VII, 1893; XV-XVII, 1897-1898.

General newspapers:
 Commercial Advertiser (New York), 1893.
 Daily Pacific Commercial Advertiser (Honolulu), 1889, 1892-1893. (In Spaulding Collection, University of Michigan).
 Birmingham *Age-Herald,* 1898.
 Buffalo *Courier,* 1893, 1896.
 Buffalo *Express,* 1898.
 New York *Herald,* 1893.
 New York *Sun,* 1897, 1898.
 New York *Times,* 1893.
 New York *Tribune,* 1889, 1893.
 New York *World,* 1893.

Portland *Oregonian*, 1893.

Sacramento *Evening Bee*, 1898.

St. Louis *Republic*, 1898.

San Francisco *Bulletin*, 1898.

San Francisco *Call*, 1893, 1898.

San Francisco *Chronicle*, 1892.

San Francisco *Examiner*, 1893.

Seattle *Post-Intelligencer*, 1898.

Washington *Post*, 1892, 1893.

Washington *Evening Star*, 1892, 1893.

SECONDARY WORKS

Adler, C., *Jacob H. Schiff, His Life and Letters*, 2 vols., London, 1929.

Alderson, B., *Andrew Carnegie: The Man and His Work*, New York, 1902.

Alexander, W. D., *History of the Later Years of the Hawaiian Monarchy and the Revolution of 1893*, Honolulu, 1896.

Bailey, T. A., " Japan's Protest against the Annexation of Hawaii," *Journal of Modern History*, III, 46-61, March, 1931.

———, " The United States and Hawaii during the Spanish-American War," *American Historical Review*, XXXVI, 552-560, April, 1931.

Beard, Charles A. and Mary R., *The Rise of American Civilization*, 2 vols., New York, 1927.

Beer, Thomas, *Hanna*, New York, 1929.

Bemis, Samuel F. (editor), *The American Secretaries of State and Their Diplomacy*, 10 vols., New York, 1927-1929.

Benton, E. J., *International Law and Diplomacy of the Spanish-American War*, Baltimore, 1908.

Bishop, Joseph B., *Theodore Roosevelt and His Time*, 2 vols., New York, 1920.

Bowers, Claude G., *Beveridge and the Progressive Era*, New York, 1932.

Brown, P. M., *Frederick T. Frelinghuysen*, in Bemis (ed.), *American Secretaries of State*, VIII.

Castle, W. R., Jr., *John Watson Foster*, in Bemis (ed.), *American Secretaries of State*, VIII.

Chadwick, F. E., *The Relations of the United States and Spain: The Spanish-American War*, 2 vols., New York, 1911.

Chambers, H. E., *Constitutional History of Hawaii*, in "Johns Hopkins University Studies in Historical and Political Science," XIV, Baltimore, 1896.

Coolidge, L. A., *An Old-Fashioned Senator, Orville H. Platt of Connecticut*, New York and London, 1910.

Cortissoz, Royal, *The Life of Whitelaw Reid*, 2 vols., New York, 1921.

Croly, Herbert, *Marcus Alonzo Hanna*, New York, 1912.

Curti, M. E., *Bryan and World Peace*, in "Smith College Studies in History," Nos. 3-4, XVI, Northampton, 1931.

Dennett, Tyler, *Americans in Eastern Asia*, New York, 1922.

———, *John Hay*, New York, 1933.

Dennis, A. L. P., *Adventures in American Diplomacy, 1846-1906*, New York, 1928.

———, *John Hay*, in Bemis (ed.), *American Secretaries of State*, IX.

Dictionary of American Biography, vol. VI, New York, 1931; vol. XVII, New York, 1935.

Dulles, Foster R., *America in the Pacific*, Boston and New York, 1932.

Faulkner, H. U., *American Economic History*, New York and London, 1924.

Fuess, C. M., *Carl Schurz, Reformer (1829-1906)*, New York, 1932.

Gibbons, H. A., *John Wanamaker*, 2 vols., New York and London, 1926.

Gresham, Matilda, *Life of Walter Quintin Gresham*, 2 vols., Chicago, 1919.

Hacker, Louis M., "The Incendiary Mahan: a Biography," *Scribner's Magazine*, XCV, 263-268, 311-320, April, 1934.

Hamilton, Gail (pseudonym for Mary Abigail Dodge), *Biography of James G. Blaine*, Norwich, Conn., 1895.

Harrington, Fred H., "The Anti-Imperialist Movement in the United States, 1898-1900," *Mississippi Valley Historical Review*, XXII, 211-230, September, 1935.

Henderson, J. B., *American Diplomatic Questions*, New York, 1901.

Hendrick, B. J., *The Training of an American: The Earlier Life and Letters of Walter H. Page,* Boston and New York, 1928.

Hibben, Paxton, *The Peerless Leader: William Jennings Bryan,* New York, 1929.

Hicks, John D., *The Populist Revolt,* Minneapolis, 1931.

Holt, W. S., *Treaties Defeated by the Senate,* Baltimore, 1933.

Hull, G. H., *Industrial Depressions . . . or Iron the Barometer of Trade,* New York, 1911.

James, Henry, *Richard Olney and His Public Service,* Boston and New York, 1923.

Jones, E., *The Trust Problem in the United States,* New York, 1926.

Joseph, P., *Foreign Diplomacy in China, 1894-1900,* London, 1928.

Kennan, George, *E. H. Harriman,* 2 vols., Boston and New York, 1922.

Lockey, Joseph B., *James Gillespie Blaine,* in Bemis (ed.), *American Secretaries of State,* VIII.

Long, J. D., *The New American Navy,* 2 vols., New York, 1903.

Millis, Walter, *The Martial Spirit,* Boston, 1931.

Morse, H. B., *The International Relations of the Chinese Empire,* 3 vols., London and New York, 1910-1918.

Mott, T. B., *Myron T. Herrick, Friend of France,* Garden City, 1929.

Muzzey, David S., *James G. Blaine: A Political Idol of Other Days,* New York, 1934.

National Cyclopaedia of American Biography, IX, New York, 1907.

Nevins, Allan, *Abram S. Hewitt, with Some Account of Peter Cooper,* New York, 1935.

————, *Grover Cleveland, A Study in Courage,* New York, 1932.

————, *Henry White, Thirty Years of Diplomacy,* New York, 1930.

New Schaff-Herzog Encyclopedia of Religious Knowledge, 12 vols., New York and London, 1909.

Olcott, C. S., *The Life of William McKinley,* 2 vols., Boston and New York, 1916.

Pratt, Julius W., " American Business and the Spanish-American War," *Hispanic American Historical Review,* XIV, 163-201, May, 1934.

————, " The Hawaiian Revolution: A Reinterpretation," *Pacific Historical Review,* I, 273-294, September, 1932.

————, " John L. O'Sullivan and Manifest Destiny," *New York History,* XIV, 213-234, July, 1933.

Pringle, H. F., *Theodore Roosevelt, a Biography,* New York, 1931.

Pyle, J. G., *Life of James J. Hill,* 2 vols., Garden City, 1917.

Rhodes, James F., *The McKinley and Roosevelt Administrations,* New York, 1922.

Robinson, Wm. A., *Thomas B. Reed, Parliamentarian,* New York, 1930.

Rubens, Horatio, *Liberty, the Story of Cuba,* New York, 1932.

Ryden, G. H., *The Foreign Policy of the United States in Relation to Samoa,* New Haven, 1933.

Sears, L. M., *History of American Foreign Relations,* New York, 1927.

————, *John Sherman,* in Bemis (ed.), *American Secretaries of State,* IX.

Schuyler, M., *Walter Q. Gresham,* in Bemis (ed.), *American Secretaries of State,* VIII.

Shippee, L. B., " Germany and the Spanish-American War," *American Historical Review,* XXX, 754-777, July, 1925.

————, and Way, R. B., *William Rufus Day,* in Bemis (ed.), *American Secretaries of State,* IX.

Smith, T. C., " Expansion after the Civil War, 1865-1871," *Political Science Quarterly,* XVI, 412-436, September, 1901.

Spaulding, T. M., *Cabinet Government in Hawaii, 1887-1893* (University of Hawaii, *Occasional Papers,* No. 2), Honolulu, 1924.

Stanwood, E., *A History of the Presidency from 1788 to 1897,* new ed., Boston and New York, 1926.

Tansill, C. C., *The Purchase of the Danish West Indies,* Baltimore, 1932.

Taylor, C. C., *The Life of Admiral Mahan, Naval Philosopher,* New York, 1920.

Tribolet, L. B., *International Aspects of Electrical Communications in the Pacific,* Baltimore, 1929.

Tyler, Alice F., *The Foreign Policy of James G. Blaine,* Minneapolis, 1927.

Volwiler, A. T., Review of D. S. Muzzey's *James G. Blaine, American Historical Review,* XLI, 554-557, April, 1936.

Weinberg, Albert K., *Manifest Destiny: A Study of Nationalist Expansionism in American History,* Baltimore, 1935.

Welles, Sumner, *Naboth's Vineyard,* 2 vols., New York, 1928.

25

Wilkerson, M. M., *Public Opinion and the Spanish-American War, a Study in War Propaganda*, Baton Rouge, 1932.

Wilkinson, Margaret S., The Maritime Canal Company of Nicaragua, MS thesis in University of Buffalo Library.

Williams, Mary W., *Anglo-American Isthmian Diplomacy, 1815-1915*, Washington, 1916.

Wisan, J. E., *The Cuban Crisis as Reflected in the New York Press (1895-1898)*, New York, 1934.

Wriston, H. M., *Executive Agents in American Foreign Relations*, Baltimore, 1929.

INDEX

Adams, Henry, 169.

Aguinaldo, E., 357n.

Alexander, B. S., 71.

Allen, Wm. V., 202, 346.

American Asiatic Association, 265, 272.

American Board of Commissioners for Foreign Missions, work of in Caroline Islands, 302; asks religious toleration in Caroline Islands, 303.

American China and Japan Association, 265.

American Federation of Labor, opposes annexation of Hawaii, 225n.

American Missionary Association, plans missionary campaign in Cuba, 300, 301.

Annexation Club, formed in Honolulu, 54 and note; mentioned, 130, 135.

Anti-imperialists, hold mass-meeting in Boston, 313.

Arion Hall, propriety of stationing troops in, 101-104.

Armenia, congressional resolution relative to protection of Christians in, 213; situation in, of concern to Great Britain and United States, 280.

Ashford, C. W., attorney-general, 41; deported from Hawaii, 199.

Ashford, Volney V., and annexation leagues, 52n., 53n.; deported from Hawaii, 199.

Asia, Christian conquest of, 281.

Atkins, E. F., opposes intervention in Cuba, 250.

Austin, Jonathan, Hawaiian minister of foreign affairs, 40, 41.

Bacon, A. O., mentioned, 346; offers amendment promising Philippine independence, 359.

Bailey, T. A., quoted, 317n.

Baptist Church, attitude toward expansion, 291-294; some papers cautious, 292-293.

Barrows, J. H., 281, 298.

Bates, G. H., on Samoa and the Monroe Doctrine, 27n.

Bayard, Thos. F., 96.

Beard, Charles A., and Mary R., on sugar as the cause of Hawaiian revolution, 159n.

Beer, W. C., makes estimate of war sentiment, 246-247n.; visits White House, 316, 334.

Beveridge, Albert J., oration on President Grant, 227-228, 231; economic basis of his ideas, 232.

Bishop, Sereno E., commends Blount, 132; says planters did not instigate revolution, 158; on evil character of native Hawaiians, 162; on morals of Liliuokalani, 163, 164; article in praise of Liliuokalani, 167-168; accuses Cleveland of conspiring with British Government, 172; on Constitution of 1894, 192-193.

Blaine, James G., ideas on expansion, 22-25; Pan American policy, 23; interest in isthmian canal, 23; on Cuba and Puerto Rico, 23-25; on Hawaii, 24-25; Secretary of State under Harrison, 25; and the Samoan question, 26-27; opposes purchase of Danish West Indies, 32; discusses new Hawaiian treaty, 37; anxious to aid Hawaii, 45; negotiates free trade treaty, 46-48; desires continuance of Hawaiian independence, 49; relations with Stevens, 50; meets Thurston, 56; resigns, 61; refuses joint guarantee of Hawaiian independence, 126-127.

Blaisdell, William, 159.

Bliss, C. N., favors retaining Philippines, 329.

Blount, James H., chairman of House Committee on Foreign Affairs, 56; meets Thurston, 56; mentioned, 81; consulted on Hawaiian treaty, 122; special commissioner to Hawaii, 124; purpose of his mission, 127; effect of Southern background, 128, 133; plans for influencing his decision, 129-130; arrives in Honolulu, 130; declines hospitalities, 130-131; terminates protectorate, 131; appointed minister, 131; conduct in Honolulu, 131-132; his investigation and report, 133-136; unfavorable opinion of Thurston, 133; leaves Honolulu, 137; report published, 137; sifts charges against Liliuokalani, 165, 168-169; attacked and defended in Senate, 177-178; action approved by Senate Committee, 183.

Bolte, C., 104-105.

Boston, U. S. S., leaves Honolulu, 76; returns, 80; troops from landed, 89.

Bradley, Mr. Justice, opinion in *Mormon Church v. United States*, 353.

Bridge, Horatio, editor of *Overland Monthly*, 223, 229.

British West Indies, acquisition of suggested, 275-276.

Bryan, W. J., and free silver, 215; presides over Trans-Mississippi Congress, 224; urges ratification of treaty with Spain, 357.

Bureau of Statistics, 277.

Burgess, John W., on Teutonic supremacy, 6-11; opposes war and expansion, 11; influence of, 20 and note; advises Dole on constitution for Hawaii, 192n.

Bush, J. E., editor and politician, 64; works with Thurston, 64-65; turns against Thurston, 75-76; talks with Willis, 142.

Business, American, opposed or indifferent to expansion, 22; attitude to war with Spain and to territorial expansion, 232-278; opposed to intervention in Cuba, 233-252; dislike of " jingoes," 235; hails economic upturn, 237-238; interest of in foreign markets, 238-239, 252-253, 257-259; fears effect of war on reviving prosperity, 239-240; sees little profit in war, 240-241; fears inflation as result of war, 241-243; Western business men less opposed to war than Eastern, 243-245; expects no great injury from war, 245-246; effect of Senator Proctor's speech, 246-247; some spokesmen regard war as inevitable, 246, 252; effect of Cuban War on investments and trade, 248-251; regards colonial expansion as a form of jingoism, 253-256; sees no value in colonies, 256-257; shows free-trade leanings, 257-259; alarmed at Count Goluchowski's address, 259-260; alarmed at European aggressions in China, 260-265; takes measures to protect interests in China, 263-265; regards Dewey's victory as giving key to Chinese trade, 266; demands retention of Philippines, 267-271; sees hand of Providence in Dewey's victory, 269; not unanimous for retaining Philippines, 272-273; converted to belief in expansion, 273-274; suggests keeping Puerto Rico and Cuba, 274-275; anticipates profitable trade with new possessions, 276-277; sees opportunities for capital and skill in same, 277-278; its reversal of position, 278.

Butler, Marion, 184.

Butler, Nicholas Murray, on Professor Burgess, 20 and note.

Caffery, Donelson, opposes annexation of Hawaii, 204; mentioned, 350, 351.

Call, Wilkinson, 178.

Cambon, Jules M., presents Spanish peace proposal to McKinley, 328; signs peace protocol, 331.

Cantacuzene, Prince, Russian minister, 125.

Carlisle, John G., 122.

Carnegie, Andrew, 238.

Caroline Islands, acquisition of suggested, 274, 303; American missionaries driven from, 290; missionary efforts begun in, 302; assigned to Spain, 303; missionaries expelled from, 303; religious toleration in demanded, 303; propaganda for annexation of, 304; sold to Germany, 304n.; proposal that Spain cede naval and telegraph station in, 340; missionary interest in, 340-341; cession of to United States discussed, 340-344; American capitalists desire island in for cable, 341; McKinley desires to purchase an island in, 341; peace commissioners desire cession of, 341; peace commissioners propose purchase of Kusaie and religious liberty in all, 342; German claims to, 342; Germany arranges to purchase from Spain, 343; Germany protests at American attempts to buy, 343-344; Germany offers cable and telegraph rights in, 343-344; Germany secures promise from Spain not to sell Carolines to United States, 344; Spanish commissioners refuse to discuss disposition of, 344.

Carr, C. E., minister to Denmark, 31; and proposed sale of St. Thomas and St. John, 31-32.

Carter, C. L., 110, 111, 123.

Carter, H. A. P., Hawaiian minister, negotiates with Blaine, 37; explains treaty negotiation, 38n.,

39n.; returns to Honolulu, 38-39; departs for Washington, 40; protests against McKinley bill, 42-43; on sugar bounty, 45; on extending reciprocity treaty, 45, 46; death of, 47; mentioned, 49.

Carter, Joseph O., 109, 143n.

Castle, W. R., 83, 110, 111, 122, 130.

Catholic Church in the United States, hopes for peaceful solution of Cuban question, 282-283, 287, 288; supports President McKinley in war with Spain, 287-288; critical of Protestant missionary fervor, 309, 310; not opposed to expansion, 309-312; some clergy see hand of Providence in war with Spain, 310-311; spokesmen of, hail civilizing mission of United States, 312.

Chamber of Commerce of State of New York, asks protection of commercial interests in China, 263-264.

Chandler, Wm. E., resolution for annexation of Hawaii, 146.

Chilton, Horace, 350.

China, European aggressions in, a threat to American business, 260-263; American trade with, 261-262; missionary opportunity in, 281; opportunity in, for civilizing work, 298; United States and Great Britain should cooperate in, 298.

Chinese immigration, obstacle to annexation of Hawaii, 118, 119; forbidden in treaty of annexation, 120; importance of to Hawaiian sugar industry, 157.

Christian and Missionary Alliance, mentioned, 284n.; accepts expansionist program, 291; asks open door for missionary work in Philippines, 315.

Churches, see Religious bodies and names of separate denominations.

Clark, Champ, ridicules plan to annex Hawaii, 321-322.

Clayton-Bulwer Treaty, disregarded by Secretary Frelinghuysen, 28.

Cleveland, Grover, withdraws Nicaraguan Canal treaty, 28; confers with Gresham and Carlisle, 122; withdraws Hawaiian treaty from Senate, 124; considers possibility of protectorate over Hawaii, 128n.; accepts Gresham's conclusions, 138; plans restoration of Liliuokalani, 140; submits Hawaiian question to Congress, 142-143, 145, 174, 175; lays Hawaiian documents before Congress, 146; how affected by charges against Liliuokalani, 170; American newspapers on his proposal to restore Liliuokalani, 172-174; policy approved by Senate Committee, 184; congratulates President Dole, 193; sends note to representatives of Liliuokalani, 194; asks consent to lease of Necker Island, 200; proposes withdrawal from Samoa, 201; opposes appropriation for cable to Hawaii, 203n.; and Venezuela, 208; and the Navy, 208; and Nicaraguan Canal, 208; opposes all schemes of expansion, 208-209; opposes intervention in Cuba, 209, 211-212; denounces treaty for annexation of Hawaii, 219n.

Coffman, Lt., 102, 105.

Colburn, J. F., secretary of the interior, 78; warns Thurston of Queen's plans, 80; mentioned, 83, 84, 85, 129, 134.

Colonial responsibilities, attitude of churches toward, 279, 290-314.

Commission, Hawaiian, to negotiate for annexation, membership and instructions, 110, 118; activity in San Francisco, 111; arrive in Washington, 111; Stevens's praise of, 111-112; negotiations with Foster, 117-120; agree to treaty, 120-121.

Commission to negotiate peace with Spain, see Paris Peace Commission.

Committee of Safety, Hawaiian, organized, 83; activities, 84-91; endorsed by mass meeting, 87; plans mission to Washington, 110.

Committee on American Interests in China, 263.

Congregational Church, is ready to accept colonial responsibilities, 300-302; special interest of in Caroline Islands, 302.

Congress, U. S. 52d, 2d session, Hawaiian question in, 146-147.

Congress, U. S., 53d, 1st session, 146.

Congress, U. S., 53d, 2d session, debate in on Cleveland's Hawaiian policy, 175-187.

Congress, U. S., 53d, 3d session, debate in on foreign policy, 200-206.

Congress, U. S., 54th, 1st session, Cuban resolutions and debate in, 210-211; "revival of nationalism" in, 212-213; votes naval increases, 213.

Congress, U. S., 55th, 2d session, issues ultimatum to Spain and declares existence of war, 227; debates and passes joint resolution annexing Hawaii, 319-326.

Constitution of 1887, proposed revision of, 78; mentioned, 136.

Cooley, T. M., 155.

Cooper, H. E., 83.

Cornwell, W. H., minister of finance, 78.

Cuba, annexation of discussed, 179, 182, 210-211; insurrection in, 209-210; Congress favors independence of, 210; popular sympathy with insurgents in, 210; Mahan on strategic importance of, 223; independence promised by Teller Amendment, 230; rumors that Spain will sell, 247 ; effects of insurrection in, on American investments and trade, 248-251 ; American flag must float there till order is assured, 275 ; business opportunities in, 277 ; moral and religious responsibility in, 282 ; to be opened to the Gospel, 287 ; offers promising field for missionary work, 300, 301, 304 ; annexation of proposed, in interest of Cubans, 305-306 ; religion of inhabitants of, 308 ; Spanish Government ready to part with, 328 ; sovereignty over surrendered by Spain, 330-331.

Cullom, Shelby M., 177, 178.

Cummins, J. A., minister of foreign affairs, 42 ; mentioned, 135 ; visits Washington, 194.

Curtis, Geo. T., 155n.

Damon, S. M., 92.

Daniel, John W., 177, 184.

Danish West Indies, acquisition of suggested, 31-32 ; Cleveland not interested in, 209 ; purchase of proposed by Lodge, 221 ; purchase of prevented by war with Spain, 226-227.

Darwin, Charles, influence on expansionist thought, 3ff.

Davis, C. K., ridicules Cleveland and Gresham, 177 ; withholds endorsement of Cleveland and Blount, 184 ; reports annexation treaty to Senate, 219 ; member of Peace Commission, 332 ; talks of dividing Philippines, 332 ; joins Reid in urging retention of all Philippines, 332, 337 ; opposes all concessions to Spain, 339n.

Day, W. R., Assistant Secretary of State, negotiates treaty with Hawaii, 218 ; promises protection for Hawaii, 221 ; not an expansionist, 326-327 ; admits uncertainty as to future of Philippines,

327 ; becomes Secretary of State, 327n. ; says no question about retaining Puerto Rico, 327 ; states that Spain may retain Philippines, 327 ; premature report of conversion of, 327-328, 332 ; signs peace protocol, 331 ; member of Peace Commission, 332 ; opposes keeping Philippines, 332 ; willing to take Luzon, 336 ; proposes concessions to Spain, 339 ; proposes that Spain cede islands in Carolines instead of Mindanao and Sulu, 341-342.

DeLome letter, 283.

Democratic Party, foreign policy of contrasted with that of Republicans, 214-215.

Denby, Charles, 262.

Dewey, Rear Admiral George, appointed to command Asiatic squadron, 222n. ; instructions for operations in Philippines, 226 ; destroys Spanish fleet, 227 ; publicity given to his plans, 228n. ; effect of his victory on business sentiment, 266, 267 ; his victory viewed as sign of divine favor, 289-290 ; points nation to a nobler goal, 308 ; victory at Manila gives new argument for annexing Hawaii, 319.

Disciples of Christ, see God's hand in war with Spain, 307.

Doherty, F. B., Paulist missionary in Philippines, 311n.

Dole, Sanford B., helps draft revolutionary documents, 83 ; agrees to head revolutionary government, 84, 90 ; replies to Willis, 144-145 ; first President of Republic of Hawaii, 191.

Dolph, J. N., on Samoa and the Monroe Doctrine, 27n., speech on Hawaii, 147, 152 ; withholds endorsement of Cleveland and Blount, 184.

Dominican Republic, project of naval base in, 30-31, 221, 227 ; Cleveland's policy toward, 209.

Douglass, Frederick, mission to Haiti, 29-30.

Doyle, A. P., suggests policy for Philippines, 311.

Draper, W. F., speech on Hawaii and sea power, 181-182.

Dunn, A. W., 337, 357.

Eddy, U. S., on Samoan question, 27n.

Episcopal Church, willing to accept colonial responsibilities, 304-307; Board of Missions commends expansion, 307.

Faulkner, H. U., quoted, 232.

Filipinos, American responsibility for, 292; warned against Protestant missionaries, 309; McKinley's intention toward, 316; thought unable to establish stable government, 333; their liberties not endangered by American rule, 355.

Fiske, John, on " manifest destiny," 4-5; influence of, 19.

Foraker, J. B., 355.

Foreman, John, 336.

Foster, John W., becomes Secretary of State, 25, 48, 50; negotiations for Samana Bay, 31 and note; on free trade with Hawaii, 48; reticent on Hawaiian policy, 70; approves recognition of Provisional Government, 115; forestalls foreign opposition to annexation, 115-116; discusses Hawaii with diplomatic corps, 116; gives qualified approval to protectorate, 116-117; negotiates with Hawaiian commissioners, 117-120; signs annexation treaty, 120; report on Hawaiian treaty, 121; seeks Democratic support for treaty, 122; resigns as Secretary of State, 123n.; sees McKinley, 216; drafts treaty for annexation of Hawaii (1897), 219.

Frazar, Everett, 272.

Frelinghuysen, Secretary, and treaty with Nicaragua, 28.

Friends, Society of, urges peaceful settlement of Cuban question, 288-289; opposes imperialism, 312-313.

Froude, J. A., 349.

Frye, W. P., remarks on Pago-Pago, 27n.; mentioned, 177, 184, 216; member of Peace Commission, 332; talks of dividing Philippines, 332; joins Reid in urging retention of all Philippines, 332, 337; proposes concessions to Spain, 339; proposes that Spain cede islands in Carolines instead of Mindanao and Sulu, 341-342.

Gage, L. J., mentioned, 242; thinks retention of Philippines unnecessary, 329.

George, James Z., 177.

German Empire, aggressions of in China, 261; ambitions of, in Carolines, thwart those of United States, 342-344.

Gherardi, Rear Admiral, sent to Haiti, 29; advises seizing Môle St. Nicholas, 29.

Glade, H. F., 83.

Gobineau, Count Arthur, on Nordic superiority, 7.

Godkin, E. L., 159.

Goluchowski, Count, Austro-Hungarian Foreign Minister, warns Europe of American competition, 259, 260.

Gordon, John B., 177.

Gorman, A. P., 122.

Grant, Ulysses S., mentioned, 152; Beveridge on his expansionist policy, 227-228.

Gray, George, defends Cleveland, 177; withholds endorsement of Stevens, 184; opposes annexations, 204; member of Peace Commission, 331-332; opposes retaining Philippines, 332, 337;

favors financial concessions to Spain, 339n.

Great Britain, not opposed to United States policy in Hawaii, 125-127; supposed designs on Hawaii, 149-150; supposed designs in the Pacific, 201, 202, 205; partnership with, in China, suggested, 298; favors retention of Philippines by United States, 329.

Gresham, Matilda, 122.

Gresham, Walter Q., mentioned, 122, 209; suspicious of Stevens, 123; motives of his Hawaiian policy, 124; consults foreign diplomats on Hawaiian question, 125-127; uninfluenced by Thurston, 137; decides Liliuokalani should be reinstated, 138; report to President, 138; instructions to Willis, 140-141, 142, 145; chivalrous attitude of to Liliuokalani, 170-171; confers with representatives of Liliuokalani, 194, 195; report of on Samoa, 201.

Grey, Sir Edward, 126.

Griggs, J. W., favors retaining Philippines, 329.

Hacker, L. M., cited, 22n.

Haiti, proposed base at Môle St. Nicholas, 29.

Hale, Eugene, 358.

Hall, Bishop, 306.

Hanna, Mark, favors annexation of Hawaii, 217; opposes intervention in Cuba, 233.

Harrison, Benjamin, foreign policy of, as President, 25-33; favors Nicaraguan canal, 28-29; seeks naval base in Haiti, 29-30; and in Dominican Republic, 30-31; policy toward Hawaii, 33, 34-73; asks correction of McKinley tariff, 44; rejects free trade treaty with Hawaii, 48; suggests closer relations with Hawaii, 69; expects revolution in Hawaii, 73; sends Hawaiian treaty to Senate, 121; desires plebiscite on annexation, 127.

Hartwell, A. S., 216n.

Hatch, F. M., Hawaiian minister, sees McKinley, 216; on Japanese menace, 217; signs annexation treaty, 219; assured of protection for Hawaii, 221; predicts that trouble with Spain will promote annexation, 225-226; fears failure of annexation and loss of reciprocity, 317; recommends that Hawaiian legislature consent to annexation by executive act, 318, 322n.; on prospects of annexation in Senate, 322.

Hawaii, relations of, with United States during Harrison's administration, 34-73; first contacts with United States, 34; reciprocity treaties of 1875 and 1887, 34; growth of foreign trade, 35; sugar plantations, 35; revolution of 1887, 35; prosperity endangered by tariff legislation, 36; government protests proposed tariff legislation, 36, 37; protectorate by United States proposed, 37, 38; new treaty drawn, 39; treaty opposed by Hawaiians, 40; treaty rejected by King, 41; injurious effects on, of McKinley tariff, 43-45; proposed free trade treaty with United States, 46-48; dual character of diplomatic relations with United States, 49; annexation movement reported in, 52-53; political events in, 1887-1892, 62-67; Constitution of 1887, 62; newspapers display interest in, 70-72; revolution of 1893, 74-109; placed under protection of United States, 114; treaty of annexation signed, 117, 120; terms of treaty, 120-121; treaty sent to Senate and favorably reported, 121; action on treaty postponed, 123; treaty recalled by Cleveland, 124; United States protectorate in, terminated, 131; conflict of parties in, 136; American newspapers on proposed annexation of, 147-152 ; as " key to the Pacific," 147 ; annexation of as a first step, 150-152 ; results of missionary work in, 162, 309 and note ; annexationists refuse to accept defeat as permanent, 173-174 ; enjoys special relations with United States, 184 ; royalists expect help in restoring Queen, 185, 190 ; Senate's declaration of policy in regard to, 186, 187 ; constitutional convention of 1894, 188-190 ; royalists denounce plan for constitutional convention, 189 ; establishment of Republic of, 191 ; Constitution of 1894, 191-192 ; prosperity in, 193 ; effect of Wilson-Gorman tariff, 193 ; republic recognized by United States, 193 ; royalist insurrection of 1895, 197-198 ; consequences of insurrection, 198-200 ; difficulties with Japan, 217 ; annexation to be by treaty rather than joint resolution, 218n. ; treaty of annexation signed (1897), 219 ; to be protected by United States pending ratification of treaty, 220-221 ; votes lacking for ratification of treaty, 225 ; joint resolution of annexation introduced, 225 ; occupation of Philippines strengthens demand for, 274 ; Baptist *Standard* opposed to annexation of, 280 ; importance of in missionary strategy, 281-282 ; annexation opposed by *Standard,* 293 ; annexed to United States, 317 ; annexation of, a by-product of war with Spain, 317-319 ; joint resolution for annexation of, passed and signed, 317, 322, 325-326 ; government suggests alliance with United States, 318 ; adopts attitude of benevolent neutrality, 318 ; effect of Dewey's victory on movement for annexation of, 319 ;

joint resolution of annexation languishes in Senate, 320 ; introduced in House, 320 ; debate on joint resolution, in House, 321 322, in Senate, 322-325 ; possibility of its becoming a state, 323 ; danger that annexation will lead to colonial expansion, 324-326 ; annexation leads logically to further acquisitions, 326.

Hawaiian cable, proposals for, 69, 200, 201, 203, 204, 206.

Hawaiian Patriotic League, 135.

Hay, John, mentioned, 327, 329 ; becomes Secretary of State, 332n., instructs peace commissioners to demand all Philippines, 338 ; authorizes cash payment to Spain, 339-340.

Heureaux, President of Dominican Republic, proposes to lease Samana Bay to the United States, 30 ; breaks off negotiations, 31 ; invites United States to seize Samana Bay, 227.

Hewitt, Abram S., 334.

Hill, James J., 271.

Hitt, R. R., speech in favor of Hawaiian annexation, 318-319, 319n. ; Chairman of House Committee on Foreign Affairs, 320.

Hoar, Geo F., makes amends to Liliuokalani, 170n. ; introduces resolutions on Cleveland's Hawaiian policy, 175 ; argues that annexation of Hawaii is not a precedent for further expansion, 324-326 ; speech against annexation of territory, 347-348, 350, 351 ; votes against ratification of treaty, 358 ; opposes McEnery resolution, 359.

Holy See, proposed arbitration by, of Cuban question, 282, 283.

Hoover, Herbert, 23.

House of Representatives, United States, adopts resolutions on Hawaii, 180, 182 ; debate on Hawaii, 180-182 ; debates and passes joint resolution annexing Hawaii, 320-322.

Hui Kalaiaina: asks new constitution, 81.

Hyppolite, Florvil, president of Haiti, 29-30.

Imperialism, Bishop Potter's attack on, 306.

" Imperialism of righteousness," 293.

" Imperial " party, beginnings of, 327.

Insular Cases, 353.

Iron, American-owned iron mines in Cuba, 250-251.

Isthmian Canal (see also Nicaraguan canal project; Maritime Canal Co. of Nicaragua), war strengthens demand for, 274.

Japan, not opposed to annexation of Hawaii by United States (1893), 125; protests against Hawaii's immigration restrictions, 217; provides incentive to annexation, 217-218; protests against annexation of Hawaii (1897), 220; withdraws protest, 221; menace of, as argument for annexing Hawaii, 319-320; menace of, cited by McKinley, 320n.; suggests alternative dispositions of Philippines, 333.

Kahunas, 160, 161, 162, 168.

Kaiulani, Princess, 121.

Kalakaua, King, accepts new constitution, 35; rejects new treaty with United States, 41; and Constitution of 1387, 62; death of, 62.

Kalua, J. W., 135.

Kidd, Benjamin, on control of the tropics, 18-19; his arguments sent to McKinley, 334.

Kinney, Wm. A., 219, 224n.

Kipling, Rudyard, 349.

Kiska, harbor in Aleutian Islands, 319.

Kohlsaat, H. H., quotes McKinley, 326 and note.

Kusaie, missionaries in, 302; peace commissioners attempt to purchase for United States, 342, 343, 344, and see Caroline Islands.

Kyle, J. H., 185.

Ladrone Islands, an island in, to be ceded to United States, 330.

" Large policy," advocated by Roosevelt and Lodge, 231; essentially an economic policy, 232.

Lee, Fitzhugh, 211.

Legislature of Hawaii, session of 1892-1893, 64-67, 74-77; changes in ministry, 65-66, 76-77; prorogued, 80.

LcLacheur, D. W., urges retention of Philippines, 315, 334.

Liberal Party, leaders favor annexation, 59, 63.

Liliuokalani, Queen, accession to throne, 51, 62; native feeling against, 58; opposed to annexation, 59; plan to remove her, 60; chooses ministers from National Reform Party, 63; names Reform ministry, 66; appoints weak ministry, 77-78; warned against playing politics, 78; plans to proclaim new constitution, 79, 80, 81 and note; prorogues legislature, 80; postpones new constitution, 82; furnishes occasion for revolution, 82; attempts to retreat, 85, 86; abdicates under protest, 93; refused permission to send representative by " Claudine," 110; protests to President Harrison, 111; provision made for annuity for, 121; refuses amnesty for revolutionists, 141-142; accepts Cleveland's conditions, 143; analysis of charges against her character, 160-171; Senator Hoar on character of, 170n.; consents to royalist uprising, 197; signs abdication, 198; pardoned, 199-200; protests against treaty of annexation (1897), 219n.

Lincoln, Robert T., 125.

Lindsay, William, 346.

Lockey, J. B., on Blaine, 23.

Lodge, Henry Cabot, cites Mahan's arguments, 21; criticizes Cleveland's foreign policy, 200, 201, 202, 206-208; preaches expansion and sea power, 204-206; defines political issues, 207-208; on Cuban independence, 211; proposes purchase of Danish West Indies, 221, 226, 275, 321; on " explosion " in Cuba, 226; helps draft instructions to Dewey, 226; reports that McKinley desires Danish West Indies, 227; says Philippines must be retained, 231; economic basis of his ideas, 232; expects annexation of Hawaii, 322; and " large policy," 325; reports conversation with Day, 327; reports probable peace terms, 331; suggests trading part of Philippines for islands in West Indies, 331n.; on blessings of American government, 355; on material benefits of expansion, 356-357.

Long, John D., thinks retention of Philippines unnecessary, 329.

Looker-on," The, on Mahan's influence, 21; on new spirit in the United States, 229.

Lottery bill, passed by Hawaiian legislature, 76; revoked by Provisional Government, 112-113; ethics of, 163, 166-167.

Louisiana Lottery Co., 166.

McCreary, Richmond, resolutions offered by and adopted, 180, 182.

McEnery Resolution, introduced in Senate, 346, 358; adopted by Senate, 359; significance of, 359-360.

McEnery, S. D., introduces resolution relative to Philippine Islands, 346, 358.

McKinley, Mrs., desires to convert Igorrotes, 316, 334.

McKinley tariff, discussed in Congress, 42; opposed by Hawaiian minister, 42-43; enacted, 43; effect of in Hawaii, 43-45, 58; modified, 44.

McKinley, William, gives little thought to foreign policy, 215; promises no jingo nonsense, 215; persuaded to support annexation of Hawaii, 215-217; consents to negotiation of treaty, 218; sends special message on Hawaiian treaty, 219; expects no immediate action on treaty, 219 and note; desires Danish West Indies, 227; sends war message to Congress, 227; receives memorial on Cuban situation, 249-250; criticized by De Lome, 283; informed of religious sentiment for expansion, 314-315; influenced by religious sentiment, 316; assures Hoar of opposition to schemes of empire, 324; not an imperialist by inclination, 326; influence of " Imperial " party upon, 327; offers terms of peace to Spain, 330; suspends hostilities, 331; confers with Peace Commission, 332; influenced by wishes of Great Britain and Japan, 333; subjected to arguments of business and religious groups, 334; weighs arguments for and against retaining Philippines, 333-338; his account of answer to his prayers in regard to the Philippines, 334n; demands cession of Luzon, 335-336; in doubt as to remainder of archipelago, 336; sounds public opinion, 337; demands cession of all Philippines, 338; adheres to decision, 338-340.

McLaurin, John L., 351, 352n.

Mahan, Alfred Thayer, philosophy of sea power, 12-13; on needs of United States, 13-17; on future of the Pacific, 15-17; on importance of Hawaiian islands, 16-17; influence of, 20-22; on expansion as an aid to commerce, 22; for annexation of Hawaii, 152-154; propaganda of, for expansion, 222-223; economic significance of his ideas, 232; says Hawaii essential for defense of Pacific coast, 319; helps convince Day of destiny in Philippines, 327-328.

Maine, U. S. S., 13, 225, 226, 236, 244, 245, 284, 285.

Mallory, S. R., 349.

Manganese, American-owned manganese mines in Cuba, 250-251.

Manifest Destiny, 1, 2, 4, 154, 279.

Manila, see Philippine Islands.

Maritime Canal Company of Nicaragua, 28, 208n.

Marsden, J., 110.

Mason, Wm. E., 346.

Melville, G. W., 319.

Merrill, G. W., 96, 154n.

Merritt, Gen. Wesley, occupies Manila, 331; on retention of Philippines, 336.

Methodist Episcopal Church, ready to do duty in war, 282; attitude of, toward expansion, 294-296.

Mills bill, 36.

Mills, Roger Q., 177, 179, 187.

Missionaries, American, arrive in Hawaii, 34; their descendants prominent in Reform Party, 62; effect of their work upon native Hawaiians, 161-162; driven from Caroline Islands, 290, 303; opportunities for, in conquered islands, 293; in Caroline Islands, 302.

Missouri, Bishop of, 306.

Môle St. Nicholas, sought by the United States as a naval base, 29-30.

Monroe Doctrine, alleged British violation of in Venezuela, 206; Cleveland's defense of in Venezuela affair, 208; upheld in Danish West Indies and Dominican Republic, 209; Congress supports Cleveland's defense of, 212; held no longer binding on United States, 307; endangered by retention of Philippines, 350.

Moore, John B., 46.

Morgan, J. P., 247.

Morgan, John T., and Hawaiian treaty, 122; mentioned, 175; writes report of Senate Committee on Foreign Relations relative to Hawaii, 183-185; and Nicaraguan canal, 208n.; accused of desiring war in the interest of silver, 242; votes for joint resolution annexing Hawaii, 326n.

Mormon Church, publication endorses expansion, 312-313n.

Morrill, Justin S., opposes annexation of Hawaii, 323-324, 326n.

National Association of Manufacturers, interest of, in expanding exports, 253.

National Reform Party, wins partial victory, 41, 62; ministers chosen from, 63; ministry voted out, 65.

Navy, United States, first modern vessels built, 13; battleships authorized, 213n.

Nawahi, Joseph, 142.

Nelson, Knute, 355.

Neumann, Paul, attorney for Queen, 112; activity in Washington, 123n.; offers compromise for Queen, 127.

Nicaraguan canal project, initiated, 28; Cleveland's attitude toward, 208; to be reopened, 221.

Nordhoff, Charles, on weakness of Provisional Government, 137n.; investigations of, in Honolulu, 165, 167, 169.

O'Keeffe, H. E., 310.

Olney, Richard, influences Cleveland's Hawaiian policy, 139-140; upholds Monroe Doctrine, 209.

" Open door," demanded in China, 269, 271, 348; should it be applied in new possessions? 276.

Opium bill, passed by Hawaiian legislature, 77n.; ethics of, 163, 165-166.

Oregon, U. S. S., 220, 274.

O'Sullivan, John Louis, 1, 2.

Page, Walter Hines, 327.

Pago-Pago, American rights at, 26, 27n.

Palmer, Julius A., Jr., investigations by, in Honolulu, 165, 169; Thurston's opinion of, 165n.; defends character of Liliuokalani, 170; describes conditions in Honolulu, 199.

Paris Peace Commission, personnel of, 331-332; confer with President, 332; divergent opinions of, as to keeping Philippines, 332, 336-337; decision as to Philippines not theirs but McKinley's, 333; negotiations with Spanish commissioners, 338-345; their ultimatum accepted by Spanish commissioners, 340; attempt to secure Caroline Islands, 340-344; sign treaty with Spain, 345.

Parker, Samuel, minister of foreign affairs, 46, 78; proposes new reciprocity treaty, 46; protests landing of troops, 89; visits Washington, 194; confers with Gresham, 195-196.

Patten, Simon N., *Theory of Social Forces,* 19n.

Pauncefote, Sir Julian, conversation with Gresham on Hawaii, 125-127.

Peace Commission, see Paris, Peace Commission.

Pearl Harbor, United States to have exclusive rights in, 34-37; loss of exclusive rights threatened, 43; proposed coaling and repair station in, 44; in proposed treaty (1891), 47; report on value of, 71.

Peterson, A. P., attorney-general, 78; mentioned, 83, 84, 85.

Philadelphia, U. S. S., ordered away from Honolulu, 196; returns to Honolulu, 198.

Philippine Islands, Roosevelt's interest in, 222, and note; retention of demanded by Roosevelt and Lodge, 231; regarded as gateway to Asiatic markets, 267, 269, 270; a portal to religious activity in Asia, 282; to be opened to the Gospel, 287; American missionaries excluded from, 290; importance in missionary strategy, 292; constitute difficult problem, 297; as a religious field, 299, 301, 304; Presbyterian missionaries in, 299n.; United States responsible for, 300; a stronghold of Catholicism, 308; Catholics to benefit from American rule in, 312; Day says Spain may retain, 327; disposition of uncertain, 327; United States troops land in, 328; McKinley's Cabinet divided as to disposition of, 329; United States to retain at least a harbor in, 329; disposition of to be determined in treaty of peace, 330; Manila surrenders to United States forces, 331; Lodge proposes trading part of group for islands in West Indies, 331n.; opinion of Peace Commissioners as to retention of, 332; progress of McKinley's thought as to retention of, 333-338; McKinley demands cession of, 338; Spanish commissioners agree to cession of, 340; constitutional argument against retaining, 346-348; Senate debate over retention of, 346-358; retention of dangerous to American agriculture and labor, 348; not suited to American institutions, 348-349; retention of dangerous to American liberties, 349; retention of likely to embroil United States in the Far East, 350; retention of commercially valueless, 350-351; retention of, a scheme of the plutocracy, 351-352; effect of hostilities in, upon ratification of treaty, 357n.

Platt, O. H., on Hawaiian treaty, 122; advocates expansion, 178-179, 204; reports sentiment for retention of Philippines, 314; argues for constitutional right to acquire and govern territory, 352-353, 354; on duty of extending Christian civilization, 356.

Ponape, missionaries in, 302; rebellion of natives in, 303; missionaries expelled from, 303; Spain agrees to sell to Germany, 343.

Porto Rico, see Puerto Rico.

Potter, Bishop, attacks imperialism, 306.

Presbyterian Board of Foreign Missions, calls interdenominational conference on missions, 299.

Presbyterian Church, attitude toward expansion, 296-300; takes lead in planning missionary work, 299.

Proctor, Redfield, speech on Cuba, 246; its effect in Wall Street, 246-247; its effect on religious press, 284.

Protestant clergy, warlike attitude of, 282-283.

Provisional Government of Hawaii, proclaimed, 91; recognized by Stevens and other foreign representatives, 92, 94; controls Honolulu, 93; initiates measures for annexation, 110; rests upon military force, 136, 137n.; re-

fuses Cleveland's demand, 144-145; dissatisfaction with, 188; calls constitutional convention, 189.

Puerto Rico, retention of demanded by Roosevelt and Lodge, 231; business interests insist on retention of, 274; business opportunities in, 277; to be opened to the Gospel, 287; volunteers for missionary work in, 301; religion of inhabitants of, 308; no question about retaining, 327; conquest of, 328; its fate settled, 329; to be ceded to United States, 330; retention of, discussed in Senate, 348.

Quakers, see Friends, Society of.

Rayner, Isidor, 182.

Reed, Thomas B., blocks action on Hawaiian resolution, 317, 320-321; permits Hawaiian resolution to come before House, 321.

Reform Party, controls Hawaiian government, 62; favors annexation, 63; fails to cement alliance with Liberals, 75; gets rid of opponents, 199.

Reid, Whitelaw, influence on Harrison, 25n.; on Samoan question, 27; says United States responsible for good government in Cuba, 230; says United States will keep Puerto Rico and Philippines, 231; member of Peace Commission and leader of expansionists, 332; favors keeping all Philippines, 332; writes opinion of majority of Peace Commission, 332, 337; probably influences McKinley's decision, 332; proposes concessions to Spain, 339; proposes that Spain cede islands in Carolines instead of Mindanao and Sulu, 341-342.

Religious bodies: see also under names of separate denominations; self-assertive spirit of, 279-282; view Cuban problem as a moral one, 282; attitude of, to intervention in Cuba, 282-286; justify war with Spain, 286-289; attitude of, confirmed by American victories, 289-290; urge acceptance of colonial responsibilities, 290-314; religious press almost unanimous for retention of Philippines, 297; influence of upon McKinley, 315-316.

Religious press, see Religious bodies and names of separate denominations.

Republican Party, espouses " manifest destiny," 2; foreign policy of, defined in platform (1896), 213-214.

Rhodes, James Ford, quoted, 232.

Robinson, Edward Van Dyke, advocates acquisition of Caroline Islands, 304 and note.

Robinson, Mark P., 165.

Roosevelt, Theodore, pupil of Burgess, 10n., 20; admiration of, for Mahan, 21; alarmed at Japanese attitude, 218; prepares for campaign in Philippines, 221-222, 222n.; praises Mahan, 222; urges securing of Puerto Rico, Philippines, and Hawaii, 231 and note, 327.

Rosa, Antone, 129, 134.

Samana Bay, sought by the United States as a naval base, 30-31; lease of, proposed by President Heureaux, 221; President Heureaux would not object to seizure of, 227; Navy Department not interested in seizing, 227.

Samoa, treaty of 1889 concerning, 26-27; Cleveland's dislike of tripartite treaty, 201; part of chain across the Pacific, 274.

Santiago, naval battle of, 328; surrender of, 328.

Schofield, Gen. J. M., mentioned, 71; for annexation of Hawaii, 319.

Schurz, Carl, opposes annexation of Hawaii, 154; receives assurances from McKinley, 215; on McKinley's conversion to Hawaiian annexation, 215n., 219n.

Senate Committee on Foreign Relations, investigates Hawaiian revolution, 176; report of, on Hawaiian revolution, 183-185; approves Turpie's resolution on Hawaiian policy, 186; reports favorably treaty to annex Hawaii (1897), 219; warns of Japanese menace in Hawaii, 319-320; reports joint resolution for annexation of Hawaii, 323.

Senate, United States, debate in, on Cleveland's Hawaiian policy, 176-180; adopts resolution on Hawaii, 187; alarmed at royalist rebellion in Hawaii, 202; reaffirms non-interference policy, 202-203; debates and passes joint resolution annexing Hawaii, 323-326; debates treaty with Spain in secret session, 345; advises ratification of treaty with Spain, 345, 358; resolutions relative to acquisition of territory debated publicly in, as substitute for public debate on treaty, 345 and note, 346-358.

Shafter, General Wm. R., 328.

Shaw, Albert, on American domination in the Pacific, 223.

Sherman, John, mentioned, 184; as Secretary of State, opposes acquisitions of territory, 215; not informed of decision to annex Hawaii, 218; signs treaty and report, 219; receives memorial on Cuban situation, 248; indifferent to European aggressions in China, 263.

Sickles, D. E., 182.

Skerrett, Rear Admiral J. S., ordered to command of Pacific station, 72; on stationing of troops in Honolulu, 104; mentioned, 131, 137n.

Smith, J. Mott, special envoy to United States, 47; agrees with Blaine on treaty, 47-48; interprets policy of United States, 49; on annexation, 55, 56; predicts delay on annexation treaty, 122.

Smith, W. O., office of, a rendezvous for opponents of Queen, 82; on committee of safety, 83; mentioned, 87, 97; reports McKinley friendly to annexation, 216.

Soper, J. H., 90, 101.

Spain, war with begun, 227; religious journals denounce policy of in Cuba, 285; war with justified by religious press, 286-289; rule of, hostile to American missionaries, 290; makes peace proposals, 328-329; attempts to safeguard sovereignty in Philippines, 330; thought incapable of governing Philippines, 333; treaty of peace with, 345.

Spaulding, Col. T. M., cited, 36n.

Spooner, J. C., 350.

Spreckels, Adolph, 111.

Spreckels, Claus, favors annexation, 111; opposes annexation of Hawaii, 156-157; says planters did not instigate revolution, 158; opposes second annexation treaty, 225n.

Spreckels family, their paper opposes annexation of Philippines, 273.

Spreckels, John, 111.

Stevens, John L.; United States minister to Hawaii, 49; advocates annexation of Hawaii, 49-51; relations with Blaine, 50; reports of conditions in Hawaii, 51-54, 67-69; asks instructions, 52; warns of British intrigue, 67; urges annexation, 68; leaves Honolulu for cruise, 76; returns, 80; orders troops landed, 89; recognizes Provisional Government, 92; conduct criticized and defended, 94; analysis of his connection with revolution, 94-109; praises character of annexation commissioners, 111-112; denounces friends of Queen, 112; reports "Hawaiian pear is now fully ripe," 113; proclaims protectorate over Hawaii, 113-115; greets Blount, 130; resignation of, 131; criticizes Blount, 132; action of condemned by Blount, 134; charges against Liliuokalani, 162, 163; denounces proposal to restore Liliuokalani, 171-172; attacked and defended in Senate, 177; action of approved by Senate Committee, 183; mentioned, 323.

Strong, Josiah: on Anglo-Saxon destiny, 5, 6; influence, 19; predicts supremacy of Anglo-Saxons, 279.

Sugar, growth of Hawaiian production, 35; proposed reduction in duties on, 36; effect of McKinley tariff on, 45; American sugar interests oppose annexation of Hawaii, 216, 225; effect of war in Cuba on sugar industry, 248, 249, 250; California sugar interests oppose annexing Philippines 273.

Sugar bounty, proposed, 36; provided in McKinley tariff, 42, 43; impossible for Hawaii to obtain, 45; interest of Hawaiian planters in, 58; asked by Hawaiian commission, 118; refused by Foster, 119; desire for, as cause of Hawaiian revolution, 156-160.

Sugar planters, Hawaiian, attitude of, to annexation, 58; 158-160.

Sugar Trust, 156, 225n.

Sullivan, Wm. V., 346.

Sulzer, William, 210.

Supreme Court of Hawaii, sustains Queen, 63.

Swinburne, Lt.-Commander, commands landing-party, 102; testimony of, 104n.

Tateno, Mr., Japanese minister, 125.

Teller Amendment, promises Cuban independence, 230; regretted by expansionists, 230; not applicable to Spain's other possessions, 230; strict adherence to, may be impossible, 275; mentioned, 300; interpreted by its author, 354.

Teller, H. M., an expansionist, 179, 204; introduces amendment promising independence to Cuba, 230 and note (see Teller Amendment); proclaims that American flag will never come down, 325; on citizens and subjects, 353; interprets his amendment, 354.

Theosophists, on American responsibility in Philippines, 312-313n.

Thurston, J. M., 236.

Thurston, Lorrin A., member of Hawaiian legislature, 54; visits Washington in interest of annexation of Hawaii, 54-57; his memorandum to Blaine on Hawaiian situation, 58-61, 61n., 158; returns to Honolulu, 61; plans to unite Reform and Liberal elements for annexation, 63; cultivates Liberal leaders, 65; says annexation not the issue, 66n.; advises stand against Queen, 80; member of committee of safety, 83, 84, 87; justifies revolution, 99-101; member of commission to seek annexation, 110; praised by Stevens, 111; private interviews with Foster, 117; seeks interview with Gresham, 123; refuses plebiscite on annexation, 127-128; attempts to influence Blount, 129-130, 134; succeeds Smith as minister in Washington, 137; fails to influence Gresham, 137; abandons hope of sugar bounty, 159; resumes work for annexation, 216n.; signs annexation treaty, 219; delegate to Trans-Mississippi Congress, 224n.

Tillman, B. R., 349, 352n.

Tracy, B. F., Secretary of the Navy, 25n.; influential with Harrison, 25n.; meets Thurston, 57; expresses wish to annex Hawaii, 72.

Trans-Mississippi Congress, 224.

Treaty of Peace with Spain, signed and sent to Senate, 345; debated in secret session of Senate, 345; ratification advised by Senate, 345, 358; debate on resolutions a substitute for public debate on treaty, 345 and note, 346-358; influences at work for ratification of, 357.

Trumbull, M. M., 155n.

Turkey, Congress pledges support for protection of American citizens in, 213.

Turner, H. G., 182.

Turpie, David, mentioned, 177, 179, 184, 185; his resolution on Hawaii adopted, 186-187.

Tyler, Alice F., cited, 44n.

Unitarian Church, opposes war with Spain, 288-289; opposes expansion, 312-314.

United Brethren in Christ, mentioned, 283; accept expansionist program, 291.

Van Voorhis, John, 182.

Venezuela, 206, 208.

Vest, G. G., mentioned, 177, 178, 179, 202; introduces resolutions against acquisition of colonies, 346; employs constitutional argument against expansion, 346-347.

Vilas, W. F., 177.

Volwiler, A. T., cited, 25n.

Walker, Rear Admiral J. G., report on unrest in Hawaii, 186n.; warns of British intrigue in Hawaii, 196.

Wall Street, anti-war solidarity of imperfect, 246-247n.

Washington, George, his isolation policy must yield to force of circumstances, 299.

Waterhouse, Henry, 105.

Weinberg, A. K., cited, 1n.

Western Sugar Refining Co., 156.

Whitaker, Bishop, 283.

White, Andrew D., encourages German ambitions in Pacific, 342.

White, Henry, 226, 231.

White, S. M., 351.

Widemann, H. A., visits Washington, 194; confers with Gresham, 195-196.

Wilcox, G. N., heads Reform ministry, 66; appointment a victory for annexation policy, 74; follows cautious policy, 74; ministry voted out, 77; supports opium bill, 165; opposes lottery bill, 166.

Wilcox, Robert W., arrested and released, 53n.; leads attempt to suppress Constitution of 1887, 62; a chronic agitator, 64; a leader of the Liberal Party, 64; works with Thurston, 64-65; favors sending commission to Washington, 74; turns against Thurston, 76; characterized by Stevens, 113; talks with Willis, 142; in royalist insurrection, 198-199.

Wilder, W. C., 83, 110.

Willis, Albert S., minister to Hawaii, 140; instructions to, 140-141; negotiations with Liliuokalani and with Provisional Government, 141-145; action of approved by Senate Committee, 184; communicates Senate resolution, 190; recognizes Republic of Hawaii, 193; warns against mob violence, 198.

Wilson, C. B., retains office as marshal of Hawaii, 75; guarantees Queen's good behavior, 86; alleged intimacy with Liliuokalani, 163; in good graces of Dole government, 199n.

Wilson-Gorman Tariff, effect of, in Hawaii, 193.

Wilson, James, favors retaining Philippines, 329.

Wiltse, Capt. G. C., promises protection to American citizens in Honolulu, 80; nature of his orders to landing party, 102.

Wodehouse, Mr., British commissioner in Hawaii, 67, 126; recalled, 196-197.

Wolcott, E. O., 355.

Wundenberg, F. W., 95n., 101.

Young, Lucien, 76n., 80n., 92n., 104n.

Zincke, F. B., 4.

DATE DUE

NOV 20 64			
5/14			
5/17			
GAYLORD			PRINTED IN U.S.A.